Hard at Work in
Factories and Mines

Hard at Work in Factories and Mines

The Economics of Child Labor During the British Industrial Revolution

Carolyn Tuttle

Westview Press
A Member of the Perseus Books Group

Copyright © 1999 by Westview Press, A Member of the Perseus Books Group

Published in 1999 in the United States of America by Westview Press, 5500 Central Avenue, Boulder, Colorado 80301-2877, and in the United Kingdom by Westview Press, 12 Hid's Copse Road, Cumnor Hill, Oxford OX2 9JJ

Find us on the World Wide Web at www.westviewpress.com

Library of Congress Cataloging-in-Publication Data
Tuttle, Carolyn.
   Hard at work in factories and mines : the economics of child labor
during the British industrial revolution / Carolyn Tuttle.
      p.   cm.
   Includes bibliographical references and index.
   ISBN 0-8133-3698-8 (hc.)
      1. Children—Employment—Great Britain—History—19th century.
2. Labor economics—Great Britain—History—19th century.
3. Industrial revolution—Great Britain.   I. Title.
HD6250.G7T88   1999
331.3'1'094109034—dc21   99-16847
                                                                                      CIP

The paper used in this publication meets the requirements of the American National Standard for Permanence of Paper for Printed Library Materials Z39.48-1984.

10   9   8   7   6   5   4   3   2   1

*Dedicated to
my son, Daniel*

Contents

Tables and Illustrations

Figures

Diagrams

Acknowledgments

I should like to express my heartfelt thanks to Joel Mokyr for his steadfast support of my research on child labor and for inspiring me to become a learned economic historian. I would like to thank Avner Offer for sponsoring me at Nuffield College in Oxford during my sabbatical and Maxine Berg for connecting me with resources and other scholars in Great Britain who could help me with my research. I am grateful for the time Helen Buchanan, a librarian at Radcliffe Camera, devoted to helping me find many of the primary sources I used for this research. I would also like to thank the participants of the Economic History Workshops at All Souls College of Oxford University, Warwick University, Nuffield College and University of Chicago for offering suggestions to strengthen my argument. Many thanks also go to Jeffrey Williamson and Lou Cain for reading and commenting on an earlier draft of this book. I feel very fortunate to have such wonderful and supportive colleagues at Lake Forest College and I would like to especially thank Simone Wegge, Diana Darnell and Kathryn Dohrmann for sharing their wisdom on several pertinent issues which needed to be addressed. My research assistant, Nicole Polarek, was extremely helpful in locating important sources and in proofreading early drafts. I am especially grateful to Kathleen Weber for giving me the support and encouragement to complete this project. I am also deeply indebted to Harriet Doud, upon whose dedication and resourcefulness I have relied throughout the editing and formatting of this book. At Westview, I had the pleasure of working with Rob Williams whose high editorial standards helped to improve the finished product. In addition, the thoughtful comments of an anonymous referee have helped to sharpen the main argument of this book.

Carolyn Tuttle

1

Child Labor in the Past and Present

The history of the economic development of Europe and North America includes numerous instances of child labor. Manufacturers in England, France, Belgium, Germany, Prussia as well as the United States used child labor during the initial stage of industrialization. In many cases, the employment of children was quite extensive and the conditions, hours and treatment appalling by twentieth-century standards. In Great Britain nearly half of the work force in the textile industry in 1833 was under the age of sixteen. Silk mills were the most extensive employers of children with 46 percent of its work force under sixteen, the cotton industry with 35 percent of its workers under sixteen and the flax and woollen industries employed roughly 40 percent of their workers under the age of sixteen. Further, children made up nearly half of the work force in coal mines (Tuttle 1986: 2). French industrial enterprises in 1845 employed 143,665 children under the age of sixteen, which constituted 11.7 percent of the total industrial work force. Seventy-three percent of France's industrial child laborers were employed in one of the textile industries. In fact, children comprised roughly one fifth of the work force in these industries with cotton blends the highest with 23.9 percent of the work force under age sixteen and cotton and woollen close behind with 18.3 percent and 18.6 percent, respectively (Weissbach 1989:16-19). A similar story can be told for Belgium where the textiles were the greatest employers of children. The linen, hemp and lace industries hired 40 percent of its workers under the age of sixteen while the cotton textiles had 27 percent of its entire work force under sixteen years of age. As in Britain, the percentage of children working in coal mines was considerable with 22 percent of its employees under sixteen (Statistique de la Belgique, Recensement General 1846). Goldin and Sokoloff estimate from a sample of firms of the U. S. Federal Census of Manufactures that 23 percent of all workers in manufacturing in the Northeast in 1820 were children. Again, they found large proportions of the labor force of textile establishments were children. Their estimates in 1820 show proportions comparable to those calculated for Britain, with half of the work force in cotton firms and 41 percent in wool firms comprised of children. They conclude that "Women and children composed a major share of the entire manufacturing labor force during the initial period of industrialization and that the employment of these groups was closely associated with production process used by large establishments across a broad range of industries" (1982:773).

Even today we hear from the International Labor Organization (ILO) and the United Nations Center on Human Rights that, "The use of child labor is endemic in virtually all developing countries" (Jacobson 1992:9). Despite the existence of child labor laws in most Third World countries, children continue to work. According to the ILO, 95 percent of all child workers in the world live in developing countries and at least 18 percent of the children and youths between the ages of ten and fourteen are working (American Federation of Teachers (AFT) 1998:1). Unlike their predecessors in Europe, they no longer work in the formal sector but have moved into the informal sector where the laws do not apply or are not strictly enforced. Consequently, today's child laborer toils in small manufacturing enterprises rather than factories or large industrial firms. They work as cheap, "sweated" labor in a variety of cultures and countries but in many of the same industries. The similarities across countries in the lists provided in both columns of Table 1.1 are striking. The first column lists industries which export to the United States where the existence of child labor is well documented. The second column lists industries where child labor abuses have occurred but documentation is scanty at best. Employment in the carpet industry, garment industry and mining industry appears to be widespread for contemporary child laborers.

It is clear from the documented cases alone that child labor prevails in the twentieth century in many industries in the Third World. Children sew cloth in the garment industry in Bangladesh, Brazil, Guatemala, Indonesia, Morocco, the Philippines and Thailand. Children tie knots to make hand-knotted carpets in Egypt, India, Morocco and Pakistan. Children spin and weave cotton, silk and wool in the textile industries of Brazil, India and Mexico. Children carry dirt and sift out precious metals in tin, chromium and gold mines of Columbia and Brazil. Can we dismiss these cases of child labor as isolated reports of a few employers? Definitely not. Millions of child laborers toil away their days. The International Labour Organization estimates that at least 250 million children between the ages of five and fourteen continue to work throughout the world (Capdevila 1998:1). Although it is difficult to obtain a precise figure for the number of children employed in specific industries, rough estimates exist for some countries which provide a benchmark for researchers. A press release from the Washington Office of the ILO showed the employment of children had reached epidemic proportions in 1992:

In July 1992, the ILO concluded in a new study that child labor is a serious and alarming problem, that as many as 25 percent of all children between the ages of 10 and 14 in some regions are estimated to be working. Asia has the highest numbers of child laborers - accounting for up to 11 percent of the labor force in some countries. India alone is estimated to have as many as 44 million child laborers. In Latin America, up to 26 percent

TABLE 1.1 Child Labor in the World

Country	Child Labor in Export Industries for U.S. Market	Child Labor in Other Industries[a]
Bangladesh	Garment Industry	Shrimp catching & processing
Brazil	Footwear, garment & textile industries, Tin mining	Leather-processing, watches, electronics, eyeglasses, handicrafts, ceramics, plastic industries, Gold mining
Columbia	Flower agribusiness	Coal & emerald mining, leather tanning
Egypt	Hand-knotted carpet industry	Textile & leather, perfumes, handicrafts, glass industries
Guatemala	Garment industry	Agricultural processing
India	Hand-knotted carpet, textiles, silk & footwear, brass & base metal, glass & glassware, fireworks	Furniture, sporting goods, garment, locks, pottery, leather & tile, Iron and steel products, shrimp & seafood processing, Granite, mica, slate mining & quarrying
Indonesia	Garment & embroidery, wood & rattan furniture industries	Food processing, shrimp & seafood processing, plastic & metal industries
Mexico	Electrical & electronic, textile industries, sporting goods, toys & furniture	Footwear & handicraft industries, Agriculture
Pakistan	Hand-knotted carpet industry, surgical instruments & sporting goods	Leather & footwear industries, Mining
The Philippines	Garment industry	Wood & rattan furniture, Gold Mining
Portugal	Garment & footwear, ceramics, granite paving stone industry	
Thailand	Garment & leather handbag, wood & rattan furniture, shrimp & seafood processing	

(continues)

TABLE 1.1 (continued)

Country	Child Labor in Export Industries for U.S. Market	Child Labor in Other Industries[a]
Zimbabwe	Chromium & gold mining	

[a]This column represents industries with alleged or definite child labor abuses, but little documentation providing specifics.

Source: *Child Labor Monitor*, (1995), pp. 4-5. Reprinted by permission.

of children may be working. In Brazil, for example, it is estimated that 34 percent of all children work (Harvey 1993:20).

After considerable work by the ILO and UNICEF "child labour has now shot to the top of the global agenda and consumer concerns in both developing and industrialized countries" (ILO 1996:5). The worldwide movement against child labor has forced government officials, politicians, capitalists and laborers to recognize the "sad exploitation of children which takes place for economic advancement" (AFT 1998:1). Increased interest in the plight of the child laborer has led to the creation of consumer groups "Free the Children" and "The Kids Campaign to Build a School for Iqbal"[1] and foundations like the RUGMARK FOUNDATION-USA[2] and campaigns such as the "UNITE Campaign against sweatshops"[3] to inform the public and rally support for the elimination of child labor. The ILO's International Program on the Elimination of Child Labour (IPEC) operates in more than twenty-five countries (ILO 1996:7). News stories of children making sneakers and sewing soccer balls in Indonesia and girls sewing clothes in Honduras have alerted American consumers to the atrocities that still exist.[4] According to the ILO, this has put needed pressure on corporations to expect "manufacturers to respect human rights" and purge any child laborers from their work force[5] (ILO 1996:5). The ILO reported that "World-renowned manufacturers such as Levi Strauss, Reebok, Sears and others in the sporting goods industry are now looking into the conditions under which their products are being produced. In Europe a number of established stores have decided not to sell products such as carpets unless they are certified as being made without child labour" (1996:5).

As an economic strategy, the employment of children has severe consequences on the future of a country. Children who work all day are unable to attend school and receive an education. Lord Ashley recognized this in 1840 as the British mortgaged its future by exploiting the young instead of educating them. As a proponent for child labor laws, he made the following argument before Parliament to set up a Royal Commission of Inquiry into the employment of children:

Sir, I hardly know whether any argument is necessary to prove that the future hopes of a country must, under God, be laid in the character and condition of its children; however right it may be to attempt, it is almost fruitless to expect, the reformation of its adults; as the sapling has been bent, so it will grow...Now, Sir, whatever may be done or proposed in times to come, we have, I think, a right to know the state of our juvenile population; the House has a right, the country has a right...The first step towards a cure is a knowledge of the disorder. We have asserted these truths in our factory legislation; and I have on my side the authority of all civilised nations of modern times; the practice of this House; the common sense of the thing; and the justice of the principle...It is right, Sir, that the country should know at what cost its pre-eminence is purchased (quoted in Best 1964:91).

The ILO is aware that history is repeating itself in many developing countries today. Nearly a quarter of the young people between the ages of five and fourteen are working in Ghana, India, Indonesia and Senegal and a third do not attend school (ILO 1996:8). The following statement by the ILO is simply a modern version of what Ashley argued over 150 years ago: "Everyone,' says the Universal Declaration of Human Rights, 'has the right to education. Education shall be free at least in the elementary and fundamental stages. Elementary education shall be compulsory.' Today, lack of education is especially damaging because both individual and societal well-being increasingly depend on literacy, numeracy and intellectual competence. A child working is therefore a future denied" (1996:8).

The problem with child labor has grown as the importance of an educated work force has become a prerequisite for economic development. Economists have long argued that economies will grow faster when the general population is literate. If all children learn to read and write, the educational base of the country grows and with it the country's possibilities for advancement. As we approach the twenty-first century, education will play a more prominent role in the development of countries because the skills necessary for working with computers and new technologies require higher levels of schooling and training (Becker 1997:22).

Information and documentation on child labor in the Third World is relatively scarce. Census data on the labor force often exclude children because the employment of children under a certain age has been prohibited by law.[6] Consequently, government agencies, international agencies and researchers have difficulty documenting the extent of child labor because there is a general tendency to conceal it. As a result, it is not possible to provide a complete picture of child labor in the world. It is possible, however, to put the issue into perspective from numerous studies completed on specific countries over the past twenty-five years.

The Anti-Slavery Society Report showed that girls in Morocco, often as young as five, are commonly employed in the carpet industry and work 60-72 hour weeks at a loom tying knots. In twenty-eight of the sixty-two private factories they visited at least one third of the employees were under the age of twelve and sometimes as many as three fifths (Anti-Slavery Society Report 1978:9). Recently the L'Union Macrocaine du Travail (UMT) estimated in 1994 between 5,000-10,000 children and youths (ages eight to fourteen) worked in the artisan carpet industry and 2,000-3,000 worked in the export-oriented carpet industry (U.S. Dept. of Labor 1994:113). Similarly, children work in the carpet industry in India, the greatest carpet exporter in the world. To support and encourage the growth of the industry, the government initiated a massive training program for child carpet weavers. By 1985, according to the government, child workers comprised 37.5 percent of the total labor force in the carpet industry.

The most recent employment statistics show that carpet manufacturing employs more than 300,000 children (Child Labor Monitor, Summer 1993:4) while an estimated 50,000 children ranging from age six to sixteen work in glass and bangle factories in India (Jacobson 1992:9). The leading industry in the Bangladeshi economy is the garment industry. Twenty percent of the workers in the garment industry are children under the age of twelve. Many of these children start working at the ages of seven and eight and work eleven hours a day, seven days a week (Child Labor Coalition, April 1993:3). In 1988, it was estimated that approximately 20 percent of the workers in gold production in Peru were young people. Boys aged eleven to eighteen pushed soil in small carts along wooden ramps from the gold panners to distant piles in the jungle of Madre de Dios (Guille-Marroquin 1988:65).

Studies on child labor in the Philippines and Columbia tell a similar story. Henk van Oosterhout uses school enrollment statistics from the Ministry of Education, Culture and Sports to calculate the number of children and adolescents working in the Philippines. He estimates between 3-8 million children are working either part time or full time (1988:109). These figures are consistent with current employment estimates of the Department of Labor and Employment (DOLE) who admit that at least 5 million children work. Estimates by UNICEF and ILO concur that between 5-5.7 million children work in the commercial and industrial sectors (U.S. Dept. of Labor 1994:136). In Oosterhout's study on deep-sea fishing he notes "to an observer in Cebu province, where the fisherman engaged in the Muro-Ami operation have their homes, that a substantial part of the population under the age of fifteen is actively engaged in earning income" (1988:110). Munoz and Palacios (1977), using census data showed that the employment of children in Columbia increased from 1951 to 1973 (102-103). In 1981, Munoz estimated that nearly 3 million children were working (1985:101). A recent government census places the number of youths (aged twelve to seventeen) employed at 800,000 (U.S. Dept. of Labor 1994:50). In a study of the quarries and brickyards in Bogota, Ayala made a comprehensive survey of elementary schools of its poorest communities in 1981. He found that the labor force participation rate of school-aged children working in productive and service activities was inordinately high at 87 percent (1982).

Child labor is not a new phenomenon nor was it new in eighteenth-century Europe. Children have worked for centuries and continue to work. Children have worked at home, on farms, in cottage industries, in family-owned businesses, in small public enterprises as well as in large public businesses. Children still work at home, on farms, in cottage industries and in small public enterprises. Young children have helped their mothers and fathers in the home and on the farm. In the home, they swept the floor, fetched water and gathered sticks for the fire. Outside on the farm they picked up rocks, weeded, fed the draught animals and picked vegetables during the harvest. As children grew older, they helped with more chores and performed a variety of tasks. Older children watched younger siblings, ran errands, took messages, cooked meals and cleaned the house. On the farm, they planted, sewed the seed and harvested the crop with the adults. As economies developed, children began to perform productive and service activities both inside and outside of the home. Some assisted in the production of a variety of goods (bonnets, baskets and clothes) while others tended to domestic duties as servants. Many children worked in their home; some children worked in other people's homes and still others worked in a shop. Once industrialization took hold many children stopped working in homes and went into the mills and factories built in the towns and cities. They became mill workers and factory workers spinning yarn and weaving yarn into cloth. Hundreds of years later children are still working in homes, on farms and for productive enterprises. In developed and developing countries, in rural as well as urban communities, children help with the everyday functioning of the household (taking out the trash, doing the dishes, and cleaning); they babysit and run errands. In rural communities and developing countries, they feed the animals, milk the cows, help with the harvest and repair fences. In developing countries, they pick cotton, spin yarn and weave it into cloth; they make shirts; they do laundry; they carry bricks; they clean shrimp; they shine shoes; they sell cigarettes and candy and harvest fruits and vegetables.

The fact that children worked during the Industrial Revolution in Great Britain was not novel nor was it unique to Great Britain. Children also worked in France, Belgium, Prussia, Germany and the United States during the early stages of industrialization. The role of child labor in the economy, however, changed as industrialization took hold. Children were no longer merely secondary workers ("helpers" or assistants) to adults but became primary workers (operators or machine minders). Children were not just casually engaged by their parents or relatives but were formally employed by supervisors and managers. More importantly, employers specifically hired children because they needed them as primary workers. Child labor was in demand. Child labor became essential in the production processes of several industries. The child laborer not only contributed to the total output of the industry but also his/her contribution was crucial.

Does this mean child labor is necessary to industrialize? Child labor was prevalent in Britain, France, Belgium and Germany as industrialization took place. Manufacturers in the United States used child labor as it industrialized. Currently, child labor prevails in many developing countries like India, Brazil, Columbia, Mexico, Pakistan and Zimbabwe. Why do we see children working at this stage of economic development? What is it about industrialization that makes child labor essential? Why do employers seem to prefer children to adults as workers?

This book will offer answers to these questions by examining the issue of child labor from a historical perspective, focusing particularly on the employment of children in Great Britain during the Industrial Revolution. This book explains the role of child labor in the British Industrial Revolution and examines how the market for child labor changed in the eighteenth and nineteenth centuries. Were the factories and mines packed with children as the pessimists claim, or was child labor negligible and declining as recent researchers argue? Data from individual factories and mines will show child labor was prevalent throughout the Industrial Revolution but was concentrated in a few industries rather than uniformly distributed across the economy. In addition, I will identify the reasons for the employment of children in Great Britain and discuss their applicability to developing countries that currently utilize child labor. Were children pushed out of the home and into the factories because their families were poor or was there something different about the production process that pulled children into the factories? Historians, economic historians, social historians and development economists have debated the causes of child labor for centuries. Some believe the existence of child labor is due to family circumstances and attributed to parents who exploited their children because they were poor, greedy, lazy or physically abusive. Others blame the industrialists for hiring children because they were a source of cheap labor and easy to discipline. I will offer evidence to support an alternative explanation, one insufficiently developed in the literature up to this point. I argue that industrialists preferred child labor over adult labor because children made ideal factory workers - they were particularly suited to operate the machines and their nature was more compatible with the new industrial regime.

This book offers an entirely different view of child labor from the most recent literature on the subject. This research will show child labor was an important component of the industrial work force of the British economy for much of the nineteenth century. In contrast, Nardinelli argues in his book, *Child Labor and the Industrial Revolution*, that the employment of children was only significant during the initial phase of industrialization (1990:108-109). I will show that children comprised a large proportion of the work force of many of the textile factories and coal mines for the first half of the nineteenth century. Nardinelli claims the employment of children was significant initially in the early rural textile factories but declined to negligible proportions by the 1830s as factories were built in towns (1990:105-109). A thorough investigation of the tasks and work environment of children in specific industries will reveal that many children worked very hard, often in confined spaces. This depiction contrasts sharply with the conclusion in Nardinelli's book that industrialization decreased the exploitation of children (1990:65-102). Lastly, I will show that the impact of technological innovation on the market for child labor is the antithesis of what Nardinelli argues. Nardinelli asserts that younger workers were merely helpers or assistants to adults and never substituted for adults as primary workers. He claims some of the new machines in the textile industry decreased the demand for children by 1835 (1990:108-112). I argue instead that industrialization brought innovations in the methods of production as well as certain inventions which increased the demand for child labor as primary workers. Employers hired children to operate the newly automated machines which could perform the work of several adults more quickly and more uniformly. Consequently, technological innovation in the British Industrial Revolution increased the demand for child labor relative to adult labor which significantly altered the work of children.

Great Britain is an especially appropriate focal point for a study of child labor and its role in industrialization for several reasons. First, Great Britain was considered a leader in industrialization (although considerable debate remains about whether what happened in England can be called an Industrial Revolution).[7] The importance of the lessons to be learned from Britain's experience are succinctly put by Mokyr: "Britain taught Europe and Europe taught the world how the miracles of technological progress, free enterprise, and efficient management can break the shackles of poverty and want" (1993:131). Second, the contribution of child labor to the industrial labor force was both prominent and controversial in Great Britain. Lastly, the employment of children during the eighteenth and nineteenth century is fairly well documented by contemporaries and Parliament.

The Employment of Children in the Economy

Whether it was working in the fields, helping around the house or assisting in the family's trade, children contributed to the family enterprise as soon as they were able. Children had worked for centuries and continued to work during the Industrial Revolution because work was part of childhood of the poor and working class. Parents had worked when they were young and the same was expected of their offspring. The practice of putting children to work was recorded in the Medieval era when children spun thread to be woven in their father's loom. Most likely the practice existed even earlier, probably on small family farms. The concept of the whole family, including wife and children, working to generate income was not viewed by parents as cruel or abusive but was recognized as necessary for survival.

Children's Employment in Pre-Industrial Britain

To understand the issue of child labor and its role in industrial development it is important to know the historiography of child labor. Child labor was not a new phenomenon invented by the capitalists or the industrialists. Farmers, households, entrepreneurs, masters and small business owners had employed children for centuries. Both rural and nonrural families expected children to work and to contribute to the family economy[8] whether farming, spinning or weaving. Children were productive members of the family, "A fifteen-year-old daughter of a medieval weaver might have spent her day spinning wool into thread, setting up her father's loom, selling cloth to customers, and completing a variety of small household and business chores; her counterpart in the nineteenth century earned a wage at a textile factory" (Bennett 1988:271). On the farm children performed simple duties - helping with the domestic chores inside the house (cleaning, washing, cooking or watching after siblings) and working outside in the fields (pulling weeds, sifting out rocks or digging up potatoes). In British towns, children were seen working alongside their parents at the loom, spinning, picking up waste cotton and reeling the cotton. Whether spinning, weaving, straw plaiting or nail making, children helped their parents by performing simple duties, fetching materials and relaying messages.

The existence of child labor prior to the nineteenth century in Great Britain has been discussed by many economic historians. Kussmaul (1981) has documented the high incidence of youths working as servants in husbandry in the sixteenth century. Youths, working and living away from home, performed a variety of tasks. Girls milked the cows, watched over the chickens, weeded and cooked. Boys cared for the draught animals, cattle and sheep in addition to ploughing and carting (34). Sharpe (1991) has documented the employment of poor children as apprentices as early as 1550. She concludes that pauper apprenticeship was a "local institution" in Colyton where children as young as eight would leave the home to work and live with others until they reached the age of twenty-one. Although the practice of "living in" declined in the late eighteenth century, the norm became "outdoor apprenticeships" where children would reside with their parents but leave each day to work for their master (265-267). Wall (1987) finds this search for employment outside the home by teens widespread in pre-industrial England from 1599-1781 but highest for children of laborers and craftsmen (91). Work was clearly the expectation of parents and youths such that "adolescence was characterized by mass movement from the parental home" to find it (91). Davin (1982) places the issue in a household context and emphasizes the subordinate role of children to their parents in eighteenth-century Britain. She described how domestic production[9] "would always utilize the labour of children from the earliest age that was practical, either as auxiliaries in production, or in odd jobs with domestic work and especially with the care of younger children" (1982:633).

Pinchbeck and Hewitt (1973) trace the employment of children from the rural farm to the urban factory, particularly highlighting the conditions and hours of work at home in the cottage industry. Pinchbeck dispels the novelty associated with factory labor by concluding that "women and children were simply doing in the factory, under different conditions, the work they had always done in their homes" (Pinchbeck 1930:197). Levine (1977) examines the demographic impact of this type of work on the age of marriage and fertility rates. He argues that the work of women and children was quite common in this stage of proto-industry or nascent capitalism in areas like Shepshed where the framework knitting industry engaged boys as winders and girls as seamers and in Colyton where lacemaking provided opportunities for women and girls (28,110). Berg (1991 and 1993) identifies another employer of children in the proto-industrial economy, the medium-sized manufactory (what she calls "small producer capitalism"). She argues these producers in the cotton industry, the metal trades, in calico printing and button making relied heavily on the labor of women and children (1991:31).

Children's Employment in Industrial Britain

The extent of the employment of children during the industrialization period in Great Britain is a matter of debate. Pessimists like Alfred (1857), Engels (1926), Horner (1840), Marx (1909), Toynbee (1884) and the Webbs (1898) believed the Industrial Revolution brought large numbers of children to work in the factories and mines. A picture was painted of the "dark satanic mills" which employed children as young as five and six years old for twelve to sixteen hours a day, six days a week without recess for meals. These "little children" toiled in hot, stuffy, overcrowded factories to earn as little as four shillings per week. Usually the worst abuses and conditions were highlighted to attract the attention of the populace and sway the sentiments of the members of Parliament to intervene on behalf of the children. As Marx observed: "Children of nine and ten years are dragged from their squalid beds at two, three or four o'clock in the morning and compelled to work for a bare subsistence until ten, eleven, or twelve at night, their limbs wearing away, their frames dwindling, their faces whitening, and their humanity absolutely sinking into a stone-like torpor, utterly horrible to contemplate" (1909:227).

Optimists, however, offer an alternative view and claim the Pessimists exaggerated the extent and conditions under which children worked during the Industrial Revolution. They argue that the main source of information cited by the Pessimists, "The Blue Books," were biased because they had been prepared by members of Parliament who wanted to pass regulations prohibiting child labor. In addition, Ure (1835), Ashton (1948) and Hartwell (1971) maintain the conditions (hours, safety, abuse) were no worse than what had existed in the home and that the wages were much better. Contrast Ure's portrayal of factory work to that of Marx's above:

> They seemed to be always cheerful and alert, taking pleasure in the light play of their muscles, - enjoying the mobility natural to their age. The scene of industry, so far from exciting sad emotions in my mind, was always exhilarating. It was delightful to observe the nimbleness with which they pieced the broken ends, as the mule-carriage began to recede from the fixed roller beam, and to see them at leisure, after a few second's exercise of their tiny fingers, to amuse themselves in any attitude they chose, till the stretch and winding-on were once more completed. The work of these lively elves seemed to resemble a sport, in which habit gave them pleasing dexterity (1835:301).

Since much of the earlier debate has relied on anecdotal evidence to make generalizations about the entire work force in nineteenth-century Britain, we must look at statistical accounts to discern the proportion of children working. Most economic historians agree that the early factory work force consisted of a considerable number of children. Freudenberger, Mather and Nardinelli found that "children formed a substantial part" of the factory labor force of 1818 in cotton. Using data from a neglected *Parliamentary Report* (1819[HL.24]CX), they calculated that 4.5 percent of the cotton workers were under ten and over half (54.5 percent) were under nineteen years of age (1984:1087). Cruickshank shows this to still be true in 1833 where the growth of the factory system meant that "children under fourteen formed a fifth or a sixth of the total work force in the textile towns. There were, for example, 4,000 children in the mills in Manchester, 1,600 in Stockport, 1,500 in Bolton and 1,300 in Hyde" (1981:51). Nardinelli, in his book, *Child Labor and the Industrial Revolution*, argued that with the enforcement of the Factory Act of 1833 between 1835 and 1838 "the number of children employed in textile factories fell from 56,000 to 33,000" (1990:107). At the same time, however, his figures show an increase in the employment of young males (thirteen to seventeen years old) over these same three years (1990:106).

In contrast, Cunningham (1990) argues that historians have gone astray in focusing on the contribution children made to their families and to the economy's labor force. Instead, he claims to have found sufficient evidence which suggests just the opposite, that idleness of children was more a problem during the Industrial Revolution than exploitation resulting from employment. He looks to the *Report on the Poor Laws in 1834* where parish after parish responded to the question, "Have you any and what Employment for Women and Children?" by saying there was "very little employment for Women and Children, not having any Manufactory" (1990:133-34). Cunningham provides statistical evidence from the *1851 Census of Great Britain* to further support the impression given by the Royal Commission on the Poor Laws. Figures from the *1851 Census* show for various counties that merely 0.2 - 11.9 percent boys and 0.05 - 21.5 percent girls aged five to nine were employed across Great Britain (Cunningham 1990:140-143). He discovers, however, the proportions are much larger for boys and girls aged ten to fourteen (ranging from 18 percent to 52 percent for boys and 8 to 51 percent for girls) and substantially higher for fifteen to nineteen year olds (Cunningham 1990:143). He concludes by saying, "It is likely, of course, that while most ten- and eleven-year-olds were unemployed, most thirteen- and fourteen-year-old boys and many of the girls, were in employment" (Cunningham 1990:143,146).

How do we reconcile these seemingly conflicting depictions of working-class children in the nineteenth century? Was idleness or employment the plight of children as Britain industrialized? In order to discern the role children and youth played in the industrialization process and the extent to which they were employed, we need to identify where they worked. Was child labor pervasive in all sectors of the British economy or was it mainly in the manufacturing sector? In the manufacturing sector, was the employment of children and youths equally distributed across industries or was it concentrated in only a few? Cunningham was on the right track when he concluded, "There was in no sense a national labour market for children" (1990:146). Instead, the labor market for children was one where shortages in some regions coexisted with surpluses in other regions. For example, while employment possibilities were negligible in the County of Sussex or East Riding, opportunities were plentiful in the County of Lancaster and Somerset. In the County of Sussex, R. William Lower reported, "We have no manufactory, or any means of employing women or children." Thomas McBride from East Riding stated, "None for those out of the workhouse; we have no manufactories requiring them." In sharp contrast, John Fisher from Preston replied, "The cotton mills afford ample employment to young girls, and considerable employment to Women and Children" and Robert Norton from the County of Somerset recorded, "The women and children are generally in full employment in the silk factories here, not on the parish account" (1834(44)XXXVI:231h, 250h,73h and 204h).

Although every region may not have employed child labor, children were working in a diverse set of occupations within certain regions. As the responses in the Report on the Poor Laws in 1834 reveal, children were employed in a wide range of activities in all sectors of the economy. Children worked outside in the fields on family farms or as outdoor servants. Children also worked in homes as assistants in the family cottage industry, as domestic servants or as chimney sweeps. Children worked in factories as parish apprentices or as "free" factory workers.[10] Children worked, moreover, underground in the coal mines and on the surface of metal mines. The extent of their involvement in the productive economy is immediately apparent in the richness of the responses of witnesses in 1834 to Poor Law Authorities. Table 1.2 tabulates the variety of responses to the question, "Have you any and what Employment for Women and Children?" in rural areas. Although Cunningham was

TABLE 1.2 Employment of Children in Agricultural Districts in 1834

Responses to Question 11 of the Poor Law Report of 1834, "Have you any and What Employment for Women and Children?"

Responses	Number	Percentage
Field work	662	47.00%
No answer	217	15.00
None	198	14.00
Lace making	79	6.00
Mining	28	2.00
Glove-knitting	27	2.00
Straw Plait Manufacture	25	2.00
Silk Mills	23	2.00
Cotton Mills	17	1.00
Spinning	15	1.00
Weaving	15	1.00
Hose Manufacture	15	1.00
Paper Mill	7	.50
Button Making	7	.50
Nail Manufacture	5	.30
Pillow Lace	3	.20
Pin Factories	3	.20
Hat makers	3	.20
Hand Loom Weaving	3	.20
Ironworks	3	.20
Calico Printing	3	.20
Domestic Service	4	.20
Unclear answer	4	.20
Housework	2	.10
Weaving Ribbons	2	.10
Flannel Trade	2	.10
Bone Lace	1	.07
China Clay works	1	.07
Earthenware Manufacture	1	.07
Glass Manufacture	1	.07
Brick making	1	.07
Prostitution	1	.07
Tile making	1	.07
Help Innkeeper	1	.07
Total	1394	100.00

Source: 1834(44)XXX, Administration and Operation of Poor Laws, Appendix B.1, pt. 1 Answers to Rural Questions.

correct in pointing out the large number of negative responses (14 percent of the respondents said "None"), there was a far greater number who gave some form of positive response.[11] Almost half (47 percent) of the respondents said there was some employment for women and children in the fields, especially during the summer months. A sizeable number responded that women and children were employed in Lace making (6 percent), Straw plaiting (2 percent), Silk throwing (2 percent), Glove-knitting (2 percent), and Mining (2 percent). The other opportunities for women and children were numerous and scattered throughout the economy in employments ranging from Button making and Brick making to Calico Printing.

The fact that children were employed in all sectors of the economy in a variety of occupations is also evident in the Occupational Abstracts of the *1841 and 1851 Census of Great Britain.* Tables 1.3 and 1.4 list the most common occupations for boys and girls in 1841 and 1851, respectively. By the middle of the nineteenth century, the most common occupations for boys and girls were the same as they had been at the beginning of the century. The vast majority of boys who worked were still Agriculture Labourers while most of the girls who worked were Domestic Servants. A large number of boys and young men were also employed as Servants (both Domestic and Farm), Cotton Textile workers, Messengers and Coal Miners. An interesting pattern emerges from the *1851 Census* once the ages of children and youths were disaggregated. A large proportion of boys aged five to ten were employed in the textile manufactories (cotton, worsted, and woollen) and in the coal mines. The concentration of boys in these industries is hardly a coincidence and will be explained in detail in Chapters 4 and 5. Although many girls and young women were also employed in Agriculture and Cotton Manufacture, instead of Coal Mines they were working in Silk Mills and Lace Manufactures. Similarly, like their male cohorts in 1851, young girls aged five to ten were more often employed in the textile factories (cotton, worsted and lace) than any other occupation except Straw Plait Manufacture. Clearly, children and youths contributed to the agricultural sector as field workers and to the manufacturing sector both in cottage industries as shoemakers and dressmakers as well as in manufactories as textile workers.

Children Worked in the Fields. Children had worked on farms and in fields for centuries and continued to do so during the Industrial Revolution. As illustrated in Tables 1.3 and 1.4, Agriculture Labourer was the most common occupation for boys and one of the fifteen most common occupations for girls in 1841 and 1851. Children either worked for their parents, for other farmers (some as servants in husbandry, others as day labourers) or for gangmasters (gang system). Most children who worked on the family farm were not hired labourers who received a wage. Instead, parents expected them to do what they were told and to help out where they could. Typically, parents rented the land from a landowner and needed to produce enough from the farm to pay off the rent and to sustain the family. As the commissioners reported, "Young girls, however, frequently work in their father's allotment or potato ground, assisting him or their mother in its cultivation, and they also help their mother in gleaning; but it is not hired labour" (1843[510]XII:28). The child's contribution usually augmented

TABLE 1.3 Most Common Occupations of Boys and Girls in 1841

Boys	*Girls*
Agriculture Labourer (196,640)[a]	Domestic Servants (346,079)
Domestic Servant (90,464)	Cotton Manufacture (62,131)
Cotton Manufacture (44,833)	Dress-maker, Milliner (22,174)
Labourer (37,756)	Agriculture labourer (14,295)
Coal Miner (32,475)	Silk Manufacture (12,539)
Boot & Shoe maker (27,320)	Weaver (11,473)
Carpenter & Joiner (20,775)	Flax & Linen Manufacture (10,898)
Tailor (19,710)	Woollen Manufacture (8,848)
Blacksmith (16,285)	Worsted Manufacture (6,185)
Woollen Manufacture (14,875)	Lace Manufacture (6,084)
Weaver (12,789)	Factory Worker (5,626)
Clerk (10,281)	Straw Plait (3,475)
Mason, Pavior (9,528)	Earthenware (3,330)
Painter, Plumber (7,042)	Spinner (2,569)
Army (6,976)	Straw Bonnet & Hat maker (2,476)

[a]Note: The numbers include all boys and girls under the age of 20.

Source: 1841(52)II, *1841 Census of Great Britain*, pp. 43-56.

TABLE 1.4 Most Common Occupations of Boys and Girls in 1851

	Ages	
Boys	*5-10*	*10-15*
Agriculture Labourer	5,546	76,713
Messenger	2,347	41,575
Farm Servant	599	33,064
Cotton Manufacture	2,243	30,985
Coal Miner	1,291	26,986

(continues)

TABLE 1.4 (continued)

	Ages	
Boys	5-10	10-15
Labourer	630	14,235
Shoemaker	322	11,320
Woollen Manufacture	1,166	10,004
Worsted Manufacture	1,655	9,089
Iron Manufacture	180	6,330
Silk Manufacture	551	6,059
Domestic Servant (general)	96	5,698
Flax, Linen Manufacture	233	5,566
Tailor	38	5,465
Earthenware	591	4,400

Girls	5-10	10-15
Domestic Servants (general)	964	57,969
Cotton Manufacture	1,706	35,352
Farm Servant (indoor)	261	12,548
Silk Manufacture	720	10,759
Worsted Manufacture	1,271	10,632
Lace Manufacture	2,644	8,997
Woollen Manufacture	826	8,002
Nurse Servant	508	7,259
Flax, Linen Manufacture	263	7,105
Dressmaker, Milliner	44	6,858
Straw Plait Manufacture	2,747	5,058
Agriculture Labourer (outdoor)	294	3,798
Glover	474	3,374
Hose Manufacture	770	3,342
Seamstress	122	2,389

Source: 1852-53[1691-I]LXXXVIII, pt. 1, *1851 Census of Great Britain*, Table 54 Classified Arrangement of the Occupations, pp. cxxvii- cxlix.

the parents' productivity. The output of the farm was the result of a collective effort of the entire family as well as any hired servants and laborers. Children performed tasks appropriate for their age and physical strength, freeing their parents to do the more arduous and difficult jobs.

Some children, however, who worked on farms were hired labor but like the sons and daughters of farmers did not receive a wage. Instead, in exchange for the work they did as ploughmen, carters, dairymaids, and stable hands, they received room and board with the farmer. These servants, as they are called in the literature, were children hired into families of their employers on annual contracts. Because they lived where they worked, their hours of work were not fixed and they provided their services whenever they were needed. Pauper children could be taken from their parents without consent by the poor law officers as early as age nine and could be apprenticed until they reached twenty-one (Hopkins 1994:14). The number of such poor law apprenticeships to husbandry declined in the nineteenth century. Kussmaul attributes the decline to three factors: (1) rapid population growth, (2) rising cost of living and (3) high grain prices (1981:120-121). Progressive farmers with large enclosed holdings began to hire "day laborers" who were cheaper (they did not require food and lodging) while only small inefficient farmers continued to hire servants. As Kussmaul documented, "By 1851, few servants in husbandry were hired in the south and east. Most poor youths worked as day-labourers; only a few were plucked from this mass and placed at the farmer's table" (1981:10). The "day-labourers," unlike their enslaved predecessors, were paid a wage and returned home at the end of a day. "The only remaining farm servants in 1851 lived to the north of Dorset, Wiltshire, Oxfordshire, Northamptonshire, Cambridgeshire, and Norfolk" (Kussmaul 1981:131).

Other children who worked on farms as hired labor received a wage but lived at home with their family. These children, however, worked in gangs and had to walk miles each day to and from work. A father from Norfolk whose child worked in the gang system at Castle Acre lamented,

> Ganging is what leads 'em into so many bad ways; that's what caused many girls to be out at nights, when they ought to be home. My girl went 5 miles yesterday to her work, turniping; she set off between seven and eight, she walked; had a piece of bread before she went; she did not stop work in the middle of the day; ate nothing till she left off; she came home between three and four o'clock. Their walks are worse than their work; she is sometimes so tired, she can't eat no victuals when she comes home (1843[510]XII:277).

The gang system was especially prevalent in areas where farms were very spread out, such as East Anglia, Suffolk, Norfolk and Lincolnshire. Usually twenty to twenty-five women and children worked under the direction of a gangmaster, moving from farm to farm under contract to do heavy work. Historians argue that gang work existed because of the destruction of cottages in "closed" parishes and the enclosure and cultivation of former marsh or open land to create more farms (Bennett 1991:21). Children began to work for the gangs as young as four and five and continued through adolescence. Their hours were longer than the children who worked on family farms and the servants in husbandry because it often took considerable time to walk to the place of work. In some cases, children left their homes at five o'clock in the morning and did not return until six or seven in the evening. What sort of work did children in the fields do?

The tasks of the child Agriculture Labourer were gender-specific and depended on the child's strength and the type of farming in that county (hops, potato, corn, husbandry, etc.). The *Report on the Employment of Women and Children in Agriculture* (1843[510]XII) provides comprehensive evidence on the nature and conditions of child labor in agriculture during this period. In general, boys and young men performed a variety of tasks ranging from bird-keeping (scaring birds) and weeding to driving horses at the plough. Young boys' chief occupation was bird-keeping, taking care of poultry or watching cattle in the fields. By the ages of ten and eleven boys were strong enough to lead horses and oxen at the plough. Young men aged thirteen, fourteen and fifteen had the physical strength to hold the plough and the maturity to attend the stable. Once a young man turned fifteen he was ready for the most difficult and strenuous jobs, that of mowing, reaping, hedging and ditching. Girls, in contrast, were confined to planting seeds and picking the ripened crop. Typically, young women were not in the field but were instead found tending the animals in the barn or doing indoor work. A commissioner summarized the activities in his district as follows, "Boys are employed to frighten crows and birds off corn; and if hired, feed cattle in the farm yards, and look after various little things about the farms; steady girls are seldom employed unless hired, and when hired generally have to feed calves, besides the in-door work" (1843[510]XII:309).

The division of field work along gender lines is demonstrated in the following descriptions from the County of Kent and the County of Sussex. In Kent, boys were employed on the Hops-gardens at "opening" - making holes for plants; "poling" - placing a pole near a plant for support; "shimming and breaking" - loosening the earth and removing weeds and "picking" - culling the fruit and dropping it into bins. Girls, on the other hand, "do little or nothing but pick hops" (1843[510]XII:167). In Sussex, boys were employed at couching[12], pulling and spudding weeds, hay-making, reaping, driving the plough, hedging and ditching. Mr. Vaughan reported that girls were employed occasionally in stone-picking, potato-planting, potato-picking and bean-dropping (1841[510]XII:171).

Boys and girls were regularly employed in farm work by the ages of nine and ten, although some boys began as early as age seven. The days were long for Agriculture Labourers, beginning at sunrise and ending at dusk. In the counties of Wilts, Dorset, Devon, Somerset, Kent, Surrey, Sussex, Yorkshire and Northumberland children and youths worked 12-hour days in the summer from 6:00 a. m. until 6:00 p. m. and 8-hour days in the winter from 8:00 a. m. until 4:00 p. m. Children doing field work in the counties of Suffolk, Norfolk, and Lincoln worked 10 hours in the summer from 8:00 a. m. until 6:00 p. m. but the same number of hours in the winter. Although the days were long, children and youths were not working constantly but had some time to rest, eat and even play. Exactly how many hours they toiled each day depended upon the weather, the season and the expectations of the parents. Work often ceased when it rained heavily and in the winter months was almost nonexistent. Wages were low and varied according to the region. They ranged from a low of three pence a day in Norfolk to a high of eight pence a day in Surrey, Norfolk, and Lincolnshire (1843[510]XII:165-289). Most children seemed to earn between four and six pence a day.

Children and youths worked on the farm because their parents expected them to help out with the family "enterprise." The number of young workers from the family (or neighbor's families) willing to work was plentiful because the tradition of work had been handed down from generation to generation. Working on the farm made sense because the opportunity cost[13] of a child working was very low since there were no other opportunities competing for the child's time. Although the work children and youths performed helped to increase the total output of the farm, it was unpaid work since parents essentially "hired" their children. The need for child labor on the farm persisted into the twentieth century and still exists on small farms today. The number of child laborers working on the farm did decline, however, with the collapse of grain prices that came with the introduction of American wheat exports at the end of the nineteenth century. The competition from America resulted in depressed conditions for British farmers such that many families left the land and migrated to the towns looking for a new lease on life.

Children Worked in Homes. Children who worked in homes were either employed as helpers in domestic production (or what is called cottage industry), as domestic servants or as chimney sweeps. Although the majority of families who were engaged in the economy were working in agriculture in 1801, the occupational distribution changed rapidly over the next fifty years. By 1831 more families were occupied in trade, manufacture and handicraft. Mitchell estimates that the families engaged in trade, manufacture and handicraft increased from 1,129,000 in 1811 to 1,435,000 in 1831 (1988:103). A complete list of all the different types of occupations within this industrial sector of the economy is provided in the *Census of Great Britain* beginning in 1841. Tables 1.3 and 1.4 give some flavor of the variety of occupations which employed children. Girls and boys were Dressmakers and Tailors, Hat makers and Painters, as well as workers making buttons, shoes, and earthenware. These "sweated trades," as they are often referred to in the literature, took place in workshops where children worked alongside parents and older siblings. The workshops were located in families' homes or attached to the backs of cottages and employed as few as three and as many as 200 workers. According to Mathias, the average workshop in 1851 was small and employed fewer than ten workers (1983:247). The workshop began as the workplace of the medieval craft guild and became the center of the spinning and weaving processes of the woollen cloth industry (Hopkins 1994:22). Despite the development of the factory system, the traditional workshop remained the standard industrial production unit until the mid-nineteenth century.

Girls began work as apprentices to Dressmakers and Milliners at age twelve. After two years of training they were paid wages. Their hours depended upon the demand for their work although Dressmakers were notorious for working very long hours. In the busiest seasons--early summer and winter--they worked 16-17 hours (from 6:30 a. m. until 11:00 p. m.) and 14 hours (from 8:00 a. m. until 12:00 midnight), respectively. Although they were given a break for meals and tea each day, they often had to stay until 2 a. m. to complete their work. The reality of these long hours is crystallized by a commissioner's description of seventeen-year-old Mary Gasson's work day:

> Has been an in-door apprentice 2 years and a half; paid a premium to be here 3 years. In the season is generally called at 4 a. m. and sometimes at half past 3 or twenty minutes to 4; at other times at half past 4 or 5. It is expected they should be in the work-room in half

an hours after being called. Leaves off at 11 p. m. regularly, except at a drawing room, when some of them have not more than 2 or 3 hours rest on the night before. Never works later than 12 on Saturday (1843[431]XIV:f216-217).

The commissioner, Dr. Stewart, was alarmed by the long hours worked by these girls. In his report on manufactures in the Counties of Dorset, Devon and Somerset he exclaimed, "These poor girls, who are at all times, except when actually enjoying their annual holiday, debarred from all desirable change of posture and occupation, and from due opportunities of improvement and relaxation, are during their 'busy season' in winter and early summer, especially prevented by the unceasing nature of their duties, from all exercise and wholesome recreation whatever" (1843[431]XIV:D2). Once the girls learned how to sew, the work was repetitive and did not require strength but produced considerable back and eye strain. In addition, the work required tremendous concentration because of its delicate nature and the demand for perfection. Apprentices did not receive a wage but instead paid a premium to the owner of the establishment for "training" in the trade as well as for food and lodging (1843[431]XIV:F31). Elizabeth Gaskell's popular novel *Mary Barton* (1848) depicts the life of a young dressmaker who lives in Manchester.

Boys and girls began to work in the pottery industry between the ages of eight to thirteen According to the *1843 Report on the Employment of Young Persons in Trades and Manufactures*, manufacturers in Lancashire employed very few children under the age of thirteen while younger children were hired by the manufacturers in Staffordshire, the center of this industry (1843[431]XIV:B38,C4). The children and youths worked between 10-1/2 and 12 hours a day, six days a week. Time was set aside for dinner and tea and unlike the Dressmakers, the children rarely worked overtime. Children worked as "jiggerers," "oven-boys," "dipper boys," "cutters," "handlers," "apprentice painters" and "figure makers." A few of the tasks were gender specific like "dipper boys" and "oven boys," while most jobs were performed by both boys and girls. "Dipper boys" dipped the ware in glaze before putting it in the ovens, while it was the sole duty of an "oven boy" to place the clay ware into the kiln. A "jiggerer" turned the pottery wheel; "cutters" cut the clay to fit the mould; "handlers" attached the handles and spouts to the ware requiring them; "painters" painted various colored ornaments upon the ware and "figure makers" made ornamental pieces (1843[432]XV:L18). Samuel Scriven provides a descriptive summary in his report, "The employments of children are various and dissimilar; in some of the rooms great numbers are congregated together, while in others there are only one or two; the painting, burnishing, gilding, flower-making, moulding, figure-making, and engraving, constitute literally schools of art, under the superintendence of masters and mistresses" (1834[431]XIV:C4). In Staffordshire, boys and girls between the ages of eight and thirteen who worked as "jiggerers," "handlers," "oven-boys," "dippers," "painters," "cutters," and "figure makers" received an average weekly wage of 2 shillings and 1/2 pence (1843[431]XIV:C4).

Boys, usually at the age of eight and nine, began working with shoemakers. They worked an average of twelve hours a day and often longer when orders came in. Boys had primarily two tasks in the process of making shoes. They were responsible for sewing the quarter pieces to the upper pieces, uniting the quarters together by the seam at the heel, called "closing" and sewing together the linings and upper leather pieces, called "stabbing" (1843[432]XV:I49). Children in West of Scotland were paid 1-2 shillings a week, increasing to 6 shillings for "closing" and "stabbing" (1843[431]XIV:I49). These tasks required skill and strength as well as considerable concentration. The difficulty of such work is captured in Commissioner Tancred's report on Shoe Manufactures in West of Scotland:

> The work is continued for about 12 hours a day, and often longer, exclusive of time for meals, and requires considerable attention, as the stitches ought to be made as regular in length as possible. The minute attention must be very irksome to children of a tender age when continued for so many hours daily; and the use of corporal punishment to compel diligence in this respect seems a general consequence of imposing a degree and kind of labour unsuited to the tender age of the workers (1843[432]XV:I49).

In summary, children began to assist their families in cottage production at slightly younger ages than they had in farming. Many children were working by the ages of seven or eight and most were helping in some capacity by age twelve. The boys and girls working in workshops worked as many hours as those working on farms. Although hours varied from industry to industry, children usually worked twelve hours with time out for meals and tea. "Usually" is the operative word, here, because in some cottage industries like Dressmaking the hours were much longer, while in others like Hat making and Lace the hours were shorter. The hours, moreover, were not regular over the year nor were they consistent from day to day. Despite a seasonal component to production, work did not stop, however, when the weather was inclement as it did in farming. It did slow down, at times, when the trade was in a slump which caused fluctuations in hours as well as employment.

It is difficult to determine precisely how many hours the children actually worked in the workshops. An eighteenth-century practice of not working at the beginning of the week and then putting in many long hours at the end of the week continued into the nineteenth century. "St. Monday," as the custom was called, effectively changed the work week to Tuesday through Saturday. Some producers had "celebrated" excessively on Monday and either did not begin work until Tuesday or got very little done on Tuesday. This put pressure on the workers to work many consecutive hours and stay late towards the end of the week in order to have the work completed by Saturday.[14] Hence, some children worked steady hours for six days a week while others worked long hours for five days a week.

Children and youths worked in the cottage industry for the same reasons they had worked on the farm - their parents expected them to help out with the family "enterprise." Just as it had been customary for children to work on the farm generation after generation, the tradition of helping the father and/or mother with the family trade or craft was firmly established. Every member of the family did what they could to increase the total output of the family "business," whether it was spinning yarn, weaving, straw plaiting or making soap. The children and youths were available for as many hours as they were needed and typically they worked alongside their parents.

Working in the cottage, like working on the farm, made sense because the opportunity cost of children working was extremely low. The need for child labor in the cottage industry gradually declined as production moved to factories and mills. The gradual mechanization and automation of many production processes lead to "technological unemployment" (Berg 1985). Many adults and children lost their jobs while others suffered wage reductions. For example, the displacement of domestic jennies by larger water frames moved the production of cotton yarn from the cottage industry to the factories at the end of the eighteenth century (Cruickshank 1981:9-12). Many of the adults working in the various cottage industries tried to sustain a living by either switching to a different trade or migrating to enter the general market for unskilled labor (Lyons 1989:69-72). With the loss of a sustainable family "business," many of the children and youths went to work in the textile factories.

Another group of child laborers worked in the home but they were not engaged in workshop production. Instead, they helped with everything else - cooking, cleaning, sewing and caring for younger children. These domestic servants, as they were called, assisted women with the management of the household. Although the wealthier classes almost certainly had domestic servants, 2 percent of working-class families also had live-in servants (F. M. Thompson 1990:63,65). As revealed in Tables 1.3 and 1.4, Domestic Service was the single largest occupation for girls and young women in 1841 and 1851. There were, however, a few male domestic servants, although males tended to be farm servants instead. The occupation was dominated by females; Kussmaul calculated the ratio of male to female domestic servants in 1851 to be 13:100 (1981:40).

Girls left home around the age of twelve to become domestic servants in the homes of artisans, traders, manufacturers and shopkeepers. The girls received a small weekly wage (1 shilling) as well as room and board. In the smaller houses, the girls were trained by the mother of the household to care for her children and do the housework. In the larger houses, the girls seldom met the owners and worked with and were trained by the older servants (Longmate 1981:80). Parents thought sending girls to work as domestic servants served two purposes. First, it fed and clothed them if the family was poor and unable to provide for the child. Kussmaul mentions this motive in the introduction of her book, *Servants in Husbandry in Early Modern England* (1981). She states that, "Because service was widely practiced, farmers, craftsmen, and tradesmen could compose their household labour force independently of the number and skills of their children; their productive households could survive the death of any of its members; parents could send the children they could not support into the household of others" (1981:3). Secondly, it gave girls an adequate preparation to become good wives and mothers. They learned all the skills necessary for running and managing a household. In some respects, girls who became domestic servants were "fortunate" as the following quote reveals: "Mothers who managed to get a place in domestic service for their daughters, instead of factory or field work, felt that they had done well for them and given them as good a start in life as possible" (Longmate 1981:82).

Domestic servants worked long hours and had little free time. They did, however, get meals regularly and were usually allowed a two-week holiday in the summer to visit with their own families (Longmate 1981:81). The novel written by Flora Thompson entitled *Lark Rise to Candleford* (1973)[1939] depicts the author's life as a servant in Oxfordshire. As girls grew up they might change employers looking for a job as a cook, housemaid or housekeeper in a larger house. Once young women married, they would leave domestic service and turn their energies to managing their own household and having children.

Girls often worked as domestic servants in other people's homes if their parents could not support them in their own home. The number of girls and young women available to maintain a well-functioning household and "attend to its personal needs" was ample because of the large family size of the poor and working class (Kussmaul 1981:4).[15] Girls would choose to work in another family's home if the value of the food, lodging and training exceeded what they would receive in their own home. Thus, the opportunity cost of a girl working as a domestic servant was low because the child's family was unable to provide her with the basic necessities for survival. Despite the fact that the servant's work was considered productive (cooking, cleaning, caring for babies, etc.), it was unpaid work because the girl received room, board and training in "domestic" skills important for marriage. The need for domestic servants persisted into the twentieth century and still exists in the wealthiest homes today. The number of girls working as domestic servants did decline, however, as "the social and economic gap between servant-supplying and servant-hiring families widened" (Kussmaul 1981:10). Girls and young women who lived and worked as domestic servants in another person's home were gradually replaced by young women who were day laborers, performing the same services by day but returning home at night.

"Climbing Boys" worked in people's homes cleaning chimneys. They rarely saw the light of day. Although this occupation is not listed among the top fifteen occupations in 1841 or 1851, the use of boys as human brushes was quite widespread. A commissioner estimated that in 1817 there were 200 Master Chimney Sweeps in London with 500 apprentices working for them (1817(400)VI:5). In 1854 Lord Shaftesbury estimates there were 4,000 "climbing boys" (Horn 1994:28). Most likely, the number peaked earlier since the Act for the Better Regulation of Chimney Sweepers and their Apprentices in 1788 and the Act for the Regulation of Chimney Sweeps and Chimneys in 1840 put a damper on the employment of boys.[16] Parents apprenticed their sons and mothers sold their illegitimate children to the master Chimney Sweep who would feed, cloth and discipline the "climbing boys" (Longmate 1981:74). Chimney Sweeps' practice of hiring young boys to clean narrow chimneys was brought to the public's attention in the *Report for the Committee on Employment of Boys in Sweeping Chimneys in 1817* (1817(400)VI). The first resolution of the committee was to improve the position of the "climbing boys." It stated, "That this Meeting is anxious to improve the condition of Climbing Boys should be taken into immediate consideration--And that the Legislature may be pleased to enact such laws as will ensure to the children employed in this necessitous business, a mild and humane treatment" (1817(400)VI:50). Additional legislation was passed in 1840 which made it illegal to apprentice anyone under sixteen or to hire anyone under twenty-one to clean chimneys. Despite the prohibitive legislation which existed, evidence that boys were still being employed by Chimney Sweeps surfaced in the

Report of the Children's Employment Commission in 1862. Mr. George Ruff, a Master Sweep in Nottingham, admitted, "The use of boys is much encouraged by the fact that many householders will have their chimneys swept by boys instead of machines" (1863[3170]XVIII:297). The boys worked twelve hours a day and began cleaning very early, usually around 4 - 4:30 in the morning. Charles Kinglsey wrote about a "climbing boy" in 1863 in a novel entitled *The Water Babies*.

The job of "climbing boys" was unhealthy and dangerous. Children as young as five began climbing chimneys. By age six and seven, they were experts at removing the thick layer of black soot which stuck to the inner walls of the chimney. Once the boys reached the age of eleven or twelve, they were too big to fit the narrow chimneys. The commissioners were appalled by the consequences of such an early introduction to work: "Stunted growth, in this unfortunate race of the community, is attributed, in a great measure, to their being brought into the business at a very early age, so early even as five years. And I have heard of instances of children four years and a half being compelled to go up narrow chimneys" (1816(397)III, Appendix:26). When children were reluctant to go up a chimney, masters were known to prick their bare feet with pins or light a fire beneath them in order to force them up the narrow space. Even without the fires beneath them, cleaning chimneys was hard and dangerous work. Initially, the boys' elbows and knees would become raw from climbing, a scab would develop and then the soot would wear away the scab. Once their skin had hardened, they could climb without pain. They had to be careful not to get asphyxiated by gases when there was debris blocking the opening.

Boys worked as chimney sweeps because their parents were poor and could not care for them. Parents felt by sending them out of the home they had a better chance of surviving, as in the case of domestic servants. The master chimney sweep not only provided them with food and clothing but he also taught the boys the art of cleaning chimneys. Working as a chimney sweep made sense because the opportunity cost of working was almost zero since there were no other opportunities for the boy's time. The boys, whether apprenticed or not, were not paid for their work because they received food, clothing and training. The demand for child labor to clean chimneys remained steady for most of the nineteenth century. The number of child chimney sweeps decreased due to three factors: (1) enlargement of chimneys in British homes, (2) invention and use of a machine that cleaned chimneys and (3) government legislation. The use of "climbing boys" to clean British chimneys was not eliminated until the Law of 1875 which required all sweeps to be licensed and imposed on the police the duty of enforcing all previously existing laws (Cunningham 1991 and Rose 1992).

Children Worked in Factories. With the introduction of water power at the beginning of the Industrial Revolution, factories and mills sprang up in the countryside to utilize this new source of energy. Consequently, the first textile mills were located in sparsely populated districts creating a shortage of labor (Collier 1964 and Redford 1926). The labor imported to the mill was of three types: (1) parish apprentices taken from workhouses who were housed, clothed and fed but received no wages, (2) apprentices on contract from their parents who received room and board as well as a small wage and (3) "free" labor living at home with their parents receiving a weekly wage (Collier 1964:39).

Most country mills employed mainly parish apprentices out of necessity. As Samuel Greg of the Quarry Bank Mill discovered, they were inexpensive to keep, physically suited for the tasks, easily trainable and readily available (Nixon and Hill 1986:20). A conservative estimate is that one third of the total workers employed in country mills were apprentices (Rule 1981:29). There are, however, indications that their numbers may have reached 80-90 percent in some individual rural mills (Collier 1964). In any case, there seems to be consensus that the practice of recruiting factory workers from the workhouses yielded an important source of labor to the country mills. Sir Robert Peel was not alone in his predicament when he replied to a question by the *Select Committee on the State of Children Employed in Manufactures in 1816,*

"Do you employ parish apprentices?" Peel replied, "There were no others I could get. When Arkwright's machinery had first existence steam power was little but known, and . . . those who wished to . . . benefit by these improvements, resorted to country places where there were great waterfalls, and consequently could not have any other apprentice labour; and I was in that situation for I had no other" (1816(397)III:135,141).

Any shortage of labor was quickly filled with "cartloads of pauper children" from the workhouses of London since,

as local people often disliked industry and a certain social obloquy met the parents of mill children, it became customary to import children from town workhouses and orphanages. The long- established but decaying custom of long apprenticeship was revived, although in fact, little training was necessary. Parish authorities gladly relieved the Poor rates by virtually selling batches of children to Northern manufacturers (Ward 1962:15).

The workhouse seemed a natural place to recruit labor because as Rule explains, "The workhouse had become a kind of factory, it was perhaps natural that the factory should be regarded as a kind of workhouse" (1981:24).

Children were bound as apprentices beginning at age nine until they turned eighteen. If children began their apprenticeships when they were older, their term never lasted past their eighteenth birthday. The mill owner was obligated to provide room and board and often housed them together as Samuel Greg did in the Apprentice House at Styal.[17] The children and youths worked twelve hours in the mills, from 6:00 a. m. until 7:00 p. m. with a little time reserved for tea and/or dinner. The life of a parish apprentice has been recorded in the heart-wrenching tales of Michael Armstrong and Robert Blincoe in Frances Trollope's *Michael Armstrong, The Factory Boy* and John Brown's *A Memoir of Robert Blincoe*, respectively. At best, conditions resembled Greg's Apprentice House where the children got pork and clean shirts every Sunday and clean sheets once a month (Nixon and Hill 1986:21). At worst, conditions were appalling and unfit for human habitation. Frances Trollope described the housing for the less fortunate:

[E]ven at dead of night the machinery was never stopped, and when one set of fainting children were dragged from the mules another set were dragged from the reeking beds they were about to occupy, in order to take their places. The ventilation throughout the whole fabric was exceedingly imperfect; the heat, particularly in the room immediately beneath the roof was frightfully intense; cleanliness as to the beds, floors, and the walls, utterly neglected . . . (1840:212).

Although there is some agreement as to the necessity of these parish apprentices for the country mills, considerable debate remains over whether they were truly a cheap source of labor. Many historians have concluded that parish apprentices were the cheapest form of labor because they were exclusively in demand by the factory masters in the country mills and were employed in large numbers (Hammond and Hammond 1920; Pinchbeck 1930; Redford 1926 and Rule 1981). Unlike free labor, however, the apprentices received housing, clothes and food in exchange for their work. Some received a dowry when the term of their indenture expired. During the nineteenth century the cost of providing the apprentices with these amenities increased. In particular, the weekly cost of keeping each apprentice quadrupled from 1790 to 1847 at Quarry Bank Mill, from 3 shillings 6 pence to 13 shillings 4 pence (Collier 1964:46). These calculations by Greg's firm led Collier to conclude that the rising cost of keeping apprentices contributed to the rapid disappearance of the apprentice system from the cotton industry and led to the employment of more "free" labor. Her conclusion, however, is challenged by other evidence. A custom existed in the early nineteenth century where mill owners would send women across the countryside to get children from their parents. In these travels, the parish overseers were the most obliging - supplying handfuls of children from the workhouses for a competitive price (Rule 1981:25). Further, once children were "purchased" they may have traveled hundreds of miles until they reached the place of employment. This implies that pauper apprentices must have been a cheap source of labor for some factory owners. At the end of the nineteenth century Edward Greg, grandson of Robert Greg, believed the apprentice system disappeared because of the "Factory Acts, 'Short Time Committees' and morbid philanthropy" (Nixon and Hill 1986:23). Whatever the reason, "free" labor from families eventually replaced the parish apprentices in the textile factories.

With the invention of Watt's Steam Engine (1769) and its application to the textile industry, factories were built in more urban areas. Most factory owners chose to locate near population centers and drew their labor force from "free" labor rather than from parishes and workhouses. Hammond and Hammond describe the transition from apprentices to "free" labor: "The millowners began by getting children from the workhouses, and this system of serf labor carried the mills over the first stages, until there was a settled population, able to provide women and children" (1937:7). Most children did not work with their parents. They left their home for the day to work in the factory. They began to work at age six in wool, flax and silk mills and at age eight in cotton factories.[18] Some children continued to work once they became adults while others left the factory for different occupations. Although they were not bound as apprentices their hours were long because the machines were powered by steam.

They were paid a daily wage which depended on their age and specific duty in the factory. Their hours, conditions and tasks are the subject of Chapter 4. As the figures in Tables 1.3 and 1.4 display, "Cotton Manufacture" was one of the most common occupations of boys and girls in 1841 and 1851. In 1841 the only two occupations which employed more children and youths than textiles were Agriculture Laborer and Domestic Servant. In addition, the other types of textile manufactories (wool, flax, linen, worsted and silk) were among the largest employers of child labor according to the Occupational Census of 1841 and 1851.

Children Worked Underground. Children worked underground in coal mines and ironstone mines and on the surface of metal mines (copper and tin). Some boys worked for their fathers while others worked for a relative, a friend or a stranger. They began to work at age four in coal mines and age five in metal mines and moved from one post to another until they were old enough to be a hewer.[19] Their hours were long and most of the work underground was done in dark tunnels, partially illuminated with lamps. Depending upon their job, they were paid by either the master of the pit or the adult with whom they worked. Their hours, conditions and tasks are the subject of Chapter 5. As the figures in Tables 1.3 and 1.4 displayed, "Coal Miner" was one of the most common occupations of boys in 1841 and 1851. In both years the number of boys employed in the coal mines nearly equalled the number of boys employed in cotton factories.

Why have so many historians of the Industrial Revolution focused on child labor in textile factories and coal mines when children were working in a variety of occupations in the fields and at home? The employment of children in the factories and mines of Great Britain was different from their work elsewhere in four important ways. First, the large number of children working under one roof or in one establishment was a new phenomenon from the scattering of children who worked in the fields, in stables, in homes or even in cottages. Second, the employment of children suddenly became highly visible both because of the centrality of location and the size of the work force employed in mills and factories. Hopkins highlighted this aspect in his discussion of the factory system: "No one in the neighbourhood could fail to notice the streams of children entering and leaving the new buildings, and many would have kith and kin working there" (1994:87). Third, the nature of the employer/employee relationship changed as children switched from working with their parents to working for strangers. Finally, children's role in the production process became more important and in some situations, essential as they replaced adult workers. Initially, child labor contributed to the family economy as well as to the local economy. As Britain industrialized, child labor contributed to the output of the national economy. To fully understand the role children and youths had in Britain's industrialization and why the factories and mines drew so much attention, an industry approach must be taken.

An industry approach allows one to examine changes in the composition of the work force, the division of labor among different ages and genders of workers, the adoption and adaptation of new technology and the wage structure at the level it was occurring.

This microeconomic approach is superior to the macroeconomic approach taken by many scholars of child labor[20] for several reasons. A considerable portion of the data that is available was collected at the firm and industry level. The first aggregate statistics on the employment of children do not appear until the *1841 Census* and are not reliable until the *1851 Census*,[21] nearly ten years after the establishment of child labor legislation. The information, moreover, on occupations for 1841 does not distinguish children from youths, recall Table 1.3. Clearly, this data is helpful in getting a sense of where children were working but it is not useful in determining how important child labor was to a specific industry. The adoption of new inventions and the application of the division of labor associated with the Industrial Revolution varied among industries and within industries. Hudson (1989) puts it very well when she argues, "Thus the process of industrialisation moved at different paces in different parts of the region (as it did in others) and the outcome in terms of such things as the nature of centralised production, sources of capital and enterprise, the extent of sweating and outwork, could vary enormously between places a few miles from one another" (70-71). Whether one factory used a new technique or divided production into many specialized but simple tasks implied very different consequences for the employment of children, women and men. The characteristics of this new industrial labor force or Thompson's "working-class" are more easily identifiable at the place of work. In terms of the younger workers, the tasks they performed, the hours they worked and the skills they embodied give us clues about why they were working and how essential was their contribution.

At first glance, what does this industry approach tell us? Table 1.5 gives the employment of children and youths in a cross-section of industries and counties in Great Britain in 1833. The employment of children and young persons is considerably higher in the textile industry than in the Pottery, Glasswork, Paper and Dyehouse industries. In the silk and flax mills, children comprised nearly one third to one fifth of the work force, respectively. When young persons are included, the figures nearly double and reveal that more than half of the work forces in silk and flax mills were nonadults. A similar pattern is also found in the cotton and woollen mills with the proportions slightly lower but still large in comparison with the nontextile industries. Nearly 50 percent of the work forces of cotton and woollen mills were under the age of eighteen compared to 16 percent in Paper, 29 percent in Glasswork and 28 percent in Dyehouses. Although the Potteries and Lace industries employed a considerable number of children and youths, their totals hovered closer to 40 percent, notably less than in the textiles.

A similar concentration of child labor existed in mining. Table 1.6 shows that children made up roughly one third of the work force in coal mines, with the largest proportion of children working in England and the fewest working in West of Scotland. As much as 40 percent of the work force in Yorkshire mines was comprised of children and youths while in Lancashire 38 percent of the workers were under eighteen. Although the mines in South Durham, England and Monmouthshire and Glamorganshire, Wales did not employ as many children, close to 30 percent of the work force in their mines were nonadults. These proportions are somewhat smaller, however, than the proportions of children and youths employed in textile factories. In

TABLE 1.5 Employment of Children in 1833

Industry and County	Mills	Children Employed as % of Labor Force		
		Under 13	13-18	Total
Cotton				
Lancashire	29	17%	35%	52%
Glasgow	43	16	24	40
Aberdeen	1	17	41	58
Belfast	2	11	39	50
Wool				
North of England	23	18	31	49
Gloucestershire	17	19	27	46
Somersetshire	3	16	23	39
Wiltshire	17	16	28	44
Aberdeen	4	12	34	36
Flax				
Leeds	4	21	42	63
Marshall & Co, Leeds	1	21	46	67
Grandholm, Aberdeen	1	15	40	55
Scotland	73	17	36	53
Belfast	1	17	57	74
Silk				
Derby	15	22	32	54
Norfolk, Suffolk, Essex	6	34	44	78
Somersetshire	4	32	30	62
Paisley	4	13	54	67
Potteries				
Staffordshire	7	10	33	43
Dyehouse				
Leeds	1	0	28	28
Lace				
Devonshire	10	12	27	39
Glassworks				
Porto Bello, Mid Lothian	1	2	27	29
Paper				
Aberdeenshire	2	0	16	16

Source: 1834(167)XIX, Supplementary Report, Part I, pp. 19-39.

TABLE 1.6 Employment of Children in Mining in 1842

Industry and County	Children Employed as % of Labor Force[a]
Coal Mines	
England	
Lancashire	38%
Yorkshire	40
South Durham	29
East of Scotland	
Mid Lothian	34
Stirlingshire	37
West of Scotland	
Various Mines	24
Wales	
Monmouthshire	31
Glamorganshire	30
Pembrokeshire	33
Ironstone Mines	
West of Scotland	
New Monkland Parish	19
Shotts Parish	23
Tin, Copper, Lead and Zinc Mines	
Cornish District	27
Alston Moor District	21

[a]Children up to the age of 18 are included.

Source: 1842[380]XV, pp. 38,198,206.

summary, children and youths comprised between one third to over two thirds of the work forces of many textile factories and coal mines in Great Britain.

Childhood and Adolescence

Economic historians, historians and development economists who study the issue of child labor must always begin by defining the term. "Child labor" invokes an image of young children, even toddlers, with dirty faces and dingy clothes slaving away in fields, in factories and mines all day. Their small stature, slender frame, and round young faces easily distinguish them from adult workers. The term "child labor" is also used when researchers are studying the employment of teenagers. For the purpose of this book, a "child" is a person who is dependent upon other individuals for his/her livelihood, whether these individuals are parents, nurses, parish magistrates or overseers.[22] To clarify the discussion and present consistent statistical information the cohort of children is disaggregated into two categories, wherever possible. A "child" refers to someone under the age of thirteen and a "young person" or "youth" to some-one at least thirteen but not yet eighteen. The age of eighteen is considered the threshhold for adulthood, although not all historians would agree. Some historians may argue the Puritan image of children and the nature of factory work meant children behaved as "little adults" (Aries 1962, Hammond and Hammond 1937 and Thompson 1966). Based on this view, children may have reached adulthood at the age of sixteen or seventeen because there was no longer any distinction between what they did and what adults did - both worked for wages, drank at pubs and visited brothels. For example, Charles Booth, a contemporary was surprised by what he saw in London. He wrote in his book, *The Life and Labour of the People in London* (1886), that poor children were seen "running in and out of public-houses carrying great jorums of beer" (quoted in Stickland 1973:208). Another contemporary, C. Turner Thackrah, mentioned the ways children participated in adult activities in his report on "The Effects of the Principal Arts, Trades, and Professions... on Health and Longevity...and Suggestions for the Removal of Many of the Agents, which produce Disease, and Shorten the Duration of Life" (1830-1859). He wrote, "The grand bane of civilized life is *Intemperance*...More shocking is the case, when the evil is found among females; - when the wife is led to imitate her husband. Most shocking, when children, nay infants, are taught to sip with the mother, and thus acquire a taste for the bane of life and health" (quoted in Stickland 1973:140). As Pinchbeck and Hewitt explained, "They (children) were indeed, looked upon as "little adults" and therein lies the essence of the explanation of much otherwise inexplicable to us today. Until modern times, children dressed as their parents and, like their parents, their dress reflected their social status" (1973II:348). This depiction, however, seems to refer more to children's behavior and attire than to suggest their independent status relative to their families.

The Beginning of Adulthood

Eighteen is a reasonable threshhold level depicting adulthood for several reasons. First, during the eighteenth and nineteenth centuries, many children had not left home by their twenties which extended the period of interdependence as well as promoted the understanding that young adults still benefitted from living with their parents (Anderson 1971 and Wall 1978 and 1987). Several economic and social factors at the time contributed to this prolonged attachment of children to their parents: (1) economic need often meant families could not survive without the children's supplementary income,[23] (2) families had established a tradition of working together in the cottage industry and placed considerable value on the concept of "family income generation,"[24] (3) people married later in Great Britain than in other western countries[25] and (4) education, which often breeds independence, was largely neglected by parents during this period.[26] Freeman's (1914) research on the conditions of boy labor in Birmingham at the turn of the century also lends support for choosing the age of eighteen as the end of childhood and the beginning of adulthood. In his study he closely and carefully examined the lives of seventy-one boys in various family and economic circumstances. In the preface to Freeman's book, *Boy Life and Labour*, Sadler claims that most of the boys in the sample were "representative of well above half of the juvenile population of the city" (Freeman 1914:x). His observations and conclusions, therefore, can provide considerable insight into the stages of a boy's life and the way in which historians at the time viewed childhood and adulthood. Freeman defines adulthood as beginning at age eighteen, nineteen or twenty rather than earlier. In his section on "The Transition to Manhood" he observes, "The youth on the verge of manhood awakes to the seriousness of his position. His parents grumble at him for not bringing home more money. He begins to think in earnest about marriage. He believes himself entitled to an adult wage, and in many cases throws his job and refuses offers of others, because he 'won't take kid's wages'" (1914:204).

Another reason eighteen is an appropriate threshhold is that contemporaries viewed eighteen as the beginning of adulthood. In reading the *Parliamentary Reports* on the Employment of Children in the Factories, factory inspectors, factory commissioners, doctors and members of parliament continually refer to boys and girls under thirteen as "children" and people between the ages of thirteen and eighteen as "young persons." In creating tables to present information on the employment of children in the factories and mines, commissioners often grouped the data into three categories - children, young persons and adults. Mr Spencer's examination of the contracts child laborers received disaggregated the data into two groups, children (ages seven to twelve) and youths (aged thirteen to eighteen) (1833(450)XX:1-77). The tables extracted by Mr. Stanway to show the distribution of operatives and average net earnings in numerous textile factories reveal a similar breakdown. He separates the data for children and adults and defines an adult as "a person who has completed the Eighteenth year of Age" (1834(167)XIX:D1 123). Within the category of "children" Stanway further disaggregates "children" into two categories: (1) "Persons above Fourteen and under Eighteen" and (2) "Children under Fourteen" (1834(167)XIX: D1 124). The same definitions of "children" and "youths" are utilized in the Commissioners' Reports on the Mines. The commissioners distinguish workers by assigning them to one of three categories, "Adults," "13 to 18," and "Under 13" (1842[380]XV:38,39 and 198). Given that the people who were examining the situation at the time consistently defined a "child" as someone under thirteen and a "young person" as someone between thirteen and eighteen, it seems appropriate that researchers studying child labor during the British Industrial Revolution today use the same definitions.

This definition, however, may not be appropriate when examining child labor in other countries. The years of an individual's life which are included in "childhood" and the ages used to distinguish one's childhood, adolescence and adulthood are affected by social and cultural forces.[27] Although biologists would consider these phases easily distinguishable, sociologists and psychologists would disagree. The *American Heritage Dictionary* gives a biological definition stating a child is "anyone between birth and puberty" and an adolescent is a person in "the period of physical and psychological development from the onset of puberty to maturity" (Morris 1981:233,17). Thus, developmental biology unequivocally says a person is an adult when he/she becomes capable of sexual reproduction. For example, menarche is used as an indicator of adolescence for girls. The biological definition, however, is not very helpful to historians because it refers more to an individual and not to an entire population. Thus, generalizations are not appropriate because the age a person becomes an adolescent may vary from individual to individual, depending upon when he/she goes through puberty.

On the other hand, social scientists have observed that the definition of a "child" and "youth" can vary depending upon the country, culture, social class and stage of economic development. In her introduction to a collection of articles in *Youth in a Changing World: Cross Cultural Perspectives on Adolescence*, Fuchs claims that the timing of the rites of passage varies from culture to culture (1976:2).[28] She argues, moreover, that the existence of a separate stage of life called "adolescence" between childhood and adulthood is linked to a country's economic development.

> The separation of young people into a recognizable period of adolescence in the industrial nations in the nineteenth and early part of the twentieth centuries proceeds from the need for more time for advanced training for the more technologically sophisticated industrial world. It was an uneven development, for the young of the lower classes were not afforded the luxury of this period, moving quickly into factories, and early adulthood; rural people also retained earlier patterns (1976:3).

In addition, she believes that as countries become more affluent and technologically efficient, the period of adolescence is stretched over a greater number of years in order to keep larger segments of the population out of the labor force and in school (1976:3). Felicia Madeira, a development economist, would concur with Fuchs' view. She also believes that the stage of adolescence may be culturally specific and intertwined with income and social class. Madeira studies youth in contemporary Brazil and gives the definition of a "young person" from the "Quem somos," a document prepared for the International Youth Year. She quotes the document: "That is why we understand that it is impossible to talk about youth in general, since we must characterize youth on the basis of its living and working conditions and the class to which it belongs. The young worker, then, is a young person who belongs to the working class and shares its living and working conditions" (1986:57). Other development economists argue that the transition from childhood to adulthood is greatly affected by culture and family, not culture and income.[29] They believe the roles of adults and children in the family and the dynamics of family interactions have an impact on the age a child becomes an adolescent and the age an adolescent is considered an adult. While examining adolescence in a matriarchal society in India, Gokulanathan argues, "Adolescence is the period of the greatest biological and psychological transitions in an individual's life, a process highly influenced by the family and the sociocultural milieu" (1976:253). Clearly, the ages and the length of the period of childhood, adolescence and adulthood may vary from country to country, within a country and over the history of a country.

Typically researchers differentiate between children and adolescents by describing the differences in their physique, emotional state and/or behavior. Children are usually physically smaller, shorter, weaker and more supple than youths because they have had less time to grow and develop. Children are both physically and emotionally dependent upon adults for their survival and therefore show very little autonomy. Youths, on the other hand, show more autonomy than children but less than adults. Their behavior, consequently, tends to oscillate between two extremes. On the one hand, they act independent because they perceive themselves as capable of performing certain tasks unassisted while, on the other hand, they act dependent because they lack self confidence and continue to seek guidance and need emotional support from adults (Madeira 1986:57). The child development literature argues that this internal emotional struggle is an essential step in becoming an adolescent. Unlike children who are submissive and docile, youths are often in conflict with adults. Thus, once children achieve a sense of independence and differentiate themselves from their parents and other adults they become adolescents. As adolescents, they form a personal identity separate and distinct from their parents (Erikson 1963, 1968). As they become independent entities they must integrate a new physical appearance, new abilities, new feelings and new roles (Whitbourne 1986). According to sociologists and psychologists, adolescence is a stage of transition from childhood to adulthood which is marked by the following five events: (1) leaving school, (2) entering the labor force, (3) living apart from the family of origin, (4) marrying and (5) establishing a new home and family (Maderia 1986:58; Schaie and Willis 1991:33). More recently, UNICEF reports in *The State of the World's Children 1997* that a few other activities have been added to this list of pivotal events. They acknowledge that all across the world country-specific age limits have been set for: (1) leaving school, (2) working, (3) marrying, (4) voting, (5) joining the armed forces and (6) being treated as adults by the criminal justice system (1997:25). Although UNICEF recognizes that the specific age limits differ from activity to activity and from country to country, the list of rites of passage remain the same. This implies that researchers should use these events and the ages at which they occur as a guide in understanding the difference between children, adolescents and adults.

The Different Impact of Employment on Children vs. Adolescents

Up until the late nineteenth century society viewed human existence as having only two phases, childhood and adulthood. Fuchs acknowledges the absence of adolescence in preindustrial societies. In her examination of the anthropological roots of "adolescence" she notes, "In pre-industrial societies, adolescence as a special period is not well defined. Generally, people moved rather quickly from childhood to adulthood. While puberty was recognized, it signified the beginning of rather early involvement in adult economic productions and preparation for marriage and parenthood" (1976:2). Hendrick makes this clear in his book on *Images of Youth* when he says, "The term 'adolescence' had little or no linguistic value in the Victorian description of youth" (1990:10). As he points out, childhood was associated with "the child irresponsible" while adulthood was associated with "the adult responsible" (1990:19).[30] The period of adolescence was not identified, developed or discussed. The emphasis of humanitarians was on children and reclaiming their childhood from the clutches of the factories and mines where they toiled day in and day out.[31] Thus, society focused on childhood and saving children rather than on adolescence as a separate age group (Hendrick 1990:17-18). This implies that it is entirely appropriate for this book to identify "child labor" with children between the ages of one and eighteen who were working in some type of activity which created goods or services that could be consumed or sold for profit. The purpose of disaggregating the data and distinguishing between "children" (under thirteen) and "youths" (between thirteen and eighteen) in this book is not to claim these two groups had dramatically different experiences but to closely examine the ages of working children and to identify any changes in the ages of child laborers among industries and over time.

Despite there being no recognition of the stage of adolescence during the British Industrial Revolution, many historians and contemporaries distinguish between the effects of employment on children and on youths. Generally, people think of children as fragile and helpless in comparison to youths who are stronger physically and emotionally. UNICEF describes this as the universal belief which currently exists, "all cultures share the view that the younger the children, the more vulnerable they are physically and psychologically and the less they are able to fend for themselves" (1997:25). The impact of long hours of monotonous work on these vulnerable human beings can be devastating. According to development biologists, brain growth spurts occur at ages 1.5-2, 9, 12 and 15 (Burke 1997:197). In addition, an individual's skeletal structure is growing and taking shape during one's childhood (Burke 1997:171-174). This implies that children who are not raised in a healthy environment and do not get the proper nutrition and sleep "grow to be smaller in all body dimensions (Galler, Ramsey and Solimano 1985)" including brain size (Stoch et al., 1982) (Burke 1997:202). Cruickshank studies the impact of factory labor on children's health and welfare. She observes that "whatever the particular circumstances of adversity, the young were especially vulnerable. In the words of an official actuary, infants were 'little blossoms which fall to the ground almost as soon as they see light'" (1981:5). She documented how children's growth was stunted, their life expectancy shortened and their health severely compromised (1981:25-30,62-70).

Freeman's defense that children should remain at school until they are at least fourteen rests on his belief of the destructive effects of employment on the physical and emotional well-being of children. He exclaims, "The child worker, however, has far more work, both mental and bodily, than he is capable of performing; he is subjected to undue physical and nervous strain; and he has insufficient sleep. The results of this over-exertion are seen in heart affection, anaemia, nervous exhaustion, deformities, and, of course, inability to study efficiently" (1914:88).

The damages to child development which occurred when children worked are irrefutablein the evidence from the factories and mines contained in "The Blue Books" as well as in contemporaries' diaries. The fact that children's growth was stunted and their bodies deformed by the work they did was obvious to parents, medical practioners, overseers and inspectors. Many of the commissioners' reports on the employment of children in textile mills and mines identified malnutrition, poor ventilation, inadequate exposure to sunlight and insufficient exercise with the stunted growth of many of the working children.

> The effects of factory labour on children are immediate and remote: the immediate effects are fatigue, sleepiness, and pain, the remote effects, such at least as are usually conceived to result from it, are, deterioration of the physical constitution, deformity, disease, and deficient mental instruction and moral culture (1833(450)XX:25).

> Is their appearance then of stunted growth, can you give the committee any information upon that subject? - Their general appearance is certainly more of knock-knees, and an emaciated countenance, than any other description of children about the metropolis (1816(397)III:10).

> In like manner, of 60 children employed as hurriers in the neighborhood of Halifax, at the average ages of ten years and nine months, Mr. Scriven states that the average measurement in height was 3 feet 11 3/10 inches while of 51 children of the same age employed in farms, the measurement in height was 4 feet 3 inches (1842[380]XV:183).

It was not difficult to distinguish between the children who worked in textile factories and mines from other children who worked in the fields, in cottage industries or in people's homes. The industrial child laborers were often shorter, skinnier and were marred with sores on their skin, curved spines or knock-knees and were plagued with deadly diseases such as pneumonia and tuberculosis.

Diaries of doctors, parents and children during this period also revealed the physical consequences of work on young children. Dr. William Buchan wrote,

> Many people imagine it is a great advantage for children to be early taught to earn their bread. This opinion is certainly right, provided they were so employed as not to hurt their health or growth; but, when these suffer, society, instead of being benefited, is a real loser by their labour. There are few employments, except sedentary ones, by which children can earn a livelihood; and if they be set to these too soon, it ruins their constitutions" (quoted in Stickland 1973:123).

C. Turner Thackrah echoes a similar sentiment in his statement on the effects of work on health and longevity:

> The employment of young children in *any* labour is wrong. The term of physical growth ought not to be a term of physical exertion. No man of humanity can reflect without distress on the state of thousands of children, many from six to seven years of age, roused from their beds at an early hour, hurried to the mills, and kept there, with the interval of only 40 minutes, till a late hour at night; kept, moreover, in an atmosphere impure, not only as defective in ventilation, but as loaded also with noxious dust...There is scarcely time for meals. The very period of sleep, so necessary for the young, is too often abridged.

Nay, children are sometimes worked even *in the night* (quoted in Stickland 1973:139).

Similarly, the description of the child laborer "growing crooked at Marshall & Co." in the unpublished "Marshall Papers" undeniably reveals the consequences of factory work on children. The employer noted in the entry that "Margaret Kendell is 16 yr. old. Came to work with us when 13 yr. old. No. 44 sweeper for 1 year or 1 1/2 year. Line spreader about 1 year. There shewed symptoms of weakness and of growing crooked" (quoted in Stickland 1973:131).

It is more difficult, however, to find statements of the distinctive problems caused by adolescent employment. Most of the references in the Factory Inspector's Reports and The Reports of the Commissioners on the Employment of Children (Mines) are about children and not youths or adolescence. Since the "discovery" of adolescence was several decades away this omission merely reflected societal views that the two groups were indistinguishable. In addition, the majority of the working-class youths who worked probably started out when they were children which made it very difficult to associate certain physical, emotional or intellectual deficiencies with employment during a certain age of childhood. Developmental biologists have found that a crucial part of an individual's physical development occurs during the "growth spurt" in adolescence (Burke 1997:178). For young men, this "growth spurt" gives them additional height and muscular strength. For young women, this "growth spurt" results in additional body mass in certain places in preparation for motherhood (Burke 1997:170-71). Therefore, young men who do not get the appropriate nutrition, sleep and exercise may become shorter, weaker and scrawnier adults. Young women, moreover, who grow up in such a compromised situation could potentially be thinner mothers. There is some scanty evidence, however, that contemporaries believed youths suffered more from the emotional and intellectual consequences of working (becoming undisciplined, irrational and uninformed) than children. A response to the question of reducing the working hours for children in "The Marshall Papers" sheds some light on this view.

These limits of working hours and the provision that no children shall be employed in factories under 11 or 12 years of age for more than 6 working hours daily, thus giving sufficient time for that first necessary of life, a good education, and also the requirement of sufficient bodily strength before the commencement of labour, we think are all that specific laws can possibly do for the protection and real benefit of the working people (quoted in Stickland 1973:134).

Freeman also argued the impact of work on the development of youths was harmful. In contrast to his earlier statement on the impact of work on children, he believed that youth's muscular power suffered when they were engaged in simple, repetitive and tedious tasks.

We must realise that the work which boys do is of a kind that rarely exercises the whole body; often it exercises merely a few of the smaller ancillary muscles. Yet it is during this period that Nature offers her greatest opportunity to the lad for physical development; it is at this time that he stands in most need of healthy exercise which will enlargen and toughen every muscle of his body. It seems probable that the great majority of the boys of this country are entering manhood physically undeveloped and unfit because of the impossibility of getting proper bodily exercise during this period (1914:187).

Several contemporaries argued that youths' intellectual development was also damaged from continuous employment. If adolescents spent the majority of their time performing unskilled work instead of attending school, their ability to be creative, think critically and solve problems would be severely limited. Freeman argued this was the greatest consequence of child labor because working youths would never have these intellectual abilities if they were not attended to in their adolescence. As Freeman concludes his chapter on "The Boy At School,"

We must think of the boy of 14 as standing at the centre of a circle, from which shoot radii towards the circumference, representing the adult environment. All of these radii are in the right direction, and if they were prolonged by continued education they would finally bury themselves in the circumference. As it is, they fall short; the boy is subjected to social and industrial conditions that speedily destroy the standards of value for which the school has created; the radii atrophy, and adequate relations between the boy and his environment are not established. The period of adolescence, during which the superstructure should be reared upon the foundation provided by the Elementary School, is devoted to commercial profit instead of training (1914:92).

Freeman, after studying the unemployment and underemployment of boy labor, believed that the years of one's youth was the ideal time to learn and become enlightened in order that a boy may have the tools to begin manhood and become a productive member of society.[32]

Hence we see developing during adolescence, reason, conscience, idealism, love, and, in fact, all the most "civilised" attributes of human nature. The limited harmony of the earlier period is broken up, and the youth is launched on the difficult experiment of fitting himself for a far more varied life than his childhood powers would permit. Hence come the instability, the "growing pains" - both physical and mental, - and the doubts and inconsistencies and difficulties, of this later stage of growth. It is man being born again (1914:95).

This period of one's youth which Freeman referred to was actually the period called adolescence. He clearly understood that children could not move from childhood to adulthood without some period of transition where they became prepared for adult responsibilities. He remarked, "To attempt to make a man of the school child is very much like trying to teach a tadpole the habits of a frog" (1914:91). Freeman used this new concept, and the definition by G. Stanley Hall, to focus on the problems of boy labor and to formulate solutions.

The idea that there existed a period between these two phases arose at the turn of the century and was formalized by the American psychologist G. Stanley Hall. Some historians believe that the problems of boy labor and "blind alley" jobs raised society's awareness of the adolescent and their economic and political role in the new industrial regime and industrial democracy (Freeman 1914:192 and Hendrick 1990:28). Others believe that the extension of child labor on a massive scale gave working children a new sense of power and autonomy which drew attention to their predicament as they grew older. Madeira argues that in developing countries today market work for children gives them a greater sense of independence and self confidence. She claims the "expansion of opportunities for paid work and formal employment strengthen ambitions and also the sense of omnipotence, and the conflicts between generations become markedly more explicit" (1986:58). G. Stanley Hall produced the seminal work on adolescence when he published his two-volume work entitled *Adolescence: Its Psychology and Its Relations to Physiology, Anthropology, Sociology, Sex, Crime, Religion and Education* in 1904. He portrayed the adolescent stage as one when there is a rapid acceleration of physical, mental and emotional growth and a new investment of energy (Hall 1904I: ch. 1-2 and Hendrick 1990:102). For Hall, adolescence had a strong biological base and was a turbulent time in an individual's life filled with "storm and stress" (Santrock 1998:9-10). Adolescence was developed as a stage of life with its own characteristics and behavior.[33] "In Hall's view, adolescents' thoughts, feelings, and actions oscillate between conceit and humility, good and temptation, happiness and sadness" (Santrock 1998:10). Discussion among sociologists, psychologists and economists eventually caused a tremendous change in societal attitudes toward children in this different stage of life. Hall's research and Slaughter's (1910) simplification of it emphasized the period of adolescence until many were convinced it was the most important period in the development of the human being. Rather than ignore youths as they went through this stage of life, many social scientists argued that they must be guided, educated and protected because they were the future parents responsible for carrying on civilization (Hendrick 1990:1-12 and Saleeby 1909 and 1911).

This book offers a new look at the multiple roles of children and the ways these roles changed once they could earn independent wages for their work. Chapter 2 examines the role of children in working-class families and how this role changed with the new opportunities for employment in the textile factories and mines. A model of a competitive labor market for children is described where the supply of child labor represents the behavior of the working-class family and the demand for child labor represents the behavior of employers. The chapter will then focus on interactions between parents and children and how industrialization changed the way labor supply decisions were made by the family. Chapter 3 will develop the other half of the labor market - the demand for child labor. Numerous explanations for hiring child labor will be explored with particular attention given to the new labor requirements of the mechanized and automated factories and larger and deeper mines. I will argue that employers' special needs for "industrial workers" increased the demand for child labor. Chapters 4 and 5 carefully develop the role of the child laborer in the production processes of the textile and mining industry. I will highlight the impact of automation and technological innovation, in the production of textiles in Chapter 4 and in the extraction of coal and metals in Chapter 5, on the employment of children. In particular, I will explore how the adoption of new machinery and the application of the principle of the division of labor in these two production process lead to a demand for child labor. Chapter 6 will investigate whether women workers were substitutes or complements to child workers in the production of textiles, coal and metal. The book concludes by identifying the factors which contributed to the decline in child labor in Great Britain. A quick look at the current increase in the use of child labor in many developing counties reveals a number of parallels with the situation in Great Britain in the eighteenth and nineteenth century. The lessons of the past are crucial if the ILO and UNICEF are to eliminate the long hours and dangerous working conditions of the children who toil in sweatshops, factories, mines, quarries and farms in developing countries today.

Notes

1. For additional information on these groups see their Web sites at the following addresses: www.freethechildren.org and www.digitalrag.com/mirror/iqbal.html.

2. RUGMARK is an international program which certifies carpets made without child labor (Child Labor Monitor July 1997:3).

3. For additional information on this campaign see their Web site at the address: www.uniteunion.org/sweatshops/sweatshp.html.

4. See Schanberg (1994:37) and Branigin (1996:A29).

5. Some manufacturers claim they are unaware of the use of child labor in their operations and have little to say in how workers are treated due to subcontracting (Berkow 1996:1).

6. The International Labour Organization convened the C138 Minimum Age Convention in 1973 and established the minimum age for employment for members at fifteen (ILO 1996:25).

7. For an excellent summary and analysis of this debate see Landes, "The Fable of the Dead Horse; or, The Industrial Revolution Revisited" (Mokyr 1993:132-170).

8. Here I am using the definition developed by Tilly and Scott: "The labor needs of the household defined the work roles of men, women, and children. Their work, in turn, fed the family. The interdependence of work and residence, of household labor needs, subsidence requirements, and family relationships constituted the 'family economy'" (1978:12).

9. Domestic Production refers to production in the home for own and market consumption. Farms used for raising and selling husbandry or those used for growing grains or vegetables were usually a family enterprise. In addition, many small businesses were carried on in the home, ranging from nail and chain making to cotton spinning and bonnet making.

10. The laborers were "free" in the sense that they were not bound by a long-term contract and could leave or be dismissed. "Free" laborers were paid wages and usually lived at home.

11. Many of the respondents separated their answers for women and children while some did not specify which group they were referring to in their answers. Consequently, we cannot use this table to conclude that child labor was present in every occupation listed. We can, however, conclude that many children were not idle but were working in agriculture, cottage industry and manufacturing.

12. "Couching" involved spreading grain on a frame or on the ground to germinate.

13. Economists define opportunity costs as the value of the next best alternative. For example, the opportunity cost of college students is the salary they are giving up if they were not in school are were working full time.

14. For an extensive discussion of "St. Monday" and its decline in the second half of the nineteenth century see Hopkins (1982) and Read (1976).

15. For a thorough discussion see E. A. Wrigley (1978:147).

16. The Act of 1788 forbade the apprenticeship of boys below the age of eight. The Act of 1840 extended the age to sixteen and fined people who permitted anyone under age twenty-one to clean chimneys.

17. People can visit the Apprentice House in Styal, Great Britain and get an idea of how the parish apprentices lived. It has been restored to its internal condition of 1830 complete with straw beds and outdoor privies.

18. For information on the age distribution of children in the textile industries see Tuttle (1986:34).

19. For information on the age distribution of children in coal and metal mining see Tuttle (1986:34).

20. Hunt (1981), McKendrick (1976) and Nardinelli (1990) utilize aggregate statistics from the Census to discern the role child labor played in the Industrial Revolution.

21. The *1831 Census* asked detailed questions regarding the occupations of adult males but it was not until the *1851 Census* that specific instructions were given on designations for the work of children inside and outside of the home. See Higgs (1989:5-85) and Tillott (1972:82-133) for an excellent history of the British Census and shortcomings associated with each year.

22. This idea of childhood originated in the seventeenth century and is developed in Philippe Aries book, *Centuries of Childhood* (1962:21-26). For a critique of Aries' work, see Burton (1989:203-229).

23. Collier (1964), Horrell and Humphries (1992) and Pinchbeck and Hewitt (1973II) discuss the importance of the children's contribution to family income in working-class families.

24. Considerable research has been done on the concept of family income generation; see the Hammonds (1937), Litchfield (1978), Medick (1976), Rule (1981) and Stone (1977).

25. Wrigley and Schofield calculate the age at first marriage in Great Britain to be 25.9 for males and 24.1 for females from 1775-1799 and 26.94 for males and 25.77 for females for 1851 (1981, Table 10.1:424,437).

26. Mitch (1982 and 1993) and West (1971 and 1978) examine literacy and the importance of schooling in the British Industrial Revolution.

27. Considerable research has been done in this area; see De Vos (1973), Eckenfels (1976), Fuchs and Havighurst (1972), Gokulanathan (1975), Havighurst (1976), Kalu (1976), Kresz (1976), Peterson (1976) and Zavalloni (1976).

28. See Kett (1977) for a discussion of these rites of passage in the United States.

29. For specific applications of this view to these stages in India, the United States, Korea and China see Kurian (1976), Maday and Szlay (1976) and Tang (1976), respectively.

30. For additional literature on childhood see Cruickshank (1981), Pinchbeck and Hewitt (1969, 1973) and Walvin (1982).

31. For a thorough discussion on Tory Humanitarianism during this period see Nardinelli (1990:14-17).

32. See Dyehouse (1981) for a construction of femininity and societal attitudes toward girls during this period.

33. Consult Gillis (1974), Humphries (1981) and Springhall (1977 and 1986) for an in-depth discussion of the stages of life and the "discovery" of adolescence.

2

The Availability of Child Labor

Children had worked during the sixteenth, seventeenth and eighteenth centuries. Parents wanted their children to work for a number of reasons. For many working-class families it was a matter of survival. The children's contribution to the family income provided more food and more coal for the fireplace. For most families it was a necessary step in their child's development. Parents knew their children needed to obtain training in a craft or trade if they were to become independent, self-sufficient adults. For others, it was what society sanctioned. Society believed that the poor and working class must adopt a strict work ethic to climb their way out of poverty and, therefore, a busy child was a "good" child.[1] By the end of the eighteenth century, however, and well into the nineteenth century the nature of child labor changed. Children were no longer merely auxiliary workers in a family enterprise; they were essential primary workers in manufactories and mines. Children who had traditionally accompanied their parents to work, now went off to work as independent wage earners. Although children had always worked, the number of children working outside the home seemed to increase dramatically during the period of industrialization. Child labor, moreover, had become a major contributor to the work forces of many textile factories, coal, copper and tin mines. The early rural textile mills imported child labor in the form of parish apprentices. Factories, once located in urban centers, continued to employ a high proportion of children and youths, mostly from families (called "free labor"). The coal mines employed miners' children underground and on the surface while the copper, tin and lead mines used youths mainly on the surface. Why were so many children and youths working in the textile factories and mines during Britain's Industrial Revolution? What sorts of explanations has the literature given for the plethora of children and youths who became independent wage earners?

The literature has offered many different explanations for the increase in the employment of children during the British Industrial Revolution. Historians have identified poverty, greed, parental abuse, large-scale operations, technological innovation and profit maximization as leading culprits for the increase in child labor.

Some of these explanations assert that the increase in the employment of children was supply induced while others argue it was demand induced. This chapter will develop a labor market model for children in order to examine the conflicting explanations for the increase in child labor during the Industrial Revolution. The supply of child labor is created in a family context using the new collective model of household labor supply. This new model provides considerable insight into how family dynamics were changing in households where children earned separate and identifiable wages. Although historical analysis provides only the ex-post result of the family's decision-making process (whether the child worked for wages), the collective model allows us to conjecture what sorts of preferences existed ex-ante in the family. The demand for child labor is created from the traditional context of the profit-maximizing firm facing capital and technological constraints. This theoretical framework makes it possible to evaluate the various explanations put forth in the literature for child labor. This chapter will focus on the supply-side factors (custom, family greed, poverty and family abuse) which many historians, economic historians and contemporaries have argued caused the increase in child labor during industrialization. In addition, the impact of the government's response on the family's and factory owner's decision to use child labor is evaluated. The labor market model will be used to access whether child labor legislation and mandatory schooling laws effectively decreased the supply of child labor.

The Market for Child Labor

Theoretically, an increase in the employment of children could result from either an increase in the supply of children, an increase in the demand for children or some combination of both.[2] As Figure 2.1 illustrates, the equilibrium of the demand and supply of labor will yield an equilibrium wage rate (w^*) and employment level (L^*) of children. This equilibrium will change as various economic, social and demographic events shift either the demand or supply curve. For example, if the supply of child labor increased, more children would be employed while their wage rate would fall. For the purposes of this analysis, the model focuses on the market for child labor in a given industry. The short-run supply of child labor represents the number of children available for work at various market wage rates. The employment decision is made in a family context where household decision-making about whether (and how many hours) the children should work in the market, work in the home, attend school or enjoy leisure (which includes time spent sleeping) is a collective process. The demand for child labor represents the number of children employers would like to hire at various market wage rates and will be fully developed in the following chapter. The decision made by the manufacturer is based on the value of the workers' additional output (or productivity). The short-run demand for child labor is a derived demand depending upon a particular level of capital services, a given price for the final product and the current state of technology.

FIGURE 2.1 The Labor Market for Children

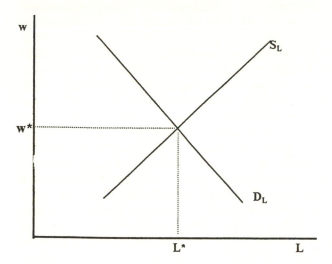

Competitive Labor Markets

The main assumption of this model is that the labor market is perfectly competitive within an industry. If the labor market is competitive then the market wage paid to workers reflects their productivity.[3] The implication of the model is that an increase in the market wage can be interpreted as an increase in the productivity of the worker receiving that wage. Therefore, if the relative wage of children to adults is increasing one can conclude that the productivity of children is increasing relative to adults. This hypothesis is tested using wage data from the *British Parliamentary Papers* in Chapters 4 and 5. In order for the labor market to be competitive, there cannot be a monopoly in the product market nor a monopsony in the labor market. First, the existence of a monopoly in the product market seems unlikely. Early industrial society in Britain is frequently characterized as one where competition was at its best (Ashton 1964[1948]). Hundreds of small producers in the cottage industry competed side by side with many medium-scale manufacturers to produce similar goods. Large-scale factories sprung up in urban centers and competed with one another to produce the cheapest and highest quality of wares. The countryside was littered with numerous stacks from coal and metal mines that were competing to extract the riches underground. The absence of a monopoly is clear in Landes's description of the cotton manufacturer in 1851 as one where "almost two-thirds of the units making returns employed less than fifty men; the average mill in England employed less than 200; and tens of thousands of hand looms were still at work in rural cottages" (1969:120).[4] Nardinelli, moreover, has shown that despite a growth in firm size for some industries, the industrial concentration remained the same (1983:8). Thus, even in the textile industries where factories were relatively large in comparison to other industries, they competed with other factories, small workshops and medium-scale manufactories for business.[5]

While this evidence appears to rule out a monopoly in the product market, further investigation is necessary to dismiss the possibility of a monopsony in the labor market. Recent evidence on wage gaps and unemployment "pockets" suggests the existence of a single national market for labor is an oversimplification.[6] Instead, regional labor markets existed that were industry based. For example, Lancashire was predominantly associated with the cotton industry, Yorkshire with wool and worsted, Warwickshire with silk, Cornwall with tin and copper mining and the Midlands with the metal trades. In this case, the limitations of travel and the segmentation of the economy could have potentially led to local monopsony power. During the nineteenth century, as industrialization spread, however, the number of employers was rapidly growing, which prevented the survival of any local monopsony. Appendix 1 presents information on the number of factories and mills for the various textile industries across Great Britain. The totals were calculated from the number of Factory Returns in 1836 and in 1850 and thus will tend to underestimate the actual number of factories which existed at the time. Despite this caveat, the evidence clearly shows that there were large numbers of textile factories in the manufacturing districts and no counties with only one factory. In England and Wales in 1836 there were 830 factories in Lancashire, 676 in Yorkshire, 120 in Gloucestershire and 35 in Cumberland. Although Scotland and Ireland had fewer textile factories, every county (except three: Wexford, Meath and Haddington) had several factories and those with only two or three had others in neighboring counties with which to compete. By 1850, the number of cotton factories in Lancashire alone was 1,235; in Yorkshire, 227; and in Cumberland, 11; while the number of woollen factories in Gloucestershire was 80, in Wiltshire, 36 and in Yorkshire, 880.

Local monopsony power did not prevail in mining either. Appendix 2 presents information on the number of collieries in Great Britain. In 1842 in England the county of Derbyshire had 48 collieries, the county of Yorkshire had 80 collieries and Lancashire had 164 collieries; by 1855 these numbers had more than doubled. In Scotland, the county of Fifeshire had 38 coal mines, the county of Stirlingshire had 15 coal mines and the county of Clackmannanshire had 11 coal mines. Such proliferation was common even in the tin and copper mines, where in 1842 there were 18 tin or tin and copper mines in the western district of Cornwall, 52 tin and copper mines in the central district and 11 in the eastern district and a total of 152 by 1855 (1842[381] XVI:766-769).[7] In addition, testimony from the *Report of the Select Committee* (1831-32(706)XV) reveals that workers moved from mill owner to mill owner and averaged a minimum of five employers over the span of their working life (Nardinelli 1988:251). Thus, workers of the early industrial labor force had choices and could move from one place of employment to another, assuring a competitive labor market.

The Supply of Child Labor

In the late eighteenth century and early nineteenth century many factory owners, mine owners, factory inspectors and parliamentarians believed that parental attitudes and actions lead to the increased market employment of children and youths. For them, the Industrial Revolution was associated with an increase in supply of child labor from poor and working-class families. Even today as historians research the use of child labor during the British Industrial Revolution, many argue it was supply, not demand, which dramatically increased the employment of children and youths in factories, mills, mines and manufactories. The supply of child labor represents the number of children and youths available for work in the market at various market wage rates. The decision of whether or not a child or youth should work in the factories and mines is made in a family context where household decision-making is a collective process. Theoretically, in the labor market model, the supply of child labor represents the preferences of the family members for leisure and consumption, where increasing family consumption can be accomplished by increasing the household's income. In order to increase family income, some or all of the members of the household will have to give up some leisure and work. The number of hours a family member works is determined by the outcome of a collective process which is influenced by their relative bargaining power within the family. If the preferences of parents or children change or if their relative bargaining power is altered, the supply of child labor could change. For example, the illness of the father would increase the family's preference for income over leisure in order to put food on the table. An increase in the family's preference for earning income could lead to the decision that the children should work for wages which would increase the supply of child labor. The existence of an alcoholic or abusive parent, on the other hand, may change the child's preference for leisure time spent at home such that the child volunteers to work in the market which would, thereby, increase the supply of child labor.

The Child Laborer in a Family Context

The economic model of the labor market for children is an application of the "new micro-microeconomics" which deals with formal models of household bargaining used in determining the allocation of the family's resources and time. The analysis is based on a synthesis of Browning and Chiappori's efficient household model (1994) and Gronau's household production model (1977). The inputs into the household production function include various family characteristics, social legislation, technology and market wage rates. The household incorporates these inputs into their decision-making process to bargain over the extent of employment for each member in the home as well as in the market (hours spent working) and the amount of education (hours per day) the children should receive. Within this framework, the household is viewed as a collection of individuals who are assumed to behave much like a firm in producing output (income, education and "home" goods[8]) from various inputs (hours worked in the home and the market, skills and school supplies). The family is assumed to maximize a family objective function which is a weighted sum of the individual utility functions of the decision-makers of the household.[9] Each member of the household is endowed with direct preferences of his/her own consumption and leisure which can be represented by an "egoistic" utility function. For simplicity, I assume the preferences of one member of the household does not depend on another person's utility. The conclusions of the model, however, do not fundamentally change when "caring" is introduced (Chiappori 1992:462-463). Undoubtedly, we would expect parents to care about their children, and in many cases, children to care about their parents.[10] In this case, the "egoistic" utility function is replaced by a joint utility function for that individual that includes the person's preferences as well as the utility function of the other member of the household. The family objective function includes the preferences of all the family members in consuming market goods and "home" goods. The weight given to each utility function is, in turn, a function of several economic variables and represents the weight of the individual in the bargaining process. In this analysis, the weight of an individual in the bargaining process depends upon prices and the wages of each household member. For a given set of parameters, every family will have a different weight function. This allows for a distinction between families who believe that children should have some say if they contribute to the family purse and families who believe nonmonetary factors like age should determine a child's influence on family decision-making. See Appendix 3 for a mathematical representation of this maximization problem.

Traditionally, the household is modeled as a group of people acting in unison with one mind and one common goal. Becker (1965, 1973, 1981) developed this unitary model which assumes the family maximizes a single utility function. Unlike the unitary models of the household, the collective models treat the household as a collection of individuals who share resources but have different, and possibly conflicting, preferences. When preferences of household members conflict, household decisions are the outcomes of agreements made by the members of the household. From this maximization problem, the family members decide how to allocate their time between leisure, time spent in school and time spent working whether in the home or in the market.[11] The allocation of time is the outcome of a cooperative process which results from maximizing the family objective function given certain technological constraints and market wage rates. Individuals arrive at collective agreements which are mutually beneficial. Although the model places minimal structure on the household decision-making process, it does assume households make pareto efficient decisions (Chiappori 1992:442). The labor force participation of family members is determined simultaneously with the allocation of time.

The efficient household model is one of several models developed from the new economics of the family. Within the new economics of the family there are two types of collective models and each portrays household decision-making as a "game" played by the members of the household. The theoretical development of these models typically depicts a two-member household that is trying to reach an agreement on how to allocate consumption goods and time. Manser and Brown (1980) and McElroy and Horney (1981) develop a cooperative game theory model where the outcome of the "game" is a Nash bargained household decision. In other words, the outcome of decision-making in a two-person household is the distribution of consumption goods that maximizes a collective utility function and is pareto efficient.[12] As Moehling (1996) points out, the problem with this Nash Bargaining Solution is that it "imposes an arbitrary structure on household objective functions" (95). On the other hand, the noncooperative game theory models developed by Rubinstein (1982), Binmore (1985) and Lundberg and Pollak (1994) illustrate what happens if cooperation between family members fail. In this case, the household does not make decisions collectively but, instead, each individual makes their own decisions simultaneously. Because the members cannot cooperate, the resulting allocations may not be pareto efficient. For example, in modeling a marriage the two people may not be able to cooperate to divide the consumption goods but they both know it is better to stay together than to get divorced because of the high emotional and out-of-pocket costs (Bergstrom 1996:1926). The efficient household model developed by Browning and Chiappori (1994) and Bourguignon, Browning and Chiappori (1995) offers considerably more flexibility than the Nash cooperative game theory approach but still requires cooperation. This theory models family behavior where the equilibrium is an agreement reached through bargaining among household members who maximize a collective utility function. Each member of the household is distinguished by his/her own preferences and because members cooperate the decisions made by the household are assumed to be pareto efficient. Although the collective approach has been used primarily to model marriages in a family, extending it to model consumption and production decisions for children and adults is straightforward.[13]

Parents and children, like husbands and wives, live in the same house and share food, heat, health supplies and other resources. It is reasonable to imagine that children and parents have different objectives, as do husbands and wives. Children may want to go next door and play with their friends while parents want to finish weaving the cloth. In addition, the options available to parents are systematically different from those available to children. Parents could sell the farm, move the family to another town, join a union or invite lodgers to live with them while children may decide whose turn it is to feed the baby. The distribution of power between parents and children, like husbands and wives, has traditionally been unequal. When there is a conflict about how certain goods should be distributed, the imbalance of power between the two members will have an impact on the outcome. Although infants and young children are still entirely dependent on their parents for survival, older children and young adults are semi-independent and are capable of living on their own. Unlike a marriage, however, one of the participants (in this case, children) finds himself/herself in this arrangement involuntarily and after a period of time has elapsed, is expected to leave.[14] This implies that the household is not a static entity but will be changing as infants are born and young adults move out of the house. Theoretically, this means the household objective function will change, which necessarily impacts the solutions reached. Empirically, this implies that tests of the existence of bargaining models where children are also decision-makers must either capture the changes in household size over time or must conduct cross-sectional studies for households of the same size.

The changing nature of the relationship between parents and children as children grow up and mature necessitates the use of a different model for children (4-13), youths (13-18) and young adults (18-24). The efficient household model seems most appropriate for depicting families with children and youths because there are relatively few options to living together. Both the cooperative bargaining models and the noncooperative bargaining models rely on the bargaining agents having access to an "outside option," which becomes the reality if negotiations break down. In marriage, the "outside option" or "threat point" of divorce seems real enough to encourage the husband and wife to try to work out a more optimal solution together. In parent-child relationships, a threat by a child that they will leave and set up a separate household is only believable if the child is mature enough to survive on their own. Young children, sickly children and immature youths would be unable to sustain themselves for any length of time. Even if the child's threat is believable, the parents may give it little credence and may not alter their decisions. Parents who have a child threaten to run away believe the child is unlikely to follow through, and if they do, will shortly return home. Similarly, in a parent-child relationship a threat by the parents to throw the child out of the house is rarely carried out. Throughout history there have been cases reported of parents leaving infants on the church doorstep or abandoning toddlers on the streets but this has never involved large numbers of children.[15] Consequently, an indirect utility function at the "threat points" for children and parents has little meaning and would hardly be sufficient motivation to resolve conflict in a bargaining "game." On the other hand, the cooperative and noncooperative bargaining models should be used to examine decision-making behavior in families with young adults. Young adults are quasi-independent and much more capable than children and youths of leaving home and establishing a separate household. Parents, moreover, having devoted their energies to preparing their sons and daughters for adulthood will be more likely to nudge a young adult out of the house. In this case, the "threat points" for young adults and parents are credible and would generate the conditions necessary for applying the Nash Bargaining Solutions.

The supply of child labor derived from the efficient household model differs from the supply of child labor derived from the unitary model. The unitary model, by assuming that households act as a unit with the head of the household making all the decisions on behalf of the family, completely ignores the impact of interactions between husband and wife as well as between parents and children on consumption and production decisions. In essence, it treats the household as a "black box" characterizing only its relationships with the outside economy while saying nothing about its internal decision processes (Chiappori 1997:440). The efficient household model, in contrast, allows us to explore economic relations within a family and how various social, political and technological factors affect the balance of power between parents and children. This implies that the supply of child labor is more complex than it is in the traditional unitary model because any factors that influence the balance of power between parents and children may alter the supply of child labor. In the unitary model, the supply of child labor will only change if the wages of household members change or the preferences of adults for leisure or income change. The interactions within the household are developed instead of ignored and household decision-making involves conflict as well as cooperation, ultimatums as well as compromises. Recent work by Davidoff underscores the importance of researching and developing a historiography of the relationships between family members. "Economic thought focuses either on the single individual *or* takes the household (family) as the unit. When household constitutes the main economic 'actor', its internal relationships are ignored, not only those of husbands and wives (as feminists have pointed out), but also those of siblings, other kin, lodgers, and servants" (1995:218).

The family in eighteenth-century England was the center of production and consumption activities, and the relationships between husbands and wives, parents and children and among siblings had far-reaching consequences for fertility, family size, class mobility and economic growth. Rather than assume that labor market decisions for children are driven by parental preferences, the newer models of the family would suggest that under some circumstances children's preferences would have an impact as well. The supply of labor is determined as the outcome of a "game" between children and adults and depends on parent's and children's preferences. The new economics of the family which models household decision-making within a collective model is more realistic than the unitary model. First, on theoretical grounds a multi-utility framework seems more appropriate to represent a household than a unitary utility function. A household is a collection of different individuals who, more than likely, have different preferences. To suppose that each unique member of the household has identical preferences or is willing to conform and adopt someone else's preferences as their own seems counterintuitive. Browning, Bourguignon, Chiappori and Lechene (1994) critique this over-simplification of the household and conclude that treating the household "as if" it were a single person contradicts the basis of microeconomic theory - individualism (1068). Secondly, there are several empirical studies which show that the resources an individual brings to the household can influence their consumption and production decisions. Schultz (1990) using Thai data on households, finds that the nonlabor income of husbands and wives has different effects on family labor supply decisions. Moehling (1996), using U.S. Bureau of Labor Statistics for 1917-1919, finds that children influence the spending patterns of the family if they are contributing to household income. She concludes that "entering the labor market gave children more input into family decisions" (123).

Within this collective model, the labor force participation of children and youths depends upon their bargaining power in the family and how much weight their preferences have when the household makes allocation of time decisions. Initially, when a child is not working and earns no income they have no bargaining power in family decision-making (in other words, w=0). In these circumstances the family reaches the initial decision to have a child work based on the family's preferences and maximizing their "egoistic" utility function. More than likely, the decision involves comparing the marginal utility of one more shilling to the "price" of children working. The marginal utility of one more shilling would be very large if the family were poor. The "price" of children working would be fairly low if there are other children at home to help out and attending school is not a viable option. If the family decides the child should work at home on the family farm or in the family business, the child still had no bargaining power because he/she did not receive a monetary reward for his/her efforts (w=0). As some industries became partially mechanized, production moved into cottages and workshops. Children and youths were often needed to assist the adults who operated the new machinery. In many cases the children and youths received a small payment for their work from the adults for whom they worked. Since this payment was greater than what they had received for helping at home or on the farm (w'>0), the family often decided they should leave home to work. Within the context of the bargaining model this payment, however small, would give the child a little bargaining power in the family. As job opportunities in textile mills and mines arose which paid a relatively high wage, this model predicts that the children of poor families would go to work (w*>w'). Children and youths left home, the farm and the cottage industry to work in the factories and mines because the wage they received exceeded what they could earn anywhere else. Once the child is working and receiving a wage, the child's bargaining power will increase in family decision-making.[16] In his book, *Boy Life and Labour*, Freeman describes this dramatic change in the position of the children relative to their parents: "At 14, the boy becomes a full-time wage earner, and, lest he should take his earnings elsewhere, he must be treated as a person of consequence by his parents. He becomes suddenly independent; and if there was supervision or control before, there will be none henceforward. 'The lad goes to bed a boy, he wakes as a man'" (1980[1914]:124). As the child continues to work they are faced with a number of places to exercise their bargaining power. The child may want to influence the family's consumption expenditures, demanding that some of the family's income be spent on their favorite foods, new shoes or a special toy. On the other hand, the child may want to work more (or less) hours than he/she is currently working which will not only impact his/her leisure time but also his/her relative bargaining power in the family. It is entirely plausible that the increased bargaining power increased their labor force participation because as they grew older, their desire for goods and services increased.[17] Thus, as the earning power of children increased, their labor force participation would have increased because the *children chose* to work. This implies that changes in the lives of children did not arise from changes in the attitudes of parents.[18] Children's lives, and in particular children's labor force participation, changed because of changes in socioeconomic factors which altered children's bargaining power in the family. I assume that the same factors influence the family's decision-making process ex-ante as ex-post of the decision to have a child work. As Chiappori pointed out we only observe the outcome of the family's decision-making process and must derive from this outcome the unobservable features of household behavior such as preferences over consumption and labor supply (1992:fn 3, 443). Thus, despite the fact that this model generates a continuum of pareto-efficient outcomes, history provides the empirical data on household behavior.

This theory of household bargaining provides insight into the changing role of children in the family economy during the Industrial Revolution - the wages children earned in the factories and mines significantly increased their bargaining power in household decision-making. Preliminary research supports this hypothesis. Chiappori

(1992) and Bourguignon, Browning and Chiappori (1995) argue that the relative wages of household members are important variables in the weighing functions. In addition, Sen (1990) found that a person's bargaining power is enhanced by his/her contribution to household income (144). Up until this point, children had worked (on the farm, in family businesses and as domestic servants) but did not receive a monetary reward for their efforts. Instead, the work of children who helped with the farm or with the family business increased the total output of the family and hence total family income.[19] The household would subsequently divide up the proceeds among family members and children would receive whatever the parents decided. The children had very little leverage to get more of the "goods" than they were allotted because their individual contribution to family income was neither identifiable nor separable from the contribution of other family members. As industrialization created a plethora of jobs for children and youths in the textile mills and the mines, the work of children and youths and the level of their contribution to family income was not only easily identifiable but it was also rather large. Consequently, the wages children earned gave them some autonomy from their parents. The fact that children were paid a nontrivial wage, enhanced their role in family decision-making which most likely altered the consumption and/or production decisions of the household. This sort of household decision-making where children negotiated with their parents to receive the fruits of their efforts stands in direct contrast to Nardinelli's paternalistic model where "the welfare of children depends on the particular mix of production, consumption and investment activities *chosen for them by their parents*" (italics are mine, 1990:40).

Observations of contemporaries and research by economic historians support modeling working-class families in the eighteenth and early nineteenth century as a collection of individuals with varying degrees of input into household decision-making. Factory owners recognized that children who worked in factories often contracted with their parents to keep some of their earnings for themselves. Their testimony is very reliable because as masters they had first-hand experience in paying the children. As early as 1816 there was evidence that children had a say in the decisions of the household. Mr. Gould, a merchant in Manchester who employed children, was concerned about the elevated position of factory children in their family and how they exercised their power. He noted, "...the children that frequent factories make almost the purse of the family, and by making the purse of the family they share in the ruling of and are in a great state of insubordination to their parents" (1816(397)III:104). Henry Ashworth, the owner of a cotton spinning firm in Lancashire, was aware of the negotiations that occurred between the youths he hired and their parents. He replied to the commissioner's question, "Do you find that at the age of fourteen many of them begin to make their own bargains, and act for themselves? - At that time many of them begin to have strong desires for finer clothing, or for other things, and they frequently stipulate with their parents for some portion of their wages" (1833(450)XX:E5).

Other adult workers observed how the clout of working youths increased tensions in the household and often lead to their permanent departure. The wages youths earned in the factories decreased their dependence on their parents and gave them the power to negotiate special arrangements with their parents. Parents with youths earning wages must have felt some of their power slip away, as they contemplated making compromises to keep their sons and daughters from leaving home. The following three quotes reveal the dynamics of the household had clearly changed from preindustrial England. Benjamin Miller, a collier in Lancashire, believed the relationship between children and parents was precarious. His reply to the commissioner reveals his concern for parents, "Do the children generally stay with their parents after they can earn enough to support themselves?- Yes, usually, especially if the father is in middling circumstances; but if the father is badly off, and does not do well to them, the children generally take advantage of it and leave him" (1842[382]XVII:204). Mr. Clarke, a cotton spinner in Manchester, described an arrangement between children and their parents that must have been common where he worked:

At what age do they usually begin to use their own discretion and receive their own wages? - I believe that every child that is employed in the mills receives his own wages, and when they receive as much money as will more than pay for their living, they contract with their parents for board and lodging, and put the rest in their pockets.

Then it is your impression that factory children are generally independent?- My impression is, that so soon as they come to receive more than will pay for their board and lodging they are thoughtless and independent.

At what ages should you think that in general takes place?- About fifteen or sixteen (1833(450)XX:D2 17).

Finally, as R. A. Arnold noted in 1864, society had become accustomed to youths leaving working-class families in areas where child labor secured a decent wage. He observed, "Children frequently leave their parents at a very early age in the manufacturing districts. Girls of sixteen, and lads of seventeen, find that they can enjoy greater liberty, and if not greater comforts, that at least they can have their way more completely in a separate house, and these partings cause little surprise or disturbance" (1864:62).

The research of several economic historians strongly suggests that changes in the earning power of household members translated into bargaining power in family decision-making. Valenze (1995) argues that the relatively high factory pay in comparison to the low wages earned in cottage industry and domestic service gave girls and young women a sense of independence from their parents. She claims that industrialization lead to the degradation of women's work and the elevation of youths' work within the family and the economy. The new factory opportunities for youths gave them a sense of freedom from "the constraints of family supervision and protection" (103). Valenze describes a change in familial relations as industrialization proceeded because working children challenged and questioned parental authority. Instead of obeying parental requests, working children began to "contract" with their parents to keep some of their earnings and started to negotiate which household chores were their responsibility. Valenze argues, "Earning wages gave young people a basis on which to 'bargain' with their parents; thus the factory could lead to different authority relations within the working-class household" (1995:107). Rose (1992) also believed that the paternalistic model of the family oversimplified the interactions among household members. Her view of the role of gender in economic relations supports using the collective model of household decision-making. Using Census data from Low Moor, Clitheroe in 1881 she shows that "wage earnings and family relations were intimately and intricately intertwined, especially for women and children" (1992:165-166). Although her empirical work is outside the time frame considered in this book, the possibility of interplay between the level of earnings and the degree of influence in family decision-making deserves investigation for any period where the relative wages of husbands and wives or parents and children changed. Rose concludes by arguing that family members had to coordinate their efforts in order to sustain themselves, "Yet, whether or not there was equanimity in their decision making and whether or not the consequence was an equal allocation of responsibilities, husbands and wives, parents and children coordinated their efforts for subsistence" (195).

Skeptics of the collective model may argue that working children's new sense of independence may have lead to unresolvable conflicts between parents and children which forced a larger number of youths to leave home. Anderson's (1971) research on Preston yields the first quantitative data on the number of children who did leave home during this period of industrialization. He finds that contrary to the comments of contemporaries, children who worked in factories were less likely to leave home. This result does not indicate, however, that children stayed home because they had no power in household decision-making. According to Anderson, the high individual wages children earned in the factories "allowed them to enter into relational bargains with their parents on terms of more or less precise equality" (131). He contrasts this to the familial relations in rural areas where the child entered a bargaining situation at a clear disadvantage because "the father had complete control over the only really viable source of income" (132). Consequently, the fact that more children were not leaving their homes, despite the wherewithal to do so, implies that children believed their standard of living would be higher with their parents than on their own. As economists we can think of this state as an "equilibrium" because both children and parents must have felt that cohabitation was better than the alternative.

The collective model of the household which examines how the bargaining power of children may affect consumption and/or production decisions can yield insights about the welfare of children, the assessment of child labor and the changing role of children in the family economy. The welfare of children who work for wages depends on the outcome of negotiations with their parents. The allocation of their time between work and leisure as well as the amount of goods and services they consume depends on their relative bargaining power in the household compared to their parents. Unlike children who did not work or did not receive any wage for their work, factory and mine children had some say in what they did, what and how much they consumed. Work for them was a double-edged sword. On the one hand, it allowed them to participate in household decision-making while on the other hand if they chose to work less, their bargaining power was reduced. The assessment of child labor, then, depends on the relative bargaining power of children to adults. If children have more bargaining power in household decision-making, then child labor may have been some benefit to the children themselves. For example, children with considerable bargaining power could secure more to eat or could convince parents to buy their favorite dessert. If, on the other hand, children had little input into household decision-making, child labor should benefit the parents initially (due to the additional wages earned) but will eventually also benefit the children and hurt the parents who have lost some control over household decisions. Child labor becomes more than "simply another input in the production of commodities that benefits everyone in the family" as Nardinelli concludes (1990:41). Child labor changes the dynamics in the household and upsets the existing balance of power.

Changes in the role of children in the family economy over time can be explained by changes in the relative bargaining power of children. When children work for wages, whether it be during the British Industrial Revolution or as developing countries compete in the world market, they are not only contributors to family income but they are also participants in household decision-making. The extent to which their power has increased relative to their parents will determine the amount of influence their preferences have on consumption and production decisions. If the relative bargaining power of children is influenced by changes in their market wages relative to their parents, any factor which affects children's wages can ultimately have an impact on the child's supply of labor and demand for consumer goods. This possibility opens up a whole new area of research on the family which may give very different answers to the questions why children work and how their welfare was affected by their employment. It may help explain why some youths left their families while others decided to stay. It will help us understand why rural families made different choices from urban families. It may also give us some insight into the changing dynamics of families as children grow older.

Children's Role in the Family - A Tradition of Working

Many social historians have argued that children of poor and working-class parents had a very different role in the family than those in the upper classes (Hammond and Hammond 1937; Hopkins 1994; Pinchbeck and Hewitt 1973; Rule 1981; Shorter 1975 and Stone 1977). Once children were able to work, they added more to the family 's income than they consumed. The more children a family had, the greater the potential income they could generate. In economic terms, children were viewed as positive economic assets that became productive after very little investment. This stands in sharp contrast to children living in developed countries today who require a considerable investment in time and money before becoming "productive" in the economy. Unlike children of the twentieth century in industrialized countries, children of the eighteenth and nineteenth centuries received very little education and were trained "on-the-job" as apprentices. The custom for children to work is apparent in Stone's research on the family: "For those slightly above the line of absolute destitution, the small holders, small tenant farmers, cottagers and artisans, children were positive economic assets, primarily for their productive labour from the age of seven until their marriage but also supports for the parents in old age" (1977:468).

As assets to the family, child labor was an essential component of the family economy and the sooner children began to work, the better. The prevalence of this tradition in the trades and manufactures is confirmed by the Commissioners' Report in 1843 when they conclude, "In all cases the persons that employ mere Infants and the very youngest Children are the parents themselves, who put their Children to work at some process of manufacture under their own eyes, in their own houses" (1843[430]XIII:195). Initially, children had no bargaining power because they were not contributing anything to the family's income. As infants and young children, they consumed rather than produced goods and service and were a burden on the family. Consequently, when they were of sufficient age they went to work because their parents told them to work. The importance of the child's contribution is revealed in the following plea of a fifteen-year-old boy from Bradford, "Have asked my father and mother to let me stop away; they said they could not do with me laiking (being idle) at home, there were so many of us laiking from not being old enough" (1833(450)XX:63).

The view that children should work had originated during medieval times and was perpetuated by the Victorian philosophy of the period. Children were looked upon as "little adults" and were expected to contribute to the family's income or enterprise. Stone's research on the family shows that the way young children dressed, what they ate and drank and how they were treated reflected the basic notion that children were rational, responsible individuals who had to work just as hard as anyone else to sustain themselves (1977). They dressed like grownups and "kept up the old way of life which made no distinction between children and adults in dress, or in work or in play" (Aries 1962:61). Many stories that circulated at the time portray children behaving as adults, drinking ale in houses and engaging in immoral activities in brothels and often in the factories themselves.[20] Although children were considered responsible and independent, they had few rights against their parents in common law whether for education, maintenance or against cruelty. Consequently, when factories offered employment to children there were few restraints to keep them at home or in school.

Parents readily accepted the employment of their children because children were viewed as a source of family income. This provides an explanation for why some children began work as early as four or five years old. "The practice of putting them to work as soon as they were able to earn a few pence" was commonplace (Pinchbeck and Hewitt 1973:390). Hopkins captures the situation of the working class perfectly when he says, "They were born into the work situation, and work and its rewards were often essential to the survival of the family. Work was the central fact of ordinary people's lives, occupying most of their waking hours during the week" (1994:93). Consequently, if the family could survive the drain on its resources while the child was fed, clothed and cared for as an infant and toddler they could enjoy a better standard of living once the child began to work. Rule describes the central position children played in the family economy: "It can be argued that the propensity of a weaving household was tied to the family cycle; with the birth of children the parents came under strain, but with their growing up the earning potential of the family reached its height, while with their leaving to marry, poverty descended once more" (1981:42).

Employment in the factories added another dimension to the concept of the family economy where children had previously received nonpecuniary benefits for helping at home or working as an apprentice; they could now make a significant contribution to the family's income. During industrialization the child generated income for the family for at least ten years instead of depleting it. Research has found that:

> Women and children whose husbands and fathers worked in factories contributed a higher share of family income than those in all other occupational categories except outworkers, with some increase during the process of industrialization. But given that few of these women themselves worked in factories, and that the factory districts afforded good employment opportunities for children, the children's contribution was probably paramount (Horrell and Humphries 1995:101).

Several social historians have argued that the Industrial Revolution by creating opportunities for children in the factories increased the returns to child labor (Anderson 1971; Davin 1982 and Levine 1985). Levine argued that employment in the factories and mines "monetized children's labor" and gave parents additional motivation to view their children as investment or capital goods (1985:181-203). If children left home for work in the market they were paid a wage which increased family income by roughly 33 percent.[21] For example, looking at average "family" income in 1843 a single man could earn 25 pounds, a married man with no children could earn 30 pounds 12 shillings and 10 pence while a married man with four children over 10 years old could double his income and earn 50 pounds 18 shillings and 6 pence with his wife and children working (Pinchbeck and Hewitt 1973II: 96). As Levine discovered in his research, "The additional labour inputs were crucial determinants of proletarian incomes during the period of industrialization" (1985:176).

Working-class children did not go to school because the loss in current earnings far outweighed the returns to education. Before 1841 only a small percentage of the labor force held occupations that required extensive formal education (Mitch 1993:fn.30, 290). Mitch found the return to education in nonfactory jobs was positive and large; 9 percent - 42.5 percent for men and between 1 percent and 16.5 percent for women (1984). He argues, however, that "it is unlikely that formal schooling contributed to the development of a disciplined factory work force" (1993:296). Sanderson's research, which is based on Lancashire marriage registers, confirms that the returns to education for factory workers must have been low. He found that the new occupations in textile factories required even less literacy and education than the old occupations (1972:89). Literacy was less useful for workers in manual occupations, like those in a textile factory or coal mine, because physical coordination, not critical thinking, was required (Cressy 1980:ch.6). Clark described the type of labor needed in the textile industry perfectly when he said, "Few tasks demanded any literacy whatsoever. Most demanded only the ability to perform the same few operations repeatedly. It might take months to acquire the necessary dexterity and stamina, but the job for most workers was highly routine" (1987:166). Therefore, families were behaving as rational economic agents by having children work in the factories and mines because the children's current earnings were higher than the expected earnings after schooling.

For the few working-class children who did get an opportunity to attend school, school was treated more like a drop-in center than an institution for learning. Children and youths who were enrolled in school had no bargaining power in family decision-making because they were not earning a wage. Without any leverage, children's preferences to stay in school were overridden by the family's preference for higher income. Consequently, if the opportunity cost of attending school increased because children's wages rose or parental income declined, the parents would pull their children out of school and send them to work.[22] Therefore, families who may have believed schooling was better for their children than working had economic forces pushing them to act in opposition to their beliefs. Despite the good intentions of the parents, the outcome of family decision-making was the same as for parents who didn't believe education was worthwhile - children went to work. If the Industrial Revolution created opportunities for children and youths to make a significant contribution to family income, utility maximizing families had no other choice but to put their children in the situation (work) where the returns were greater.

Parental preferences for poor and working-class children to work were strong for other reasons as well. Many parents believed work during one's childhood was not only necessary for the family's survival but was essential for the child's development. As Hopkins put it, "Starting work, after all, was a rite of passage, the beginning of an entry into a more adult world, and as the children grew older, they would keep part of their earnings" (1994:89). Children acquired the skills and lifelong habits in their childhood which they would need to become independent, self-supporting adults (Davin 1982:633). Work was a central part of childhood for the poor and working class. Through work, children learned how to be responsible, dependable, productive members of society. Parents of poor and working-class children knew it was essential to have skills that would generate income. They felt strongly that putting their children to work was better than allowing them to be idle. In this way parents were giving their children the best chance they could for survival in their adult lives. These pragmatic attitudes are expressed in the following two quotes by mothers of field laborers:

> I think boys are better regularly employed. I do not let them go long to school, for they must be earning something (1834[510]XII:67).

> We had little parish relief when our children were quite young, but none since the eldest boy when out, which was when he was about 7 or 8. All my boys worked at that age. I think boys and girls are always better when they are out at work. It makes them better behaved (1843[510]XII:70).

Although it had been a tradition for children to work, many contemporaries postulated that the innovations in production and the organization of the work place associated with industrialization changed parents' motives for wanting their children to work. Rather than being sensible and concerned for their children's future, parents who sent their children to work outside the home were seen as selfish and self serving. Some members of society began to think that the Industrial Revolution brought with it opportunities for parents to exploit[23] their children.

Parents' View of Child Labor - Was it Greed, Poverty or Abuse?

The Pessimists believed that the country was industrializing on the backs of children and that they needed protection. They argued to the members of Parliament that children needed protection from the factory owners, the overseers, the proprietors of mines but, most of all, from their parents. Because they had not understood that children and youths had been working in the home for centuries, they believed that child labor was a new phenomenon. They concluded, moreover, that children and youths who worked in the factories and mines must have had parents who were either lazy or greedy. They believed that the new employment opportunities in factories and mines changed parental attitudes about childhood. Children were no longer "little adults" to raise but instead became workhorses to exploit. Factory commissioners were certain of where to place the blame for the predicament children were in: "It is, unhappily, to a painful degree apparent throughout the whole of the evidence, that against no persons do the children of both sexes require protection as against their parents" (1865[3548]XX:xxv). Stories circulated that children were becoming the breadwinners of families and that the only work for fathers was to carry their children to and from the mill each day.

According to the Pessimists, the textile mills and mines increased the opportunities for poor and working-class parents to exploit their children to achieve a higher standard of living. Children and youths working in factories, however, did not seem objectionable to most of the British population because child labor had been such an integral part of the family economy for centuries. According to Pinchbeck and Hewitt, "A good deal of this sort of complacency regarding the exploitation of children sprang from the notion, supported by religious sanction that in society there was a place for everyone, and, everyone should remain in his place" (1973II:357). The exploitation, however, seemed particularly severe during the Industrial Revolution.[24] The days were longer, the tasks physically demanding and the working conditions oppressive. Recognizing these changes, social historians have since denounced this exploitation of children and characterized parents during this time period as greedy caretakers.

> The idea of the family wage as the economic unit, though not of course explicitly formulated, governed men's thinking about the industrial system, and thus factories seemed to offer special advantages to the poor by providing employment for their children (Hammond and Hammond 1937:20).

> Handworkers had difficulty in obtaining alternative employment; the factories required women and children mainly. By 1830 the only labour for many men was to carry their children to the spinning mills, to earn the family's livelihood (Ward 1962:13).

> It was not so much the capitalist employers who drove little children down mines or into factories for fourteen hours a day or more, it was the parents who eagerly pushed them into it, in part admittedly because of the fall in the price of their own labour (Stone 1977:468).

Factory Inspectors of this period echo this sentiment when commenting on the indifference of parents to their children's education. In Derbyshire Mr. Fellows says the interests of parents is "to make all they could off their Children at as early an age as possible without regarding their future welfare" (1843[430]XIII:193). Similarly, in Lancashire Mr. Austin notices in witness after witness that parents "will not send them (their children) to school, but put them at very early ages to work; and that they are apprehensive of any alteration which should have a tendency to deprive them of their profits of their Children's labour" (1843[430]XIII:193). Mr. Jones concludes after interviewing children and parents in Wales that "this apathy results in many cases from the selfishness and dissipated habits of the parents, and in others from their ignorance of the benefits of education" (1843[430]XIII:193). Such statements, however, may reflect the prejudice of the factory inspectors as much as it reflects the true motivation of parents. The difficulty of interpreting these types of statements is revealed in the following summary report of Inspectors Thomas Tooke, T. Southwood Smith, Leonard Horner and Robert Saunders on the "Moral Condition of the Children and Young Persons employed in Collieries and Mines or in Trades and Manufactures" in 1843:

> That the parents, urged by poverty or improvidence, generally seek employment for the Children as soon as they can earn the lowest amount of wages; paying but little regard to the probable injury of their Children's health by early labour, and still less regard to the total neglect of their education; seldom, when questioned, expressing any desire for the regulation of the hours of work, with a view to the protection and welfare of their Children, but constantly expressing the greatest apprehension lest any legislative restriction should deprive them of the profits of their Children's labour; the natural parental instinct to provide, during childhood, for the Child's subsistence, being, in great numbers of instances, wholly extinguished, and the order of nature even reversed-the Children supporting, instead of being supported by, their parents (1843[430]XIII:199).

This summary report suggests that parents valued total income and were prepared to take whatever action was necessary to secure more income for the family.[25] This apparent change in parental attitudes, which placed increasing income as paramount, increases the likelihood that families would decide to have their children work. If parents initially were earning more than their children, they may have exercised their greater bargaining power in household decision-making in order to send their sons and daughters to work for wages. Once their children were contributing to the family purse, however, some bargaining power shifted over to the children who were now able to influence household decisions.

Linda Pollock, on the other hand, argues that parental attitudes toward children did not change during the Industrial Revolution. Her research concludes that parental attitudes and parent-child relationships changed very little from the sixteenth century to the nineteenth century (1983:268). To examine the attitudes of parents about their children's growing employment opportunities during industrialization, she examines the statements made by eighteen parents who were interviewed by Sadler's Committee investigating *The Employment of Children in Mills and Factories* in 1831-32 (1831-32(706)XV). Far from encouraging children to work, parents were "desperately unhappy about the situation their children were in" and were "horrified by the conditions in which their children toiled" (1831-32(706)XV:63,64). Parents felt, moreover, the factories were "having a damaging effect on the morals, health and capacity for education of their children" (64). Although these statements of parents provide insight into parental attitudes during a critical period, generalizing about all parents seems unwarranted. Two basic problems exist with Pollock's research: (1) the sample is small and (2) it may not be representative of the working-class population.[26] Additional research in this area could be quite fruitful.

More recently, several economic historians have argued that it was poverty, not greed, which forced children into the mills, factories and mines during industrialization. They hypothesize that the effect of the demographic revolution was to put enormous economic pressure on the family.[27] Wrigley and Schofield have shown that the demographic revolution in the early eighteenth century disproportionately increased the number of youths in the population, thereby increasing the dependency ratio. Furthermore, it is plausible that families could reduce the growing economic burden if their children worked for wages in the market to supplement the household's income. Medick (1976) characterized this behavior for the proto-industrial family economy as one of "self exploitation" because children often had to work in order to establish a balance between production and consumption within the family (299). He asserted that both of these functions became more and more dependent on the market as the family adjusted to the loss of their agrarian base during industrialization. In the context of a collective household model, this behavior would be considered the outcome of bargaining between the parents and the children. Instead of interpreting the result as "self exploitative" as Medick has, the new models of household decision-making would describe it as pareto efficient. Parents gave up some control over household decisions in exchange for additional income to spend on goods and services.

Exploring the motives operating within families, the Hammonds have looked to the economic incentives within the household to explain the "dreadful" behavior of parents who carried their children to the mills at five o'clock each morning. They concluded that "factories seemed to offer special advantages to the poor by providing employment for their children" (1937:20). Market employment for children put the dream of crawling out of poverty and increasing the family's economic position within reach. Theoretically, when the child has little or no bargaining power, a change in parental preferences toward income over leisure would necessarily increase the supply of child labor. Collier's research on working-class families from 1784-1833 confirms the reality parents faced:

> [T]he most important social effect of the factory system was the increase it made possible in the earning power of the family which had an adult male employed in a factory but, even when this were not the case, the higher earnings of women and children, meant a substantial increase in the incomes of the families to which they belonged (1964:16).

Factory children who could earn, on average, a third of adult men's wages made a significant contribution to household earnings. Anderson (1971) argues that the combined effect of the low wages of the late eighteenth and early nineteenth centuries and large families meant that children had no choice but to work and that even loving parents found themselves sending their children off to the mills and mines for wages. Horrell and Humphries' recent article on the contributions of women's and children's earnings to family income lends further support for this view. They find that within factory families the contribution of children to family income increased relative to other household members from 1787 to 1845 and was "probably paramount" (1995:13-14). They also discover that miners' children contributed more to family income until 1841 and then less thereafter, the decline attributed to the Mines Regulation Act of 1842 which prohibited underground work for children (1995:13).

This argument, however, does not address the question of *why* - why factories and mines? What were these "special advantages" the factories and mines offered? The supply-induced argument is based on circular reasoning. If families had more children because of the employment opportunities in the market, what created these employment opportunities in the first place? If children had been contributing to the family income for centuries by working in the home or as paid outworkers, what made these market opportunities so different as to cause family size to increase? Indeed, if poverty was the main factor driving children out of the home and into the market, we would expect to find children employed in all types of trades and manufactories. Instead, we find children and young persons concentrated in only a few industries as Table 1.5 has shown. Furthermore, the concentration of children and youths in the textiles and mining industries persists over time, as Tables 1.3 and 1.4 demonstrated.[28] The predominance of industrial occupations employing young people is consistent from 1841 to 1851. Apart from the most common occupations for young people during this period, domestic servant and agricultural laborer, cotton manufacture and coal mining were among the six most predominant occupations in both censuses, with the other textiles not lagging far behind. Additional evidence is provided by the poor law authorities and parishes who reported that children were employed in counties with manufactories but unemployed and idle in other counties (1834(44)XXXVI:16h-261h). Furthermore, we learn from Levine's work on family formation that family size did respond to changes in the demand for labor of children and women, but it increased only in those villages where opportunities in industry were present. He finds a family strategy that resulted in zero population growth for Bottesford (a rural agricultural village) during the period 1650-1799 and one of rapid population growth for Shepshed (an industrializing village) during the period 1750-1824 (1977:95,77).

Nardinelli approaches the supply argument from a totally different perspective and argues it was the children making the decision to leave home and work in the market. He claims that children left home voluntarily to avoid systematic abuse by their parents. Although he admits parental abuse was not widespread, in the case of an alcoholic parent, children could escape and actually improve their situation by leaving home and going to work in a factory (1988:265). This theory rests on two rather unrealistic assumptions: that children acted independently in a household during this Victorian period and that the abuses within the factories were less severe than those within the home. The first assumption contradicts much of the child development literature which demonstrates that Victorian children had a prolonged attachment to their parents. In addition, considerable evidence has been presented in this chapter to show that children and parents collectively made allocation of time decisions. This points to an inconsistency in Nardinelli's theory. While on the one hand he uses the unitary model to show that parents make all the decisions for children, he claims on the other that children act as independent individuals who make their own decisions. Nardinelli's second assumption rests on a dubious presumption that children would be better treated in the factories than in their homes. Documentation in an earlier paper of Nardinelli's on corporal punishment suggests, however, that "the Royal Commission found widespread corporal punishment in the manufacturing industries of Great Britain and Ireland" (1982:285) whereas evidence of systematic abuse of children in the home has not been confirmed.

Most recent historians concur that brutality was not common in the working-class home. Parents may have demanded obedience and conformity, but they did not usually whip their children into submission. Discipline was extremely important but took many forms, ranging from the word to the stick. Obviously, what method parents used varied from family to family and may have even changed from one child to the next within a family. But the goal was the same, to establish and maintain a sense of order in the household.

> The family - that congeries of a father, mother, aunts, uncles and servants - taught the creed of obedience, morality, loyalty. Discipline lay at the heart of socialization. Each child must learn order and self-restraint through encouragement and suppression. Enforcement of the culture was simple and direct, manliness, honor, duty, deference, the orderly life. God sanctioned it. The family taught it. The world approved (Black 1974:200).

Despite the images created by Pinchbeck and Hewitt (1969), Plumb (1975) and Stone (1977) of battered children, Pollock (1983) finds little support for their argument that harsh treatment was the norm in society. She agrees, however, with Stone that "parents in the early 19th century were imposing a stricter discipline on their children than in the 18th" (184). Based on her interpretation of ninety-two diaries and nineteen autobiographies, Pollock concluded that "child abuse was not as prevalent as many historians have claimed" (266) and that "the majority of children were not subject to brutality" (268). Hopkins' findings, like Pollock's, also challenge Stone's classification of the cottager and artisan parent as "brutal but careful" (Stone 1977:468). Other historians, like Lofts, argued that parents were inclined to use ruthless punishment on their children. Lofts claimed that "exact obedience was expected from Victorian children and any departure from this was severely punished" (1979:165). After weighing the evidence, Hopkins concludes that although "a certain degree of physical correction was generally accepted," most working-class children were not subject to cruel and brutal treatment at home (1994:117). He believes that parental brutality and cruelty highlighted by earlier historians must have been the exception, not the rule. This type of behavior was more likely to be present in the homes of "the more degraded and sometimes drunken parents" and not in the majority of dwellings (1994:117).

Whether it was family greed or poverty that made families decide to have children work in the market or parental abuse that drove the children from the home, an increase in the supply of labor would theoretically reduce the equilibrium wage. An increase in the supply of labor, ceteris paribus, which is illustrated by a rightward shift in S_L puts downward pressure on the original equilibrium wage (w*) as more children competing for jobs offer to work at a slightly lower wage until a new equilibrium is reached with a lower equilibrium wage for the children employed (w'), see Figure 2.2. Much of the evidence on wages during this period, however, indicates an increase, not a decrease in the equilibrium wage. Tables 2.1 and 2.2 present the nominal wages of children for various jobs in the textile and mining industry. In all industries given in Table 2.1, except silk, the trend in children's wages from 1839 to 1859 is upwards. Therefore, the supply-induced argument is not supported for the textile industry by the evidence on wages. In coal mining, however, we do not find wages increasing but instead decreasing in three collieries in Scotland, refer to Table 2.2. It is possible that wages were rising in coal mining by 1850, as in Manchester in Table 2.1, but with an incomplete list of wages it is impossible to prove this. It is possible, however, that the supply-induced argument has some credence in explaining the increase in child labor in mining. Further investigation into wages in the mining industry is necessary and will be explored in Chapter 5.

Child Labor Legislation and Schooling - A Deterrent?

If parents' desire to send their children out into the work force met with strong resistance from the government, the increase in the supply of child labor might have been modest or negligible. Therefore, proponents of the supply-induced argument claim that the only way to reduce child labor was to pass laws that kept the supply of child labor from increasing. Government legislation prohibiting children of certain ages from working or fixing the hours children could work had the potential of keeping some children out of the labor force. In addition, legislation that established schools and required children of certain ages to attend could have decreased the supply of child labor or at least may have prevented the supply of child labor from increasing. If effective, child labor laws and mandatory schooling laws would act as deterrents to parents wanting to send their sons and daughters into the factories and mines for work.

Despite the gallant efforts of several individuals, government intervention on behalf of working children occurred neither swiftly nor smoothly. Proponents of child labor laws met considerable opposition from within the government as well as from the outside. Debates took place on the floor of the House of Commons and the House of Lords between the Whigs, Tories and Peelites.[29] In addition, battles raged on the factory floor between the operatives and the owners. Before any bill passed both the House of Commons and the House of Lords, data were collected, commissions formed and more data were collected. This took time and generated new discussions centered on the validity of the data, the subjectivity of the reports written based on the data and the motives of the authors of these reports. The end result, child labor laws, were passed years after their first reading and contained compromises which had important implications for the effect of the laws on the people they were designed to protect - the

FIGURE 2.2 An Increase in the Supply of Child Labor

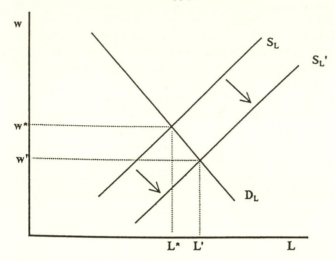

TABLE 2.1 Children's Nominal Wages Paid Weekly for Various Occupations

Industry	Occupation	1839 s. d.	1849 s. d.	1859 s. d.
Manchester				
Cotton	Card minder (boys 14-18)	6 0	6 6	7 0
	Throstle spinners (girls 14-18)	4 0	4 6	5 0
	Doffers to spinners (boys)	5 0	5 6	6 0
	Pin winders (girls)	5 6	6 0	5 6
	Doffers to doublers (girls)	4 0	4 6	5 0
	Powerloom helpers (b & g)	3 0	5 0	5 0
Silk	Spinners (boys)	7 6	7 6	10 0
	Preparers (girls)	8 0	7 0	6 9
	Flax spinners (girls)	8 0	7 0	7 0
Coal Mining	Drawers (boys)	12 0	9 0	12 0
Huddersfield				
Wool	Winders (young girls)	5 0	6 0	8 6
	Reelers (girls)	6 6	7 6	8 6
	Servers and Feeders (b & g)	6 0	7 0	8 0
	Billy piecers (b & g)	4 0	4 6	5 0
	Mule piecers (b & g)	5 0	5 6	7 6

Source: Commercial Department of Board of Trade, "Miscellaneous Statistics of the United Kingdom," 1859[2563]XXIX, pp. 2-4 (300-302) and 1861[2895]LXII, pp. 260-261.

TABLE 2.2 Children's Nominal Wages in Coal Mining, East of Scotland

Wages Paid per Week

Year	Elphingston Colliery Putter s. d.	Clackmannan Colliery Putter s. d.	Elgin Collieries Putter s. d.
1812	8 0	1 6	16 6
1814	8 0	1 6	16 6
1822	9 0	1 3	11 0
1823	9 0	1 3	11 0
1831	9 0	1 4	11 0
1832	7 0	1 4	11 0
1834	7 0	1 4	11 0
1836	5 10	1 4	11 11
1838	5 10	1 4	14 8
1840	5 10	1 4	12 10
1841	5 10	1 4	12 10

Source: 1842[381]XVI, pp. 391-392.

children. As many as fifteen laws were passed in the nineteenth century regulating some aspect of child labor but only four were thought to have contributed to improving working conditions.[30] The labor laws of 1833, 1844, 1847 and 1850 were turning points in the history of government regulation of the employer/employee relationship as it pertained to the child laborer. Table 2.3 provides a historical overview of child labor legislation in Great Britain. Initially, regulation was aimed solely at parish apprentices who had been bound to textile factories and by mid-century legislation protected "free" children and youths as well as women.

One goal of the Reformers in passing the Factory Acts was to eliminate the employment of young children and reduce the working hours of youths. They had hoped that the establishment of fines and the threat of getting caught would deter employers from hiring children and parents from sending their children to factories and mines. Similarly, mandatory schooling legislation can have the same intended

TABLE 2.3 Summary of Child Labor Laws in Great Britain

Act of 1782
  encouraged paupers to engage in industry work

Act of 1788
  improved conditions of children working in chimneys

Pitts Bill of 1796
  created "schools of industry" for pauper children

First Factory Act of 1802
  set maximum hours for children at twelve and improved conditions in cotton mills

Cotton Factories Regulation Act of 1819 (Peel's Act)
  set minimum working age to nine and maximum hours at twelve in textile factories

1825 Bill
  prevented evasions of 1819 Act

1831 Bill
  limited factory hours to twelve in cotton mills for all persons under eighteen

Regulation of Child Labor Law 1833
  set maximum hours for children at nine, prohibited night work and allowed inspections

Mining Act of 1842
  prohibited girls and women from working in mines

Factory Act of 1844
  limited hours for children in textiles to six and a half a day

The Ten Hours Bill of 1847
  limited hours to ten for women and young persons

Act of 1850
  prevented evasions of Ten Hours Bill, set work day hours

Act of 1853
  included children under coverage of 1847 Act, regulated their work day hours

Factory Act Extension Act of 1867
  extended 1847 Factory Act to all manufactories

Agricultural Gangs Act of 1867
  prohibited children under eight from working in gangs, separated the sexes in gangs

Act of 1874
  raised the minimum age of employment in factories to nine and limited hours to ten

(continues)

TABLE 2.3 (continued)

Consolidation Act of 1878
  combined all previous regulations under one law

Act of 1893
  set minimum age for factory and workshop employment at eleven

Act of 1902
  raised minimum age of employment to twelve years old

effect on the labor force participation of children. A government can reduce child labor by requiring children to go to school until a certain age, thus removing them from the labor market. Unfortunately, education laws were not a deterrent to child labor in Great Britain because elementary education was not compulsory until 1881. Although local school boards had the authority to require attendance as early as 1870, schooling for working-class children and youths was not widespread. It was not until 1891, moreover, that schools became available to all classes without having to pay fees.[31] If mandatory schooling requirements exist and are enforced, the employment of children can be severely curtailed.

According to our labor market model, the existence of legislation prohibiting children from working or requiring them to attend school can be interpreted as affecting the supply of child labor. The laws raise the opportunity cost of children's time by imposing fines which reduce the net wage received by working children. This would lower their contribution to family income and reduce their relative bargaining power in household decision-making. In the case of child labor laws, the existence of fines (averaging 1.5 pounds per offense) and the cost of reporting imposed an implicit tax on the factory owners' demand for child labor. The implicit tax equalled the probability of getting caught times the fines and fees if they were caught. This tax would increase the cost to factory owners of employing children as well as reduce the take-home pay of the children (Nardinelli 1980:7). Hence, the Factory Acts by establishing a constraint on the number of children who were eligible for work (age minimums) and the number of hours employed children could spend working (maximum hour provisions), attempted to reduce the overall level of children employed. In the case of mandatory schooling requirements, the existence of fines (5 shillings) and school fees (1 or 2 pence per week) imposed an implicit tax on the family's supply of child labor. This tax would decrease the potential income the child could generate for the family because the family would have to pay a fine and school fees if authorities caught their children working instead of attending school. Graphically, the regulations on children and youths could be depicted as a reduction in the supply of child labor, as depicted in Figure 2.3.[32] The difference between the gross wage rate, w_g, and the net wage rate received by the children, w_n, is the implicit tax, t. Employment is reduced due to the tax from L to L'. The size of the shift and its impact on the level of employment of young people depends upon the size of the fines and fees and the degree of enforcement. For the Factory Acts, the underlying assumption is that the penalties are levied on the millowner who weighs the cost of

FIGURE 2.3 The Impact of Legislation on the Market for Child Labor

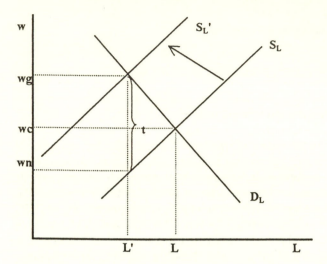

getting caught with the benefits of employing children. The higher the fines and the greater the chance of paying them, the larger the implicit tax, and the larger the reduction in the employment of children resulting from the legislation. In the case of mandatory schooling requirements, the fine and school fees are levied on the family who weighs the chance of getting caught and paying the fines with the income received from the child if they work.

Judging from the evidence, both the Factory Acts and Education laws were ineffective deterrents to manufacturers and families. Nardinelli shows that the cost of getting caught was sufficiently small that "the enforcement of the Factory Acts imposed no direct burden on factory-owners" (Nardinelli 1980:108). Between 1835-1880 there were a total of 33,520 prosecutions and 50,692 pounds collected in fines. The annual averages across all industries in Great Britain were 713 convictions and 1,079 pounds a year (Nardinelli 1980:100-110). It appears that the Education laws were as ineffective as the Factory Acts in deterring families from making the collective decision for children to work. Fines rarely exceeded five shillings, which would hardly reduce the average child's income at eight pounds a year in 1870. Enforcement was also a problem, as it was with the Factory Acts. The rate of conviction was less than 5 percent and of 66,882 violations reported in 1873, only 2,751 resulted in a conviction (1875[c.1184]XVI). This suggests that the reduction in the supply of labor resulting from the Factory Acts and schooling laws may have been modest at best.

It was customary for children and youths to help their family by working at home, out in the fields or in other people's homes. For centuries there had been a strong sense of a family economy among the poor and working class. Everyone who was physically able pitched in and did what they could. Children were no exception; they needed to contribute to the family's enterprise as soon as they were old enough. They could watch their baby brothers and sisters, clean the house, fetch water, pick weeds, spin cotton thread or work as a servant in someone else's home. The employment of children in textile factories and mines, however, seemed different from the employment of children on the farm or in cottages. The number of children and youths working outside the home increased dramatically. Although some children still helped around the house and worked as farm laborers and domestic servants, many children filled the new occupations of textile worker and miner. In addition, there had never been so many children and youths working together in one place, under one roof. Children who had worked on the farm or in a cottage industry were scattered across the country, working in small family establishments. Children who were employed in the mills, factories and manufactories worked under one roof alongside many other children. The concentration of children and youths into identifiable work places drew public attention to this new use of child labor. Inhabitants of textile towns were familiar with the sound of their little feet pattering on the streets at day break as they made their way to the factories and at night when they dragged themselves back home. The long hours they worked and its toll on their physical stature and emotional state were visible to the entire British population. Child labor may not have been a new phenomenon, but it took on an entirely new dimension.

The increase in the number of child laborers, moreover, could not be explained by an increase in the supply of child labor. Impoverished families needed their children to work, whether it was during the preindustrial era or during the Industrial Revolution. Unless new evidence is discovered that shows a dramatic increase in poverty during this period, poverty cannot explain the increase in the employment of children and youths. In addition, parents had not changed their attitudes about their children during the Industrial Revolution and suddenly become greedy or abusive. Families decided their sons and daughters should work when the wages they brought home exceeded the cost of having them work (value of home work, leisure and schooling). There is no evidence, moreover, that the number of alcoholic parents increased such that children were working in factories and mines to "escape" abuse at home. How do we explain the fact that the textile factories and mines were filled with child laborers? Why was the employment of children and young persons concentrated in some industries and not in others? The next chapter develops a theoretical framework to address these questions. The argument focuses on demand, not supply, as the reason for the increased employment of children and youths. The model highlights how the new labor requirements faced by employers arising out of the technological innovations associated with the British Industrial Revolution increased the demand for child labor.

Notes

1. A petition of the woollen laborers on the use of scribbling machines in the *Leeds Intelligencer* (June 13, 1786) clearly connected the idleness of children with a future of criminal activity (Reprinted in Crump 1931:314-316).

2. Empirically it is very difficult with ex-post data on employment to determine the source of the change (called the identification problem) although, theoretically, we can separate the changes in supply and demand in our analysis.

3. According to labor theory, in a competitive market the wage rate equals the value of the marginal product of the worker.

4. In 1815-16 the two centers of the cotton industry had numerous mills with several hundred employees each. The average number of employees in 43 mills in Manchester was 301 (1816 (397)III:374-375) and in 41 mills in Glasgow averaged 244 (Clapham 1964I:184) and by 1835 the average for all cotton mills was considerably smaller at 175 (Ure 1835:481).

5. In 1830 the average size of the work force of coal mines in Tyneside was close to 300 while the average number of workers employed in the tin and copper mines of Cornwall was 160 in 1838 (Clapham 1964I:186-187).

6. Williamson (1985) argues that factor market distortions lead to large wage gaps between rural and urban areas during the 1830s and 1840s and Cunningham (1990) asserts the employment of children was high in towns with manufactories and extremely low in areas without one.

7. Note that the term collieries and pits are not synonymous. Each colliery was a company and some had 2 or 3 pits while others had between 11-50 pits (1842 [382] XVII:94-95).

8. "Home" goods are consumer goods (like bread, hats and shirts) produced in the home with materials from the home and market.

9. Most economists have applied these types of models to an examination of marriage. For an excellent summary of this literature see Bergstrom (1996:1903-1934).

10. Becker (1981) first introduced the possibility of "caring" in his theoretical models of marriage.

11. Recently, household production has been introduced into the collective models such that a distinction has been made between work in the home and work in the market (Apps and Rees 1997 and Chiappori 1997).

12. The collective utility function is the product of the difference between each person's utility if they remain in the household and each person's utility if they leave the household.

13. McElroy (1985) extends the model to show how young men and their parents jointly determine work, consumption and household membership. Moehling (1996) uses the model to test whether the employment of children in the U.S. changes the composition of household expenditures (88-124).

14. The exception to this would be in countries where the marriage is prearranged.

15. An obvious exception to this would be the "selling" of children to employers (called bonded labor) by poor families in many developing countries (India, Pakistan, Nepal, Thailand, Sri Lanka, Kuwait, Bolivia, Columbia, Brazil, the Dominican Republic and parts of West Africa)(Springer 1997:34).

16. Theoretically, as w_c increases $\propto$ falls and $(1-\propto)$ increases.

17. Freeman, in his examination of boy labor in Birmingham, states that a boy who received relatively high wages enjoyed keeping a portion which will "suffice him for many hitherto little-tasted pleasures" (176).

18. Nardinelli arrives at a similar conclusion using Becker's (1981) model (1990:37-45).

19. The children who worked as domestic servants in someone else's home usually received room and board as payment for their services.

20. This view is developed in more detail in Hammond and Hammond (1937:300), Thompson (1966:307) and several *Parliamentary Reports*, 1819(HL.90)XCVI, 1833(450)XX and 1842[382]XVII. This perpetuation of the medieval concept of childhood was apparent only in children of the working class. Children of the noble and middle class began to dress differently (in robes and false sleeves) in the seventeenth century.

21. On average, children's wages in textiles were one third of adult male wages (1833(519)XXI:33-37).

22. The motive to increase family income is extremely strong as evident in some developing countries today which pay families a daily allowance to send their children to school. In Campos, Brazil minimum-family allowance programs were very popular but children went back to work as soon as the government funding ran out (Franca 1996:11).

23. "Exploitation" is defined as the use of another person in an unjust manner for personal gain or profit (Nardinelli 1990:65).

24. See Tuttle (1998) for support of this position.

25. Theoretically, this implies that income was an important component of the parents' utility function.

26. Hopkins argues Pollock's conclusions are not applicable to working-class children because her data primarily represent middle-class beliefs and behavior. For much of the sixteenth and seventeenth century, most people in the working class could not write and those who could did not keep journals (1994:2).

27. For a more detailed development of this view see Hohenberg (1991), Lazarus (1969), McKendrick (1976), Mitch (1982), Pinchbeck (1930) and Stone (1977).

28. Although the *1841 Census* underestimates the number of children employed inside the home, it does accurately capture children working in the textiles and mines outside the home.

29. For a complete discussion of the child labor debate see chapter 2 of Nardinelli (1990).

30. Nardinelli (1990) has a thorough discussion of the Factory Acts in chapter 5 of his book.

31. An entire body of literature which discusses the history of education in England and its role in the Industrial Revolution (Landes and Solomon 1972, Mitch 1982 and 1993, Sanderson 1967 and 1968 and West 1978).

32. Theoretically, a tax that increases the gross wage paid by factory owners and decreases the net wage received by children can be depicted graphically as either a decrease in the supply or demand for labor.

3

Wanted: Child Labor

Although families had offered their children for employment for centuries, the demand for child labor changed dramatically with the Industrial Revolution. Much of the work children had been doing on the farm, in family enterprises, in other peoples' homes and in small cottage industries could be done by workers of any age. Parents and children shared the work and when children were not available, adults performed their tasks. In other words, there was nothing special or peculiar about the work the children were doing that made it necessary for children to perform certain tasks. Adults could just as easily plant seeds, weed crops, fetch water, spin thread, clean house and make bonnets. Child labor was used because it was available and allowed parents to complete other tasks which increased the overall output (harvested crop, thread, bonnets, etc.) of the family. Children's work was considered simply an auxiliary by-employment. The Industrial Revolution affected the market for child labor such that this was no longer the case. Industrialization brought innovations to the production process as well as certain mechanical inventions which increased the demand for child labor. Applying the principle of the division of labor and specialization to the production of textiles, to the extraction of coal and to the isolation of copper ore, created jobs for children. In addition, several inventions in the textile industry lead to machines which gave children a comparative advantage over adults. Thus, industrialists preferred child labor over adult labor because children made ideal workers - they were particularly suited to operate the machines and their nature was more compatible with the new industrial regime.

The Demand for Child Labor

It was demand, not supply, which dramatically increased the employment of children and youths in certain leading industries during the British Industrial Revolution. The Industrial Revolution is associated with an increase in the demand for child labor by factory owners, overseers, butties, masters of mines and by the operatives working in these establishments as well. The demand for child labor represents the number of children and youths employers would like to hire at various market wage rates. Theoretically, in the labor market model, the demand for labor represents the preferences of employers in hiring workers to combine with capital in the production of some product or service. The decision made by the manufacturer is based on the value of the worker's additional output (or productivity). The short-run demand for child labor is a derived demand depending upon a particular level of capital services, a given price for the final product or service and the current state of technology. If any of these three factors are altered there will be changes in the demand for child labor by employers.[1] For example, the installation of new machinery in a factory could potentially increase the productivity of children which would increase the demand for child labor. Innovations in the production process, moreover, could create new jobs which would also increase the demand for child labor. The Industrial Revolution in Great Britain had an impact on the demand for child labor because several new inventions in the textile industry and innovations in the production process of making cloth and extracting coal increased the productivity of children and youths. As children and youths became more productive, the demand for their services rose. This increased demand for child labor came from factory owners, manufacturers, overseers, managers and tributers not parents. Hence, industrialization not only increased the demand for child labor, it changed who demanded child labor. The employer was no longer the child's parents or a member of their family. The employer was an outsider who hired children and youths on a contractual basis as employees of a profit maximizing enterprise. Thus, with the evolution of textile factories and the surge in coal pits during Great Britain's industrialization, the nature of the employer/employee relationship was altered forever.

Children and youths involved in domestic manufacture worked with and for their parents. Supervision, regulations and punishments were decided by the parents and were administered by them with no intervention by any third party. In the factory children and youths were no longer "protected" by their parents, their livelihood depended on the disposition of the factory master. Suddenly the "relations between employer and labourer were becoming both harsher and less personal" (Thompson 1966:199). Some masters were "heartless" while others made sure the children washed and took breaks regularly (Cruickshank 1981:52). As a factory laborer a child's work was no longer considered an apprenticeship but instead formal market employment with established hours, fixed breaks and regular monetary payments.

Table 3.1 summarizes the terms of employment which existed in several factories in Great Britain where each entry represents a single factory or mill. Children and youths spent roughly thirteen hours a day in the factory, working eleven or twelve of those hours with two brief recesses for breakfast, dinner and tea. Although such long days were typical for families deriving their earnings from cottage manufactures, the amount of time actually spent working was almost certainly less than the hours worked by factory children.[2] One explanation for the irregular work hours is that children and youths followed the rhythm of their mother or father; whereas, in the factory they followed the rhythm of a ceaseless machine. In addition, even the strictest of parents must have allowed their children to stop to eat, sleep and play,[3] but at the factory child

TABLE 3.1 Conditions of Work in Textile Factories

Type of Mill	Percent of Young People Employed	Work Hours	Recess (hours per day)	Number of Holidays (days per year)
Cotton	43%	6 am-7:30 pm	1.50	4.50
Cotton	n.a.	5:30 am-7 pm	2.00	6.50
Cotton	27	5:30 am-7 pm	2.00	6.50
Cotton, silk, & worsted	15	7 am-7 pm	1.00	10.00
Cotton	31	6 am-7 pm	2.00	4.00
Silk	32	6 am-7 pm	2.00	8.25
Silk	54	6:15 am-7 pm	2.25	13.00
Silk	71	6 am-7 pm	1.65	6.50
Silk	36	5 am-7 pm	1.55	8.50
Lace	55	5 am-7 pm	1.55	8.50
Unknown	51	6 am-7 pm	2.00	10.00

Source: 1833 (519)XXI, Tabular Examinations of the Health of Factories, Dr. Hawkin's Report, pp. 255-270.

workers were allotted only two short recesses for meals and rest, and often did not take these but ate while cleaning the machines. Children and youths, moreover, worked six days a week and had a set number of "holidays" a year, ranging from four to thirteen. The transition from parent-child to master-child did not occur all at once with industrialization but happened gradually as more and more factories were built in urban centers and as power shifted from parents to factory managers.

Children and youths had become more than auxiliary by-employments; they were independent wage earners. Children no longer worked for their parents, relatives or neighbors but instead were hired and paid by employers who set their work hours, determined their duties and deducted fines from their pay (in the case of infractions of the rules). In the factories, masters or overseers were responsible for the recruitment of the work force except in the case of "piecers" for the common mule. Usually the adult spinner would hire their own "piecers" and a few were members of the same family. In the mines, tributers or masters recruited the labor for surface work and many jobs underground. On the other hand, a few underground jobs remained in the family because hewers hired their own assistants, "putters." A discussion of the different employer/employee relationships in the textile and mining industry is developed in Chapters 4 and 5. In the few cases where children and youths were hired by members of their own family, the competitive labor market model breaks down. Children are no longer independent wage earners who offer their services in the market to the highest bidder but instead are hired by their parents. In these circumstances children may or may not receive a wage commensurate with their productivity because their wage would be deducted from their parents' earnings. It is possible they may not have received any wage at all for their work. Instead, their parents' earnings would be higher reflecting the child's contribution. As the child's productivity increased, moreover, the parents' earnings would increase. Little research has been done on whether children were paid a wage when they worked for their parents. Wage data from the numerous *Parliamentary Reports* reveal wages paid to children performing various tasks but do not give any specifics on the arrangement made within families. An investigation of individual wage books from factories or mines would be very illuminating.

As industrialization occurred, children who for centuries had worked as a helper on the family farm or as an apprentice in the family business or as an assistant in the cottage industry, were now employed as primary workers in one of the countries' manufactories. The contribution the children made to family income became quantifiable and the contribution the child laborer made to the manufactories' output was measurable. Child labor became an important and necessary ingredient in the production process of several British industries. What was so special about younger workers that industrialists wanted to hire them? Was it that younger workers had the necessary attributes for the new production methods? Rather than think of all workers as homogenous, a study of child labor must draw out the differences between the child worker and the adult worker. From the industrialist's perspective, adults and children were not perfectly substitutable in the production process. Children and youths seemed better able to cope with the changes in the organization of work that accompanied industrialization. Work moved out of homes and cottages into one central location and the work day was no longer flexible, but instead, determined by the rigid beat of the factory clock. In order to understand why managers were especially interested in hiring child labor, we need to examine the distinctive features of children and youths that helped them to conform to the demands of the new industrial regime.

The Child Worker

Children and youths have different physical characteristics, skill levels and mental aptitudes from adults, making them particularly suited for some jobs and certain work situations. They are physically smaller, more supple, and have quicker physical reflexes than adults. They have smaller hands and nimble, little fingers. They can move quickly and can squeeze through, duck under and maneuver around obstacles without any injury to their limbs. In addition, children and youths have keen eyesight and senses that are highly sensitive to outside stimuli. As any parent knows, children seem to have an unlimited supply of energy and are in constant motion. This implies that younger people can work harder and longer than adults. This advantage acts as a double edged sword, however. On the one hand, it means that in the short run children may be more productive workers in the new industrial regime than adults. On the other hand, the long term physical damage to their health is higher than it is for adults because their bodies are still developing.

Child labor is almost invariably unskilled labor. Workers acquire skills throughout their life from formal and informal training. People become proficient in their jobs through various avenues: by studying and attending school, by watching others perform similar operations, by trial and error and by practicing. Adult workers usually begin a job with a certain level of skill which they have acquired as youths through education and/or training. As they work their expertise grows with on-the-job training and learning-by-doing. The opportunities for training and learning are severely limited, however, when a child begins to work at the age of seven or eight. Children and youth work instead of receiving any type of education (informal or formal). If they work eleven hour days, six days a week, they have no time for school after work or on weekends. Investment in the child's human capital during this period in Great Britain was restricted to Sunday school and on-the-job training. Although Sunday school was pervasive throughout England and Wales by 1833, it was not a substitute for formal education. The purpose of Sunday school was "to train up the lower classes in habits of industry and piety" (Lawson and Silver 1973:239). Unlike apprenticeships and formal day schools, Sunday school may have only marginally increased children's human capital.[4] On-the-job training, moreover, received by children was brief and task oriented. They learned quickly because their job required dexterity and coordination, not creativity and critical thinking. In many industrial jobs, children were taught simple, repetitive tasks on a specific machine.

It is plausible that it may have been easier to teach children simple tasks requiring dexterity and endurance. A child's mind acts like a sponge, ready to absorb new information and react to new stimuli. The combination of curiosity and naiveté embodied in children makes them eager to face and conquer any challenges confronting them. When placed in front of a door, they figure out how to open it; when confronted with stairs, they learn how to climb them. The same principle holds for work - which is essentially learning how to complete a task. When placed in front of a spinning machine, children figured out what to do by watching someone else perform the task. When handed a sieve full of dirt and copper, children learned that shaking it back and forth separated the two substances. Children were ideally suited for these types of tasks because their undeveloped minds gave them a greater ability to withstand monotony - a characteristic of automated and mechanized work. Adults with a higher mental aptitude are more likely to get bored performing repetitive, simple tasks. Unlike children who simply require physical stimulation, adults need mental stimulation to stay alert and interested in what they are doing. Marx highlighted the comparative advantage of children when he wrote, "Even at the present day, where the system is perfectly organized and its labour lightened to the utmost, it is found nearly impossible to convert persons past the age of puberty, into useful factory hands" (1909:424).

Not only were children and youths easier to train, but they were easier to recruit, supervise and less likely to cause trouble than adults. Since water-driven or steam-powered machinery lacked any physical limitations regarding the amount of work it could perform, a continuous mode of production was adopted in many manufactories. Subsequently, the worker was required to perform his/her duties constantly, with few breaks, around the clock to keep up with the relentless machinery. Ure described this new factory discipline in his book, *The Philosophy of Manufactures*, "The grand object therefore of the modern manufacturer is, through the union of capital and science, to reduce the task of his work-people to the exercise of vigilance and dexterity, -faculties, when concentrated to one process, speedily brought to perfection in the young" (1835:20). To find a worker willing to submit to such toil was extremely difficult for the first industrialists. Pollard identified this as a major problem for managers in recruiting labor for the early factories, "the aversion of workers to entering the new large enterprises with their unaccustomed rules and discipline" (1965:160). Reluctant to work in the first factories, many adults working in the cottage industry preferred starvation to employment in the country mills. They were too free-spirited to be slaves to the automated machines. According to Pollard, workers had to be "broken in" to the new factory discipline. "Once at work it was necessary to break down the impulses of the workers and to introduce the notion of 'time thrift'" (1965:183).

Artisans, Handicraft workers, hand-loom weavers and farmers were accustomed to working when they wanted for however long they wanted. They worked hard but at their own pace, stopping when they were tired or hungry and taking a holiday when they wanted.[5] Children, however, seemed to be the perfect candidates because they could be dragged to the factories without consent and would follow managers' orders. Children, by definition, are not independent. They depend on adults for their physical, emotional and psychological needs. When children are young, their parents make decisions for them. Parents, not children, decide whether a child will work, play or go to school. As children develop and mature into youths, they offer their input and use various methods of persuasion to impact the outcomes which affect their lives. During this period working-class parents raised their children to be submissive and obedient to adults and people of authority. If parents told their children to go to the factory and work, most children did so.

The docile and submissive nature of children made the job of an overseer or manager considerably easier. If the overseer told a child to work at their station from 6:00 a.m. until 12:00 noon when they would break for lunch, the child did. If the overseer told a child to work faster, he/she did because he/she was afraid of being scolded, slapped, whipped or fined.[6] Children were easier to supervise because they were less likely to refuse to work, less likely to organize against employers (and form Unions) and more likely to respond to punishment.[7] Several historians recognized this fact,

It was much noted at the time that women and children more willingly accepted the discipline of the factories, and submitted more easily to the long hours (McKendrick 1976:184).

They (children) were preferred, too, for other more conclusive reasons. Their weakness made them docile, and they were more easily reduced to a state of passive obedience than grown men (Mantoux 1928:410).

In addition, contemporaries often attributed employers' preference of hiring children (and women) to their docility;

. . . masters finding a child or woman a more obedient servant to himself, and equally efficient servant to his machinery (P. Gaskell 1836:146).

The labour of adults is infinitely more regular in machinery than in manual employment, but can never be controlled and reduced to the uniformity of attendance of children (P. Gaskell 1836:136).

In some factories none but women are allowed to labour, excepting a few men, such as managers, overlookers, and one or two, in a very important department to the master, viz., "the bating book," in the warehouse; not because the women can perform the work better or turn off a greater quantity, but because they are considered to be more docile than men under the injustice that in some shape or form is daily practiced upon them (Leach 1844:11-12).

There are, however, several problems with hiring juveniles as workers. Although they have a lot of energy, children tend to tire easily and need rest to revitalize. Unlike adults with stamina, children are more accident prone when they are exhausted and sleep-deprived. This would not be a problem for children working at home or on the farm because they could rest or take naps. The factory children and child miners, however, had no such luxury. The new factory discipline required them to work continuously for six hours and after a short meal break, another continuous six hours. Although it may have been possible for children to rest during their meal break, many witnesses from Sadler's Report said children worked and cleaned machinery while they ate their meals (1831-32(706)XV:5,53,102,148,157,192 and 195). Sadler's Report and the Commissioners' Report contain evidence that children did tire toward the end of the day. Overlookers confessed to hitting children to wake them, young workers mentioned getting fined and beaten for falling asleep and medical officers reported accidents and injuries which resulted from children getting sucked into machinery (1831-32(706)XV:37,75,103,108,112,128,142,163,192,475,503,522 and 534). At the same time, children were more likely to respond to corporal punishment than adults. Submissive children who feared "the stick" would have tried to work longer and harder for the overseers. In addition, child laborers may have missed more work than adults because they are more susceptible to sickness. Unlike adults whose immune system is fully developed, children cannot fight off disease as well and are more likely to get ill. The factory regime compounded the problem because children did not get proper nourishment or sleep (Rubin and Farber 1988:327-334 and Dubey and Yunis 1991:190-196). Consequently, children may have missed more days of work than adults due to illness. This could present problems to the overseer who was responsible for the production line running smoothly and at full capacity. Given the nature of the production process in the factories and mines, however, this would not have caused any grave concern for managers. As Chapters 4 and 5 will show, the tasks children performed were easily and quickly learned such that other children (either already employed in the establishment or looking for work) could replace sick children without much difficulty. Despite the fact that children may have been more likely to grow weary and fall ill, adults would have protested the long hours and refused to give in to the factory regime. Thus, the advantages of hiring children appeared to outweigh the disadvantages.

Cheap Labor, Obedient Children or The Dilution of Skill?

Although many historians would probably agree that young workers have special physical and emotional features that make them especially productive workers doing monotonous, repetitive, simple tasks, few have examined the issue in conjunction with technological change. They prefer, instead, to focus on only one factor which made child labor valuable to the industrialist. They argue the employer's preference for children over other laborers was attributed to one of four explanations: (1) children were a cheap source of labor, (2) child labor solved management problems, (3) children were passive workers and (4) the new inventions used unskilled labor. Many contemporaries believed that children were hired by industrialists because they were cheaper than adult labor. It seemed obvious to them that the profit-maximizing behavior of factory owners and proprietors of mines lead to the increase in the demand for child labor in order to minimize costs. Children's wages were considerably lower than adult men's and employers could hire two or three children for the same cost of one adult male.[8] John Kennedy hints at this motive for hiring children when he read his "Observations on The Influence of Machinery upon the Working Classes of the Community" before the Literary & Philosophical Society of Manchester on February 10, 1826: "In proportion as machinery is improved in simplicity, and becomes more uniform in its action or motion, a lower class of labour is required for its management; and as women and children are thus enabled to produce those fabrics, which it formerly required all the ingenuity, skill, and labour of the very best workmen to furnish" (43).

As feminist economists have pointed out, his reference to a "lower class of labour" refers as much, if not more, to their relative earning power than it does to the technical expertise necessary for the job (Rose 1992 and Valenze 1995). If the new opportunities in the manufactories did not require any special training and industrialists had a choice of hiring adult men, women or children, women and children were preferred because they could be paid less to do the same work as adult men. Early millowners recognized this competitive strategy in recruiting labor for the first rural spinning mills located near rivers. George Unwin (1924) argues that Robert Owen and Samuel Oldknow's spinning mills in Stockport were built with the intention of hiring children as cheap labor.

More usually the beginner sought to utilize the advantages of water power in conjunction with the cheaper labour of women and children (117).

As soon as the mill was built and at work, the social and economic problems involved in the formation of the new community assumed an entirely different form. The demand for adult male labour rapidly decreased. What was needed was an increased supply of the labour of children and young persons (166).

Further, some economic historians argue that the reduction of labor costs was the motivation for adopting certain new machines. Chapman viewed the adoption of the self-actor and adaptations to lengthen its frame (increasing the number of spindles) as cost saving because child labor could replace adult labor. He argued that, "The object of early attempts had been to construct a machine capable of being tended by children, but when the mules became longer and one man began to manage two, this incentive was removed and the reduction of labour cost still further was commonly thought to be impracticable" (1904:69).

The fact that child labor was cheap is not disputable. The argument that children were in demand because they were cheap is. Children had always been a cheap source of labor. On the farm, in small workshops, in cottage production and in domestic service children rarely earned a subsistence wage. Since the low relative wage of children compared to adults was not a new phenomenon how could it explain the increase in the demand for child labor during industrialization? Employers would not hire workers just because they were cheap if they could not perform the necessary tasks. Children could be free and still be of no use to industrialists if they were unable to be productive. The explanation that children were in demand because they were cheap is insufficient because it does not explain why the employers thought child labor could be of any use in their factories, mines and manufactories. To understand why employers wanted to hire children instead of adults, one must examine the changes taking place in their establishments. The cheap labor argument only makes sense when coupled with an understanding of the technological innovation during this period and how technology changed the face of labor.

Several economic historians have given the cheap labor theory credence while arguing changes in technology were at least as important, if not more important, in altering the demand for child labor. Berg (1991) and Thompson (1966) both argue it was a combination of technological innovation and cost which pulled children into the textile factories. Thompson describes a demand-driven labor market, "The first half of the nineteenth century must be seen as a period of chronic under-employment, in which the skilled trades are like islands threatened on every side by technological innovation and by the inrush of unskilled or juvenile labour" (1966:243). He recognized the role of technology in changing the skill requirements for the factory work force which then made it possible for owners to replace expensive labor (adult men) with cheap labor (women and children). Thompson asserted that, "Manufacturers in the first half of the nineteenth century pressed forward each innovation which enables them to dispense with adult male craftsmen and to replace them with women or juvenile labour" (1966:248). Berg gave considerable weight to the role the new machines and production process played in making the employment of children feasible in the cotton industry, the metal trades, calico printing and button making.[9] She believed that women and children were highly productive when working with the new machines in the small and medium-scale manufactories. She argued that, "In the English workshops and small factories of the eighteenth century, a specific labour force was targeted not simply because it was cheap, but because it formed part of a package with the new technologies and organisation" (1991:32). The role of technology and its impact on the labor force will be developed thoroughly in the second half of this chapter. While Berg and Thompson appear to have been on the right track in identifying technology as an important factor affecting the employment of children, more recent research has attempted to dispute links between technology and child labor.

Bolin-Hort (1989) argues the use of child labor in the cotton industry was driven by labor relations not technology. He believes it was the efficient strategies of managers and desires of adult workers who brought children into the textile mills during the Industrial Revolution, not technological innovation. He points out that it was difficult and costly for managers to recruit, train, supervise and discipline the factory work force. The subcontracting system which had persisted on the common mule turned out to be an efficient and useful employment strategy because "the mule-spinner recruited, trained, and fired his own piecers and scavengers" (51). The workers also preferred this system because it gave them the power to regulate the entrance of new workers into their occupation as well as to hire their own children or children of friends (51,52,300). Although Bolin-Hort's argument is intuitively appealing, the evidence he offers in support of his theory is unconvincing. First, he purports that the majority of children who were employed in the textile industry were "piecers." Although many children working in textile factories were "piecers" who assisted spinners, Chapter 4 will show that there were many children employed in other jobs as well. Consequently, how does industrial relations explain the employment of the rest of the child laborers? Second, Bolin-Hort's evidence does not disprove the notion that there is a link between technology and child labor. His comparative analysis is quite interesting but overlooks the differences in spinning technology between England, Scotland and the United States. The fact that the work forces of textile mills in these three countries were quite different may reflect the different labor requirements of the mule, the throstle and the ring frame rather than variations in management and worker strategies.[10] Other economic historians who also focused on recruitment strategies have argued that it was the characteristics of children, not industrial relations, which lead managers to employ children.

Both Redford's (1926) and Pollard's (1965) research suggests that the supply of labor near factories was quite limited and that bottlenecks existed for factory owners both in rural and urban labor markets. They argue that the recruitment of labor was especially difficult since the demands of factory work were quite different from those of the cottage industry. The new work discipline in the factory required regular fixed hours, punctuality, constant attendance, cleanliness and sobriety. Adults who had worked on the farm or in their home were accustomed to having autonomy, working irregular hours and not working on "St. Monday." Wadsworth and Mann noted the changing working regime in their examination of the cotton textile industry, "Whatever else the domestic system was, however intermittent and sweated its labour, it did allow a man a degree of personal liberty to indulge himself, a command over his time, which he was not to enjoy again" (1965:391). Many adults were simply unwilling to submit to the authority of an overseer or succumb to the long, fixed hours and tedious tasks performed in the factories. Additionally, the adult workers who did enter the factory turned out to be trouble for the factory owners. Their attendance was irregular and "St. Monday" and feast days were persistent problems for managers (Pollard 1965:182).

Consequently, some children and young persons who were passive, submissive and obedient, worked in the factories because that is what their parents told them to do. Although they must have had some bargaining power because they were earning wages, either they placed considerable value on pleasing their parents or their own preferences were identical to their parents. This sense of obedience was founded in the principles of the religious movement at the time and had become a pillar of Victorian society. Children learned to do what they were told and not to question authority. It was not uncommon for children to work where their parents refused to go. Lyons (1989) finds this to be especially true among the hand-loom weaver's families in Lancashire. Despite falling wages which began in 1815, hand-loom weavers were still unwilling to go into factories due to "the new economic order needed . . . part humans: soulless, depersonalized, disembodied, who could become members, or little wheels rather, of a complex mechanism" (Pollard 1965:161). Although this explanation is quite plausible, it tells only part of the story. The fact that some children were submissive and obedient to their parents explains why, once the opportunities arose in the factories and mines, parents sent their children (and children went) to work in places other workers would not go. It does not explain, however, why these opportunities for children arose or what made children able to perform these jobs as well as or better than adults.

Von Tunzelmann (1981) points to "labour dilution" created by the use of new machinery as the reason employers began to hire unskilled labor in place of skilled labor, and women and children in the place of adults (161). Chapman describes three stages in the recruitment of labor for the mills. In the first stage factory owners needed skilled workers to build the mill and in the second stage skilled workers to build the machinery. In the third stage, however, "once the mill building was completed and the machinery built most of the labour force required were unskilled women and children" (1967:165). Smelser argues that at first entire families and then later just children were drawn into the textile industry because of the technological change. When identifying the workers needed for each type of spinning or weaving machine he concludes that "practically all these occupations required attentiveness rather than strength" (1959:204). Berg takes the argument one step further and claims that the new technologies changed the sexual division of labor as well. Berg rejects the traditional definition of skill and believes "the very definitions of skilled and unskilled labour have at their root social and gender distinctions of far greater significance than any technical attribute" (1985:151). Thus, some work, particularly in machine spinning, began to be associated as "women's" or "children's work."[11] Berg develops the argument further in her recent paper and suggests that the increase in the demand for women (and girls) in textile factories was attributable to a "gender-typing of innovation" (1993:35). Berg argues that manufacturers at the time preferred women and girls because they had "a greater 'natural' aptitude for the manual dexterity and fine motor skills required by the new technologies" (35). The basic argument is that technological change, by altering the expertise necessary to operate the new machines, tended to increase the proportion of children working in factories. I extend and expand on this idea by concentrating on the technological requirements of both specific machinery and work situations which necessitated the use of children and youths.

The Theory of Biased Technological Change

The industrialization process in Great Britain is characterized by, among other things, the coupling of automation with the division of labor to medium- and large-scale production. Theoretically, this would increase the demand for labor in general and would not necessarily favor the employment of children and youths over adults.[12] It was the nature of the technological change that tipped the scales toward children and youths. The technological change in certain industries favored or was "biased" toward the employment of child labor over adult labor. The new technology that arrived with the Industrial Revolution made special use of young people in three different ways. Some innovations increased the number of assistants necessary in the production process. Still others increased the possibilities of substitution of unskilled for skilled labor (e.g., children for adults). And finally, certain inventions and work situations required the labor of small workers.

The Industrial Revolution in Great Britain is associated with many important inventions and innovations.[13] Some inventions were "dramatic new departures that opened entirely new technological avenues by hitting on something that was entirely novel and represented a discontinuous leap with the past" or what Mokyr called "macroinventions" while others were "microinventions" or "small, incremental improvements to known technologies" (Mokyr 1993:18). Innovation involves the subsequent diffusion and implementation of these (either macro or micro) inventions. Certain innovations which occurred in the modern or dynamic sector of the British economy favored the employment of children and young persons over adults in three ways. The first involved labor-intensive technology which increased the demand for children as helpers. Marx observed this "labor intensity" of British industry and said, "Nowhere do we find a more shameful squandering of human labour power for the most despicable purposes than in England, the land of machinery" (Marx 1906I:430). In describing the new workshops of the eighteenth century Samuel associated the introduction of machinery with the creation of "a whole new world of labour-intensive jobs" (1977:8).[14]

The application of the principle of the division of labor to the production processes of making cloth and extracting coal increased the number of secondary workers. The process of making cloth had been separated into four stages and carried on in different cottages: the preparation of the material (cotton, flax, silk and wool), the spinning of thread, the weaving into cloth and the finishing (cleaning, bleaching and dyeing). With the factory and new machinery all these stages were under one roof and each had been further subdivided into numerous simple tasks. Children assisted in every stage as "pickers," "batters" and sweepers in preparation; as "piecers" and "bobbin doffers" in spinning and as "dressers" in weaving. Similarly, underground the process of extracting coal was divided into many distinct but interconnected tasks with children assisting the adult colliers by controlling the air doors so waggoners could pass ("trappers"), and youths placing the pieces of coal into the wagons ("putters") as well as transporting the coal from the pickers to the shaft ("hurriers," "pushers" and "trammers"). In this setting the benefits Adam Smith had attributed to the division of labor became a reality for many factory owners and proprietors of mines.[15] The division and specialization of labor increased the demand for children and youths because their quick and nimble fingers made them particularly dexterous workers and consequently very good at these simple tasks.[16] In addition, a few inventions like Crompton's Common Mule and Cartwright's Combing Machine used in textile production increased the number of assistants necessary to work with the adults operating the machines.

This labor-intensive technology which increased the number of assistants utilized in the production process would increase the demand for child labor as illustrated in Figure 3.1. Children are considered complements to the production process and as the demand for labor increased, the number of children employed would increase (to L') as would their wage rate (to w').

The second type of technological change that increased the demand for child labor was inventions and innovations which made it possible to replace adults with children and youths. The degree of substitutability between children and adults varied greatly depending upon the industry and even within a given industry. Many substitution possibilities arose in the textile and mining industry but for very different reasons. In textiles the employment of children as primary workers depended upon the machines utilized in the production process and on the improvements that had been made to the machines. It was Arkwright's macroinvention of roller spinning that revolutionized the process of spinning, replacing the movements of the human hand with machines. His water frame, by reducing the level of strength and expertise required to spin, replaced the adult spinner on the wheel with a machine "minder." Furthermore, several microinventions made improvements on machines that made it possible for children to replace the adult they had been assisting. Robert's automation of the common mule and Cartwright's automation of the hand-loom dramatically reduced the effort and strength required to operate these spinning and weaving machines, eliminating the need for strong, skilled operators.

Contemporaries, in describing the new manufactories, were struck by the power of these machines and often fearful of their effects on the work force.[17] Andrew Ure describes what was happening in the factories:

whenever a process requires peculiar dexterity and steadiness of hand, it is withdrawn as soon as possible from the cunning workman, who is prone to irregularities of many kinds, and it is placed in charge of a peculiar mechanism, so self regulating, that a child may superintend it. . .on the automatic plan, skilled labour gets progressively superseded, and will eventually, be replaced by mere overlookers of machines (Ure 1835:19-20).

FIGURE 3.1 Labor Intensive Technologies: Children as Helpers

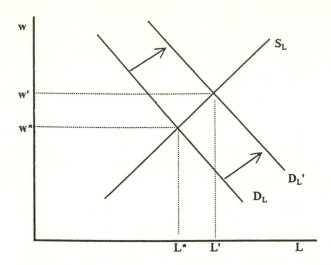

Robert Owen, a critic of the factory system, believed the increased productivity from the technical change entailed the exploitation, misery and moral degradation of labor (Owen 1969:211-215). P. Gaskell, another pessimist, surmised the point of new machinery and its adoption was to eventually "do away with the necessity of human labour" and therefore to lessen its value (P. Gaskell 1836:315-316). The *New Moral World* in reporting the impact of the new machinery in 1836, declared, "If the value of human labour be reduced, the benefit must, says the intrepid Doctor, be grasped by the masters, who secure it by substituting the industry of Women and Children for that of men, or that of ordinary labourers, for 'skilled artisans'" (1836:640-641).

In mining, the increase in the possibilities of substitution between children, youths and adults occurred not because of new macro or microinventions but instead due to the innovation of the division of labor as applied to surface work. Children and youths proved to be very good substitutes for adult workers on the surface of coal and metal mines. In coal mining the process of "preparing the coal" or "screening the coal" had been divided into two separate tasks. Each task involved a simple one-step procedure that required little strength and was repeated over and over and then passed on to the next step in an assembly-type line. Similarly, in metal mining (lead, copper and tin) the procedure of "dressing the ores" had been broken down into eight separate tasks and was as easily performed by children as adults.

These new opportunities for children and youths which arose in the textile factories and on the surface of mines increased the demand for child labor. Theoretically, the increasing substitutability between children and adults in the production process would increase the elasticity of the demand for labor. This is illustrated graphically in Figure 3.2 by a new demand for labor curve, $D_L{}^\wedge$, which is flatter than the original. The new equilibrium yields a higher level of employment for children ($L^\wedge$) and increases their wage rate ($w^\wedge$).

FIGURE 3.2 Labor Substituting Technologies: Children as Workers

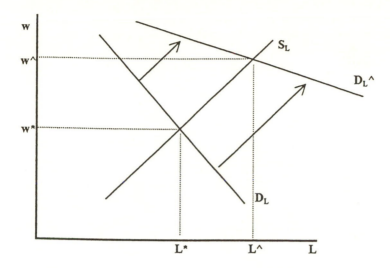

Finally, the third type of technological change that favored children were inventions and work situations that had special technical requirements. In this case, children had a comparative advantage in working in some situations and with certain machinery because they could work in tight spots. For example, children could maneuver in smaller openings and spaces in underground tunnels of coal mines which often stood only three feet high (1842[380]XV:47-65). In this instance, children were essential because of their size and agility which enabled them to perform work in situations where adults simply could not fit or maneuver. In addition, some of the first machines used in textile mills, like the water frame, stood very near to the ground and were ideally suited for children but not for adults. They were so low that the backs of adults would have been severely injured after one day of stooping down to tend these machines and even some of the children who worked with them were often deformed for life. Still other machines, like the power-loom, were situated so close to one another on the shop floor that only workers of small and thin stature could pass freely and perform the necessary operations.

These special technical requirements increased the demand for child labor, specifically for younger (and smaller) children. At the same time, these specific technical requirements meant that there were fewer substitutes for children in these tasks. Theoretically, the demand for child labor would both increase and become less elastic. This is illustrated in Figure 3.3 where the new demand for child labor curve has shifted rightward and become steeper, represented by $D_L\sim$. Although the modus operandi is different, the effect on the level of employment and wages is the same as in the other two cases - both increase.

In conclusion, the employment of a large number of children and youths in the textile mills and mines of Great Britain during the Industrial Revolution was remarkably different from the child labor employed on the farms and in cottages.

90

FIGURE 3.3 Labor Specific Technologies: Children Working in "Tight Spots"

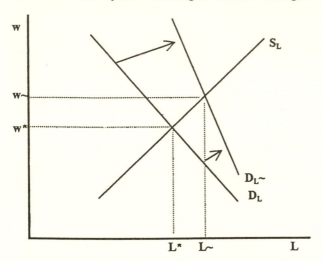

Although children and youths had worked for centuries on the farm and in cottage industry, the nature of their work, the employer/employee relationship and its impact on their role in the economy had changed. Children and youths worked longer hours with barely any time to rest or eat in a highly-regimented system for people they did not know. The specialization and technological innovation, moreover, which occurred in the textile and mining industry created a demand for child labor. The technological change was biased toward the employment of children and youth, and therefore, employers not only wanted to hire younger workers but also in some cases needed to hire children and youths for their factories and mines. As the demand for child labor increased, their role in production became essential to the growth of the industry. Employers needed, wanted and had to hire child workers. This preference for child labor is clear in the following advertisements: the first, asking for cotton workers in 1787 for Thomas Evans' factory in the Midlands and the second, asking for silk workers in 1825 for a silk factory in Macclesfield:

<u>Darley Cotton Mill</u>

Wanted, Families, particularly women and children to work at the said mill. They may be provided with comfortable houses and every necessary convenience either at Darley or Allestry; particularly a milking-cow to each family. It is a very good neighborhood for the men getting work who are not employed in the manufactory (Chapman 1967:159).

<u>Wanted</u>

Wanted immediately from 4 - 5,000 persons from seven to twenty years of age to be employed in the throwing and manufacturing of silk. The great increase of the trade having caused a great scarcity of workmen, it is suggested that this is a most favorable opportunity for persons with large families and overseers who wish to put out children (Warner 1922:133-34).

P. Gaskell noticed that in places where the spinning and weaving machinery had been adopted "there is no employment to be found for adult males; on the contrary, they are becoming daily more and more a clog in the way of masters" (1836:172). Samuel Oldknow, who owned several cotton mills, spent considerable time and effort finding employment for the fathers and husbands of his cotton operatives in order to maintain his labor force (Unwin 1924:166-170). Consequently, employers competed with one another for children and youths, thereby bidding up the market wage. This relatively high wage increased the bargaining power of children in the family and subsequently impacted the consumption and labor supply decisions of the household. To support this view we must move from a theoretical analysis to a historical analysis and thoroughly examine the technology and work situations in the textile and mining industries. Chapter 4 explores the textile industry while Chapter 5 analyzes the mining industry. In each chapter, the three sources of the increase in the demand for child labor will be developed and the wages of children and youths during this period examined.

Notes

1. According to the economic definition of capital, capital is further disaggregated into two types: (1) fixed capital and (2) circulating capital. In the short run we assume that fixed capital (e.g., the buildings) cannot change but circulating capital (e.g., tools and machines) can.

2. Berg, Hudson and Sonenscher argue that the "casual" method of earning which persisted for families involved in domestic production created "casual" habits of living where leisure preferences were almost universal (1983:2). They point out that the possibility existed for each worker to stop working to feast or play, an option not available to factory workers (19).

3. The existence of games, dances and sports provide indirect proof that children still enjoyed some leisure time while they worked with their families in the cottage industries (Thompson 1966). Thompson argues that if they had worked the long hours that the factory children worked there would be no time to enjoy any of these activities and historians would have documented the absence of games and parks in this period.

4. Mitch argues that Sunday school did not improve literacy rates, as measured by signature rates at marriage (1992:147).

5. See Hopkins (1994) for a thorough discussion on the differences in working hours between agriculture, workshop industry and the factory (24-26).

6. Corporal punishment was not uncommon in textile factories. Children's faces were slapped, hands struck with a stick, heads were hit and ears were smacked by overseers on the factory floor. Evidence presented before the Factory Inquiry Commission in 1833 reveals that children who worked in the factories were ill-treated (1833(450)XX and 1833(519)XXI).

7. Nardinelli shows that corporal punishment was widespread in the factories using child labor. In addition, he argues that children who were subject to corporal punishment were paid a compensating differential. He estimates that it raised children's wages by 16-18 percent (1982:288-295).

8. Pinchbeck and Hewitt calculated an average family income in 1843 and found children's wages were one fourth of adult male wages (1973II:96) while Mitch claims children could earn between 10 - 30 percent of an adult wage in the middle of the nineteenth century (1982:293). For original data on wages see The *Return of Wages 1830-1886* (1887(c5172)LXXXIX).

9. Rose (1992) makes a similar argument to explain the employment of so many women in the hosiery, lace and carpet industry during British industrialization (6, 29).

10. There were variations within each country, spinning in England was done primarily on the common mule and then the self-actor, spinning in Scotland was done primarily using the throstle (water frame) while ring spinning was most popular in New England, which could explain the need for child labor (Benson:1983).

11. A more thorough discussion of the gendered meaning of "unskilled" labor or "women's work" is found in Chapter 6.

12. All references to adults refer to adult males. The role of women in the Industrial Revolution is developed fully in Chapter 6.

13. The literature on technological change during the Industrial Revolution is rich and bountiful, see Ashton (1948); Berg (1979); Landes (1969); MacLeod (1988); Mantoux (1928) and Mokyr (1990).

14. Blaug (1961), MacLeod (1988) and Von Tunzelmann (1981) have sufficiently discredited conventional wisdom and have shown that many inventions associated with the Industrial Revolution were not labor saving. Although some machines multiplied the movement of the hand, the size and speed of the machines required many laborers to tend them. Before these machines were perfected, increasing the size (for example, the number of spindles on a water frame) and/or the speed (for example, the number of picks per second on the power-loom) often increased the number of breaks in the thread.

15. Smith believed the increase in productivity of labor resulted from three factors; the increased dexterity of the worker, the decreased lost time from passing from one species of work to another and the increased number of machines which enabled one worker to do the work of many (1976[1776]:9-11).

16. Sokoloff found this to be true for industrialization in the United States. He argues that factories "favored" the employment of children due to the more extensive division of labor and that it was easier to maintain an intense work regime with children because of their submissive nature (1984:358).

17. There is considerable literature on what is called "The Machinery Question." The technological innovation which accompanied the Industrial Revolution changed the jobs workers performed, redefined and displaced skill as well as increased the speed of the production process. See also Berg (1980); Engels (1845); Hobsbawn (1964); Mill (1965[1848]); Pollard (1965); Thompson (1966) and Ure (1861) for additional discussion.

4

The Textile Industry

The importance of the textile industry in defining, describing and determining the nature of the British Industrial Revolution has been established by contemporaries and modern historians alike.[1] The term "revolutionary" is appropriately applied to characterize the machinery, the techniques of production, the organization of workers and the levels of output associated with the silk, cotton, and later, worsted and woollen industries. The woollen industry had its roots in the twelfth century and woollen goods were Britain's main export until the nineteenth century. In 1742 the English woollen goods were described by Daniel Defoe as "the richest and most valuable manufacture in the world" (1742:Letter 3). The worsted industry, which utilizes the longer staple wool fibers, was particularly successful because "the rich pastures of England and of Belgium seem to be more favourable to the growth of long combing wool than any other country of the world hitherto tried" (Ure 1835:130). The exports of the cotton, woollen and worsted, and silk manufactures for the first half of the nineteenth century are given in Appendix 4. The export of woollen and worsted goods was highest in 1815 and then fluctuates, peaking again in 1822 and 1836 but never regaining the levels exported in 1815. The export of woollen yarn, however, steadily increased from 1819 to 1845 and remained high through 1850. The silk industry, which had been given statutory protection in the fifteenth century, made its mark in 1721 when Thomas Lombe designed and built the first water powered mill for throwing silk. The new machines in his factories produced organzine, a high twist yarn, which up to this point, had been imported from Italy at considerable expense (Bush 1987:5). The export of silk thread more than quadrupled from 1815 to 1850, despite a significant drop in the 1840s. The production of flax thread made from the bark covering of the linum plant, began using the Saxony wheel in the late Middle Ages. The Saxony or flax wheel was used to spin flax until spinning machinery was invented in 1787. Although the industry's output pales in comparison to that of cotton and wool, it became quite profitable by the 1820s with the application of automated machinery (Clapham 1964:242). The production of flax increased with the application of steam.

Cotton's dominance is obvious even in 1815, where the export of cotton piece goods was 253 million yards and that of wool and worsted was only 12,173 yards. By 1850 the export of cotton thread was 300 times the export of woollen yarn. Subsequently, cotton has been dubbed a "leading industry," a "pace making industry" in the Industrial Revolution and the cotton mill a preeminent model of the factory system (Thompson 1966:192). As Hobsbawn declared, "Whoever says the Industrial Revolution says cotton" (1969:56). One of the explanations for the rapid climb of cotton textile production and the success of the new cotton factory was the technological innovation in spinning and the evolution of a new type of work force - factory laborers.

Employment of Children in Textile Factories

Many of these factory laborers were children and youths. Initially, most of the children who worked in the early country mills were apprentices, although some mill children were members of a family and lived at home. As industrialization progressed, a very large proportion of the factory work force in towns consisted of this type of child labor - children from working-class families. The youthful composition of the labor force of textile mills shown in Table 1.5 was not an aberration. This becomes clear when examining the results of the returns of Saunders, a factory commissioner for a very large district in England.[2] Tables 4.1 and 4.2 present information collected from hundreds of mills producing cotton, wool and worsted and upwards of eighty mills producing flax and silk in his district. In all of the textile industries the proportion of the work force under eighteen is close to 50 percent for the entire period. In other words, on average, almost one out of every two workers in a textile factory was a child or youth. Worsted and silk mills employed the highest percentage of non-adults while cotton employed the lowest percentage after 1835.

If one looks closer at the age and gender stratification of these child laborers, as presented in Table 4.2, several interesting patterns emerge. More girls than boys were employed in every industry, except wool. The silk industry had the highest percentage of girls in its work force, ranging from 33-42 percent, while the wool industry had the

TABLE 4.1 Employment of Children in the Textile Industries

% of Labor Force under 18

Industry	1835	1838	1839	1843	1845
Cotton	49%	46%	46%	39%	40%
Wool	47	50	50	42	46
Worsted	64	59	60	43	46
Flax	58	55	54	48	53
Silk	56	56	62	47	46

Source: 1835, 1839:1840(227)X, p. 119. 1838, 1843, 1845:1845[639]XXV, pp. 51-52.

TABLE 4.2 Employment of Children in Textile Industry by Age and Gender

% of Labor Force under 18

Industry		*1835*	*1838*	*1839*	*1843*	*1845*	*1850*
Cotton	M	(8)[a] 21%	(4) 19%	(4) 22%	(3) 16%	(5) 17%	(4) 17%
	F	(8) 28	(4) 23	(5) 28	(4) 23	(4) 23	(4) na[b]
Wool	M	(13) 29	(8) 30	(8) 30	(6) 25	(8) 27	(8) 25
	F	(9) 18	(6) 20	(6) 21	(4) 18	(5) 19	(5) na
Worsted	M	(10) 23	(6) 18	(6) 18	(4) 13	(7) 15	(7) 16
	F	(15) 41	(8) 41	(9) 42	(5) 30	(8) 31	(7) na
Flax	M	(9) 20	(6) 19	(5) 18	(5) 19	(6) 21	(4) 15
	F	(11) 38	(4) 36	(4) 36	(3) 28	(6) 32	(3) na
Silk	M	(9) 15	(9) 16	(9) 15	(7) 14	(6) 13	(4) 11
	F	(17) 41	(13) 40	(15) 42	(13) 33	(10) 33	(9) na

[a] The number in parenthesis refers to the percentage working under thirteen years of age.
[b] The totals for females in 1850 are not available because the returns gave totals for females ages thirteen and up.

Source: 1835,1839:1840(227)X, p. 119. 1838,1843,1845:1845[639]XXV, pp. 51-52. 1850:1851[1304]XXIII, p. 64.

lowest, ranging from 18-21 percent. More than twice as many girls as boys were employed in the worsted (except in 1835) and silk industries during this period. The gender differences are most pronounced for youths (aged thirteen-eighteen) working in all of these industries.

Several explanations for these gender differences in employment practices emerge. As children grew older, the physical strength of boys became more pronounced and steered them toward other more strenuous occupations, like carpentry, masonry, and road building. Alternatively, young men may have left factory work to pursue other occupations which had traditionally been dominated by males, like mining, engineering, and shopkeeping. Young girls, on the other hand, had fewer employment opportunities and were expected to stop working after marriage. There is a stronger presence of young girls on the shop floor in the silk and worsted mills, but the distinction is significant in silk where almost twice as many girls under thirteen are working than boys of that age. The work in silk mills was considered the lightest but most delicate of the textile trades. Silk manufacturers quickly realized that the thin and graceful hands of girls were far superior to the large and clumsy hands of boys in winding, twisting and piecing.

The large proportions of children and youths employed which are presented in Tables 4.1 and 4.2 are alarming because these totals represent free labor - not apprentice labor; the new industrial labor force - not merely the early labor force of the rural factories; and all textile industries - not solely the cotton industry. Despite the factory legislation, moreover, of 1833 and 1844, which meant to curtail the employment and hours of child labor, the percentage of the work force under eighteen started increasing in 1843, after a period of decline. The employment of children peaked earlier in cotton and flax (in 1835) and almost five years later in wool, worsted and silk (in 1839). By 1845, although the proportions were not as large as they had been at their peak, at least two-fifths of the labor force of these mills were still non-adults. Furthermore, the evidence on children and young men indicates these high proportions still existed in 1850, although they had waned somewhat in the flax and silk mills. Why did these factories and mills use such a large proportion of child labor? What sorts of tasks did the children perform in these factories and mills? Did the children work on their own or were they helpers to the adult workers? The answers to these questions lie within the diverse resources available to the historian from this period.

A plethora of materials exists which provide evidence on the organization of labor, the utilization of technological innovations and the participation of children in the factories, mills and mines of Great Britain during the eighteenth and nineteenth centuries. The State Papers at the Public Record Office (PRO) include petitions by the inventors for patents. These statements often contained justifications or defenses of the patent that were particularly revealing of the type of labor required to work the machine and the type of labor which might be displaced by its adoption. Despite the fact that the machines finally adopted by the factory owners may have been different from the ones described in the patents, the intentions of the inventor are clear and illustrative of the basic principle of the machine. There are also dictionaries and cyclopedias of manufactures (by Baines, Clapham, Crump, Rees, Ure, and Warner) which provide detailed descriptions of the latest machines and techniques used, accompanied by sketches and plates which give an indication of size and scale. These are extremely reliable sources of information because they are objective and meant to be factual. In addition, the trade newspapers (like the *Manchester Guardian*, the *Gentleman's Magazine* and the *Westminster Review*), the daily newspapers (like the *Leeds Mercury* and the *Leeds Intelligencer)* and the periodical publications of the Royal Statistical Society (JSS) documented the changes taking place in the textile industry both in terms of mechanization and the employment of workers. The newspapers report technological breakthroughs as well as workers' responses, although slightly tainted by the political view of the reporter. The authors of the journal articles, however, had acquired expertise after researching the industry and typically saw their duty as one of presenting facts and figures rather than hypothesizing or proselytizing.

Similarly, many contemporaries' (Gaskell, Guest, Kennedy, McCulloch, Ogden and Radcliffe) observations are particularly relevant because they wrote with reverence about the new machines and methods of production after visiting a factory or descending into a mine.[3] Their accounts, however, were more subjective than the researcher and laden with emotional language and personal interpretation on the effects of the new techniques. Therefore, these accounts must be used cautiously and the facts carefully separated from their opinion. The Factory Inspectors' reports contain a wealth of information on the output, occupations, employment and earnings within factories and mines. Despite the probable bias in the selection of child witnesses parading before Sadler's Committee in 1832, their comments on the type of work children did and how they worked with the new machinery was free from any bias.[4] Who could better talk about the tasks and machinery than the children who tended them or the supervisors who oversaw their operation? Who could better understand the costs and benefits of these innovations than the manufacturers who were familiar with the expense of their new machinery and its productivity? In many ways the workers' statements were autobiographies of the child laborer, yielding considerable insight about their work experience.

Finally, the employment statistics and wages collected in the Board of Trade, House of Commons and House of Lords papers permit the economic historian to tell the story yet another way and connect theory with practice. Unfortunately, we get only snapshots of certain years from this period dependent on persistent factory commissioners and dutiful factory owners. But fortuitously, these snapshots represent the activities of hundreds of factories. Until the *1851 Census*, they provide the closest thing to a systematic analysis of the period we can obtain.

In describing the role of child labor in the textile industry, particular attention is given to the cotton industry because many of the inventions and innovations in the production of textiles were first applied to cotton. The application and adaptation of machines to production, however, was uneven both within the cotton trade and among different trades. For example, the mechanization and automation of spinning was faster than in weaving. The new inventions and innovations in cotton were more slowly adapted to the worsted and woollen trades. Some of the new machinery was more easily altered for different types of raw material (like carding engines, the spinning jenny, and the self-actor) than others (like the water frame and common mule). Even within a given industry, the old and new technologies often coexisted under one roof. According to contemporaries, it was not unusual to see hand mules and self-actors side by side in the spinning rooms of cotton factories or hand-looms and power-looms in the weaving department of silk and woollen mills.[5] Thus, mechanization was not uniform nor simultaneous in all mills in the textile industry (Clapham 1939I:143). When the machinery changed and techniques improved, so did the skills of the labor required to operate the machines and perform the new tasks. In many cases, the new labor required was child labor.

Children worked at every stage in the production of cloth: assisting adults, tending some machines and operating others. There are four main stages in producing cloth: the preparing of the raw material, the spinning of the raw material into thread, the weaving of the thread into cloth and finally, the finishing of the cloth for sale. Each stage involves one or more processes with several variations, depending upon the raw material. See Appendix 5 for diagrams of the production processes for cotton, wool, flax and silk. In general, the first stage involves cleaning, sorting, and carding or combing the raw material to produce a loose rope of fibers called a sliver. The second stage is spinning, where the sliver is pulled and twisted to form a strong thread. The threads are produced in various counts depending upon their strength, thickness and smoothness.[6] In the third stage, the weft (the crossway threads) is woven using variations of the "over and under" motion with the warp (the lengthwise threads) which unwinds from a beam of the loom. Finally, in the last stage the cloth is cleaned and then bleached, dyed or printed and sold. The increase in the demand for child labor in each of these stages occurred because the technology adopted was biased toward the utilization of children. Children were hired because the macroinventions and innovations in the new textile factories could be classified as either labor intensive technology, labor substituting technology or labor specific technology. Each component tilted the employment scales toward children and youths and together they explain the increase in child labor during this period.

Labor-Intensive Technology: Children as Helpers

As factory owners adapted the new spinning and weaving inventions into water or steam-driven factories, the division of production into many separate and distinguishable tasks took place.[7] This innovation in the division of labor resulted in an increase in the number of helpers or secondary workers required for production. As Ure declared, "This tendency to employ merely children with watchful eyes and nimble fingers, instead of journeymen of long experience, show how the scholastic dogma of the division of labour into degrees of skill had been exploded by our enlightened manufacturers" (1835:23). In general, the "watchful eyes and nimble fingers" of children were ideal for the simple one-step tasks which required little or no training and were performed over and over. Consequently, children assisted in every stage of the production of cotton, wool and worsted cloth and in three of the four stages of silk manufacture. The diversity of jobs performed by children and youths is apparent in Inspector Horner's Directory of the Departments in a Cotton Factory in 1842, replicated in Table 4.3, giving the occupations, ages and gender of factory workers.[8] Although ages and occupations probably varied from one factory to another, the presence of youths in every stage of production is undeniable. Table 4.3 also reveals another interesting feature of factory organization - several tasks were often gender specific. The segregation of occupations by gender is most salient for youths while younger boys and girls appear to be interchangeable. For youths, the distinctions are pronounced in the preparation stage with young men working as "card tenters" and young women working as "can tenters." In spinning, the segregation occurs only in throstle spinning where young women are spinners and young men are doffers.

In the preparation stage, children were hired as "pickers" and "batters" in removing the waste and dust from the bales of raw cotton. This process was the first to be mechanized and was performed by a carding engine (invented in 1775 by Richard Arkwright) tended by children. Boys ("card tenters") would feed the lap into the machine and girls ("can tenters") would replace the full cans of sliver with empty ones. The cotton was fed into the back of the wooden machine and combed by millions of metal spikes on a revolving drum. "In Arkwright's day they were set in leather by children, who were paid a pence for every three thousand, a task which usually took

TABLE 4.3 Directory of Workers in a Cotton Factory

Preparation Department

    Card tenters, are boys from 13 to 16 years of age
    Can tenters, are girls from 13 to 16 years of age
    Drawing-frame tenters, are females from 16-20 years of age

Mule Spinning Department

    Scavenger, is a boy or girl from 9 to 13 years of age
    Big piecer, is a young person of either sex from 15 to 20 years of age
    Mule spinners, are generally men from 25 years and upwards; frequently women
        when the mules are small

Self Actors

    Minder, is a young person of either sex from 18 and upwards
    Cipher, the same

Throstle Spinning

    Throstle spinner, is a female from 16 to 20 years of age
    Doffers, are boys from 14 to 18 years of age
    Reelers and winders, are females from 16 and upwards
    Jobbers, are males from 18 and upwards

Weaving Department

    Weaver, is a male or female of either sex from 16 and upwards
    Helper, is a boy or girl from 13 to 16 years of age
    Dresser, is a man from 21 years of age and upward

Source: 1842(31)XXII, p. 85.

about four hours" (Aspin 1981:6). Similarly, children worked with wool as "scribbler fillers" placing the wool on the feed sheet of the scribbling machine and as "carder fillers" placing the fleece from the scribbler into the carding machine. In the preparation of flax, breaking (cutting the fibers into three pieces) and sorting (sorting the heckled flax) were performed by children; whereas, feeding the automatic heckling machine was reserved for young men who were called "machine boys" or "machine minders." Unlike in the preparation of cotton and wool, however, feeding the tow of flax into the carding engine was a task done by women not children. Although preparing the raw silk for spinning involves a completely different procedure from carding, the winding and cleaning was still primarily the work of children. Children worked as "piecers" to the winding engine and were supervised by a woman overseer called the "danter." In 1831 Dionysius Lardner wrote in his *Treatise on Silk*

Manufacture that, "...the constant attendance of children upon this winding machine is requisite, in order to join up any threads which may be broken in winding, and when the skeins are exhausted to place new ones upon the swifts" (Bush 1987:14). In cleaning the silk, young children were also "piecers" to the operators of the scissor mechanism which removed knots from the thread. David Davies wrote of the Lombe silk mill in Derby; "the cleaning machines wind the silk from one set of bobbins to another. In this part many children are employed whose nimble fingers are kept in continual exercise by tying the knots that break, and removing the burs and uneven parts" (1811:167).

In the next stage, boys and girls aged eight to twelve assisted in the spinning process by piecing together broken threads and changing bobbins on the spinning jenny and on the common mule. In the spinning of cotton and worsted thread, the child workers who performed these operations were called "piecers," "minders" and "doffers" while in wool they were called "winders" and "warpers" and in flax "little doffers." Contemporaries felt these tasks simply required dexterity and children could easily spot broken threads or full bobbins on several machines at the same time. As P. Gaskell observed, "Factory labour, in many of its processes, requires little else but manual dexterity, and no physical strength; neither is there anything for the mind to do in it; so that children, whose fingers are taught to move with great facility and rapidity, have all the requisites for it" (1836:66). In a medical report on wet and dry flax spinning, Sir David Barry describes the superb performance of child "piecers" with extraordinary detail,

> It is quite impossible to give an adequate notion of the quickness and dexterity with which these girls joined their broken threads; shifted the pirns; screwed and unscrewed the flies, etc. To supply the place of such artists by new adult hands would be utterly impracticable, and difficult in the extreme to find relay hands equally expert, under present circumstances. There is no sameness of attitude- no standing still; every muscle is in action, and that in quick succession (1834(167)XIX: A3 5).

Similarly, Ure in describing the process of flax spinning reveals the relative proportion of "doffers" to spinners and depicts the task of a "doffer," "There was, before the late Factory Bill passes, a class of very young children employed in the flax mills, under the name of little doffers, forming generally a troop of from four to ten in each spinning room, who, the moment they perceived the bobbins of any frame or side of a frame exhausted of roving, ran together and furnished it with full ones as quickly as possible" (1835:223). Furthermore, the younger children worked as sweepers and scavengers in cleaning around and underneath the machines after a day's work.

In weaving, youths provided general assistance to the weaver or became "drawboys." Youths aged sixteen to eighteen prepared shuttles of weft, tied broken threads, wound the warp onto the beam and assisted the weaver in dressing the warp with a starch solution (also called sizing). Silk weavers used the draw-loom, which required two people, a weaver and a "drawboy," to operate it. The "drawboys" were seated on top of the loom to lift groups of drawstrings or harness cords to form a pattern in the cloth. Both boys and girls, beginning at age nine, worked as "drawboys" and the number employed was significant. For example, in Worcestershire 25 percent of the 1,821 people employed in twenty-two Weaving Manufactories were youths and 14 percent were children (1843[430]XIII:22).

In the last stage of the production process, children and youths worked as "trimmers," "darners," "tenters," "carpers" and "preemers." In the cotton mills girls worked with the finishing frame trimming edges, removing knots and imperfections and cutting up cloth. Unwin discovered from Samuel Oldknow's wage books that each finishing frame was worked by two experienced girls and three "improvers" or four "learners" (1924:109). Oldknow's finishing operations at Heaton involved, "The most important work carried on comprised the trimming of the 'float' or figures of the pattern woven; and the cutting of ballasore and romals into handkerchief size. The apparatus of this department was simple, consisting of 30 finishing frames and several darning frames. The staff comprized 81 girls and a foreman or forewoman" (Unwin 1924:109). In the woollen industry, children helped with several tasks in the finishing of the cloth. Youths were hired as "tenters" to carry the cloth outside from the fulling mill where it was stretched and hung to dry. In the next step, called teasling, the loose fibers are raised into a nap and the children helped as "carpers" and "preemers." Children of both genders prepared the thistle-teasels used in this procedure, while primarily boys, cleaned the teasel rods and handles. This sexual division of labour occurred because the overseers thought "preeming is a much harder and more disagreeable work than carping" (Ure 1835:202). As this process was partially mechanized by Atkinson's Gig-mill and as lewies were used in the cropping room, young men replaced children (Ure 1835:203). Bleaching and dyeing (of cotton and flax) was considered a more dangerous job which employed primarily women while printing was considered a skilled art reserved for adult men. Children were employed, however, in bleaching and dyeing establishments from the age of eight and assisted the women (1857(151)XI:16). Defoe was impressed with the beauty created by the bleaching season in Lithgow (Scotland) when he reported, "The whole green, fronting the lough or lake, was covered with linen-cloth, it being the bleaching season, and, I believe, a thousand women and children, and not less, tending and managing the bleaching business" (1742:214). The best silken material was dyed before it was woven while the cheaper goods were dyed by the piece. Like cotton and flax, the process of dyeing silk was reserved for the older workers.[9] In addition, silk finishing which involved hot pressing and steaming, was the work of skilled adults not children (Warner 1922:449).

As helpers in the production process, children's tasks were essential in preserving the rapid and uninterrupted pace of machinery. If children stopped, the productivity of the adult spinners and weavers would suffer if not cease altogether. Many contemporaries, proprietors of mills, overlookers and adult workers recognized this complementarity of child workers to adult workers. This interdependence became abundantly clear in discussions on the Ten Hours Bill to limit the hours of children working in factories. The factory commissioners Thomas Tooke, Edwin Chadwick and Thomas Smith asked overseers, adult workers and factory owners the following question: "Would turning away those under eighteen years of age, after ten hours of work, compel the master to turn away the grown-up workmen also and stop the machinery?" The responses were similar and in the affirmative in witness after witness, "I think it would compel them to stop their mill in a general way;" "Certainly, as one half of our hands are under eighteen, it would be impossible to keep spinning on without the piecers" and "It is almost sure in some cases that the Ten Hours Bill would stop the work in the whole factory" (1833(450)XX:D2 3 D2, 29-30 and C2 34). Similarly, the crucial role of children is also revealed in P. Gaskell's position on the Ten Hours Bill when he said,

> Of this Bill it may be truly said that it is an absurdity, being founded upon the most singular ignorance of the interior economy of the mills. This economy consists of a series of operations in which the child performs an essential part. There is a mutual dependence of the entire labourers one upon the other; and if the children who are employed principally by the spinner are dismissed, his work ceases, and the mill is at a stand still (1836:168).

The predominance of children employed as helpers is supported by the information documented by factory owners during this period. In Yorkshire, 296 manufacturers and mill owners were asked to state the processes in which the greatest number of young children are employed in their works. Their overwhelming response was "piecers" as shown in the Table 4.4 but they also identified "doffers," "pieceners," "feeders," "winders," "tenters," "screwers" and "carpers." An examination of Benjamin Gott's Woollen Factory, Bean Ing, in 1813 also confirms children worked alongside adult workers in preparing, spinning and weaving woollen cloth (See Table 4.5). In the upper and lower scribbling rooms, there were forty-two and forty-six children, respectively, working as helpers ("pieceners," "fillers" and "cleaners") with only ten adult workers in each department. Similarly, in the spinning and weaving rooms there were many "winders" and "warpers" assisting the spinners and weavers. The organization of labor in a Flax Mill in the Lancashire District also reveals the utilization of children and youths as helpers. Table 4.6 shows in the Throstle spinning room there were seven "jobbers," seventy-two bobbin "doffers" and six bobbin carriers

TABLE 4.4 Responses to Question 23 in 1834 Supplementary Report

"Does the nature of your work require the employment of children under twelve years? State the processes in which the greatest number of young children are employed in your works."

Responses	*Number of Manufacturers*
Piecers	120
Spinners	44
Pieceners (on cardings)	30
Doffers	19
Winders	9
Feeders	7
Other	18
No Response	60

Source: 1834(167)XIX, Supplementary Report, p. C1.

TABLE 4.5 Factory Organization at Bean Ing (Woollen Factory) in 1813

Wool Room
    1 Overlooker
    5 Boys
    4 Sorters
    33 Moaters

Upper Scribbling Room
    1 Overlooker
    8 Slubbers
    25 Pieceners
    8 Carder Fillers
    7 Scribbler Fillers
    2 Cleaners
    1 Willower

Lower Scribbling Room
    1 Overlooker
    2 Slubbers
    6 Pieceners
    4 Fillers
    4 Fillers
    5 Blanket Spinners
    21 Pieceners
    9 Fillers
    2 Cleaners
    2 Willowers

Spinners' Room
    1 Overlooker
    17 Spinners J.G.R.[a]
    16 Spinners B.H.
    8 Spinners B.R.
    4 Spinners J.D.
    3 Spinners J.M.
    2 Mule Spinners
    2 Boys
    10 Warp & Listing Winders
    7 Warpers

Weaving Shops
    49 Weavers B.R.
    46 Weavers B.H.
    38 Weavers J.G.R.
    21 Winders B.H.
    15 Winders B.R.
    14 Winders J.G.R.

[a]Initials of "masters" given for spinners and weavers.

Source: Crump 1931, p. 307.

TABLE 4.6 Factory Organization at a Flax Mill in 1834

Heckling Machine Room	1 Overlooker 11 Boys[a] 7 Girls[b]
Line Preparing Room	1 Overlooker 1 Boy 16 Women 22 Girls
Throstle Spinning Room	6 Overlookers (men) 7 Jobbers (boys) 11 Throstle spinners (women) 4 Throstle spinners (boys) 66 Throstle spinners (girls) 3 Bobbin Doffers (boys) 69 Bobbin Doffers (girls) 6 Bobbin Carriers (boys) 1 Roving Carrier (woman) 1 Roving Carrier (boy)
Weaving Room	2 Overlookers 4 Winders (women) 8 Winders (girls) 2 Weavers (women) 1 Dresser (man) 1 Twister-in (man)

[a]"boys" refers to boys and young men (under 18)
[b]"girls" refers to girls and young women (under 18)

Source: 1834(167)XIX, pp. 152-154.

assisting the eighty-one Throstle spinners (many of whom were also youths). The tasks appear to be gender-specific because only boys were jobbers and bobbin carriers while the majority of bobbin doffers and winders were girls and young women. Similar proportions of adults to assistants are apparent in the factory returns from 151 manufactures in 1833. Mr. Stanway's report shows a large proportion of children working as helpers in the cleaning, carding, spinning and weaving departments of cotton factories. Table 4.7 summarizes these returns and disaggregates them by age and gender. Several interesting patterns emerge. The largest number of children and youths are found in mule-spinning, working as "piecers" and "scavengers" and they outnumber the adults in all but one district (Duckenfield and Stayley Bridge). These "piecers" and "scavengers," moreover, are predominantly boys and young men, not girls. On the other hand, there are more females under eighteen working than males in carding, reeling and weaving. Overall, the totals indicate a reversal in the gender of occupations of traditional cottage workers - where spinners were female and

TABLE 4.7 Employment in Cotton Factories by Department in 1833

Department Employed in	Adults		Children under 18	
	Males	Females	Males	Females
Manchester and Immediate Neighbourhood				
Cleaning & Spreading	92	493	152	69
Carding	783	1,352	412	620
Mule-spinning	1,745	606	2,523	1,298
Throstle-spinning	90	388	190	304
Reeling	67	1,446	37	280
Weaving	1,127	1,407	448	854
Stockport and Heaton Norris				
Cleaning & Spreading	78	13	20	1
Carding	254	434	180	261
Mule-spinning	556	37	692	60
Throstle-spinning	30	161	95	78
Reeling	4	114	--	35
Weaving	1,276	1,408	562	1,010
Duckenfield and Stayley Bridge				
Cleaning & Spreading	16	39	5	17
Carding	292	406	55	108
Mule-spinning	538	129	466	169
Throstle-spinning	6	5	4	2
Reeling	15	135	--	32
Weaving	333	528	22	128
Brinnington, Hyde				
Cleaning & Spreading	30	11	15	2
Carding	310	358	175	308
Mule-spinning	512	31	801	61
Throstle-spinning	8	63	35	43
Reeling	2	77	2	22
Weaving	1,009	1,901	291	1,102
Tintwistle, Glossop				
Cleaning & Spreading	13	--	--	--
Carding	163	198	77	135
Mule-spinning	381	46	461	198

(continues)

TABLE 4.7 (continued)

| Department Employed in | Adults | | Children under 18 | |
	Males	Females	Males	Females
Throstle-spinning	7	18	10	9
Reeling	7	244	–	57
Weaving	127	166	23	107
Oldham				
Cleaning & Spreading	14	13	9	4
Carding	166	222	104	279
Mule-spinning	488	64	461	155
Throstle-spinning	15	16	49	45
Reeling	40	208	5	64
Weaving	506	299	184	272
Bolton				
Cleaning & Spreading	26	117	8	5
Carding	341	438	284	458
Mule-spinning	847	227	1,086	673
Throstle-spinning	34	35	17	39
Reeling	9	285	1	80
Weaving	95	162	28	66
Warrington				
Cleaning & Spreading	1	2	–	–
Carding	31	61	18	20
Mule-spinning	66	33	74	32
Throstle-spinning	3	2	4	25
Reeling	–	43	–	3
Weaving	86	92	44	51

Source: 1834(167)XIX, pp. 24-131.

weavers, male. In 1851 the number of unskilled workers among children was still substantial. In a sample from the *1851 Census*, 22.3 percent of working children were employed as factory helpers and unskilled textile workers. The sample consists of 13,000 children (of which 2,726 had market employment) from eighteen counties of Great Britain.[10] The total number of children working as "bobbin putters," "burlers," "piecers," "reelers," "winders," "rovers," "combers," "pickers," and "strippers" was 253, not much less than the more traditional employers of children, agriculture (314), domestic service (532) and family-owned trades (385).[11]

The number of child helpers also increased because several inventions during this period were labor intensive. The inventions of Crompton's Common Mule (1779), Stockport's Slubbing Billy (1786) and Cartwright's Combing Machine (1792) reduced the number of skilled workers required while increasing the number of assistants. The common mule was used primarily in cotton spinning and required strength and technical expertise to operate. It combined the stretching motion of the water frame with the winding motion of the jenny to produce a smooth, strong, fine yarn that could be used for warp. The attendant worked a pair of mules and needed to use both hands to throw the carriage back and forth while at the same time turned a wheel that rotated the spindles and wound the thread onto the spindles. When the mule was first invented in 1779, it had forty-eight spindles but by 1800, machines with 400 spindles were in production (Rees 1819:"Cotton"). The mule was a labor substituting device because it replaced the job of male spinners, as one mule replaced forty-eight spinners at the wheel, but increased the number of assistants necessary. Because the drawing out and intermittent action often broke threads, child "piecers" worked with the adult spinners tying broken threads before the yarn was wound on the spindles.

As the mules were lengthened and stacked (called doubling or coupling) the number of spindles increased, such that the number of assistants more than quadrupled.[12] J. William Longston, a manager of a cotton mill in Stockport, compiled statistics on the number of mules and spindles in sixty-five cotton mills and concluded: "The number of spindles in the mills ten years ago, seldom ran above 200 or 216; in the document just put in, they are frequently found to be 432; again one of them is 500" (1831-32(706)XV:432-33). Smelser believed the effects of the longer mules was to create technological unemployment for adults through the increased productivity of the machines and the increase in the number of assistants per spinner (1959:196-197). He discovered from the *Parliamentary Reports* that in 1819 the ratio of "piecers" to spinners was 2:1 (on two mules with 504 total spindles), in 1832 the ratio was 3:1 and more than doubled by 1833 (198). By 1834 a factory commissioner claimed that "the improved mules would change the ratio of assistants to adult spinners from 4:1 to 9:1" (1834(167)XIX:386-8).

Although this may have been a slight exaggeration it could not have been too far from the truth.[13] According to calculations made by Mr. Cowell in the *Supplementary Report* (1834(167)XIX), the coupling of mules caused the ratio to more than double. The relevant figures are replicated in Table 4.8 showing the projected effects of coupling mules on the number of spinners and "piecers" required. By pairing the mules and hence doubling their productive power, the ratio of "piecers" to spinners increased from 4.48:1 to 9.3:1 in Mill A. Similarly, for Mill B the ratio increases from 4:1 to 8.7:1 and in the largest mill, Mill C, the ratio increases from 3.9:1 to 8.8:1. His conclusion supports observations made by contemporaries, that the mules containing more spindles increased the demand for child labor, "The effects of improvements in machinery, not merely in superseding the necessity for the employment of the same quantity of adult labour as before in order to produce a given result, but in substituting one species of human labour for another,-the less skilled for the more skilled; juvenile for adult, female for male, causes a fresh disturbance in the rate of wages" (1834(167)XIX, Supplementary Report, Part I:D1 119h). Thus, the proportion of child "piecers" to adult spinners was increasing dramatically in the spinning

TABLE 4.8 Mr. Cowell's Estimation of the Effects of Coupling

MILL A

Mules 25 pairs = 50
Spinners 25

Piecers 112   128 spindles/ piecer
Spindles 336/mule: Total= 16,800

after improvement,

Mules 13 pairs
Spinners 13
Piecers 121   128 spindles/piecer
Spindles 636/mule: Total = 16,800

MILL B

Mules 20 pairs = 40
Spinners 20
Piecers 80
Spindles 324/mule: Total = 12,960

after improvement,

Mules 10 pairs
Spinners 10
Piecers 87
Spindles 648/mule: Total = 12,960

MILL C

Mules 103 pairs = 206
Spinners 103
Piecers 403
Spindles 312/mule: Total = 64,272

after improvement,

Mules 50 pairs
Spinners 50
Piecers 444
Spindles 648/mule: Total = 64,800

Source: 1834(167)XIX, Supplementary Report, Part I, pp. D1 119i-119k.

departments equipped with the common mule. This trend is aptly summarized by John Redman, an overseer of a Manchester Cotton Spinning Factory, "A spinner employs from two to eight or nine piecers, according to the size of the mules and the fineness of the cotton thread that he spins. Where the mule is widest, or rather where there is the greatest number of spindles, and the thread is the finest, the spinner requires the greatest number of piecers (1833[450] XX: D1 43).

Stockport's Slubbing Machine or "Billy" used in the woollen industry had a similar effect on the amount of child labor required in the factory. Mr. Stockport's invention became important in the spinning of wool because it improved upon the mule by making the spindles stationary (Kennedy 1830:63). The "Billy," which looked like Crompton's mule, reduced the cardings by drawing them out in length and then joined them in a continuous spongy cord to form a slubbing or roving. Like the mule, it was manually driven and required several assistants to every operator. Typically four "pieceners" worked with one "slubber" on one billy machine (with an average of 60 spindles), a ratio of 4:1. The job of the "piecener" was, "...to take the cardings and lay them on the sloping billy-board, joining their ends by rolling them together for a moment with the palm of the hand. Each piecener have fifteen ends to piece, collects several cardings at once, which he lay over his left arm, and walks alongside of the billy, joining each end successively with his right hand" (Ure 1835:178).

Cartwright's Combing Machine, used in the worsted industry replaced the arduous task of the hand comber with a machine tended by one adult working with several assistants. The machine, often called "Big Ben" because it replicated the gestures of a prizefighter of that name, was far from perfected and still required the wool to first be combed into slivers by hand (Aspin 1982:18). Despite these problems "Big Ben" reduced the preparation time for worsted and substituted child helpers for skilled adult combers. Sitting within the circle of the comb table, the children's small fingers removed the short and broken fibers from the teeth of the combs (Rees 1819: "Worsted"). Chapman recites a statement about "Big Ben" made by the workers "according to the combers, 'one machine only with the assistance of one person and four or five children, will perform as much labour as thirty men in the customary manual manner'" (1967:193).

In summary, once the division of labor had been applied to the production process of making cloth, the demand for child labor increased. The division and specialization of labor created many simple one-step tasks that required almost no skill, but instead, quickness and constant attendance. Innovations like the common mule, the slubbing billy and the combing machine replaced the work of many adult workers relying on only one skilled operator and several assistants to keep the machines running. The experience and work habits of the traditional skilled artisan were ill-suited for the long, steady hours and relentless activity of the machines. Instead, it was the high energy, quickness, "watchful eyes and nimble fingers," dexterity and docility of children that were required by this new factory system. As more and more mills adopted this new system and as other textile trades adapted the principles and machinery to their raw material, the demand for child labor grew.

Labor Substituting Technologies: Children as Workers

Another source of the bias of technology toward children arose from several inventions which increased the possibilities of substituting children and youths for adults. In the textile industry, there were several technical breakthroughs which reduced the level of skill and the amount of strength needed to perform processes in the stages of production. A single water wheel had first been used to move all the silk spinning and twist mills in 1717 by Sir Thomas Lombe. The idea of water power, however, lay dormant for nearly seventy years until a new breed of factory owners (Arkwright, Greg, Oldknow, Owen, Strutt) built cotton mills with huge water wheels along the rivers. The unpredictability and seasonality of river water made steam power an attractive alternative. Initially, the steam engine was used in rural factories to enhance the supply of water running over falls by pumping water back up over the wheel. The first steam-driven spinning mill was built in 1785 and by 1838, eighty percent of English cotton mills were steam powered (Berg 1980:23). Once many of the new machines, like the water frame, the common mule and the loom, were automated, the job of the skilled operator was replaced by that of an unskilled "minder." Consequently, children's opportunities for employment extended into areas previously dominated by adults. They were soon replacing adult workers in spinning and weaving of cotton, worsted and wool, "Children employed in factories, as a distinct class, form a very considerable portion of the infant population. We have found that the numbers so employed are rapidly increasing, not only in proportion to the increase of the population employed in the manufacturing industry, but, in consequence of the tendency of improvements in machinery to throw more and more of the work upon children, to the displacement of adult labor" (1834(167)XIX:55).

Contemporaries and newspapers recorded the displacement of adult workers with either a tone of amazement for the advances in technology or of disgust for the plight of the unemployed breadwinner. Both Ellis (1826) and Kennedy (1826) wrote about the effects of the new inanimate powered machinery on the happiness of the working classes and highlighted the problems arising from the substitution of child for adult labor. Kennedy captures the sacrifices made in the name of progress in his speech before the Literary and Philosophical Society of Manchester:

In the first place, the object of all manufacturing machinery being the substitution of some power in the place of human labour, its immediate tendency is to diminish the necessity for manual exertion, or to render it less burdensome, and as a direct consequence of this to enable the younger and more delicate members of the community to perform those operations, which only the skillful and robust where wont to execute. Hence it is that wind, water and steam have been applied as moving power in the place of human or horse labour, and that women and children are enabled to execute those tasks which formerly required the ingenuity or the strength of men (1826:40-41).

Ten years later, P. Gaskell observed a similar trend but was more worried about its eventual impact on the position of the male breadwinner within the family. He asked the question, "Why, why had adult labour been displaced?" His answers consistently point to the use of new machinery in spinning and weaving that made a child or a woman a more productive and obedient servant of the machine than men (1836:145-147). As he compared the productivity of children to adults he concluded, "...-that, in consequence of machines, thus impelled, requiring merely feeders or watchers, and those watchers or feeders, being not, of necessity, strong in body or intellect, -that adult male labour having been found difficult to manage, and not more productive, - its place has, in a great measure, been supplied by children and women" (1836:147). In contrast, Ure (1835) was astonished by the changes that were taking place in the textile factories and excited about their potential. As he walked through the cotton, worsted and flax mills his observations mirrored those of a capitalist or manufacturer concerned with output, productivity and profits, "It is, in fact, the constant aim and tendency of every improvement in machinery to supersede human labour altogether, or to diminish its cost, by substituting the industry of women and children for that of men; or that of ordinary labourers, for trained artisans" (23). Ogden, on the other hand, was impressed by the accomplishments of technology and automation and viewed these new machines as an artist would a painting. As he described cotton spinning in Manchester during the eighteenth century, he spoke of the water frame, "The improvements kept increasing till the capital engines for twist were perfected; and it is amazing to see what thousands of spindles may be put in motion by a water wheel, and managed mostly by children, without confusing, and with less waste of cotton than the former methods" (1887:90). Newspapers like the *Union Pilot* and *Westminster Review* documented these different attitudes towards the new machinery, "There were those who thought that labour would be absolutely dispensed with, for invention might be carried so far as to supersede manual labour entirely" (*Union Pilot*, April 17, 1830).

Mechanization was applied to the first three stages of production in every industry. In the first stage of preparation, the application of machines led to the substitution of child labor for adult labor. In silk, girls tended the winding engine which replaced the hand process that had previously employed women in the cottage (Davies 1811). In worsted, boys fed the long wool into a machine called the "plucker" which cleaned and separated the fibers. In flax, boys tended the automatic heckling machines which were used to divide, clean and straighten the fibers (Ure 1835). In wool, boys and girls fed the combing machine and in cotton, the carding engine. In the second stage, children proved to be good substitutes for adults spinners with the invention of the water frame and self-actor. In weaving, youths operated the power-looms which quickly displaced the less productive hand-looms. Considerable evidence exists which supports the increasing elasticity of the demand for labor. In particular, the invention of the water frame, the self-actor and the power-loom challenged the position of adult spinners and hand-loom weavers.

Arkwright's Water Frame. Modern historians believe the water frame was operated by children and the only role for adults was as supervisor (Berg 1985:254; Fitton and Wadsworth 1958; Hills 1979:123 and Wadsworth and Mann 1965[1931]:417). Little, if any, documentation has been provided to support this important claim, however.

Fortunately, this assertion can be substantiated by the historical evidence. In spinning, children could mind the water frame because no special skills were needed to operate this machine and its continuous action was initially powered by a water wheel (hence the name "water frame") and later a steam engine. The water frame, based on a new principal of roller-spinning, was labor-saving and replaced the skilled spinner with unskilled "piecers" and "doffers" who minded the machine.[14] Invented by Arkwright and patented in 1769, it began with four spindles but quickly grew to as many as 1,000 spindles per machine. It produced a good strong warp and by 1845 was adapted for worsted and flax but was never used for spinning wool (McCulloch 1847:679). The water frame was operated primarily by children and this is articulated by Rees in his description in the *Cyclopedia*, "When the frame has been so long at work, that the bobbins become filled with thread, the child in attendance, by the handle of the lever, disengages the binder of the four spindles from its axis and then they, as well as the head of the rollers belonging to them, stop, and the child breaks the thread; then pulling off or unscrewing the flyer, he lifts the bobbin, puts on an empty one, ..." (1819: "Manufacture of Cotton"). In fact, the attorney general in issuing a patent to a predecessor of Arkwright's machine, Lewis Paul's roller spinning machine (in 1741), mentioned child labor in his justification to grant the patent.[15] In describing the spinning machine he says:

> ...and it is to be worked without the handling or fingering the matter to be wrought after the same is once placed in the Machine and requires so small a share of skill that any one after a few minutes teaching will be capable of Spinning therewith and of altering the same to greater or less and to any Degree of size, or twist as often as he shall think fit and can also do the work with greater Expedition than by any of the Methods now in use and even Children of five or six Years of age may spin with the same by which means the poorest of the Clothiers will be enabled to supply their customers (PRO, SP 36/41:213).

In addition, John Wyatt, a co-inventor of Paul's roller spinning mechanism, boldly confronts the problem associated with adopting an automated spinning machine.[16] The solution, as in the citations above, involved employing children instead of adults. Wyatt begins by summarizing the problem: "The grand objection to our project that we are apprehensive of is the diminution of the labour of a certain set or class of our people." He responds with an elaborate calculation showing that by "adopting the machine, a Clothier formerly employing a hundred spinners might turn off thirty of the best of them but employ an additional ten infirm people or children previously supported by the parish" (Wadsworth and Mann 1965[1931]:417 quoting Wyatt MSS, i:31-2). When Arkwright petitioned for a patent, Strutt, a factory owner, was very impressed with the water frame and eager to use it. He also mentioned the potential for employing children to spin cotton on this machine (Fitton and Wadsworth 1958:71).

As a result, by 1788, cotton manufacturing employed a disproportionate number of children spinners; 26,000 males weavers, 31,000 women spinners, and 53,000 children spinners (Rees 1819: "Cotton"). Although the figures are not available, the same pattern existed in worsted mills. As James, a scholar of the worsted industry noted, "In the worsted mills, on the other hand, the spinners were chiefly children or young persons, for there Arkwright's water frame was in use" (1857:549). Both P. Gaskell (1836) and Chapman (1904) noticed this increase in the number of child spinners using the water frame while maintaining that skilled spinners were still required to operate the improved jennies and the common mule. Chapman said the water frame used a "lower class of labour - unskilled adults, male and female, young persons and children" but did not "displace skilled cotton spinners in any appreciable degree" (53). It may, however, have had a greater impact than Chapman realized because the unemployment of many adult spinners was a growing problem. The spinners blamed their plight on the water frame and banned together to protest.[17] In 1780, a group of disgruntled spinners issued the following statement in a pamphlet entitled "An impartial representation of the case of the poor cotton spinners in Lancashire," "...together with the rapid increase of the number of these [Arkwright] Machines, which require so few hands, and those only children, with the assistance of an overlooker...and performing upon a moderate calculation, with the attention of a child, as much as would, and did upon average, employ ten grown-up persons" (2-3).

Robert's Self-Acting Mule. In mule spinning, which had been primarily an adult male occupation, youths were being employed once the self-actor was in place. Robert's Self Acting Mule (1829) made the common mule fully automatic (with water or steam power) and continued the dilution of skill reducing the number of adults required and replacing them with "minders" and "piecers." The self-actor was considered one of the most remarkable inventions of the nineteenth century and could spin the very finest of threads. It was used in cotton, worsted and woollen factories and eventually replaced the spinning jenny and water frame. Once connected to a water wheel or a steam engine the frames were lengthened and contained between 720 and 960 spindles (per pair) by 1833 (Wood 1910:141).

Although several modern economic historians have argued that children did not operate the self-actor, the historical evidence indicates that child labor was prevalent. Contemporaries like Ure, P. Gaskell, Baines and Chapman all recorded the substitution of child for adult labor when factories adopted the self-actor. Ure observed that "the effect of substituting the self-acting mule for the common mule, is to discharge the greater part of the men spinners, and to retain adolescents and children" (1835:23). Automation made the substitution of children for adults possible. The strength needed to push and pull the carriage back and forth on the mule was managed by the power created by falling water or steam not human muscle. Consequently, the job of the spinner was eliminated while the task of the "piecers" remained. This radical departure from the spinner-piecer system of the common mule is highlighted in Baines' description of the self-actor, "Mules have been constructed, which do not require the manual aid of a spinner, the mechanism being so contrived as to roll the spindle-carriage out and in at the proper speed, without a hand touching it; and the only manual labour employed in these machines, which are called self-acting mules, is that of the children who join the broken threads" (1835:205). Since the self-actor provided for the automatic return of the carriage as well as the spinning and winding of the yarn, the "duty of the spinner was reduced to the mere supervision of the headstocks and piecing" (Chapman 1904:69).

This was clearly advantageous to the factory owners who could dispense with the adult spinners who commanded higher wages and were more difficult to discipline than the children. In volume II of Ure's *Dictionary on the Cotton Manufacture* he reproduces the "Sketch of the Origin, Progress, and Present State of the Spinning Machine, termed 'The Self-Acting Mule'" by an eminent Factory Engineer. The engineer's writings confirm this motive for adopting a self-actor, "In considering the advantages resulting to the proprietors of cotton-mills from the use of self-acting mules, it may be stated that, although the only, or at any rate the principal benefit anticipated, was the saving of the high wages paid to the hand "spinner," and a release from the domination which he had for so long a period exercised over his employers and his fellow work-people..." (Ure 1861:155). The difficulty of employing jenny or mule spinners was familiar to the inventor as well. As proprietors of several cotton mills, Messieurs Sharp and Roberts listed as advantages in using the self-actor, "The savings of a 'spinner's wages to each pair of mules, piecers only being required, one overlooker being sufficient to manage six or eight pairs of mules or upwards" (Ure 1861:156).

Earlier in 1792, William Kelly (a factory owner of the Lanark mill) made a self-actor with the intentions of employing children. Mr. Kelly explains his invention in a letter to Mr. Kennedy dated January 8, 1829. He writes, "From the above date I constantly had in view the self-acting mule, and trying to bring it into use; and having got it to do very well for coarse numbers, I took out the patent in the summer of 1792. The object then was, to spin with young people, like the water twist (frame). For that purpose, it was necessary that the carriage should be put up without the necessity of applying the hand to the fly-wheel" (Baines 1835:206). His machine was unsuccessful because as the number of spindles were increased it became quite bulky and cumbersome and the "saving by spinning with boys and girls was thus superseded" (207). The financial benefits from hiring children instead of adults were also recorded in newspapers and magazines. Alfred Mallalieu, the author of an article on "The Cotton Manufacture and the Factory System" in Blackwood's *Edinburgh Magazine* chose Roberts self-actor as an example of a machine where child labor was replacing adult labor. He states:

> At present every improvement in machinery tends, and has invariably tended, to the exclusion, more and more, of the adults hands from operations which formerly could only be managed by them, but now can be equally well attended to, and at a much lower rate of wages by children. The result threatens to be their entire exclusion from manufacture . . . accompanied as that is with the invention of more finished machines for simplifying the processes of skilled labour, such as the self-acting mule of De Jong and Roberts (Part II, XL, July 1836:11).

Thus, the adoption of the self-actor in spinning increased the possibilities of substituting children and youths for adults. In contrast to the case of the water frame, adults were not totally replaced by youths. But as the number of spindles increased, there were more and more opportunities for youths and fewer for the adult spinner. In addition, since children were paid less than adults and adjusted better to the factory regime, managers wanted to hire children. As a result, the demand for child labor increased.

Nardinelli, however, argues just the opposite in his book on child labor. He claims that the adoption of the self-acting mule meant a reduction in the number of child assistants (or "piecers") required because it broke fewer threads. Bolin-Hort has proven this argument fallacious by pointing out that the number of breakages (and hence, "piecers") was dependant upon the speed of the machinery, the length of the mules and the quality of the roving (1989:105). Although it is difficult from the reports to discern the speed of the self-actors, it is clear that "piecers" had more to do because the number of spindles per machine were increasing.[18] Additionally, Nardinelli overlooked the technical changes which made the self-actor easier to operate. Berg (1985) and Lazonick (1979), however, recognized these technical changes and the potential for child labor but argued that children were barred from employment due to existing industrial relations. The essence of their argument is summarized when Berg concludes, "The self-acting mule did not displace the skilled mulespinner, for existing workplace organization embodied in the minder-piecer system remained and successfully blocked a redivision of labour which might have allowed capitalists to use workers with lower subsistence wages" (1985:194).

Bolin-Hort's recent book (1989) develops the role of labor relations more fully but gives conflicting information on who operated the new machines. Based on a comparison of the work forces of mills using hand-mule spinning and self-actor spinning, he finds a much larger proportion of children working in the mills with self-actors and refutes Nardinelli's claim that children were not employed on the self-actor (1989:104). Bolin-Hort concludes that "the immediate result of the adoption of this new spinning technology was therefore a marked increase in the proportion of young workers in this part of the labour process" (104). He argues, however, that initially children operated the self-actors but eventually labor market pressures and managerial strategies forced a return to the subcontracting system where adults operated the machines and children assisted as "piecers." Citing evidence from the returns of the Quarry Bank Mill in Styal and Birley's Mill in Manchester, he concludes that "the self-actors were initially staffed entirely with young workers" (104). Additionally, he offers the testimony of a number of manufacturers from *The British Parliamentary Papers* who ran self-actors using only child "piecers" (104). He concludes, however, that the subcontracting system which linked spinners and "piecers" on the common mule was reinstated on the self-actor. According to Bolin-Hort, children gave up their position as machine minders and became "piecers" because it was an efficient strategy for recruiting, training and disciplining a factory work force for managers as well as adult spinners (51,111-112). The evidence he provides to support this assertion, however, is scanty and inconclusive. He purports that "in many urban factories roughly 90% of the children were "piecers" in the mule-spinning process" (49). This figure is grossly exaggerated and derived from the personnel records of three "fine spinning" mills in Manchester. In these three mills, the proportion of children working as "piecers" was 75 percent, 78 percent and 75 percent, respectively. Although this is not "roughly

90%," the number of children working as "piecers" was still quite high. Data from other mills, which are more likely representative of textile mills than the three mills used for Bolin-Hort's calculation, show a number of children worked in other occupations (see Table 4.7). According to the factory commissioner, the three mills were chosen to demonstrate "the effects which improvements in machinery actually produce on the price of labour" and specifically focused on how "piecers" replaced spinners when the mules were lengthened (1834(167)XIX:119i-119m). In addition, Bolin-Hort uses evidence from one mill, the Quarry Bank Mill in Styal, to show that labor on the self-actor had been reorganized around the minder-piecer system. Based on the reorganization in one mill he concludes that "the managerial strategy of staffing the self-actor with cheap female or juvenile labour was soon abandoned in Lancashire" (110). Although this may have been a trend, the returns of other mills reveal that children and youths were still minding the self-actor and had not been displaced by adults.[19]

Although the minder-piecer system may have still been intact, the system became distorted as child "piecers" far outnumbered adult minders. The organization of labor on the self-actor resembled more an overseer-piecer system than a minder-piecer or a minder-cipher system. More and more youths were being hired and the number of adult males declined. Evidence from 35 mills compiled by John Leach, a Manchester operative in 1844, confirms the displacement of the adult spinner was widespread among cotton factories using the self-actor. He compares the number of spinners and spindles in 1829 and 1841, before and after the adoption of the self-actor in Manchester. It is clear from Table 4.9 that in every mill that acquired self-actors, the number of adult spinners declined. In twenty-one of the mills, moreover, less than half the spinners were still employed in 1841 and in five mills no adult spinners remained at all. Quite disturbed over this triumph of machine over man Leach writes, "The free-traders do not tell you what has become of the sixty-seven men (in Houldsworth's mill) out of the 127 that had been thrown out of employment by the improvements in machinery since 1829" (1844:29).

Similarly, statements made by manufacturers support the position that it was adult labor being displaced by the self-actor, not child labor. Samuel Greg, the owner of several spinning mills, provided the factory commissioners with the following description of the self-acting mule for their report, "it requires older and better piecers, but acts without a spinner" (1834(167)XX:D2 191). Another mill owner, John Jellicorse, proud of his modern production methods also confirms the predominance of children as spinners on the self-actor, "This mill has now been established three years; the machinery is of the newest construction, and possesses every advantage from the latest inventions; indeed, I believe it is the only entire mill in the kingdom where the self-acting mule is worked to the total exclusion of the common hand-mules; hence the great proportion of children to adults employed in the mill" (1834(167)XX: C1 74).

Cartwright's Power-Loom. The improvements in weaving lagged behind those in spinning so that adult hand-loom weavers comprised the majority of weavers until the 1820s. Although Cartwright's power-loom was invented in 1785 it took thirty years

TABLE 4.9 Effects of Automation in Manchester Cotton Mills

Employer	1829		1841		No. of Men Thrown Out of Work	No. of Self-Actors
	No. of Spinners	No. of Spindles	No. of Spinners	No. of Spindles		
Hanover Mill	18	22,608	4	22,608	14	14
H. Ewart's Mill	53	16,148	25	16,148	21	1
Becton's Mill	36	16,320	28	16,320	8	6
Ogden's Mill	36	23,880	4	23,880	32	32
Clark's Mill	21	10,550	0	10,550	20	21
Birch and Gough's Mill	36	14,688	9	15,552	27	0
Guest's Mill	48	16,240	17	16,240	21	8
Beever's Mill	13	8,736	0	8,736	30	13
Pooley's Mill Temple St.	20	12,480	1	13,932	19	19
Chapel's Mill	14	6,221	6	7,776	8	9
Dodson's Mill	5	2,800	0	3,080	5	5
Norris's Mill	30	12,600	0	12,600	30	30
Wrigg's Mill	15	9,544	7	15,728	8	2
Ardwick's Mill	8	4,680	6	5,760	2	0
Crowdson's Mill	14	4,128	5	4,128	9	9
Pooley's Mill	23	15,264	15	38,160	8	8
Kenedy's Mill	106	65,712	52	65,712	54	20

(continues)

TABLE 4.9 (continued)

Employer	1829		1841			
	No. of Spinners	No. of Spindles	No. of Spinners	No. of Spindles	No. of Men Thrown Out of Work	No. of Self-Actors
Barton's Mill	8	4,592	6	5,656	2	0
Pooley's Mill Hulme	52	23,800	15	23,800	38	38
Birley's Mill	213	82,892	0	82,892	213	213
Houldsworth Mill	127	83,376	60	84,886	67	–
M'Connell Mill	200	126,816	87	132,192	113	–
Murray Mill	147	90,936	62	100,296	85	–
Ogden Mill	138	88,744	52	88,744	86	–
Plant Mill	43	27,432	16	27,432	27	–
Belhouse Mill	36	31,804	30	47,644	6	–
Barnes Mill	43	36,888	29	41,624	14	–
Moore Mill	25	16,704	19	27,648	6	–
Marsden Mill	23	13,720	8	11,920	15	–
Caruthers Mill	16	10,488	9	13,300	7	–
Greys Mill	65	52,604	26	52,604	39	–
Rhodes Mill	9	6,480	3	6,480	6	–
Faulkner Mill	29	18,280	11	18,280	18	–
Williams Mill	42	22,992	23	32,448	19	–
Beesley Mill	57	46,810	52	50,630	5	–

Source: Leach (1844), pp. 28-29.

to be efficiently integrated into production. Nevertheless, once perfected, the power-loom changed the industry so dramatically that children became employable as productive steam-loom weavers. The few economic historians who have researched the employment of children in power-loom weaving, however, arrive at different conclusions. Berg (1993) and Hammond and Hammond (1920) claim that the majority of power-loom weavers were women. Both Berg and the Hammonds acknowledge the employment of children as power-loom weavers but suggest their numbers were small. Speaking with authority on cottage production, the Hammonds assert that, "The early power-loom weavers were all women or boys. In the case of spinning, when work left the cottage for the factory, men in factories with the help of children replaced the women domestic spinners: in weaving, when the change from the domestic to factory industry took place, women and boys in factories replaced men who had worked at home" (1920:72).

Although this gives a general idea of the work force, without documentation it is difficult to discern whether the women and children worked together or were substitutes for working the power-loom. Smelser examines the industrial relations in factories closely and believes children were in demand, not women. In fact, he actually blames the disruption of the family organization on the power-loom. He argues that the power-loom, unlike other new machinery, not only demanded young persons but also changed the relationship between workers. Once children operated the loom independently, parents or operatives no longer recruited the youths but the masters did (1959:200). Evidence from the *Parliamentary Papers* on wages paid to workers lends some support for Smelser's view. Weavers, unlike mule spinners, were primarily in the direct employ of masters, not operatives, in the factories included in Mr. Stanway's Report for eight major manufacturing districts. In Manchester, 758 of the workers under eighteen were employed by masters whereas only 544 were employed by operatives and the same was true in Stockport, 835 compared to 737 and in Bolton, eighty-eight compared to six (1833(519)XXI:123-133). What made the power-loom so different from the other machines? Is there evidence that children did become weavers once the power-loom was adopted?

Cartwright's first power-loom invented in 1785 required considerable strength to operate and had to be constantly stopped for dressing the warp. After the invention of Radcliffe's dressing frame and several technical improvements, youths aged fourteen or fifteen could manage two steam looms and weave three and one half times as much cloth as the best hand weaver (Baines 1835:239). Rees confirmed this in his description of weaving when he concluded the,

> Great part of the intellectual skill required in weaving is in the dressing and beaming of the warp; the mere mechanical part of throwing the shuttle, & etc. is soon acquired, even by a boy. A more accurate division of labour, by reducing the beaming and dressing to a system by which they are better, more economically, and more expeditiously performed than before has removed the great difficulty in the art of weaving and rendered it in a great measure the employment of children (1819: "Cotton").

William Radcliffe, the inventor of the "new system of warping, sizing, dressing, drying, winding on to the beam, drawing, and twisting-in" realized the impact his improvements would have on the hand-loom weavers (1828:13). In a letter to Mr. Horrocks of Preston he apologetically explained that although children were working his looms now, they were meant to employ families in their cottages, "I further stated, that though at the time I was obliged to bring such a number of boys and girls into the factory to work the looms, yet, when the hands had been taught to work them, it was my intention to disperse all these looms into the cottages of the weavers throughout the country, in lots, proportioned to the number of children in the families" (1828:30).

The number of power-looms in England and Scotland increased dramatically between 1820 and 1835 which displaced the traditional hand-loom weavers with young power-loom weavers. In 1820 there were reported 12,150 power-looms in England and by 1835 as many as 97,564 (Chapman 1904, fn. 1: 28). By 1845 the power-loom was used in the manufacture of cotton, wool, worsted and flax (McCulloch 1847:679). The power-loom changed both the age and gender of weavers such that a primarily adult male occupation became one reserved for girls and a few boys. This striking shift in the work force of weaving departments is apparent in the writings of P. Gaskell in 1836, "The multitudes of adults now dependent on hand-weaving must be pushed from the market; no extension in this department can absorb the operatives, because the power-loom does not require adult labour; whilst it is so greatly more productive, that the very cheapness of its produce must, when it is in general use, completely supersede hand-manufacture in the home and foreign market" (330). Other contemporaries were struck by the remarkable increases in output when comparing the hand-loom weavers with the power-loom weavers. Along with these figures were precise descriptions of the workers who tended the machine:

> A very good Hand Weaver, 25 or 30 years of age, will weave two pieces of nine-eights shirting per week, each twenty-four yards long, and containing one hundred shouts of weft in an inch, the reed of the cloth being 44, Bolton count, and the warp and weft 40 hanks to the pound. A Steam Loom Weaver, fifteen years of age, will in the same time weave seven similar pieces.

> In 1823, a steam-loom weaver, about 15 years of age, attending two looms, could weave seven similar pieces in a week.

> In 1826, a steam-loom weaver, about 15 years of age, attending two looms, could weave twelve similar pieces in a week; some could weave fifteen pieces.

> In 1833, a steam-loom weaver, from 15 to 20 years of age, assisted by a girl about 12 years of age, attending four looms, can weave eighteen similar pieces in a week; some can weave twenty pieces (Baines 1835:240).

Thus, children and youths were performing some of the tasks their parents had performed: the spinning and weaving of cotton, worsted, wool and silk. The factory returns from nine manufacturing districts in 1833 highlight the presence of children and youths in spinning and weaving. Out of 1,846 workers employed in throstle-spinning, over half (964) were under the age of eighteen.[20] Since the only types of operatives in this department are overlookers and spinners, it is safe to conclude that these younger workers were, in fact, spinners, not helpers. Out of a total of 16,040 workers in the weaving departments (including an overlooker, warpers, weavers and dressers) there were 1,631 males workers and 3,674 female workers under the age of eighteen. According to the descriptions on the forms, most of these young workers were weavers (1834(167)XIX:124-125). Returns from thirty-seven silk mills in Macclesfield, Congleton and Manchester also reveal the employment of young spinners ("throwers") and weavers. The predominance of younger workers in the spinning departments of textile factories and mills was clearly not an aberration. In the mills included in List I and List II of Table 4.10, 73 percent of the silk throwers were children and youths. The ratio of females under eighteen to males was nearly 2:1 for List I and 1.75:1 for List II. Even in the weaving department where most adult workers were employed, 30 percent of the weavers were children and youths. In a sample of the 1851 Census, 9.1 percent of the workers under eighteen were employed as spinners and weavers. In this sample, there were almost as many youths working as skilled workers (249) in the textile industry as there were unskilled (253). The category of "skilled in the textiles" includes children and youths who worked as "cotton spinners," "self-acting cotton spinners," "power-loom weavers" and "steam-loom weavers." Clearly, the replacement of children and youths for adults was not uncommon. As these new job opportunities arose, the demand for child labor increased.

Labor-Specific Technology: Children Working in "Tight Spots"

The final source of technological bias towards children was situational. Children were not only particularly suited for the machinery, but some machinery and work situations especially suited children. When the first factories, both rural and urban, were built they had two structural features which biased the type of labor that could work within

TABLE 4.10 Employment in Silk Mills by Department in 1833

Department Employed in	Adults		Children Under 18	
	Males	*Females*	*Males*	*Females*
List I: 18 silk mills in Macclesfield, Congleton and Manchester				
Throwing	394	768	1075	2130
Weaving	325	269	70	189
List II: 19 silk mills in Macclesfield, Congleton and Manchester				
Throwing	563	1072	1667	2929
Weaving	412	413	97	242
Engineers & Mechanics	53	—	—	—

Source: 1834(167)XIX, pp. 146, 149-150.

them. The two attributes were: (1) the machines were made of wood and situated close to the ground and (2) the rooms were small and compact with little space between machines. As a result, "little people" had a comparative advantage working with the early wooden machinery. As P. Gaskell observed, "The simplicity of the first machines adapted for spinning and their small size, fitted them for being tended by children" (1836:137).

Low Wooden Machinery. The backs of adults would have been severely injured after working a week in the textile mills constantly stooping over to work the machinery situated so close to the ground. Hence, factory owners preferred children to adults and younger children to youths when hiring workers to tend these machines and clean underneath them. This preference was revealed frequently in the replies of manufacturers to questions posed by the Factory Commissioners regarding the impact of the factory law to restrict younger children from working. When asked, "Does the nature of your work require the employment of children under 12, and why?" they responded:

My work does require the employment of children under twelve years of age, because they are best adapted to the work, being short and not obliged to stoop (1834(167)XX:B1 41).

Children of small stature are requisite for the purpose of cleaning and keeping in order those parts of the machinery which large persons could not reach (1834(167)XX: D1 224).

The roller-joining or piecing does require the employment of young children, as after they attain an age much beyond twelve years they are too large, their work being near the ground (1834(167)XX: B1 107).

Yes; for this reason worsted machinery is low, and those of nine years of age will manage the work with as much ease, or more, than those of twelve years (1834(167)XX:C1 43).

Just how low was this machinery? Based on replicas on display at The Museum of Science and Industry in Manchester, Hargreaves' spinning jenny, Arkwright's water frame, and the Self-Acting Mule stood between three and five feet tall with the threads (to piece) and the spindles (to doff) were placed only two feet from the ground. Specifically, their spinning jenny on display was 830 mm or 2 feet 9 inches tall, their water frame 1420 mm or 4 feet 8 inches tall and their self-actor 1690 mm or 5 feet 6 inches tall. The spindle mechanism on the water frame stood 1150 mm or 3 feet 9 inches from the ground and the spindle mechanism on the self-acting mule was considerably lower at 450 mm or stood only 1 foot 6 inches from the ground.[21] It would be erroneous to generalize from these dimensions because the various machines made by the numerous machine makers, and factory mechanics were not standard or uniform. Nonetheless, they are illustrative of how small the early wooden machines were in the textile mills. In addition, advertisements in newspapers to sell off machinery give dimensions which are consistent with the hypothesis that the early machinery was built close to the ground. The *Leeds Intelligencer* on March 1, 1802 carried the following announcement (Crump 1931:323):

Machinery (to be sold by Auction)

one	3'4" single scribbling engine
3	4' double scribbling engine
one	4' double carder
4	30" carders

Only the youngest and shortest children could work these machines comfortably. Even then, the lowest machines, like the water frame and the "Billy," caused deformity in some children that worked them. As Cruickshank noted in her book on *Children of Industry* "children using low-built frames were deformed for life" (1981:17). A common complaint of the children and parents of "pieceners" who worked with the water frame in the worsted mills was "crooked legs," "knock-knees" and "weak knees" (1831-32(706)XV:1-455). John Hall, an overlooker in a worsted mill, provides damning evidence on how widespread the problem was. When asked, "Have you remarked that cases of deformity are very common in Bradford?" he replied, "They are very common; I have the names and addresses of, I think, about two hundred families that I have visited myself, that have all deformed children, and I have taken particular care not to put one single individual down to whom it had happened by accident, but all whom I judge to have been thrown crooked by the practice of piecening, and of throwing up the right shoulder and of bending the right knee" (1831-32(706)XV:116). Joseph Shepley, a machine-maker highlights the problem in his response to the question: "Why was your machinery less liable to produce deformity than other machinery?", "I can tell you what kind of machinery makes cripples, that is, the old kind of water-frame, which was built very low in the spindle-boxes to accommodate young children" (1834(167)XIX:10).

Why was the machinery built so close to the ground? Did inventors and machine makers have children in mind, ex ante, when they built these machines or did they build these machines and then, ex post, find that children could best work them? A few machine makers and manufacturers believed as Shepley did - the machines were constructed with children in mind (1834(167)XX:C1 79,343). John Hansen, a domestic woollen manufacturer who had two girls employed in the factories in Huddersfield reveals this viewpoint directly in the following exchange with a factory commissioner who asked:

Has the result that these inventions chiefly have been carried into effect, the object of which has been the employment of children, though the known result of such employment has been to deprive part of the adult population of their work? -Yes; and I recollect that at present they are making machines lower than they use to; I think, on purpose that they may employ children of younger ages than formerly, so that lesser (younger) children may be enabled to work those machines for still lower wages.- You mean that the machines are made to stand at a less distance from the floor? -Yes; it is children's labour which is most in requisition now (1831-32(706)XV:400).

Several of the early machines may have been constructed with the intention of employing child labor. Berg and Hudson (1992) hint at this possibility when they take a fresh look at the productivity of women and children during this period and declare, "The peculiar importance of youth labour in the industrial revolution is highlighted in several instances of textile and other machinery being designed and built to suit the child worker" (36). MacLeod's research on the English patent system tackles this issue directly. She discovers from patent records that several inventors claimed within their patents to replace skill or effort with machinery so the young, sick, or very old could be employed (1988:163).[22] Two of the four patents she cites as examples of this were forerunners to the machines herein highlighted for employing child labor. Haines' spinning engine (1677) worked on a similar principle to Hargreaves' spinning jenny patented almost 100 years later and Paul and Wyatt's machine for roller spinning (1741) resembled Arkwright's water frame patented twenty-eight years later. In addition, she found that, "...another 3 patentees, in 1798-9 claimed the replacement of adult male workers by women or children as an advantage of their machines. Since this was at the heart of much resistance to new technology, it was a bold step indeed to voice it" (168).

In particular, the case of Hargreaves' spinning jenny has created considerable debate in the literature. Hargreaves' original spinning jenny (1767) was built small and light and required little strength to operate.[23] On the first machines, the spinner turned a horizontal wheel which moved eleven spindles simultaneously. It was used first in cottages and then mills to spin cotton into weft although an improved version was adapted for spinning wool which was used long after the common mule had replaced it in cotton spinning. Although it was still powered manually like the spinning wheel, it was said to "multiply human hands" (S. J. Chapman 1904:53). Because of the horizontal wheel it was difficult for adults to operate, but children were known to work it with as many as forty spindles with relative ease. Rees emphasizes this fact in his description of the jenny in the *Cyclopedia*, "the original machine, which from its form was inconvenient and tiresome to grown up persons, though girls of twelve and fourteen managed it with ease" (1819: "Cotton"). Contemporaries like P. Gaskell and Ogden made similar note of the peculiar construction of this new spinning machine, "These were first used by the country people on a confined scale, twelve spindles being thought a great affair at first, and the awkward posture required to spin on them, was discouraging to grown up people, while they say, with a degree of surprize, children, from nine to twelve years of age, manage them with dexterity" (Ogden 1887:87).

Although most economic historians agree that the improved versions of the jenny required adult labor, some historians doubt the original machine could be operated by children and youths.[24] In particular, Aspin argues that the early jenny required considerable skill to operate. His conclusion is based almost exclusively on conversations with museum personnel who reconstructed the jenny from Hargreaves' patent specifications (1964:43-58). Once constructed, the staff had considerable difficulty in operating the jenny and concluded that jenny spinners must have been highly skilled laborers. He writes of this Helmshore Jenny, "The world's first successful spinning machine can hardly be said to have been the work of a mechanical genius; at one point in the winding, the operator is required to turn the driving wheel with his right hand, push forward the draw bar with his left hand and move up the deflection wire with his toe" (1964:43). A similar conclusion was drawn by the women who demonstrated spinning on a reconstructed jenny at Greg's Mill and Museum at Styal. After having the machine operable for only a month, they showed me that they could fill only five to eight spindles simultaneously and even then at a very slow and erratic pace. Is this sufficient evidence to refute what inventors, cyclopedias, and contemporaries were saying about the jenny? The fact that several adults could not efficiently operate the jenny actually lends support for what contemporaries were saying: children could work the machine, while adults had considerable difficulty. In addition, these adults did not have the benefit of growing up in a family where spinning was a way of life and where skills were passed from generation to generation and spread from house to house as new techniques were utilized. Could it be the case that once taught how to operate the jenny, children were able to spin "with relative ease?" Aspin has since revised his answer in a more recent article entitled "New Evidence on James Hargreaves and the Spinning Jenny" (1968). He found documents which confirm that youths could and did operate the original jenny. Mary Burgess, Hargreaves' daughter, wrote a letter to Mr. Brotherton on August 28, 1822 and in it she recalls, "Soon after this I began to spin on the Machine, being then about 14 years of age, and my father made two more, one for my brother George and another for a Mr. Kenyon" (120).

The preceding documentation has confirmed that children could operate the original spinning jenny and tend the water frame, the self-actor and the power-loom. In addition, the evidence suggests that the inventors of these and similar machines, people like Hargreaves, Roberts, Radcliffe, Haines, Paul and Wyatt, and Strutt recognized this fact. Technological change may have been steered towards utilizing child labor when inventors realized that children were ideal factory workers - cheap and easy to supervise. Certainly, this is a plausible interpretation of the evidence and one which suggests that some technological change was endogenous. At the same time, the laws of physics imposed certain constraints which implied that some technological change was exogenous. The argument is simple and straightforward and has, until this point, been entirely neglected in the literature. At its core is a principle universally known among engineers and mechanics about wooden machinery. The early spinning and weaving machines were made out of wood. A wooden frame with rapidly moving parts has a tendency to wobble back and forth while it is running. The taller the legs on the machine, the more it vibrates and shakes. Ergo, the shorter the legs on the machine and hence the closer to the ground it stood, the less vibration there was. Finally, the less the machine vibrated, the better it operated and the longer it lasted. Once the machines were built it became obvious to the inventors, machine-makers and entrepreneurs that the low construction made them more suitable for short and small people, i.e., children. If children had not been productive workers, wooden machines could have been placed on blocks of wood or metal anvils in order to make them more comfortable for adults to operate. The evidence, however, indicates that the wooden machines were constructed low to the ground and that they remained that way for decades. Therefore, it appears there was feedback between the supply of labor, social factors and technology. The laws of physics imposed certain constraints on the construction of the early wooden machinery which steered technology toward using "little people" and this bias was reinforced because children were cheap and obedient laborers. Technology was not entirely exogenous nor was it completely endogenous.

As iron and other metals began to replace wood in the 1820s, the frames became secure and the machine's vibrations were minimized. Consequently, the newer versions of these machines were higher off the ground and more easily operated by taller people. Children no longer had a comparative advantage because of their small stature in working with the modern textile machinery. P. Gaskell quoted a witness who stated to the Committee on the Employment of Children in Manufactories, "As the children grew to be adults, notwithstanding their acquired expertness, they became too big for the machinery, and their labour too expensive. In consequence of the introduction of the revolving steam engine, factories were established in manufacturing towns; the establishments in manufacturing towns were more calculated for adults, and machines of greater size and complications were constructed for the more difficult and finer kinds of spinning" (1836:136).

Compact Factory Floors. Many of the early wooden machines took up very little room because they were small and low to the ground. Accordingly, the early mills and factories were built on a smaller scale with low ceilings and compact rooms. Greg's Mill, said to have dimensions typical of early cotton mills, was 30 feet by 90 feet (The National Trust 1985). As P. Gaskell noticed, "The construction of the first mills was, of course, fitted only for small machines; they were consequently small, and the rooms were low, and of very contracted dimensions" (1836:138). An early woollen mill, The Hebble Mill, near Halifax had very similar dimensions with several even smaller rooms. It was 3 stories high, with 3 rooms, each 32 feet by 86 feet and 3 other rooms, each 24 feet by 50 feet and the other 36 feet by 50 feet (*Leeds Intelligencer*, August 13, 1804 in Crump 1931:323-33). William Brown, manager of the East Mill (flax) in Dundee, was struck by the awkwardness of the construction and floor plan of his mill, "In size the mill house is 98 feet long and 26 wide within walls, exclusive of room for the steam engine, and contains three floors and a garret. The house in general is clumsy, ill arranged and ill proportioned; its width is ten feet less than it ought to be; the doors, windows, stairs and partitions are irregularly placed" (Brown 1980[1819]:8). The same was true for silk mills as Malmgreen's research has uncovered. She studied the silk industry in Macclesfield during the period 1750 to 1835 and concluded that the "ceilings tended to be low" in the early silk mills built around 1758 (1985:16). This is in sharp contrast to a newly constructed mill in 1810 which was a "'skyscraper' of its day" and was "six storeys high and rectangular in plan (34' by 74', with a 10' floor-to-ceiling height-loftier than in the older mills) it had an engine and boiler accommodated in lean-to sheds attached to the main block" (20). Because of the limited space and requisites of water or steam power, machines were placed close together and in rows.[25] The Floor Plan of the Canal Street Factory in Preston collected as evidence in the *First Report* (1816(397)III: 258-259) illustrates this nicely. Both the number and the arrangement of machinery in the carding rooms

The Floor Plan of Canal Street Factory in Preston

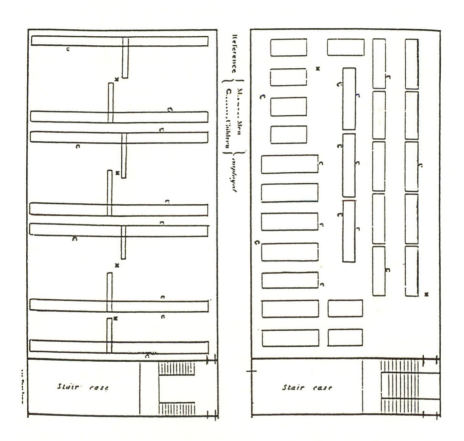

Source: 1816(397)III, pp. 258-259.

leaves little space between machines. In addition, the positioning of child workers between the frames (denoted by the letter C) in the spinning rooms contrasts sharply with the central location of adult workers. Once again, the advantages of smallness were apparent. Children could more easily maneuver between, around and underneath machines. Since many of the tasks involved tending a row of machines, as in piecing and doffing, children performed their duties quickly and efficiently without getting snagged or stuck between spinning frames. These problems are highlighted in one manufacturer defense for employing children under twelve, he explains, "The nature of the work requires the employment of young children; tall and stout children would be in each other's way, and would not perform the work so lightly" (1834(167)XX:208). The same was true in weaving rooms where the power-looms stood very close together. The weaving rooms at the Quarry Bank Mill have been reassembled to represent weaving sheds during Greg's time and have looms "packed together as closely as they would have been at the turn of the century" (The National Trust 1985).

In summary, the third component of the increased demand for child labor arose because of their small stature. Young children and small children were just the right size to work the wooden machines situated close to the ground. They could piece broken threads and dress the warp without stooping over. They could move swiftly down the narrow passageways removing and replacing full bobbins off the water frame and mule. They could turn the horizontal wheel on the original spinning jenny and piece together wool slivers on the billy-board. They could crawl underneath the spinning machines and sweep up the waste cotton. Children were able to perform certain jobs and tend machines with a degree of ease and comfort that adults could not match. This gave them a comparative advantage over other workers and created an increase in the demand for child labor.

In conclusion, the increase in the demand for child labor came from three sources. Children and youths worked as both secondary and primary workers in the textile industry, and their contributions were important to the overall operation. This is evident in P. Gaskell's depiction of the changes in cotton production, "Girls tend the throstle which produce the warp; boys tend the mule which produce the weft; girls tend the loom which produce the cloth; - mechanisms dress it and mechanism dyes it" (1836:332). The first factor to increase the employment of children was caused by certain innovations in preparing, spinning and weaving cotton that were labor intensive instead of labor-saving. The division of labor into many simple one-step tasks increased the number of workers involved in the production of cloth. At the same time, mechanization lightened the work and reduced the skill necessary to perform the various tasks. Factory owners hired children for as many jobs as possible because they could easily perform the work and were more likely to adjust to and obey the new factory regime of long, steady hours, day after day. In addition, several inventions like the common mule, the slubbing billy and the combing machine increased the number of assistants required to work with adults. Thus, even the adults who worked in the factories needed children as "piecers" and "doffers" in order to produce output of high quality. It was, moreover, their natural qualities of quickness, agility, energy and perfect vision which allowed them to perform these tasks efficiently. Although children had helped their families for centuries, the interdependence between adults and children reached new heights during the Industrial Revolution. The second source of the increase in demand for child labor arose from several innovations that were labor substituting. The water frame, the self-actor and the power-loom completely eliminated the need for a skilled operative and instead required merely a minder or tender. These machines, powered by the water wheel and the steam engine, required someone to watch the machine and perform simple procedures. As cheaper and more docile factory workers, children and youths began to substitute for adults.

Finally, the third source of bias toward the employment of children arose due to a feature in the construction of the new machines and factories. Most of the newly invented machines were constructed of wood and built close to the ground to reduce vibrations. Inventors may have had children in mind when they constructed these machines. Knowing that children were a cheap source of labor would give manufacturers who adopted their machines a competitive advantage. Children of a small stature were able to work comfortably with these machines and did not have to stoop. They could stand erect as they changed bobbins on the frame, or fed roving into the "billy" or turned the wheel of the original spinning jenny. In this case, the comparative advantage of children over adults was most pronounced. Not only were children preferred to adults but in some cases they were the only workers capable of performing the necessary tasks. Each of these three components lead to an increase in the demand for child labor. Together they provide an explanation for the large proportions of children and youths found within the work forces of many of the textile mills in Great Britain.

Rising Relative Wages of Children to Adults

If the increase in the employment of children was caused by an increase in the demand for child labor and not an increase in the supply, their wages would increase. If the demand, moreover, for children was increasing relative to adults because of their comparative advantage (or higher relative productivity), we would expect children's wages to rise more than their adult counterparts (or not to have fallen as fast if the trend was downward). The implication is based on the assumption that if the labor market was competitive, an increase in the marginal productivity of children would be reflected in a higher wage, ceteris paribus. A measure of the relative wage of children to adults would reveal how the wages of children and adults fluctuated over time while eliminating any distorting effects of prices changes. The wages in each region come from the same factories for the period of time specified. Assuming that the workers in these factories aged together over time reduces the possibility of an upward bias. Since wages were linked to the worker's age as well as their productivity, children's wages would increase as they got older regardless of changes in productivity. Adult's wages also gradually increased with age. Therefore, by calculating relative wages the bias is reduced because the wages for both sets of workers would be increasing over the period. Consequently, an increase in the relative wage of children to adults can be interpreted as reflecting an increase in their relative productivity. The figures in Table 4.11 can be used to test the hypothesis that there was an increase in the demand for child labor during the Industrial Revolution. The relative wages were derived from actual weekly earnings of "boys," "girls" and "children" ranging in age from nine to eighteen and adult men working in the same mill assimilated in the *Return of Wages 1830-1886* (1887[C.5172]LXXXIX) and Wood's *History of Wages* (1910). When children performed different tasks from those of their male counterparts, it is indicated in the column description where the first job refers to the child's task (for example, cotton "piecer") and the second to the adult's task (for example, cotton spinner).

The evidence presented in Table 4.11 shows the wages of children were rising relative to adults from the 1830s to 1860, supporting the hypothesis that the demand for child labor was increasing during this period. In the cotton textiles of Manchester, the relative wage of a power-loom worker increased from 0.45 in 1844 to 0.52 in 1848. Similarly, between 1833 and 1848, cotton "piecers" wages doubled relative to the spinners they assisted, the ratio increasing from 0.21 to 0.42. Outside of Manchester in Bolton, Yorkshire, Lancashire and Oldham, child "piecers" wages were increasing relative to spinners as well. The wages of youths, moreover, increased relative to adults as apparent in Yorkshire and Lancashire where the ratio of big "piecers" to self-actor spinners rises. The evidence from woollen factories in Bradford and Huddersfield exhibit a gradual but consistent increase in the relative wages of children to adults. This was not the case in worsted factories, where the relative wage of children to adults fell for weavers and fluctuated considerably for wool sorters. Because the data, however, ends in 1831 when the adaptation of the new machinery had just begun in worsted, the figures do not capture the impact of the new technologies on the demand for child labor. In silk mills it appears that the relative wages of child spinners to adult "throwsters" fell from 1839 to 1849 but rose from 1849 to 1859. Without more data from other occupations or other areas, it is unwise to make any generalization regarding changes in the demand for child labor in the silk industry.

Critics may argue the labor market for factory children was not competitive because families worked together and parents hired their own children. Consequently, the child's wage would not reflect changes in children's productivity. This implies that an analysis of the movement in the relative wages of children to adults would not necessarily capture changes in the demand for or supply of child labor. A different model would have to be developed to incorporate the interdependence of the child's and adult's labor supply and their earnings. Did parents hire their own children to work with them in the factories? Anderson (1971) and Smelser (1959) have argued that they did. Subsequent research has shown that this practice only applied to children working in the early rural mills (Edwards and Lloyd-Jones 1973).

Contemporaries gave conflicting reports in the *British Parliamentary Papers* with regards to the prevalence of family-based employment in the textile industry. Charles Hindley, an owner of a cotton spinning factory in Manchester, told commissioners that family employment was prevalent in the mills. "In factories we may be said to have family labour, most of the members being employed at the same mill; and even if it were possible to make the time of children less than the time of the adult, in many

TABLE 4.11 Relative Wages of Children/Adults in Textiles in Great Britain

County	Description	Year	Relative Wage
COTTON			
Manchester	cotton card room	1832	0.41[a]
	cotton card room	1874	0.52
	cotton powerloom	1844	0.45
	cotton powerloom	1845	0.46
	cotton powerloom	1846	0.48
	cotton powerloom	1847	0.41
	cotton powerloom	1848	0.52
	cotton powerloom	1849	0.50
	cotton piecer/spinner	1832	0.26
	cotton piecer/spinner	1833	0.21
	cotton piecer/spinner	1848	0.42
	cotton winder/reeler	1806	0.16
	cotton winder/reeler	1839	0.63
	cotton winder/reeler	1846	1.18
	cotton winder/reeler	1849	0.65
	cotton winder/reeler	1859	0.59
	cotton minder/grinder	1839	0.46
	cotton minder/grinder	1849	0.50
	cotton minder/grinder	1859	0.54
	cotton throstle spinner	1839	0.46
	cotton throstle spinner	1849	0.60
	cotton throstle spinner	1859	0.55
Bolton			
	cotton piecer/spinner	1833	0.16
	cotton piecer/spinner	1841	0.35
	cotton piecer/spinner	1850	0.31
	cotton piecer/spinner	1855	0.28
	cotton piecer/spinner	1860	0.25
Yorkshire			
	big piecer/SA spinner	1837	0.27
	big piecer/SA spinner	1841	0.23
	big piecer/SA spinner	1859-61	0.39
	big piecer/SA spinner	1886	0.45
Lancashire			
	big piecer/SA spinner	1833	0.35

(continues)

TABLE 4.11 (continued)

County	*Description*	*Year*	*Relative Wage*
	big piecer/SA spinner	1840	0.44
	big piecer/SA spinner	1850	0.40
	big piecer/SA spinner	1860	0.41
	big piecer/SA spinner	1874	0.42
Oldham			
	cotton piecer/spinner	1833	0.24
	cotton piecer/spinner	1841	0.29
	cotton piecer/spinner	1860	0.39
	cotton piecer/spinner	1874	0.43
WOOL			
Bradford			
	wool spinner/weaver	1823	0.26
	wool spinner/weaver	1824	0.27
	wool spinner/weaver	1825	0.29
	wool spinner/weaver	1826	0.32
	wool spinner/weaver	1827	0.33
	wool spinner/weaver	1828	0.32
	wool spinner/weaver	1829	0.37
	wool spinner/weaver	1830	0.36
	wool spinner/weaver	1831	0.38
Huddersfield			
	mule piecer/spinner	1839	0.20
	mule piecer/spinner	1849	0.22
	mule piecer/spinner	1859	0.28
	billy piecer/slubber	1839	0.17
	billy piecer/slubber	1849	0.19
	billy piecer/slubber	1859	0.21
	winder/powerloom weaver	1839	0.58
	winder/powerloom weaver	1849	0.61
	winder/powerloom weaver	1859	0.63
WORSTED			
Bradford			
	wool weaver	1823	0.89
	wool weaver	1824	0.74
	wool weaver	1826	0.73
	wool weaver	1827	0.73

(continues)

TABLE 4.11 (continued)

County	Description	Year	Relative Wage
	wool weaver	1828	0.75
	wool weaver	1829	0.78
	wool weaver	1830	0.79
	wool weaver	1831	0.79
	wool sorter	1824	0.24
	wool sorter	1826	0.37
	wool sorter	1827	0.24
	wool sorter	1828	0.23
	wool sorter	1829	0.30
	wool sorter	1830	0.27
	wool sorter	1831	0.29
	wool comber	1824	0.33
	wool comber	1826	0.45
	wool comber	1827	0.44
	wool comber	1828	0.43
	wool comber	1829	0.48
	wool comber	1830	0.48
	wool comber	1831	0.46

SILK
Manchester	silk spinner/throwster	1839	0.68
	silk spinner/throwster	1849	0.54
	silk spinner/throwster	1859	0.59

ªEach figure in Table 4.11 was obtained by converting the Earnings per week to a standard unit of pence per week. It was assumed that there are 20 shillings per pound and 12 pence per shilling. The relative wage was then calculated by taking the average weekly earnings for children in pence and dividing it by the average weekly earnings for adults (usually men) in pence.

Sources: 1887[C5172]LXXXIX, Return of Wages 1830-1886. G. H. Wood 's *The History of Wages in the Cotton Trade* (1910), pp. 17-19, 22-25, 58, 91, 95 and 131.

cases they would be left without the care and attention of the parent, who must remain employed at the mill" (1833(519)XXI:D2 49). One cannot discern, from Mr. Hindley's remarks, how widespread family-based employment was nor to what extent the children and parents worked **together**. According to Thomas Worsley, who had worked for years in cotton factories, children did not work with or for their parents. He stated, "...and even if the law could be enforced, supposing times for breakfast were different, much unnecessary injury would be done to such parents as have several children working in different mills (and this is the case with most parents), and who must provide them with their breakfasts at different hours" (1833(450)XX:D1 16).

Smelser documents a minder-piecer system in the textiles from statements made in the *British Parliamentary Papers of 1816 and 1819* and trade union articles which state that spinners hired their own assistants ("piecers" and scavengers) and chose their wives, children or near relatives. He argues the system became trade union law because spinners wanted to secure the family economy which had existed in the cottage industry (1959:189). Smelser erroneously concluded that most factory children worked for their parents and that the traditional family structure remained intact. His conclusion, however, is based on evidence from only two wage books; that of Robert Peel's at Bury in 1801-02 and those of McConnel and Kennedy at Manchester in 1795 (Edwards and Lloyd-Jones 1973:308). Anderson's analysis of the *1851 Census* for Preston identifies textile factories with the highest proportion of sons (under twenty years of age) who worked in the same industry as their fathers (1971:121). Although this parent-child system did exist for some families, Anderson himself notes that "the proportion of factory children employed by family and kin was not high" (1971:117). When the factories moved to urban areas, the likelihood that children worked for a parent or a relative was considerably smaller. *The Report of the Twelfth Meeting of the British Association for the Advancement of Science* found that, "By 1840 an average of four piecers were employed to every spinner in Manchester, with only 15 per cent of the children related to the adult workers" (Shuttleworth 1843:93).

The returns from factories, moreover, reveal that the extension of the family into textile mills was not widespread. Despite the fact that the minder-piecer system prevailed in many textile mills, roughly half the children working in factories were hired by the master or owner of the factory and not an operative. As Table 4.12 illustrates there were only two occupations in textile factories, spinning and weaving, where the child workers were hired by the operative and not the master. The vast majority of children and youths in mule spinning (3,205) were employed by the workers. This subcontract system was also common among weavers (544) but not as pervasive as among mule spinners (except in the factories of Warrington). About half of child workers in textile factories, however, did not work for a parent because they were hired and paid by the master. In cleaning and spreading, children are exclusively hired by the master. In carding, throstle spinning and reding the majority of child laborers were hired by the master although a few were hired by an operative.

In conclusion, the evidence presented here on the relative wages of children to adults supports the hypothesis that the demand for child labor was increasing relative to adult labor. In a competitive labor market model an increase in the demand for child labor, ceteris paribus, will lead to an increase in their market wage. If the supply of children increased more than demand, we would have found children's wages falling relative to adult wages. It appears that children were being rewarded as their productivity increased with the new spinning and weaving machines. Whether it was their "nimble fingers," their "keen eyesight," their small stature or their ability to do monotonous tasks quickly, the textile mills wanted and needed child labor.

Table 4.12 People who Hire Child Workers in Factories

Number of Children Hired By

Employed in	Manchester		Stockport & Heaton Norris		Dukenfield & Stayley Bridge		Brimington, Hyde		Tintwistle, Glossop		Oldham		Bolton		Warrington	
	Mᵃ	Oᵇ	M	O	M	O	M	O	M	O	M	O	M	O	M	O
Cleaning & Spreading	220	0	18	0	18	0	11	3	0	0	13	0	13	0	2	0
Carding	983	44	423	11	107	35	468	15	158	33	344	35	717	25	38	0
Mule Spinning	597	3,205	60	692	51	580	244	587	31	615	1	604	57	1,702	0	106
Throstle Spinning	467	21	116	2	5	0	78	0	19	0	88	6	56	0	29	0
Reding	313	1	34	0	19	12	20	4	53	1	59	10	81	0	3	0
Weaving	758	544	835	737	127	23	1,277	166	107	23	197	192	88	6	28	67

ᵃM = In the direct employ of Masters
ᵇO = In the direct employ of Operatives

Source: 1833-34(19)XXI, Factories, Employment of Children, Mr. Stanway's Report, pp. 123-133.

Notes

1. The classic literature on the role of the textile industry in the British Industrial Revolution includes Baines (1835), Chapman (1904), Floud and McCloskey (1981), Hobsbawn (1964), Landes (1969), Wadsworth and Mann (1931) and Ure (1835 and 1861).

2. The district included the following counties and parts of counties: Berks, Bucks, Cornwall, Derby, Devon, Dorset, Essex, Hants, Herts, Kent, Lincoln, Leicester, Middlesex, Norfolk, Northampton, Nottingham, Suffolk, Surrey, parts of Oxford, Somerset, Stafford, Wilts and Yorkshire (both in East Riding and West Riding).

3. Peter Gaskell, the historian, not to be confused with the novelist, Elizabeth Gaskell.

4. Optimists believe that the witnesses were chosen to expose the worst abuses of the factory system and contained a disproportionate number of young children working very long hours.

5. For documentation of these dual technologies in silk see Warner (1922) and in woollen see J. H. Clapham (1907).

6. The number of counts of yarn represent the number of hanks per pound of spun yarn. For example, one pound of no. 40 would contain 33,600 yards of yarn (where 1 hank=840 yards).

7. The separation and division of different operations had begun in cottage industry but "in the small compass of a single family, division of labour could not be carried far" (Kennedy 1819: 6).

8. The absence of the work of younger children by 1842 is understandable since Peel's Act of 1819 set the minimum working age at nine and the Regulation of Child Labor Law of 1833 appointed inspectors to enforce the labor laws.

9. Silk dyeing was the second most important branch of the manufacture of silk goods (weaving was the first). All materials dyed by the dyers were examined by government officials (Warner 1922:446).

10. For a detailed discussion of this sample refer to Tuttle (1986:167-180) and Anderson (1988).

11. In addition, there were 355 children whose occupation stated "helper" or "assistant" but did not specify the type of work involved.

12. When two 300-spindle mules were attached together to form one 600 spindle mule it was called "coupling" or "double decking." This allowed a pair of mules to be operated by one spinner instead of two (1842(31)XXII: 86).

13. Smelser points out that the demand for "piecers" may have fallen because the longer machines were more efficient and broke fewer threads (1959, fn. 3: 198). Bolin-Hort argues convincingly that faster and longer mules increased the number of breakages thereby increasing the need for "piecers" (1989: 105).

14. MacLeod concludes from patent documentation that Arkwright's water frame was a labor-saving machine (1988: 162).

15. Paul and Wyatt's spinning machine failed because it did not separate the drawing stage from the spinning stage. Arkwright's machine separated the two stages (Hills 1979:117-123).

16. Baines believed Wyatt (not Paul) invented roller spinning but that it was Paul's invention that got patented in 1738 (1835: 119).

17. Rioters in Lancashire were said to blame the jennies and water frames for their job loss (Wadsworth and Mann 1965[1931]: 499 and Hobsbawm 1964:7-22).

18. The number of spindles increased dramatically once longer mules could be moved by water or steam power. Thus, the self-actor which began with 48 spindles increased to 60 and than 120 by 1832 and had 1,000 spindles by 1850 (1831-32(706)XV:180 and Blaug 1961:366).

19. It seems more likely, as Bolin-Hort argues in his conclusion, that once child labor laws were enforced in the late 1830s and 1840s the minder-piecer system became more widespread.

20. The throstle machine is similar to the water frame but moved faster and had fewer parts. It was an improvement on the water frame because all the spindles move in unison (instead of groups of four).

21. I would like to thank the curator, Nick Dixon, at the museum for providing me with these measurements.

22. The purpose of such employment was to relieve the parishes from having to financially support the "impotent" poor.

23. Whether Hargreaves' intention was to employ children is unclear, refer to Appendix 6 for a history of the patent.

24. S. D. Chapman (1967) and Hills (1979) argue the spinning jenny required skilled labor, whereas, Berg (1985) believes it was best suited for young children.

25. A system of line shafts (overhead rods) and belts was developed to drive the machines using only a single source of power (a water wheel or steam engine) located in the basement of the factory.

5

The Mining Industry

Coal provided the power behind Britain's Industrial Revolution. The economy's transition from animate to inanimate power was crucial for expanding and sustaining the high levels of output associated with this period. Although nothing "revolutionary" happened within the coal industry as it did within the textile industry, an "industrial" transformation was underfoot. As many historians and economic historians have recognized, the growth of the coal industry was vital to the industrialization of Great Britain. Britain was a world leader in producing coal because "throughout the seventeenth and eighteenth centuries coal was dug in Britain on a scale without parallel elsewhere" (Wrigley 1988:54). This abundant supply of coal produced in Great Britain fueled the process of mechanization and enabled small manufactures to grow into large industries. More industries began to burn coal to create energy such that "the British economy that entered the Victorian era was indeed a coal-based one" (Flinn 1984:456). The steam engines that powered the spinning and weaving machines in the textile factories used coal. Similarly, coal produced the heat for the steam-powered ovens used in iron-making, nonferrous metal smelting and firing and glazing pottery. Even flour-milling and brewing were coal-dependent industries by 1830 (Flinn 1984:456). The number of collieries producing this coal more than quadrupled between 1842 and 1856. In 1842 there were 567 coal mines in all of Great Britain (recall Appendix 2). By 1856 there were 1,704 coal mines in England alone, 306 in Wales, 368 in Scotland and 19 in Ireland (Hunt 1856:206). The output of British coal mines increased by a factor of ten from 1750 to 1850 from 4,356 tons to 46,337 tons. Pollard's estimates put the largest increase in production after 1830 when coal output increased from 32,379 tons (1830-1840) to 46,337 tons (1840-1850) to 64,513 tons in 1854 (Pollard 1980:229). During the first half of the nineteenth century, production in the Northumberland and Durham region accounted for nearly one fourth of total coal output while Lancashire and Cheshire accounted for between 10-15 percent, South Wales 10-13 percent and Scotland 11-15 percent (Pollard 1980:230). According to Pollard's regional estimates, the rate of growth of coal mining in the nineteenth century was faster than earlier estimates of Clapham (1964), Deane and Cole (1967) and Hoffmann (1955).

Great Britain was also blessed with rich deposits of metal, especially copper and tin.[1] Hunt's research uncovered several documents which place the discovery of tin in England before the Christian era. Apparently, the Phoenicians discovered tin in some small British islands, among them, the west of Cornwall, and traded it with the rest of the world (1887:3-7). Centuries later in 1690, the ore of copper mines was first extracted and began to be valuable in Cornwall. By the mid-nineteenth century the metal mines of Cornwall were "heading the list of production of the copper and tin ores of the world" (Jenkin 1927:302). The produce of British tin mines doubled from 1790 to 1855 while that of copper ores more than doubled from 1796 to 1852, refer to Appendix 7. The road to prosperity for miners, however, was filled with years of poverty as the output of tin and copper fluctuated considerably during this period.[2] During the mid-eighteenth century, more mines were dug and developed as new veins (or lodes) of ore were discovered. All this underground activity was visible to the eye as the tall, thin smokestacks seemed to grow like wild flowers across the countryside. In 1801 there were seventy-five mines, presumably copper and tin, at work in Cornwall (R.C.P.S. 1900:71 in Jenkin 1927:171). By 1856 there were 220 Copper mines in England, 12 in Wales, 15 in Ireland and 130 Tin mines in England (Hunt 1856:206). Who worked in all these coal and metal mines? The mining work force was quite diverse and included British men, Scottish women, Irishmen, English lads, Cornish "bâl maidens" and English, Scottish and Welsh children.

Employment of Children in Mining

The proportion of children and youths employed in the mining industry during this period was high but considerably less than in the textile industry. Unfortunately, the available data makes it more difficult to trace the employment of children and youths in mining from the eighteenth to nineteenth century. Several contemporaries, however, provided estimates that give a general indication of the use of child labor in the industry. Table 5.1 provides a summary of these estimates for the coal, tin and copper industry. Although the figures are rough estimates and are not strictly comparable because they are from different sources, they are consistent with one another and with actual returns from the *Parliamentary Papers* in 1842. With these caveats in mind a coherent story emerges when examining trends instead of individual totals.

Child labor was prevalent in coal mines at the turn of the nineteenth century. In 1842 the proportion of children and youths of the total work force ranged from 19 percent to 40 percent in the mining districts (1842[380]XV:38). By 1851, children and youths (under twenty) comprised 30 percent of the total population of coal miners in Great Britain. In metal mining, the number of children working was steady during the nineteenth century. In 1838, Jenkin estimates that roughly 5,000 children were employed in metal mines in Cornwall, and by 1842, the returns from mines in the *First Report* show as many as 5,378 children and youths worked in the mines. Henwood's

TABLE 5.1 Employment in Metal and Coal Mining in Great Britain

Year	Colliery	% of Miners aged 11-20	Source
1802	Howgill	22.2%	Flinn (1984)
1812	Felling	48.7	Flinn (1984)
1841	all	28.4	1841 Census
1851	all	30.6	1851 Census

Total Number of People Employed

Year	Tin	Copper	Sources
1787		7,000	Boulton and Watt MSS
1801	16,000		Jenkin (1927)
1827	5,836	13,737	Spackman (1827)
1837		19,035 total 11,282 men 7,743 women and boys	Lemon (1838)
1838		30,000 total 18,000 men 5,000 women 5,000 children	Jenkin (1927)
1839	10,000		Carne (1839)
1842	28,000		Leifchild (1857)
1842		30,000 total 18,472 men 5,764 women 5,764 children	Henwood in Leifchild (1857)
1842		19,505[a] total 12,580 men 2,157 women 5,378 children	1842[381]XVI:770
1862		50,000	Jenkin (1927)

[a]These totals represent the returns of mines in Dr. Barham's district (Cornwall and Devonshire) and therefore underestimate the total mining population.

estimates of the total number of children working in Cornish mines are quite close to the returns tabulated in Dr. Barham's report. Dr. Barham's totals may, moreover, have underestimated the total number of children working since the figures are based on returns received and may not include all mines. Whether there were 5,000 or 5,764 children employed in Cornish mines, it is clear child labor was no stranger to the mining industry. How widespread was the phenomenon of using child labor? Were most of these children working in small mines or instead were they in a few large mines?

The first detailed and disaggregated employment statistics on the mining industry were gathered and printed in Lemon's article in the *Journal of the Royal Statistical Society* in 1838. His statistics on the employment of men, women and children in metal mines in Cornwall provide concrete evidence on the widespread use of child labor in metal mining. The totals from the returns he received are converted into percentages in Table 5.2 to show the relative proportion of women and children working in each mine. Eighty-five percent of the 124 tin, copper and lead mines in Cornwall employed children.[3] In the 105 mines that employed children, children comprised from 2 percent to 50 percent of the work force with a mean of 19.24 percent and two modes (bimodal) of 11 percent and 19 percent. Children worked, moreover, in establishments of all sizes from the tiny mines of Baldue, Copper Valley and Glebe to the larger and more notorious mines of Levant, Dolcoath and Consols and United Mines. A more comprehensive study of the employment of children in the mining industry which included coal, lead and ironstone mines was published in the 1842 *Parliamentary Reports*. By 1842, one third of the underground work force of coal mines was under the age of eighteen and one fourth of the work force of metal mines (including tin, copper, lead and zinc) was children and youths. As Table 5.3 reveals, there were regional differences in employment; the coal fields of Yorkshire and East Lothian had the highest percentage of children and youths working (40 percent) while Leicestershire, Derbyshire, South Durham and Fifeshire employed 10 percent less (29 percent). Fewer younger children worked in the ironstone mines in West of Scotland and the metal mines of Cornwall. Commissioners believed that more children were employed in coal mining because they could assist in cutting the coal underground which required considerably less strength than extracting the precious metal imbedded in hard rock. Jobs on the surface in metal mines, however, were found which could easily be performed by the younger and weaker children. Were these children working independently of their family as in the textile mills, or did they work alongside their parents and siblings?

Unlike the textile industry, many children and youths who worked in the coal and metal mines had parents and siblings who also worked in the mines. Family-based employment was prevalent because of the nature of underground work, the location of mines and the payment system. Underground work in coal mines was labor-intensive with a division of labor which encouraged colliers to hire child helpers. Colliers who excavated the coal discovered their yield increased if they had assistants who would gather the dislodged pieces of coal together and take them to the main shaft of the mine. Hence, the colliers who could focus their time and efforts exclusively on excavating, enjoyed the productivity benefits of specialization. Fathers who hired their

TABLE 5.2 Employment in Tin, Copper and Lead Mines in Cornwall in 1837

Mine	*Percent of Work Force*		Total Employed
	% Women	% Children	
North Roskear	30%	23%	640
South Roskear	45	16	380
Binner Downs	26	10	390
Trewavas	26	11	161
Great St. George	10	15	340
Wheal Leisure	6	22	95
Wheal Prudence	27	18	73
Wheal Virgin	34	23	392
Wheal Buller	27	19	155
Wheal Busy	45	25	112
Levant	8	34	550
Perran Consols	14	6	100
Consols & United Mines	27	19	3,196
East Crinnis	20	27	232
Pembroke	9	37	139
Wheal Gorland	14	24	86
Wheal Damsel	2	27	40
Wheal Providence	9	26	93
Wheal Harriette	24	12	33
Wheal Maiden	30	30	37
Unity Wood	19	33	424
Carharrack	35	21	96
North Downs	12	21	24
Cardrew	15	25	40
Fowey Consols & Lanescot	18	19	1,680
Great Work	11	18	418
Morvah & Zennor	2	24	116
Gwallon	12	15	136
Tiedarva	19	31	16
St. Ives Consols	5	19	313
Wheal Reeth	8	28	231
Balnoon	7	15	80
Boscaswell Downs	2	24	246
Wheal Mary	8	19	163
Stray Park	16	12	189
Dolcoath	37	12	590
East Wheal Crofty	40	14	1,004
East Pool	39	8	211
Wheal Friendship	16	9	115
Wheal Prosper	7	7	80
Wheal Darlington	16	16	317
Rospeath	8	11	52
Great Wheal Fortune	7	13	207
Trevaskus	21	8	144

(continues)

TABLE 5.2 (continued)

Mine	Percent of Work Force		Total Employed
	% Women	% Children	
Trevarthen Downs	44%	19%	16
Owen Vean	5	8	72
Penberthy Crosts	8	8	27
Providence	14	23	132
East Wheal Strawberry	16	25	120
Holmbush	4	20	191
St Austell Hills	12	22	109
North Ciaze	11	11	9
Rocks	9	13	95
Carrygian Roche	3	11	35
Charlestown	15	32	814
Polberran	7	17	478
Wheal Coit	25	25	16
Polgooth	5	25	202
Wheal Vor	28	22	1,174
Wheal Andrew	–	22	9
Boscean	–	27	89
Bosorn	–	20	20
Baldue	–	17	6
Ballowall	–	25	36
Wheal Budnick	24	19	172
Wheal Bolton	8	–	70
Cornwall Great United	10	11	197
Cardaze	–	43	14
Carn Brea	19	9	723
Copper Valley	–	20	5
Copper Bottom	29	11	72
Wheal Clinton	–	20	5
Creigbraws	12	24	41
West Dolcoath	–	20	5
East Downs	–	25	8
Friendly	17	17	12
Gunnis Lake	8	21	88
Godolphin	14	8	480
Glebe	–	50	4
Hallenbeagle	10	26	192
North Hallenbeagle	15	10	40
Wheal Julia	17	15	148
Wheal Jewel	15	26	359
West Wheal Jewel	8	28	124
Wheal Kitty	20	4	258
Wheal Martha	25	10	40
Wheal Maitland	–	2	26
South Wheal Mary	–	21	14

(continues)

TABLE 5.2 (continued)

Mine	*Percent of Work Force* % Women	% Children	Total Employed
Marazion Mines	21%	24%	401
Wheal Owles	--	16	131
Wheal Osborne	11	11	52
Wheal Prosper	--	28	14
Wheal Pye	33	17	6
South Polgooth	11	16	126
Pentuan Stream	--	22	23
Pheonix (Padstow)	--	7	14
Relistian	27	18	250
Redmoor Consols	11	16	151
South Rose	--	29	41
Streamers (Camon)	1	31	212
Tresavara	24	--	33
Turnavoore	--	20	5
West Tincroft Consols	--	11	37
Wheal Triumph	--	17	12
Wheal Trenwith	5	18	109
Wheal Tamar & South Hooe	5	19	110
United Hills	25	--	359
Wheal Vyvyan	24	23	103
Wheal Amelia	--	--	4
Wheal Brothers	--	--	2
Camborn Consols	--	--	4
East Cornwall	--	--	6
Wheal Fire	--	--	6
Wheal Friendship	--	--	4
Gurnett's Head	--	--	24
Wheal Neptune	--	--	4
Perran Downs	--	--	41
Polbreen	--	--	80
Wheal Rose	--	--	4
Wheal Speed	--	--	10
Wheal St. Just	--	--	2
Wheal Sarah	--	--	12
Trebilzue	--	--	19
Wheal Trevannance	--	--	12

Source: Lemon (1838) Tables XVI and XVII, pp. 78-79.

were dependent upon mining families to work their mines. The livelihood of families in mining towns, moreover, depended upon the mines. As new pits were excavated, employment opportunities grew and the discovery of a large coal bed or a rich mineral deposit meant prosperity for the miners. Once the pits had been exhausted of their coal or metal ore, unemployment resulted and families sought jobs in other nearby pits

TABLE 5.3 Employment of Children in Mining in 1842

Industry and County	Children Employed as % Work Force		
	Under 13	13-18	Total

Coal Mining (Underground)

Industry and County	Under 13	13-18	Total
England			
Leicestershire	13%	16%	29%
Derbyshire	12	17	29
Yorkshire	17	23	40
Lancashire	13	25	38
South Durham	13	16	29
Northumberland and North Durham	13	18	31
East of Scotland			
Mid Lothian	9	24	33
East Lothian	12	28	40
West Lothian	15	23	38
Stirlingshire	15	21	36
Clackmannanshire	12	24	36
Fifeshire	8	21	29
West of Scotland			
Various Mines	7	17	24
Wales			
Monmouthshire	11	21	32
Glamorganshire	12	18	30
Pembrokeshire	10	23	33

Ironstone Mines (Underground)

	Under 13	13-18	Total
West of Scotland			
Whiterigg, New Monkland Parish	6	13	19
Shotts, Shotts Parish	10	13	23

Tin, Copper, Lead, Zinc Mines (Underground & Surface)

	Under 13	13-18	Total
England			
Cornwall, Western District	8	12	20
Cornwall, Central District	9	20	29
Cornwall, Eastern District	9	17	26
Devonshire	11	22	33

Source: 1842[380]XV; First Report of the Commissioners on the Employment of Children (Mines), pp. 38,198,206,236. 1842[381]XVI; Appendix to Report and Reports and Evidence: Part I (Mines), pp. 766-770,778.

the family on the prosperity of the industry and increased the reliance of parents on or moved to a new area where mines showed promise of rich deposits. The isolation of the mines which required a highly mobile work force increased the dependence of their children's labor. Adults (usually men) performed the strenuous work of hewing while the children helped in a variety of ways both underground and on the surface. Some children were employed by the owners while others were hired by the hewers or colliers who supervised them.

A subcontract system similar to the one which existed between spinners and "piecers" in the textile factories, was used in the coal and metal mines. Humphries argues this system arose due to shortages of labor in mining districts and persisted because it placed the task of recruitment and supervision on the hewer instead of the mine owners or agents (1981:11-16). She believed this decentralized system "provided a positive inducement to employ women and children" because the miners did not have to share their earnings with outsiders (14). Drawing from his research on the textile industry, Thompson asserted that subcontracting was predominant in the mining industry as well (1966:243). As Table 5.4 shows, youths who were "putters" and "drawers" in coal mines were paid by those they assisted rather than by the master. Child workers who worked underground (as "trappers" or horse drivers) were paid by the master because they worked alone and when they performed their task many workers benefitted. The subcontract system, however, did not exist in the Ironstone mines because the ores were freed with the use of gun powder. The process of

TABLE 5.4 People Who Hire Child Workers in Mines

Type of Mining	*Classes of Workers*	*How Paid*	*Who Paid By*
Collieries	Colliers under 18	Piece	Master
	Putters and drawers	Day	Workmen
	Trappers	Day	Master
	Horse drivers	Day	Master
	Engine boys	Day	Master
Ironstone Mines	Miners under 18	Piece	Master
	Female drawers under 18	Day	Master
Iron Works	Pig moulders at furnaces	Day	Workmen
	Catchers at forge-rolls and heaver-ups	Day	Workmen
	Straighteners and staff carriers	Day	Workmen
	Door drawers	Day	Master
	Pudlers' underhands under 18	Day	Workmen

Source: 1842[380]XV, p. 158.

isolating and procuring the valuable ore was more of a group activity than in coal mines where a single hewer worked on a certain area of the face. On the other hand, the subcontract system was prevalent above ground in the Iron Works. Youths who worked on blast furnaces received their wages from those they assisted, not the masters or owners of the mines. Whether this practice was common is not clear, but we can get some clue from the Commissioners' summary in their *Second Report*, "In the majority of instances, the young people, while in their place of work, are under the care and control solely of the adult workmen, by whom they are generally hired and paid" (1843[430]XIII:200). In many cases these adults were the children's parents, but there were instances in which children worked for a family friend or even a stranger.

Children and youths worked primarily for their parents in the coal mines in West of Scotland and South Wales and the metal mines in Cornwall. In most coal mines in England (South Staffordshire, Shropshire, Warwickshire, Derbyshire, Durham and Northumberland) and North Wales the children were hired and paid by the contractors or butties or charter masters (1842[380]XV:39). On the other hand, in the mines located in Ashby-de-la-Zouch, West Riding of Yorkshire, Lancashire, Cheshire, Oldham and Cumberland hewers or colliers hired and paid the young "drawers," waggoners and thrutchers (1842[380]XV:39). Children and youths worked for their father in the coal mines in West of Scotland and South Wales (1842[380]XV:40). As T. Tancred reports for the mines in West of Scotland, "In this district the drawers to colliers are generally their own Children or younger brothers or sisters, and are paid by the adults whom they assist" (1842[381]XVI:336). Similarly, Mining Commissioner R. H. Franks observes the strong familial tie in the coal mines located in South Wales, "The collier boy is, to all intents and purposes, the property of his father (as to wages) until he attains the age of seventeen years, or marries; his father receives his wages, whether he was an air-door boy of five years or a hauler of fifteen" (1842[382]XVII:482). The subcontract system was used almost exclusively in Cornwall in the tin and copper mines. Children were brought to the mines by their parents in search of employment opportunities. As one commissioner noted in his report, "The first introduction of a Child to mining labour in the Cornish districts usually consists in its being brought by the parent with a request for work; or, if the father is employed, he is probably allowed to put a child into any opening which may occur" (1842[380]XV:784). All the boys working underground as "putters," haulers and "fillers" were employed by the men except the boys who worked the machines and drove the horses. Since their jobs involved more general work which benefitted more than one miner they were hired and paid by the masters. Children and youths were brought to the mines by their parents to work on the surface but did not work side by side in preparing and dressing the ores.[4] In contrast to Cornwall, children and youths were hired and paid by contractors in the metal mines of Scotland, North Wales and Ireland (1842[380]XV:230). In conclusion, it appears that the subcontract system was more prevalent in the mining industry than the textile industry during industrialization.

Children were usually hired and paid by the adult with whom they worked and in many cases this adult was their father. Although children received wages, they were not independent wage earners in the same sense as the spinners, "doffers" and weavers in the textile factories. Instead, the children and youths working in the mines were dependent on the colliers or hewers who hired them in the same way the "piecers" were dependent upon the adult spinners. The dependence, however, was two-sided. The output and earnings of the hewer depended upon the endurance and productivity of their "putters." When the adult was their father, the subcontract system extended the family economy outside the home and beyond cottage production. Therefore, children worked with adults and for adults and often with family members. There is evidence that some fathers took advantage of their children and paid them less than they deserved. W. R. Wood, the commissioner of collieries in Bradford and Leeds, reported that the contract between collier and "putter" in the same family is "disadvantageous to the children in many cases, from the parent laying out upon the child a less sum than he receives for its labour, and applying the surplus to his own purposes, generally those of intemperance" (1842[382]XVII:H5). Since this behavior was not mentioned by other commissioners, it is probably safe to assume that such exploitation was not widespread. The fact that it did happen to some children is noteworthy because it implies some children had almost no bargaining power in the household.

The competitive labor market model is no longer applicable in the situations where fathers hired their sons (or daughters) to work for them. In this case, the demand for child labor represents the desires and needs of fathers rather than employers to enhance the production process. By assisting their father, children increased the amount of coal or ore they were able to excavate and raise to the surface (i.e., increasing the father's productivity). Thus, the decision made by fathers to employ their children was based not only on the value of the children's additional output (or productivity) but also on the desire to maximize the family's income. As Humphries noted, hewers who hired their own children did not have to pay children of other families and brought home the majority of what they earned (1981:14). In some instances, despite adding very little to the final output, young children were hired because their mere presence in the pit put more money in their father's pocket. This was the situation in the coal mines of Lancashire and Oldham because the general practice for payment encouraged fathers to employ even their youngest children. Colliers were paid based on the amount of coal hewed each day. Rather than create separate piles of coal on the surface for every hewer underground, all the excavated coal was put into one pile and the colliers determined the portion of the pile each hewer should get. According to several coal surveyors, commissioners and colliers the portion "assigned" to each hewer depended upon the number of people (where children depending on their age, counted as different fractions of adults) who had worked together in the pit.[5] Hence, a collier would be "assigned" a larger portion and receive a higher wage the more children he had working with him, regardless of their output. The existence of this payment system provides additional justification for the prevalence of family-based employment in the mines.

> But the colliers' boys are taken down into the pits so soon as they can be of the least service, and often before, in order merely that they may count as assistants. The collieries

being in all ordinary times overhanded, the proportion of coal which each man's labour shall get is regulated among themselves; and his assistants being reckoned as so many fractions of a man, if he can have down another member of his family he will be at liberty to count it as a sanction for getting a certain portion of coals, and receives wages accordingly, although the child may really have done very little of the labour (1842[382]XVII:820).

It is not clear from the First Report (1842[380]XV) or the *Second Report* (1842[381]XVI) on the mines if parents actually paid their children or simply said they did when asked by Inspectors.[6] Theoretically, the demand for child labor becomes a doubly derived demand and is not directly measurable in the labor market. In other words, the demand for child labor is a derived demand from the demand for the father's labor which is derived from the demand for the final product. This has important implications for wages which are discussed at the end of this chapter. What types of jobs did the children perform on the surface and underground?

Children worked in most, but not all, stages of coal and metal mining. The process of mining has two main subdivisions of work: underground and surface labor. Within each subdivision, there are several stages. See Appendix 8 for a diagram of the production process of mining coal and metal. The three main stages or steps involved in bringing the coal or ore to the surface are hewing, loading and hauling. In coal mining, the hewer used a pick, wedge and mallet to remove the coal in large pieces from the coal bed. Gunpowder was often used in metal mining because the veins or lodes of ore were imbedded in hard rock. Once broken apart, the hewers used picks and hammers to break up the large rock and isolate the valuable ore. Underground, children and youths worked as assistants to the adult hewers in loading and hauling the coal or metal ore which had been loosened from the earth's clutches. After the coals or ore-filled rock reached the surface, they underwent several procedures before they were ready for sale. In general, the process of "preparing the coals" and "dressing the ores" involved isolating, cleaning and purifying the valuable product for sale. The surface work for metals involved three times as many steps than for coals, and employed a large number of youths as primary workers. In contrast with the textile industry, the increase in the demand for child labor in mining was the result of expansion rather than significant changes in technology. The increase in the demand for child labor to work above ground as well as underground occurred as the demand for coal grew. The industry experienced considerable growth as there was expansion into new coal fields and enlargement of existing ones. As the scale of operations expanded with the application of the steam engine to draining, the method of extraction and preparation became more labor intensive and children and youths filled the new positions. There were a few microinventions, however, which improved the method of underground hauling that increased the possibilities of children and youths substituting for adults. In addition, children were the only workers who could work in some underground situations, particularly where the subterranean roads were low and narrow. Together these three components explain why child labor was important in mining during the first half of the nineteenth century.

Labor Intensive Technology: Children as Helpers

As the demand for coal increased, more opportunities arose for children and youths working underground and on the surface. In mining, as with textiles, the industry grew by expanding the scale of operations and applying the principle of the division of labor to the production process. In contrast to textiles, mechanization of the process of extracting coal and dressing metal ores was limited. Instead, increases in output were created by increases in labor, not capital. The changes in scale and industrial organization were, however, closely connected to capital and to one of the macroinventions of this period, the steam engine.

The steam engine was adopted and adapted in coal and metal mines long before it was fully integrated into textile factories. Thomas Savery invented a pumping engine in 1698 to meet the needs of tin and copper miners in Cornwall. Ten years later, Thomas Newcomen invented the "fire engine," an improved, self-acting, atmospheric engine which was adopted in coal and metal mines (Ashton 1964:27). In 1769, Boulton and Watt patented an improved steam-pump with a separate condensing unit. In 1775, there were 321 Newcomen pumping engines in the coal mines of England, Scotland and Wales (Flinn 1984:122). Kanefsky and Robey estimate that between 1,014-2,500 new steam engines of all makes were erected in coal mines during the eighteenth century (1980:168-169). In the tin mines of Cornwall, the number of steam engines increased from 24 in 1813 to 58 in 1837, and the average duty more than doubled, from 19,456,000 to 47,087,374 (Lemon 1838:67).[7] In 1849, James Sims, a mining engineer who owned Sims and Sons, a prominent engine-making firm in Cornwall remarked: "that the Cornish steam-engine, or rather the steam-engine as used in Cornwall, is the most economical; is in fact, now so generally known that it scarcely needs a remark" (102-103).

Steam power was used for three main purposes - to drive the pulleys which raised and lowered the coals or ores and miners in the main shafts, to move the fans which enhanced ventilation underground and to drive the pumps that removed water from the pits. The development and application of these three improvements in working the mines had a significant impact on the mining industry. Economic historians believe that the application of steam power to coal and metal mining increased the "scale of operations while leaving the technology of hewing unchanged" (Ashton 1964:27 and Samuel 1977:21). The improvement in underground drainage allowed miners to go deeper than they had before, which increased the size of the pit. The miners expanded their work underground, digging deeper and developing a complex system of shafts, winzes, levels, cross-cuts and adits.[8] In addition, mines close to the shore and even under the ocean (at Land's End and Penzance) could now be explored to their potential. Consequently, both the number and size of mines had increased by the nineteenth century.

The increasing size and depth of mines where steam engines were in use was highlighted by several contemporaries (Leifchild 1853 and Taylor 1837). In the 1770s, coal mines in the Northeast reached 100 fathoms, and by 1800, they had penetrated 133 fathoms. A survey of mines in 1828 showed depths ranging from 20-

180 fathoms with an average depth of 90 fathoms (NEI Buddle 25/111:4-15 cited in Flinn 1984:79). In 1834, the Monkwearmouth mine was 263 fathoms. Further, the Consolidated Mines had 826 men and boys working at and below 100 fathoms, at an average depth of 229 fathoms (Lemon 1838:68). By the 1840s, many of the metal mines of Cornwall like Wheal Vor, Dolcoath, Cook's Kitchen, Gwennap United and Fowey Consols were 300 fathoms deep (Jenkin 1927:221). The consequences of this expansion on the work force were twofold. More mines and bigger and deeper mines increased the demand for labor and increased the possibilities for the division and specialization of labor.

Because of the limited opportunities of mechanizing and automating the extraction process, bigger and deeper mines meant more hewers and "putters" were needed. The hewers were cutting more coal and the "putters" had more coal to transport and longer galleries in which to travel (Samuel 1977:21). Since "putters" were typically young men (or lads) between the ages of fourteen and eighteen, the number of youths working underground increased. Leifchild describes this group of workers as he descends in a coal mine; "Here we come to a new set and sort of lads and boys, who may be called generally "putters." This term signifies the boys who push, or put, the trains of coal from the places where the hewers fill them, to the crane, where they are hoisted upon the rolleys, or waggons for transporting the coals from the crane to the shaft" (1853:156). The demand for children to work underground with the hewers is apparent in the following statements made by Inspectors of the Mines in the *First Report of the Midland Mining Commission.*

. . .such is the demand for children amongst the butties, that there are not boys in the Union Workhouses at Walsall, Wolverhampton, Dudley and Stourbridge, and there is not a school master at any of these establishments (1843[508]XIII:xi).

The nature of the employment will always secure an ample supply of young hands who, whilst earning good wages, will have the opportunity of acquiring the skill and experience necessary to rise from step to step in their trade (1843[508]XIII:xli).

As pits got larger and the underground workings more complicated, the benefits from dividing and separating tasks became more profitable. The employment opportunities for children and youths increased as the process underground and on the surface was divided into numerous simple well-defined tasks. During the eighteenth and nineteenth centuries, hewers used one of three methods of excavating coal; the pillar-and-stall system, longwall working and panel-work system (Leifchild 1853:128-130). The extent of the division and specialization of labor depended upon which method was used. There were three classes of workers in the longwall system (also called Shropshire method): hewers, "drawers" and "slackboys." All of the coal was extracted by a single process and the roads were fortified by stone or wood. This method was used in ironstone mines and coal mines with thin seams. The pillar-and-stall method had several more classes of "drawers" but did not use "slackboys" because coal was left to form the pillars or roof support. This system was used on larger and deeper beds of coal. Consequently, the underground workings resembled an ant farm where tunnels were built on various levels and at great distances from the opening to the surface. "Hurriers," "drawers" and "putters" traversed these longer galleries from the coal face to the shaft. By the early 1800s, this system was replaced by the panel-work system (or Newcastle system) which permitted a high degree of specialization. The underground workings were divided into quadrangular panels, resembling blocks in a city square. The panels were interconnected by a system of roads which facilitated the hauling of coal and the coursing of air. Like the pillar-and-stall method, this Newcastle system required several classes of haulers. At the same time, the new system of ventilation created another task, that of opening and closing the air doors (Leifchild 1853:128-129).

The method used for excavating metal ore, however, was quite different. The process was slower and more arduous because the metals of tin, copper, lead and zinc are found in very hard rock. Often gun powder was used to separate the ore from the solid granite, slate and clay-slate. The excavations in working a mineral vein were formed either vertically or pursued laterally while the advanced points tended progressively downwards. This was the reverse of the mode of working a coal seam and meant many subterranean roads were on an incline (Leifchild 1857:138). The unique method of working the metal mines in Cornwall and Devon encouraged a division of labor that included hiring children as assistants to the hewer. The system of tribute where the workmen contract for a "setting" every two months and are paid by the "pitch" (so many pence or shillings to the pound) produced incentives for the miners to dig only what would bring them income and to hire as many children at low wages to assist them.[9] Taylor mentions these incentives in reference to the method of paying the miners and workmen and claims it, "...not only instigates the miner to discover and produce as much as he can, but leads him to consider every circumstance which may diminish the expense of returning it, or may enable him to produce the greatest quantity of each metal at the lowest charge of dressing as well as raising" (1814:24). Many of these children were the sons and daughters of the miners, brought to the mine to do whatever they could to earn a wage and to learn the trade. The boys became "putters" and haulers and transported the coal or ore in the pits from the miners to the shafts. The girls usually worked as "riddlers" and "pickers" on the surface separating the valuable portions from the rocks and dirt. A commissioner for the mines, H. H. Jones, made this observation about the boys employed in North Wales:

> They are for the most part the children of colliers, and from infancy become familiar with the idea of underground work, and anxious to go below and begin to work. This wish of course meets with no opposition from parents, who, lured by the wages, are never backward in sending their children to the pits as soon as they can get them into employ (1842[382]XVII:367).

In both types of mining, the job of a hewer required strength and was considered dangerous due to underground explosions and cave-ins. It was the work of strong men between the ages of twenty and forty, although commissioners questioned a few miners as old as eighty-two (1842[381]XVI:450-512). Children and youths were employed in the next three stages in coal and iron mining: loading, hauling and hooking. In tin, copper and lead mines fewer children and youths are found working underground and most are employed on the surface. Children under thirteen working underground comprised between 7-17 percent of the workers in coal mines while only between .2-1.5 percent of the workers in tin and copper mines were under thirteen. Similarly, the employment of youths underground was quite prevalent in coal mines where they comprised between 16-28 percent of the work force but not in tin and copper mines where only 1.5-5.1 percent of the worker were youths.[10]

Workers on the surface were responsible for getting the product ready for sale, supplying workers underground with necessary materials and keeping the engines running. Youths performed the first of these duties which had been reduced to several distinct steps. In metal mining, the process of "dressing the ores" was labor intensive and employed children and youths as "riddlers," "pickers," "cobbers," "jiggers" and "washers."[11] The description, age and gender of workers in Tables 5.5 and 5.6 illustrate the types of work children and youths performed in collieries in Great Britain. Table 5.5 lists all the workers of South Hetton Colliery, a coal mine, in 1853. This division of labor is typical of the larger collieries since South Hetton was considered a "first-rate northern colliery establishment" (Leifchild 1853:183). The labor is separated into three distinct groups: the managers, the workers above ground and the workers below ground. On the surface, the lads working as "screeners," "wailers" and "for sundry miscellaneous duties" comprise one third of the work force. Underground the ratio is closer to one half because there are as many "putters," "foals" and "half-marrows" as hewers.[12] The organization in smaller mines, like the one shown in Table 5.6, was nearly identical except for the number of managers. The number of boys under eighteen in each occupation is given explicitly for the Walbottle Colliery. There are fewer boys working on the surface (28) of this colliery, but the proportion underground is considerably larger than in the South Hetton Colliery. Nearly two thirds of the workers underground were child "trappers" and youths working as "putters" and drivers. The information regarding the organization and relative numbers of workers in these documents are fairly representative of the coal mines during this period. The sexual division of labor and the complete exclusion of any girls or women, however, seems exaggerated. In some parts of England (West Riding of Yorkshire, Bradford and Leeds, Halifax, Lancashire and Cheshire and North Lancashire) and in East of Scotland and South Wales, girls did work underground and many young women worked on the surface (1842[380]XV:24-31). In relation to the nature of children's employment in these districts, the commissioners remarked that there were no divisions of tasks by gender. A few seemed shocked by this and were astonished to see girls in trousers with muscles protruding from short sleeved shirts "putting" the coal just like the boys (1842[381]XVI:181).

The youngest children aged six, seven and eight began work as a "trapper" and opened the air-doors so waggoners could pass and then quickly closed them to preserve the airflow necessary to keep the tunnels ventilated. Upon descending Pemberton's Coal pit in Monkwearmouth, Leifchild is surprised by what he sees:

But what in the world have we got here? A little mite of a boy, sitting behind this door,

TABLE 5.5 Organization of Labor at South Hetton Colliery

Superior Officers

Manager	1
Viewer (chief mining superintendent)	1
Under Viewer	1
Overman and Wasteman	2
First Engineer and Second Engineer	2
Surgeon	1
Clerks	4

Workmen Above Pit

Joiners and Sawyers (to keep the works in repair)	13
Engine Wrights (to repair or make machinery)	7
Enginemen (to keep machinery running, clean etc.)	8
Firemen (to attend to the boilers, fires, coals etc.)	9
Smiths (to prepare the iron-work in rough)	18
Masons (to build engine-houses, etc.)	8
Labourers (to masons)	6
Cartmen (carting all work)	11
Horseman	9
Saddler	1
Waggon-wrights (to lay down and men rails on railways)	6
Waggon-riders (one conductor per train)	11
Staithmen (to attend to shipping place of coals)	4
Banksmen (to work at pit-mouth, delivering coals)	8
Screeners of coal, and waggon-fillers	12
Wailers (boys who pick out stones and slates from coal)	9
Corves, or basket-makers	4
Heap-keepers (looks to quality of cleaned coals)	1
Storekeeper (over a vast quantity of stores for all men)	1
Attendants on railway (engineers and furnace-men)	8
Trimmers (to fill the holds of vessels with coal)	8
Boys, for sundry miscellaneous duties	39

Workmen in the Pit

Hewers (to hew down, blast, and get the coal)	140
Putters (to put or push coals in trains, with many assistants of different styles and ages)	140
Deputies, ventilators, shifters, and several other subordinate officers below ground	36
Total below ground	316
Total above ground	212
Total of Colliery Establishment	528

Source: Leifchild (1853), pp. 182-83.

158

TABLE 5.6 Organization of Labor at Walbottle Colliery in 1841

Above Ground Establishment

	Boys	Men
Blacksmiths	--	11
Engine-wrights and joiners	--	8
Waggonway-wrights	--	4
Masons and labourers	1	4
General labourers	--	4
Cartmen	--	4
Waggonmen	--	10
Wailers and screeners (the boys aged about 14)	6	4
Pick-carriers and way-cleaners (aged from 10-12)	5	--
Banksmen	--	4
Brakemen	--	3
Plugmen	--	7
Firemen	--	7
Corvers	--	4
Heapmen	--	2
Staithmen and off-putters	--	4
Keelmen (the boys aged about 15 to 18)	16	32

Under Ground Establishment

	Boys	Men
Hewers	--	95
Putters (aged from about 14 to 18)	36	--
Drivers (aged from about 11 to 14)	30	--
Trappers (aged from about 7 to 10)	14	--
Shifters	--	12
Overmen	--	3
Overmen's deputies	--	7
Rolleyway-men	--	5
Cranemen	--	5
Onsetters	--	3
Horse-keepers	1	2
Wood and water leaders (aged from about 12 to 16)	4	--
Wastemen	--	2
Furnace-men	--	2
Total below ground	85	136
Total above ground	28	112
Total in Colliery Establishment	113	248

Source: 1842[381]XVI, p. 557.

crouched up in a corner. Looking anything but like a free, joyous boy of playful propensities! What can he be doing here? This is the little "trapper boy", the youngest piece of humanity employed in the mines: his duty is to pull open the door with this cord, whenever he hears the drivers or trains of coal waggons coming on one side or the other (1853:151).

The need for a trapper arose from improvements in the ventilation system utilized in medium- and large-scale operations. Initially, ventilation had been achieved by putting a pipe or tube down the shaft and along the roof of the gallery until it reached the miners at work (Davies 1811:90). Subsequently, a new system was created based on creating drafts with fires. The heated air which ascended through the chimney was replaced by the cold air from the shaft, which pulls air up from the lowest part of the mine (Davies 1811:105). In 1760, James Spedding devised a system of air circulation known as "coursing the air" where a draft was directed through all parts of the workings by a route created by trap doors and deliberately blocked passages. Buddle improved upon this system and developed elaborate split courses to move the air underground.[13] Both innovations increased the need for young children to work as "trappers" (Flinn 1984:330). In particular, a mine utilizing the panel-work system, as shown in Diagram 5.1, required "trappers" between every panel to control the flow of air. As the diagram illustrates, the number of "trappers" needed increases with the number of panels worked.

Slightly older children, usually boys aged nine to twelve, worked alongside the hewers and loaded the coal or ore. They worked as "fillers" and "pitchers" in getting all the large and small pieces of coal and rock loosened by the adult hewers into the "skips" (waggons or corves). For the longwall method, once this step was complete "slack-boys" raked the small coal and coal dust into baskets and threw it into the empty spaces or the "gobbing." Boys were then used as human asses to either pull (called "hurriers," "trammers" or "drawers") or push (called "pushers," "putters" or "thrutchers") the "skips" of coal or ore from the workings to the horseway or to the foot of the shaft. As one commissioner remarked in 1842:

> But by far the greatest number of Children and person employed in coal mines are engaged in propelling and drawing tubs laden with coal, from the face to the pit-eye, or the main-levels in those pits where they have horses (1842[380]XXV:81).

> But the work which employs the greater part of the younger boys underground (in tin and copper mines) is what is termed by them 'rulling', that is, rolling or wheeling barrows, loaded with the ground removed from the place where it has been excavated to that from which it is to be taken to the surface. This occupation is always laborious (1842[380]XV:215).

The job of the "putters" (as they were generally called) required strength. The amount of exertion necessary depended upon the weight of the waggons and the condition of the subterranean roadways. The weight of these waggons varied from two cwt. to nine cwt. and could be filled in accordance with the lads strength. Often two lads would

DIAGRAM 5.1 "The Coursing of Air" in Coal Collieries

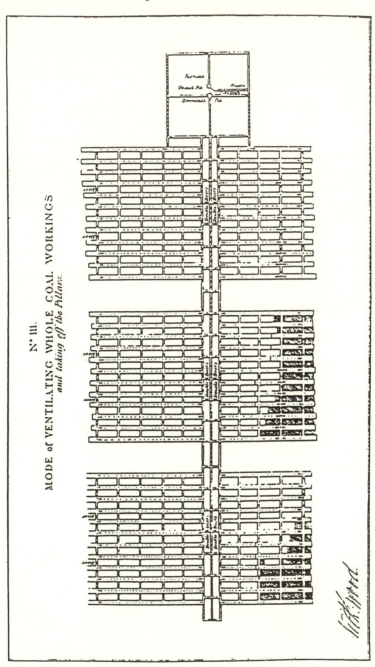

Source: 1835[603]V:Plate II

move the "skips" of coal, one pulling from the front and the other pushing from the back. As Mr. Fletcher reported to the Commission on Mines:

The 'waggoners' of the larger tubs are youths of seventeen or eighteen, when one person has to manage the whole load; but younger boys often join two together, to 'make a waggoner,' receiving the pay of one, and dividing it between them, according to their relative ability; the younger one calling himself a 'thrutcher' only, and designating the older one his 'butty' (1842[382]XVII:825).

Several methods existed for raising the coal and rock with metallic ore to the surface. In the larger coal and metal mines, the product was raised to the surface by horse or steam power in corves. Young boys (called drivers) usually drove the horse "whim gin" because the work was easy and monotonous since the horses knew where to walk (Jenkin 1927:234 and 1842[381]XVI:10). Similarly, the engineers who managed the high pressure steam engine on the surface were often boys aged twelve to fourteen (1842[380]XV:66). Some mines used a machine called a jig and the "jiggers" were typically young boys.[14] Mr. Kennedy, a commissioner, had this to say about their performance: "I am told that these little boys, for they are generally not more than 10 years old, become exceedingly expert, and will stop the machine at the proper place with the greatest precision" (1842[382] XVII:167). In the smaller mines of England and Scotland, the coals were brought to the surface on the backs of women and boys, called "coal-bearers." Simonin, a contemporary who studied and compared the French and British system of working the coal had this to say of their toil: "Like the mendits (in France), they acquire great skill in this work, and draw with ease an average weight of three hundred pounds of coal at each journey; but it is not a pleasant sight to witness" (1869:119). Similarly, in the smaller tin and copper mines of Cornwall, the ore was "brought to the grass" on the backs of women and youths who climbed a series of ladders or levels to the surface. The sacks or baskets were filled with ore according to the strength of the workers carrying it. Such primitive technology was also used in the Ironstone mines in Forest of Dean where, "The ore from these little mines is carried to the surface in billies, on the backs of young boys, who crawl along the galleries and climb into the daylight with the address and activity of monkeys" (1842[382]XVII:5).

In addition, the surface of coal and metal mines offered many opportunities for girls and young women to work. The process of "preparing the coals" or "screening the coals" was light work which required very little strength or skill.[15] The process was broken down into two simple steps, "slating" and screening. In the first step, the girls who separated the coal from the stone and the large coal from the small coal were called "wailers." In the next step, the "screeners" separated the pieces of coal from the dirt and dust with large metal sieves. The *First Report of the Commission of the Employment of Children in the Mines* confirms this: "At almost all the collieries in this district an operation is carried on at the surface which gives employment to great multitudes of children under 13, and of young persons between the age of thirteen and eighteen, namely, that called 'screening the coals', which is a plan by which the large coal is separated from the small coal and dust" (1842[380]XV:88). The number of surface workers increased as more coal was brought to the surface and consequently the demand for child labor grew.

The pressure to keep up with the underground workers and increase the amount of product for sale was even greater in metal mining. Because most metallic minerals are found in veins or fissures of rock and not beds like coal, the process of "dressing the ores" is more tedious and requires many procedures. The process had been divided into seven separate tasks, most performed by young women although there was work for the weaker young men who could not work in the pits. Most of the work, except bucking, required no strength and was considered superior employment because it was performed outside. After ascending from a copper mine in Cornwall, Leifchild reveals his enthusiasm for this "grass-work": "What a congregation of women and children, all engaged in this surface-mining work! And how happy and healthy they look compared with children in coal pits and colliery work! There they sit, 'spalling, jigging,' 'buddling and trunking', and doing all manner of mining mysteries, and delighting in them too" (1857:164). In Cornwall these young women were called "bâl maidens."[16] The tasks were simple and repetitive but required good eyesight and stamina. The hours were longer for surface workers than pit workers, nine to ten hours compared to six to eight hours per day (1842[380]XV:216-217, 239-241). Working in sheds with protection only overhead, their work was performed every day, often in the rain and bitter cold. According to Taylor in 1837, the sheds were an improvement on earlier conditions when the "dressing the ores" took place in the open air. In noting the progress with surface work he wrote, "Whoever inspects a large mine in Cornwall will now observe, that for the persons who work on the surface, a great proportion of which are young women, sheds are provided, to protect them from the weather, and thus to allow their labour to proceed without interruption" (1837:42).

The sexual division of labor on the surface of metal mines meant many tasks were gender-specific. The first process of separating the larger ore from the smaller ore was called "riddling" and was typically performed by girls sixteen and over. In the next step, called "picking," the valuable portions of smaller ore were separated by hand from the worthless material. The quickness and keen eyesight of the "pickers" was important in determining the yield and profit of the mine. The "pickers" were usually girls ranging in age from fourteen to eighteen. The valuable portions were passed on to the young boys who cleaned the stones in wooden troughs, a process called "washing up." The next two steps were considered the hardest work on the surface but were still performed by girls. The girls, usually over fifteen years of age, broke the stones open with a hammer (cobbing) and then further reduced the size of the stones using a hammer, anvil or a grinder mill (bucking). Once pulverized, boys separated the valuable portions of the ore by suspending a sieve in water. The ore which had been reduced to a powder was then washed approximately 100 times. The monotonous job of washing employed multitudes of girls and boys. Finally, the ores were prepared and divided for sale by women (1842[380]XV:66).

The large proportion of children and young women working on the surface was highlighted by contemporaries and recorded by commissioners. Contemporaries' descriptions of the countryside often included remarks on child labor above ground. In 1795, Aikin describes the life of a copper mine in Staffordshire which was "neglected as unprofitable" in 1780 but "re-opened by a Cornish miner" who discovered new ore deposits 200 yards deep. His employment estimates of this mine show the division of labor and children working above ground, "More than 300 persons, men, women and children, are employed in the works; the men in digging, the women and children in breaking and picking the ore" (104). Davies' *A New Historical and Descriptive View of Derbyshire* (1811) contains a commentary on the lead mines in the area: "All the ore that comes from the mine, is beaten and knocked into small pieces, and afterwards washed and sifted before it is sold: this part of the business is performed by women and children who are employed by the miners for a very trifling renumeration" (86). *In A Londoner's Walk to the Lands End and a Trip to the Scilly Isles* (1855), White commented on the surface labor in tin mines and compared it to the factories he had seen, "Here greater supplies of ore; every minute the heavy heaps from below poured out from the ascending kibble, and men wheeling it away to larger heaps, while more women, and young boys and girls, pick and separate the various qualities. All red, and all busy; for here the labour goes on as in a factory" (280).

The presence of children and youths on the surface is apparent in the figures given in the *Reports on Children's Employment in the Mines in 1842* (1842[381]XVI). Returns from ninety-four Tin and Copper mines in Cornwall and Devonshire confirm the prevalence of child labor in surface employment. Children and youths working on the surface comprised from 15 to 35 percent of the total labor force employed in these mines (1842[381]XVI:770). In a different report, the specific duties of children and youths on the surface of copper, tin and lead mines was recorded for several districts. Table 5.7 aggregates the information by the type of mine while preserving the age, gender and occupational subdivisions.[17] The employment of children and youths on the surface appears to be more pronounced in copper mines and tin mines than in lead mines. The sexual division of labor is abundantly clear: girls and young women were exclusively involved in separating the rocks from the ore ("riddling" and "picking") and in breaking the rocks open to expose the ore (spalling, cobbing and bucking). Boys and lads, on the other hand, worked in jigging, trunking slimes, buddling and tying.[18] The only exception to this occupational segregation is found in the tin mines where both boys and girls were "framers."

In summary, the growth of the mining industry in Great Britain meant an increase in the demand for child labor during the eighteenth and nineteenth century. To meet the increase in demand for coal, collieries needed to excavate more. Meanwhile many new lodes of tin and copper were discovered in Cornwall and some at depths which had not been considered workable. The application of the steam engine to winding, ventilating and most of all, pumping, made all this possible. Subsequently, more and more mines were sunk while those in existence became bigger and deeper. Because the process of "getting the coals" or "bringing the ore to the grass" was labor intensive, more workers were required. Close to half of these workers were children and youths because traditionally the mines had been worked by adult hewers and child "putters." In addition, as mines expanded, the innovation of dividing the process into many separate and distinct tasks occurred, which also increased the number of workers required. Since many of these tasks were simple and required no skill, children and

TABLE 5.7 The Number of Children Performing Various Tasks in Metal Mines

Processes		Copper Mines		Tin Mines		Lead Mines	
		Under 13	13-18	Under 13	13-18	Under 13	13-18
Riddling	M	--	--	--	--	--	--
	F	--	27	--	--	--	--
Picking	M	--	--	--	--	--	--
	F	65	66	--	6	16	5
Spalling	M	--	--	--	--	--	--
	F	2	23	--	8	--	--
Cobbing	M	--	--	--	--	--	--
	F	1	10	--	--	--	--
Bucking	M	--	--	--	--	--	--
	F	--	31	--	--	--	3
Jigging	M	41	90	--	--	--	21
	F	--	--	--	--	--	--
Trunking	M	42	7	111	15	--	--
	F	--	--	1	--	6	1
Buddling	M	40	33	28	59	--	--
	F	--	--	--	3	--	--
Tying	M	20	17	5	1	--	15
	F	--	--	--	--	--	--
Framing	M	--	--	26	6	--	--
	F	--	--	18	62	--	--
Rolling		--	--	19	54	7	3

Source: 1842[381]XVI, Table 17, p. 778.

youths were hired to assist the hewer underground or "prepare the coal" or "dress the ores" on the surface. In the coal mines of England and Wales, the proportion of children and youths working at numerous collieries often exceeded one third while in Scotland the ratio was closer to one fourth (1842[380] XV:38). In the Ironstone pits, the proportion was substantially higher, exceeding two fifths (1842[381]XVI:8). On the surface of tin and copper mines in Cornwall, the ratio exceeded one third in two districts while approaching one fifth in the others (1842[381]XVI: 766-770). Clearly, the employment of children and youths as secondary workers in the production process was far from trivial.

Labor Substituting Technology: Children as Workers

There were fewer possibilities of substituting child labor for adult labor in the mining industry than in the textile industry. The mechanization of the various stages of production was severely limited in mining. The process of hewing required considerable strength and human discretion and even to this day remains an adult male occupation. The method of hauling, however, progressed during the eighteenth and nineteenth century until children and horses were replacing adult males, shown in Diagram 5.2.[19] Originally coal and metallic rock had been transported in sledges (wooden boxes) which were dragged along the barren floor. Once filled with coal these sledges were too heavy to be drawn by children, and only muscular youths and adults called "barrowmen" could move them from the workings to the shaft. By the middle of the eighteenth century, the labor of the hauler had been lightened as changes

DIAGRAM 5.2 Different Methods of Hauling from 1600 -1850

Seventeenth Century

(continues)

166

DIAGRAM 5.2 (continued)

Eighteenth Century

Nineteenth Century

in the waggons and underground roadways were made. In some mines, wooden planks were laid down and wheels added to the sledges while in others, wooden rails were constructed to carry carts with grooved wheels. Although none of these improvements would be considered technological breakthroughs, they did make it possible to employ children and more youths as haulers. Ashton and Sykes (1929) highlight these substitution possibilities in analyzing the changing composition of the mining work force, "The introduction of the wheeled corf and the tramway lightened the task of the putters, and so brought it within the powers of young children" (173).

The employment of children and youths as haulers was widespread by 1842, but the use of rails was by no means universal. The youthfulness of "hurriers," "pushers" and "trammers" is apparent in Table 5.8 which summarizes the methods of hauling utilized in the various coalfields. Both boys and girls pushed wheeled corves on rails (called "trammers") in the coal mines of Warwickshire, West Riding of Yorkshire, Lancashire, Cheshire, Oldham, South Durham, Scotland and Forest of Dean. James Wilson, a managing partner of Clackmannan Colliery, gave a common reply to the Commissioners' questions on children's employment when he said: "Children are employed to hurry the corves [carts] on the rails; the weight of coal or ironstone therein varies from 4 cwt. to 7 cwt." (1842[381]XVI:491). Similarly, in mines without underground railways, boys pushed wheeled carriages and waggons (called "pushers" or "hurriers") through the subterranean roads in Staffordshire, Leicestershire, Derbyshire, Halifax, North Durham and Northumberland. "In proportion to their strength, boys were also employed in rolling or wheeling stuff in barrows in places where underground tram-roads had not been laid down" (1842[381]XVI:765). The substitution possibilities, however, were not present in all mines and therefore the increase in demand for young children was unevenly distributed. As apparent in the superintendent's descriptions, wooden or iron railways had not been widely adopted by 1842 (1842[380]XV:67-105). Tram-roads had been introduced in the metal mines of Gwennap Consols, Poldice, Treskerby and Wheal Damsel as early as 1824 (RGSC III:65 in Jenkin 1927:223). By 1849 the system was still imperfect.[20]

The introduction of ponies and horses underground lead to substitution possibilities which both increased and decreased the demand for child labor. On the one hand, the adoption of horses for hauling meant drivers and "putters" replaced "barrowmen." Young boys between the ages of ten and eleven were usually hired to drive the horses in the pits (1842[380]XV:66). Commissioners documented children driving horses in the coal mines of Leicestershire, Derbyshire, the southern part of West Riding of Yorkshire and South Wales (1842[380]XV:66-106). Ashton claims that the substitution of boys for men reduced the cost of extracting coal, "The introduction of ponies, greatly reduced the cost of coal, for it meant the barrowmen (who formed the majority of underground workers) could now be replaced by boys whose wages were relatively low" (1964:46). In addition, the use of horse traction reduced the length of the galleries the "putters" traversed by creating a system of main roadways (or horse-ways) and secondary roads (or waggon-roads and tramways). Consequently, boys and young men were hired to drag the corves from the workings to the horse-ways. In Derbyshire, three sets of boys were used to haul coal to the shaft. Young boys drove the horses, other boys dragged corves to waggon-roads where it was placed on wheels and then a pair of boys took the waggons to the shaft (1842[380]XV:69). This subdivision of labor among the haulers was not uncommon (also found in Oldham, South Durham and Forest of Dean), and it increased the demand for child labor underground. At this stage, horses and children were complements in the removal of

TABLE 5.8 Methods of Hauling in Coalfields in Great Britain in 1840s

Mining District	*Methods of Hauling*
South Staffordshire	boys push carriages
North Staffordshire	youths push and draw skips
Shropshire	boys and young men draw carriages by Girdle and Chain method
Warwickshire	boys push waggons on rails
Leicestershire	boys drive horses, push and pull corves
Derbyshire	boys drive horses, drag corves, and push waggons
West Riding of Yorkshire	boys drive horses, push corves on rails
Bradford and Leeds	girls draw by Girdle and Chain
Halifax	children drag wheeled carriages
Lancashire and Cheshire	boys & girls push waggons on rails
Oldham	children push tubs or draw by Girdle and Chain, youths push waggons on rails
North Lancashire	children draw by Girdle and Chain
Cumberland	no children putters or hurryers
South Durham	youths push trams on rails
North Durham & Northumberland	boys push corves
East of Scotland	girls and women carry on backs
West of Scotland	children and youths draw or push whirleys along rails
North Wales	children and youths draw or push waggons with chain
South Wales	youths drive horses and haul, boys drag skips
Forest of Dean	children and youths drag corves, two lads push waggons on rails
South Gloucestershire	children tug tubs by Girdle and Chain
Ireland	no children or youths are pushers, young men drag sledges

Source: 1842[380]XV, pp. 66-106.

coal and together were substitutes for adult men. The practice of using a combination of horse power and child power was widely adopted by the early nineteenth century in coal and metal mines with sufficient capital and adequate roof support.

On the other hand, as the application of horses traction extended into more and more mines and in more and more levels, the need for child "hurriers" diminished. Leifchild recognized this in 1853 when he mused over the effects of progress on the mining labor force, "Amongst the possible improvements of the putter's labour, is the introduction of Shetland ponies into mines. They would do the work well in many mines, but then this improvement would altogether exclude the putters from work" (161). At this point, horses became substitutes for the lads who had been "pushers," "pullers" and "trammers" and the demand for child labor decreased. As the commissioner in the Northumberland and North Durham collieries remarked:

> There is a practice now in use at Hetton and other collieries of substituting for putters small ponies, drawing a different kind of carriage, and taking the coals direct from the hewers to the shaft bottom. The plan is likely to answer and witness thinks of trying it here. It is much cheaper, and would render it possible to do entirely without putters (1842[381]XVI:587).

In the Cumberland coalfields where horses had been widely adopted because "the height of the coal-seams admits of horses being brought up to the workings," no children or young persons were employed in trailing, hurrying or putting (1842[380]XV:87).

There were a few cases, therefore, where children substituted for adults in the mining industry because of the application of new technology. The creation of wheeled corves, waggons and rolleyways to replace wheelbarrows and sledges lightened the labor of haulers. As these innovations were adopted and adapted into more and more mines, the age of "hurriers" gradually decreased, and the demand for child labor grew. By mid-nineteenth century, most coal mines employed boys or girls as "pushers," "pullers" and "trammers." In fact, the proportion of children and youths underground ranged from one fourth to two fifths and most of these were haulers. These numbers, however, were almost certainly smaller by the end of the century. Improvements in rail technology and the innovation of using horsepower underground lead to a substitution of capital for labor. Eventually, horse-drawn carriages on iron rails replaced the child "hurrier." By 1850, however, the use of railways and the substitution of horses for children and youths was far from universal and the employment of children as human asses was still rampant. Although technology may have had contrary effects on the demand for child labor, mother nature did not. In certain situations underground, children were able to perform tasks that were best suited for "little people" and nearly impossible for adults.

Labor Specific Work Situations: Children Working in "Tight Spots"

In the underground coal and metal mines, children could maneuver more easily in tunnels standing only three feet high and operate in small nooks and crannies where adults of larger stature would not have been able to move. Developments in mining during the Industrial Revolution created certain work situations in the pits that increased the demand for child labor which could not be satisfied by men, women, animals or machines. Like the textile industry, young children were in demand for specific tasks because they were small, short and thin and could be more productive than adults. In mining, however, it was not the machinery that gave "little people" the advantage, but it was the nature of the work space underground. The hewers often worked in a contracted space while cutting the coal or working upon the course of the vein. Depending upon the size of the colliery and the method of excavation used hewers worked standing, sitting on their knees or lying on their side. The "putters" or haulers were similarly constricted while traversing the underground levels or roads connecting the workings to the shaft. The tunnels varied in height and width with the largest roads clearing five feet and the smallest less than three feet high. In the latter, where the roadways were so small and narrow that it was difficult for adults to maneuver there was a demand for child labor. Children and in particular, small children, could move freely and haul the coal or rocks with relative ease. As the commissioners concluded in the *First Report on Children Working in the Mines*:

> But when the main ways are under four feet, the coals can no longer be conveyed along these roads by ponies or asses, or even by adults or young men; they can only be conveyed by children. Yet it is in evidence that, in many mines which are at present worked, the main gates are only from twenty-four to thirty inches high, and in some parts of these mines the passages do not exceed eighteen inches in height. In this case not only is the employment of very young children absolutely indispensable to the working of the mine, but even the youngest children must necessarily work in a bent position of the body (1842[380]XV:45).

Why were some roadways so small? In developing the underground workings of the pit the miners digging passageways could have made them larger but chose not to. Why? What factors contributed to the decision to make some roads tall and others tiny?

Digging and securing shafts and internal roadways required time and capital and often included constructing an underground tramway for haulage and stalls for ponies in large pits. The larger the coal bed or thicker the vein of copper, the larger and more complex the pits. Although shallow pits could be sunk in a matter of weeks, very deep pits could take up to four years (Flinn 1984:191). In either case, the size of the underground roadways depended upon the method of haulage to be used and the strength of the strata overhead. Flinn concluded from his research on coal mining for this period, "It was uneconomic to construct roadways of a larger cross-section than was absolutely necessary. Heights and widths were determined by the dimensions of the conveyance used for hauling" (82). There were several ways to haul the coal or ore from the workings to the shaft. In the smaller and more primitive mines, baskets were filled and carried on the worker's back or wheelbarrows filled and pushed along the barren floor. Larger establishments used wooden sledges (called "trams") or wheeled corves which ran along wooden planking. The most progressive collieries built an underground railway (called "rolleyway") using wooden or iron rails. These "trams," corves and waggons were either moved by humans or horses. If powered by human muscle it was typically the muscles of boys and young men that were used to haul the coal and ore filled rock. Thus, there was an increase in the demand for child labor in mines which chose human asses over horses. Why would the management make such a choice? Certainly children could not have been more productive than horses. In what situations was this a rational cost-minimizing decision?

Boys were chosen over horses in the smaller collieries, in collieries with limited capital and where the seams of coal were thin. In the smaller collieries because there was less coal or ore to extract, less time and capital was spent on developing the entrances and subterranean roads. Thus, in trying to minimize tutwork and excavate only that which was valuable, work spaces tended to be more compact and passageways narrower.[21] Proprietors, managers and viewers, moreover, would have expected smaller revenues from smaller mines. Regardless of how accurate their predictions were, the initial development of the mine and the method of haulage adopted was based on this assumption. When comparing the wages of boys with the expense of buying, feeding and caring for horses, hiring boys seemed the cheaper alternative in the short run. The additional expense, moreover, of paying miners to dig higher and larger tunnels so the horse could pass was avoided. Flinn believes this was quite costly and served as a deterrent for substituting horse power for human power (1984: 96). Based on the *Reports of the Mining Districts I* the cost of enlarging the subterranean roadways was substantial for some mining establishments. A commissioner, in reporting the impact of the Mining Act of 1842 in Scotland, highlighted the financial consequences of the law:

> The proprietors . . . published notices of the Act, and called upon their work-people to conform to its provisions. This was possible in some works without occasioning much expense to the proprietor; in others a considerable outlay was rendered necessary for the purpose of heightening the road-ways, and so preparing them, as to enable men or horses to draw the coal from the spot where it was worked, to the bottom of the shaft of which it was to be drawn (1844[592]XVI:1).

Although horses could haul heavier loads, the rate of return was lower because the revenues were expected over a shorter period of time and the costs were higher. Consequently, the passageways were narrower than those found in medium- and large-scale establishments and more suitable for child labor. E. P. Thompson identified the advantage of using child labor in small-scale pits because "the roadways were sometimes so narrow that children could most easily pass through them" (1966:331). This was the case for the small mines in the Oldham district where the superintendent of the mines noted:

> The mines in the thin mountain-seams in the higher parts of Oldham and Rochdale parishes are, with few exceptions, worked on a very small scale, and in a very rude manner. . .Many have insufficient drainage; ways so low that only very little boys can work in them, which they do naked, and often in mud and water, dragging sledge-tubs by the girdle and chain (1842[380]XV:55).

This was also true for many of the mines in East Scotland, Wales and the southern part of West Riding of Yorkshire where the seams were between twenty-two and twenty-eight inches thick. The commissioner noted young children worked in extremely narrow tunnels, "It is obvious that in such collieries all the coal obtained must be conveyed the whole distance from the workings to the foot of the shaft, through a space not greater than that of a common drain" (1842[380]XV:52).

Underground roadways also tended to be small and narrow in establishments with little capital. For many of the adventurers[22] in Cornish mining and the proprietors in coal mining, using horsepower underground required more capital than was available. Capital was necessary to sink shafts, to dig roadways and levels, to drain the mines, to ventilate the workings and to raise the coal or ore to the surface. For example, Leifchild put the cost of sinking a single shaft (11 inches in diameter and 300 yards deep) between 2,000 pounds and 2,500 pounds (1853:100). Flinn documents that in 1775 it cost an estimated 10,836 pounds to develop a new pit at Limley on the Wear, and in 1809, the total investment in building Elswick Colliery was 25,000 pounds (1984:192-199). Horses were already used on the surface to lower and raise the workers, the coal or ore and the buckets used for drainage. Managers aware of the costs and benefits of horsepower must have realized the use of horses for underground haulage was an expensive proposition. A horse would cost 15 pounds and would live and work for twelve to fifteen years (Flinn 1984:96). A continual outlay of funds, however, was necessary because the cost of maintenance was extremely high. Horses had to be fed and cared for daily and since they were usually kept underground, this involved buying feed and hiring boys to look after them.

Several contemporaries who were quite familiar with mining recognized these tradeoffs and made the connection between inadequate capital, low passageways and child labor. Leifchild noticed that the tin and copper mining operations in Cornwall that were barely profitable had especially small subterranean roads. He commented, "In mines which are not very prosperous, some of the passages are very low and confined places" (1857:149). Dr. Mitchell observed that mines with inadequate supplies of capital took advantage of "little children." In his observations about the mines in Warwickshire, he conveys the connection, "In the very small collieries, where a man without capital is endeavoring to get on, and cannot afford the proper means of working his pit, little children are sent into holes in the mines with baskets to get the coals to bring to the foot of the shaft, and they drag them along on their hands and knees" (1842[381]XVI:62). Thus, hiring children who ate and slept at home and received low wages was a cheaper short-run solution to the problem of hauling for some owners and adventurers.

In coal mining, the dimensions of the subterranean roads depended upon the thickness of the seams of coal. To maximize the yield of coal and minimize costs, when the seam of coal was thin the roads tended to be low and narrow and were only widened enough to permit the passage of the waggons and corves. This practice is evident in the following statement made by the Commissioners Thomas Tooke, T. Southwood Smith, Leonard Horner and Robert Saunders: ". . .but then as the thickness of the seam diminished it rapidly becomes more expensive, in proportion to the quantity of coal to be procured, to make the roads for carrying on the operations of the mine a convenient height; and the cost of doing this is materially affected by the nature of the strata both above and below the seam" (1842[380]XV:44). Even the corves were built according to the thickness of the seams. This is conveyed in the comment of a commissioner of the coal mines in Northumberland and North Durham,

"The lowest height which boys are compelled to work is the minimum height of the corf, which is about 3 feet 9 inches in this district. The corf is made to suit the height of the seam, and not, within witness's observation less than 3 feet 8 or 9 inches" (1842[381]XVI:567). In some instances when the seams are too narrow to allow for any passage, the roads are heightened by cutting away both the roof and floor of the seam. When the roof is hard the height was usually 4-1/2 to 6 feet (1842[381]XVI:381-32). Sketches of these underground tunnels were placed in the *Parliamentary Reports* by several commissioners and are reproduced in Diagrams 5.3, 5.4 and 5.5. Despite the rather isolated view of each picture, together these illustrations give a sense of how small and compact some of these tunnels were. If children worked in a crouched or bent position when dragging these waggons, clearly bigger and taller adults would have to crawl on their stomachs to accomplish the same thing. Therefore, the thinner the seam, the smaller the roads and the greater the need for child labor.

DIAGRAM 5.3 Child "Trapper" Working Underground

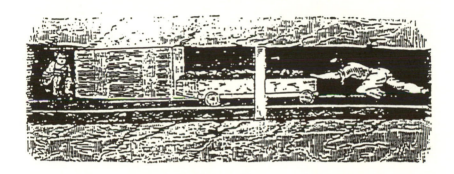

DIAGRAM 5.4 Child "Putter" Working Underground

DIAGRAM 5.5 Child "Drawer" Working Underground

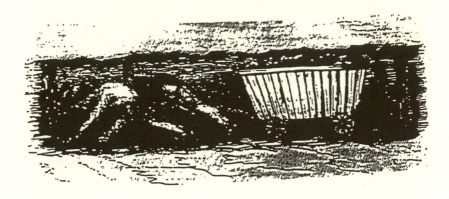

Contemporaries, commissioners and miners recognized the comparative advantage of using children to put and haul the coal from the face to the main roads when the seams were thin. In the *First Report on Children Working in the Mines* the commissioners concluded:

> There is, however, one case of peculiar difficulty, viz. that in which all the subterranean roadways, and especially the side passages, are below a certain height: by the evidence collected under this commission, it is proved that there are coal mines at present in work in which these passages are so small, that even the youngest children cannot move along them without crawling on their hands and feet, in which unnatural and constrained posture they drag the loaded carriages after them (1842[380]XV:259).

Individual colliers expressed a similar sentiment when asked about the necessity of employing children underground. In West Riding a collier stated, "In these places (thin seams), then, the youngest children must necessarily crawl on their hands and feet; and in this posture they drag after them their loaded corves of coals, without wheels, along roads without trams" (1842[380]XV:52). In Yorkshire a collier replied concisely:

> In the thin pits the necessity for, and temptation to employ young children, is manifestly much greater than where the larger sized gates or passages can be easily traversed by larger children; but where the gates vary from two to three feet in height, the posture in which they go along is one which certainly can be easily acquired after nine years of age. The feeling is nearly universal on this point in the districts (chiefly in the Wakefield and Huddersfield Unions), where the thin coal-beds prevail (1842[381]XVI:164).

The tunnels were especially narrow in Ironstone mines because the beds were quite thin, usually from two to three feet in diameter. John Reid, a contractor for Crofthead IronStone Pits, had this to say about the dimensions of the subterranean roads: "Men who are wrought upon iron-stone make their own roads, which rarely exceed 54 inches high, and, from the softness of the roof, soon settles down to 40 inches" (1842[381]XVI:472). Consequently, the proportion of boys to men underground was considerably larger, 70 boys to 100 men in Ironstone pits compared to 30 boys to 100 men in coal pits (1842[381]XVI:8). Making the connection between child labor and thin seams an Ironstone miner commented: "In consequence of the thinness of the beds, horses and asses cannot be employed in bringing the ironstone from the workings to the foot of the shaft, and consequently a proportionately greater number of Children and Young Persons are required for this purpose" (1842[380]XV:196).

The argument that the demand for child labor was greater in coal mines and ironstone mines with thin seams is supported by the information collected in the *Reports on Children's Employment in the Mines*. The *First Report* contains a description of the seams and subterranean roadways of the districts with coal pits and the types of labor employed underground (men, children and/or horses). This information is summarized in Table 5.9. Of the twenty coal mining districts in Great Britain, twelve had some seams and roads under three feet and ten of those say they required the employment of children underground.[23] Unfortunately, the number of children actually employed in each district cannot be traced to verify these claims made by the superintendents. Fortuitously, this information is available for the individual pits in Yorkshire in the *Second Report*. Thirty-four of the eighty mines listed worked seams less than three feet in thickness. In these thirty-four mines, on average, 29 percent of the work force underground was children under the age of thirteen and 31 percent youths between the ages of thirteen and eighteen. Thus, in the mines with very thin seams more than two thirds of the workers underground were under the age of eighteen. On the other hand, the percentages of children and youths employed in mines with seams of five feet or more in thickness were substantially lower. In these fifteen mines, on average, only 11 percent of the work force underground were children and 23 percent youths (1842[381]XVI:Appendix B:210-211).

In order to test the strength of this relationship, a correlation coefficient was calculated for the average thickness of the seam and the percentage of the work force under thirteen and between the ages of thirteen and eighteen in these eighty coal mines. The correlation coefficient for seam thickness and child labor was negative (-.472) as hypothesized but does not indicate a very strong linear relationship. The correlation coefficient for seam thickness and youth labor was also negative (-.205) and indicates a weaker relationship exists. This is not surprising since the argument rests on the small size of children and the thinness of seams; whereas, many older youths would be taller and would no longer have the comparative advantage in working in extremely "tight spots." The results from a cross tabulation of the size of the seam and the percentage of children employed indicate that a systematic relationship does exist.[24] The Chi-Square of 32.515 is significant at the 99 percent level and indicates that the relationship between the size of the seam and the number of children employed is not random.[25]

TABLE 5.9 The Seams and Subterranean Roadways of Coal Mines in Great Britain

| District | Height of Seams and Roads | | | Labor Used |
	Under 3'	3 - 5'	Over 5'	
South Straffordshire			X	Horses
Shropshire	"so thin"			Children
Warwickshire			X	Horses
Leicestershire	"sufficient thickness"			Children, Horses
Derbyshire		X	X	Asses, Ponies
W. Riding of Yorkshire	X	X	X	Children, Horses
Halifax	X			Children
Lancashire & Cheshire	X	X		Not stated
Oldham	X	X		Children, Horses
North Lancashire	X	X		Not stated
Cumberland			X	Horses
South Durham	X	X	X	Horses, Boys
North Durham & Northumberland	X	X	X	Children, Horses
East of Scotland		X	X	Children, Horses
West of Scotland	X	X	X	Not stated
North Wales	"low and narrow"			Not stated
South Wales		X	X	Horses, Lads
Forest of Dean	X	X		Children, Horses
South Gloucestershire	X	X	X	Children, Horses
Ireland	X			Not stated

Source: 1842[380]XV, pp. 47-65.

The historical evidence has supported our intuition that several jobs in the coal and metal mines were particularly suited for people of small stature. The demand for child labor underground was high in coal and ironstone mines because the children were better suited for working in "tight spots." These "tight spots" arose in small mines, establishments with little capital and collieries where the seams were thin. In order to keep costs down and maximize returns, the adventurers and viewers of these establishments chose human haulage over horses. As a result, the underground levels and roadways were small and narrow allowing only a small waggon or corve to pass. The small, short but brawny bodies of boys were ideal for dragging, pulling and pushing the waggons from the hewer to the main roads or to the shaft. As young boys, they doubled up to accomplish this feat, but as they grew older and stronger, they were able to manage the corves on their own. Boys and lads had become productive workers underground in situations where adults would have been useless.

In concluding this chapter, the importance of child labor in the mining industry of Great Britain during the Industrial Revolution should be clear. The increased output of coal and tin and copper during this period was produced by increasing labor and much of this was child labor. The demand for child labor increased because more workers were needed to work the growing number of coal fields and metal mines.

Additionally, as the existing mines grew in size and depth, more workers were hired to work above and below ground. The demand for adult labor also increased because the method of extraction was very labor intensive - the proprietors hired more hewers and more "putters." Although technological change did not play nearly as large a role in the employment of children in mines as it did in factories, there were a few innovations in mining that favored the employment of children over adults. The use of the steam engine for draining mines permitted miners to dig deeper mines and explore deposits which had once been abandoned as unprofitable. Bigger and deeper mines meant that tasks could be divided and laborers could specialize. This created a host of new jobs that children could fill. Due to a shortage of adults, the increase in the demand for labor was met when the butties, hewers and tributers brought their sons and daughters to the mines. Children worked as "trappers," "haulers," "fillers" and drivers underground and were "pickers," "riddlers," "cobbers," "washers" and "screeners" on the surface. They worked alongside adults as "putters" and independent of adults, as the "trappers" and surface workers. With the advances in the technology for hauling, younger children could also be used to haul the corves and waggons full of coal and ore. Younger haulers could transport coal and iron ore when wheeled waggons and tramways replaced the wheelbarrows and sledges. Additionally, more haulers were needed to traverse the complex network of main roads and auxiliary passageways as the underground workings of mines expanded. In some cases, adults and women could have performed these duties if there had been a sufficient supply. In certain situations, however, children were the only workers who could be productive in small, narrow underground tunnels. When the passageways were less than three feet high, even children had to pull and push the waggons on their hands and knees or in a bent over position. Such "tight spots" were present in the smaller mines where the deposits were meager and in mines with limited capital where the coal and ore were removed by the crudest methods. Additionally, the subterranean roads tended to be particularly small in collieries working thin seams of coal. Subcommissioners even noticed the comparative advantage of using children in these places because their "size is suited to the contracted space" (1842[382]XVII:31). These three components increased the demand for child labor and explained why the work forces of coal and metal mines were comprised of between 20 and 40 percent children and youths.

Rising Relative Wages of Children to Adults

If the increase in the employment of children was caused by a greater increase in the demand for child labor than the increase in the supply, their wages would increase. But was the increase in demand for child labor due to the expansion of the industry or work situations or some combination of both? If the increase in the demand for children is mainly attributed to an increased demand for workers due to the large increase in the demand for coal then the relative wage of children to adults will not increase. On the other hand, if the productivity of children was increasing relative to adults because of their comparative advantage of working in "tight spots," we would expect children's wages to rise more than adult wages. The figures in Table 5.10 can be used to test these alternative hypotheses. Was the demand and productivity of children rising more than the demand and productivity of adults in the mining industry or did they rise together? The figures were derived in the same manner for Table 5.10 as Table 4.11 in Chapter 4. The relative wages were derived from actual weekly earnings of "boys" and "lads" ranging in age from nine to eighteen and adult men working in the same mine as assimilated in the *Return of Wages 1830-1886* (1887[C5172]LXXXIX).

The evidence presented in Table 5.10 shows the relative wage of children to adults changing very little in the mid-nineteenth century. Since adult wages were relatively stagnant during this time, changes in the relative wage can be attributed to changes in children's wages.[26] Children's wages are rising relative to adults after 1855 in the Ironstone mines of Staffordshire but fall and then rise in the coal mines of Manchester. The relative wages of boys to men in the Ironstone mines rose slightly from 0.34 to 0.38 during the period 1855 to 1860. In Manchester coal mines, a reduction in the ratio of children to adult wages was followed by an increase suggesting the relative productivity of "hurriers" and "drawers" rose only during the period 1849-1859. This implies an increase in the demand for child labor in mining may have occurred after the period under consideration. This may have been true for youths, but it is highly unlikely that there was an increase in the demand for children after the passing and enforcement of the 1842 Mines Regulation Act. Additional employment data is necessary to discern if there were more youths employed in mining after 1850.

Another more viable explanation for the trend in relative wages involves the implications of family employment. If fathers hired their sons as "hurriers" and "drawers" the competitive model cannot be used to draw conclusions about movements in wages. As stated earlier, the demand for child labor is no longer a derived demand from the final product but instead a derived demand from the father's demand for labor. The assumption that employers hire workers up to the point where their wage equals their marginal product is not valid. Consequently, changes in the child's productivity will not necessarily be reflected in changes in the child's wage. Instead, changes in the child's wages may be reflected in the adult's wage if the two are related and contributing to the same family income. This would imply that the relative wage of children to adults could fall despite a rise in the productivity of the child. Simply put, as a child gets more hauling done, the father earns more money but does not pay his son more. The net result on family income is the same regardless of whether the child's earnings have risen and the father's have fallen or the child's earnings remain the same while the fathers have risen. Consequently, in the case of "hurriers" and "drawers" who may have been employed by their parents, a decline in the relative wage could occur with an increase in the demand for child labor. A definitive conclusion will depend on what proportion of the children work for their fathers. Research on individual wage books of coal mines would be especially fruitful to address the issue of how children were compensated in subcontracting with family members.

The competitive labor market model may also not apply to the demand for "putters" in mines East of Scotland. Some "putters," like "hurriers" and "drawers," may have

TABLE 5.10 Relative Wages of Children/Adults in Mining in Great Britain

County	Description	Year	Relative Wage
IRONSTONE MINES			
Staffordshire			
	Ironstone works	1855	0.34[a]
	Ironstone works	1856	0.36
	Ironstone works	1857	0.35
	Ironstone works	1860	0.38
COAL MINES			
East of Scotland			
	putter/hewer	1812	0.40
	putter/hewer	1814	0.40
	putter/hewer	1822	0.36
	putter/hewer	1823	0.36
	putter/hewer	1831	0.50
	putter/hewer	1832	0.37
	putter/hewer	1834	0.37
	putter/hewer	1836	0.36
	putter/hewer	1838	0.36
	putter/hewer	1840	0.36
	putter/hewer	1841	0.36
Manchester			
	hurrier/miner	1839	0.48
	hurrier/miner	1849	0.45
	hurrier/miner	1859	0.48
	drawer	1839	0.71
	drawer	1849	0.64
	drawer	1859	0.71

[a]See Table 4.11 for an explanation of these calculations.

Source: 1887[C5172]LXXXIX, Return of Wages 1830-1886.

worked for their parents. Therefore, changes in children's productivity and demand for their labor would not necessarily be captured by changes in their wages. Thus, although the figures indicate that the wages of children did not rise and may have even fallen relative to adults, it is still possible that the demand for child labor increased. There are several plausible explanations for why the change in relative wages was negligible, from 0.40 to 0.36, over the entire period. On the one hand this may indicate there was little change in the productivity of miners working underground and the increase in employment of children was due to scale effects, not changes in productivity. As the demand for coal grew, more hewers (adults) and more "putters"

180

(children) were hired to work the mines implying very little change in their relative wage, ceteris paribus. It is also possible that the wages in Scotland are not reflective of miners' wages in England because of their greater reliance on women workers as "coal bearers" and "drawers." Another possibility is that most of the "putters" were sons of the hewers and the competitive model is not applicable. If the market is not competitive, changes in the child's productivity and/or demand for their labor will not be reflected in their wage. Without more data from other areas and information on the familial ties between workers, it is impossible to discern what is behind the downward trend in relative wages found in East of Scotland.

In conclusion, the complexity of the labor market for children in mining makes it difficult to discern whether the productivity of children was rising relative to adults. In contrast to the textile industry, it was not uncommon to find families working together in the same mine. Traditionally, a father took his sons into the mine at a young age to teach them his "trade." Young boys worked their way through the various jobs underground which were stratified by age, beginning as child "trappers" and "putters" and eventually becoming adult hewers. Young girls accompanied their mothers on the surface where they performed a number of tasks in "preparing the coals" or "dressing the ores." As the demand for coal increased during the British Industrial Revolution, the demand for labor to extract the coal also increased. An increase in the demand for adult hewers meant an increase in the demand for child "trappers," "putters" and "drawers." In a competitive labor market, this would imply that the productivity of children increased. In a family-based employment model, the increased productivity of children would translate into an increase in the productivity of adults. Based on the evidence on relative wages presented in Table 5.10, neither hypothesis can be ruled out. The evidence on the relative wages of boys to men does not strongly support the hypothesis that the productivity of children was rising relative to adults because the relative wage ratio fluctuated over the time period. The argument has not been refuted, however, and is plausible in the case of Ironstone workers in Staffordshire and coal miners in Manchester. For these workers, the ratio of children to adult wages falls and then rises again, indicating that an increase in the productivity of adults may have been followed by an increase in the productivity of children. This may be two sides of the same coin if adult miners hired their own children as assistants and did not adjust their pay as their productivity increased. At the same time, the stagnant ratio of children's wages to adult wages in the coal mines in Scotland may also be misleading because of the practice of hewers hiring their own children as "putters." Fathers demanded "putters" and were responsible for hiring and paying them, not the owners. In cases where familial arrangements replace market contracts, a closer look at cost book accounts of mining companies is in order. Additional research and data on the extent of familial employment and the wages of child and adult miners are necessary to understand the rising employment of children and youths in the mining industry. The competitive labor market model continues, however, to be appropriate for many child laborers who worked in the mines. The demand for surface workers, drivers and "trappers," as well as haulers in "tight spots" represented the desires of masters and owners, not workmen. Whether children worked for the masters and owners of the mines or their own parents, it is indisputable that child labor was in demand in the mining industry in Great Britain.

Notes

1. Coal is deposited in beds of varying thickness while copper and lead are usually found in masses and tin in veins (or lodes) of rock.

2. The historians of Cornish mining argue that the output of mines increased when the price of tin or copper increased and when the cost of tools fell (Jenkin 1927:Chapter 4).

3. Since Lemon does not define what ages constitute "children" we cannot say with certainty whether these figures include youths or not. Consequently, these figures may underestimate the number of children working according to the definition of a "child" used in this book.

4. Most of the tasks on the surface were performed by children and youths. Only the weaker men and women worked on the surface in the two tasks which required some strength.

5. For example, a collier would get three tons for a kale (or turn) for a days work. If he brought his child who was between the ages of six and ten into the pits, he would receive an additional one eighth of a kale. If his child was fourteen years old, he received an additional one half of a kale; sixteen years old, he received an additional five eighths of a kale and so on (1842[382]XVII:209).

6. Wages are quoted for children performing a variety of tasks, including "putters" and "drawers," where they were most likely to assist their father (1842[380]XV:158 and 221).

7. The duty is measured by the pounds of water raised one foot by the consumption of a bushel of coal.

8. A shaft is a pit open to the surface while a winze is a pit sunk from one gallery to another. Levels are horizontal galleries excavated in the mineral veins and cross-cuts are horizontal galleries excavated in rocks. An adit is the principal gallery used for drainage of the mine.

9. The payment by tribute or pitch was similar to paying by piece rates in the textiles because it encouraged the miners to be both productive and cost efficient.

10. The figures for coal mines were taken from Table 5.3. The ranges for tin and copper mines were calculated from the employment returns of Dr. Barham's Report in 1842[380]XV:206 and 1842[381]XVI:770.

11. "Riddlers" and "pickers" separated the rock containing ore from worthless pieces and "cobbers" broke the rock open with hammers. Once the ore was pulverized, the "jiggers" and "washers" separated and washed it using a sieve and water.

12. A "foal" was the youngest hauler and preceded the tram full of coal. A headsmen pushed the tram along with a "foal" situated at the front. Alternatively, a pair of youths, each called a "half marrow," worked at each end of the tram, pushing it to the shaft.

13. See Buddle's testimony in 1835[603]V:134-137 and Plate II for a description of his split air coursing.

14. "Jiggers" control the winding machine that brings the material from the pits to the surface.

15. Screening was sometimes done underground but more often above ground. It required a lot of space and when done on the surface meant the waste and invaluable material was raised at cost.

16. The word "bâl" is the Cornish word for mine.

17. The mining terms contained in this table have the following meaning. Jigging is the process where a sieve is suspended in water to separate out the more valuable part of the pulverized ore. Trunking slimes involves clearing out the slime pits in which the mineral mud is collected and wheeling it to the frames. "Framers" then rake a portion of the metalliferous mud in shallow wooden frames using a gentle stream of water. Buddling is a coarser kind of framing (1842[380]XV:234-239).

18. Burke argues the sexual division of labor began at age twelve while these figures show it occurred earlier (1986:183).

19. The use of illustrative materials in the *Parliamentary Papers* was unusual. Commissioner Dr. Southwood Smith asked that graphic wood engravings be included in the *1842 Reports on the Mines* to convey information not captured by words. Most likely, the sketches were done by the Commissioners Scriven, Kennedy and Franks, with the help of someone experienced with geological drawings (John 1980:46).

20. Sims surveyed the mines in Cornwall and concluded that many existing railways were defective and poorly maintained (1849:99-100).

21. Sinking shafts, driving levels and main roads was paid by "tutwork" or task work where workers would get so much per fathom for a given area cleared.

22. The people who financed the working of a mine were called adventurers and each owned shares in the mine.

23. The other two districts did not state what type of labor was used.

24. See Appendix 9 for the results of the cross tabulations.

25. The Chi-Square statistic at the 99 percent level for 4 degrees of freedom is 13.28.

26. To understand trends for men's wages see the seminal article on the standard of living debate by Williamson and Lindert (1983). According to their estimates, colliers' nominal annual earnings were stagnant from 1815-1851 (Table 2:4).

6

The Role of Women Workers

Women and children....were they easily interchangeable as workers in the eyes of the factory owner, the manager, the overseer, the adventurer and the tributer? Did women and children fill the same occupations and perform the same tasks in the textile factories and mines, or did they have quite different duties? Contemporaries commented on the new faces of the industrial labor force, but only a few historians tried to understand and explain the changes that were taking place (Engels 1926; Gaskell 1833 and 1836; Marx 1909 and Ure 1835 and 1836). P. Gaskell connected the new faces with the technological innovation in the textile industry and remarked despairingly in 1836:

> Yet a change is rapidly taking place in the condition of the operatives, and a disposition is developing itself to have recourse to the labour of women and children in preference to adults. The causes which have led to this are the great improvements which are taking place in machinery, and its application to an infinite variety of minute operations, requiring the nicest management, the requisite power being given by steam (143).

Charles Bray in writing *The Industrial Employment of Women* in 1857 also observed the changes and had this to say: "But our industrial system has now absorbed both wife and children, and to retrace our steps will be very difficult, if not impossible" (14).

Recently, several economic historians have begun to reexamine the work of women and children during the Industrial Revolution, but still very little light has been shed on the relationship of child labor to women's labor (Berg and Hudson 1992; Horrell and Humphries 1992 and 1994). Current researchers have followed in the footsteps of their predecessors in their basic approach to these constituents of the labor force. In the literature, women and children have been treated as either two totally separate groups of laborers or as one homogenous group of workers. Pinchbeck's insightful research in 1936 on the role of women workers in industry during the eighteenth and nineteenth century rescued the history of women's labor from oblivion. Subsequently, the complexities of women's employment outside the home have been developed by

Berg (1993), Hill (1989), Humphries (1991), Lown (1990), Rendall (1990), Roberts (1988), Rose (1992), Scott and Tilly (1976 and 1978) and Valenze (1995).[1] Meanwhile, the story of the child laborer and their participation in the industrialization of Great Britain has been told by Cruickshank (1981), Cunningham (1990), Nardinelli (1990), Pinchbeck and Hewitt (1973) and Tuttle (1986).

Preoccupied with establishing a historiography of the woman worker and the child worker, researchers rarely discussed the similarities and differences in their work-related experiences. Several historians have recognized their paths crossed but have presumed away any differences by considering the work of women and children as though it were one and the same (Hammond and Hammond 1920; Rule 1981; Smelser 1959 and Thompson 1966). Neither approach is satisfactory because each ignores the question of whether or not child labor was somehow "special" to the factory owners, overseers and mining agents. If, as I argue, the demand for child labor was increasing during the Industrial Revolution because children possessed qualities and characteristics that made them ideal workers in certain industries, then women and children were not one homogenous group. Children were small and could squeeze and maneuver in tight spaces where adults could not even move. Children by nature were more passive, docile and obedient than adults and usually did what they were told. Children had an unlimited supply of energy and would be in motion for longer periods of time than adults. At the same time, the women and children who worked in the factories and mines had more in common than either group had with the adult male workers. Women, like children, were more docile and less pugnacious than men and hence less likely to organize and engage in collective action against the employers. Women, like children, had greater dexterity in their hands and fingers and were especially talented in detail work (i.e., needlepointing and embroidery). In addition, women like children, were a cheaper source of labor because their wages were less than men's wages. Did women workers have enough in common with child workers that they were considered close substitutes to employers? Or did child laborers have a number of distinctive qualities that made them "special" and consequently better suited for certain jobs?

To adequately address these questions an examination of the jobs and tasks of women working in the textile factories and mines of Great Britain is necessary. Understanding the role working women had relative to the child laborer places the issue into perspective by illuminating to what extent the work of children was unique because of their "special" qualities. If women and children performed primarily different tasks within a given industry then the employment of "women and children" must be reinterpreted by modern historians to account for their separate roles and contributions in production. If women and children were substitutes in the industrial work force then one must explain why more children and youths worked than women. In addition, we would expect to find women replacing children in the factories and mines once child labor laws were effectively enforced. This chapter sheds some light on the relationship of women and children in the production processes of making textile cloth and extracting coal and metal. In these two industries, there were as many differences as there were similarities in the types of work women and children performed during the Industrial Revolution.

The Employment of Women

Many women were working alongside children and youths in the textile factories and mines of Great Britain. Our first hint of the dominating presence of women and children in the textile industry comes from a *Report on the State and Conditions of the Children Employed in the Cotton Manufactories of the United Kingdom* in 1819. As Freudenberger, Mather and Nardinelli discovered, "Women accounted for a little over half of the workers, and children formed a substantial part of the labor force" (1984:1087). The cotton factory employed more women than men; 21.4 percent of the factory labor force were females over the age of twenty compared to 19.6 percent who were male (1087). Dr. Mitchell, a factory inspector, collected returns from 269 textile mills and factories in 1833. In these textile factories, women comprised between 18 percent and 40 percent of the work force. The figures in Table 6.1 are derived from the same source as Table 1.5 in Chapter 1. In this case, however,

TABLE 6.1 Employment of Adults by Gender in Textiles in 1833

Industry and County	Women, Men Employed as % Labor Force	
	% Adult Females	*% Adult Males*
Cotton		
Lancashire	27%	26%
Glasgow	33	21
Aberdeen	38	10
Belfast	40	18
Wool		
Leeds	21	34
Gloucestershire	23	33
Somersetshire	27	38
Wiltshire	22	38
Aberdeen	35	24
Flax		
Leeds	22	20
Marshall & Co., Leeds	18	14
Scotland	39	14
Grandholm, Aberdeen	37	14
Belfast	21	10
Silk		
Derby	34	17
Norfolk, Suffolk, Essex	24	1
Somersetshire	39	4
Paisley	33	7

Source: 1834(167)XIX, pp. 21-30.

the number of females eighteen years and over in the numerous mills in the various districts were compared to the total number of workers in those mills in each district. The number of women working in the cotton, wool, flax and silk mills is significantly less than the number of children and youths employed, often half in many cases. The number of adult females employed, however, exceeds the number of adult males in all but woollen manufactories. The gender differences are greatest in the silk industry where women comprise between one fourth to one third of the work force while men in only one district (Derby) comprise more than one tenth of the work force. It is not surprising that the woollen manufacture was the only textile industry with more men working than women and the lowest percentage of children and youths. Work in the woollen industry had traditionally been reserved for men because combing wool required strength and stamina. Additionally, many of the processes were still done by hand as the adaption of the new machinery to woollen fibers was difficult. The cotton industry, on the other hand, employed a large percentage of women. Almost one third of the cotton laborers were women in Lancashire mills while in mills in Scotland and Ireland the proportions reached two fifths. The practice of employing more adult females than adult males in the textile industries was widespread and continued for decades.

In 1835 and 1839, the factory returns from Dr. Saunder's districts showed the same employment pattern, shown in Table 6.2. In cotton, there were 4,918 females and only 2,945 males working in 1835, and by 1839, the difference had grown even larger where 5,751 females were working compared to 3,156 males. The same was true in the flax and silk factories; whereas, in wool the number of adult males far exceeded the number of adult females - 9,590 men to 3,312 women in 1835 and 10,030 men to

TABLE 6.2 Employment of Adults by Gender in Textiles in 1835 and 1839

Industry	*No. of Mills*	*Employed in 1835*		*Employed in 1839*	
		Females	*Males*	*Females*	*Males*
Cotton	154	4,918	2,945	5,751	3,156
Wool & Worsted	106	1,446	821	1,994	907
Wool	362	3,312	9,590	2,961	10,030
Worsted	193	3,688	1,585	8,308	2,160
Flax	81	2,431	1,363	3,130	1,122
Silk	87	3,653	1,405	4,268	1,125

Source: 1840(227)X, p. 119.

2,961 women in 1839. In 1847, Dr. Horner produced aggregate statistics on the number of workers employed in all cotton factories in Great Britain. In England, there were 98,950 female and 78,783 male cotton operatives employed. The proportion of women to men, moreover, was substantially higher in Scotland and Ireland than England. There were 16,868 females and 5,796 males employed in cotton factories in Scotland and 1,849 females and 954 males employed in cotton factories in Ireland (1850[1141]XXIII:183-4,221,265). Clearly, the textile factories of Great Britain employed a considerable number of women in the nineteenth century.

Not surprisingly, the mining work force was dominated by men and not women. The job of a hewer began as an occupation for the strong and adventuresome males of society and the bonding, apprenticing and training of young lads assured that it remained that way. Despite these mechanisms, however, women were employed underground in the coal mines and on the surface of metal mines. The death of Abigail Jackson in a pit explosion at Gateshead in 1705 shocked the British people (Ashton and Sykes 1929:171). Similarly, Cornish families anguished over the loss of Elizabeth Goyne who was killed in a boiler explosion at the United Hills Mine in 1830 (Vivian 1990:20). But were women regularly employed in mining or were these just a few isolated cases? One might conclude the employment of women was quite extensive after reading many of the comments of the inspectors and witnesses in the *1842 Report on the Employment of Children in the Mines*. R. H. Franks recorded what he saw in the collieries in the East of Scotland: "The coal-bearers are women and children employed to carry coal on their backs in unrailed roads with burdens varying from 3/4 cwt. to 3 cwt." (1842[381]XVI:384). Similarly, he reported women working underground in the collieries in Pembrokeshire, South Wales: "These windlasses are worked by women, and their labour is certainly severe, though only of eight or ten hours of duration" (1842[381]XVI:475). Joseph Fraser, a coal-hewer in the East of Scotland gives an emotional response to an inspectors' query on the employment of women underground. He said disapprovingly, "When women are encouraged to work below they get husbands very early, and have large families, and the children are as much neglected as they have been themselves. There are a vast number of women who work in the pits, and the employment very much unfit them for the performance of mother's duties" (1842[381]XVI:442).

Many historians, however, have considered the case of Scotland and parts of Wales exceptional and argued the employment of women underground was not widespread but varied considerably by region (Ashton and Sykes 1929; Flinn 1984; Humphries 1981; Hunt 1981; John 1980; Nef 1966 and Pinchbeck 1969). The figures in Table 6.3 confirm this. The percentages are derived from information submitted in the *First Report of the Commissioners of the Employment of Children in the Mines* in 1842. The proportions in the report are based on Returns from the "highest class of employers" and are believed to underestimate the number of females employed underground (1842[380]XV:38). Despite this caveat, the commissioners argue that "a sufficient number of Returns have been received to justify the conclusion that they afford a near approximation to the truth" (38). Supposing these totals represent a lower bound for the employment of women, the regional variations are still quite pronounced. Less than 1 percent of the work force of English coal fields were women

TABLE 6.3 Proportions of Women, Children and Youths Working in Coal Mines in 1842

Country and District	Adult Females	Children	Youths
England			
Leicestershire	--	**13%**[a]	**16%**
Derbyshire	--	**12**	**17**
Yorkshire	1%	17	23
Lancashire	.05	13	25
South Durham	--	**13**	**16**
Northumberland and			
North Durham	--	**13**	**18**
East of Scotland			
Mid Lothian	16	9	24
East Lothian	15	12	28
West Lothian	10	15	23
Stirlingshire	12	15	21
Clackmannanshire	11	12	24
Fifeshire	11	8	21
West of Scotland			
Various Mines	--	**7**	**17**
Wales			
Monmouthshire	--	**11**	**21**
Glamorganshire	1	12	18
Pembrokeshire	20	10	23

[a]The numbers in bold highlight those places where no girls were employed.

Source: 1842[380]XV, p. 38.

and in the majority of districts no women were employed at all. If one looks solely at the adult population underground, the ratio of women to men was 1 to 45 in Yorkshire while in Lancashire it was as high as 1 to 12 (1842[380]XV:39). On the other hand, women workers were nearly absent from other English coal mines as they were in the West of Scotland and in Monmouthshire, Wales. In sharp contrast, women were employed in all of the districts in the East of Scotland where they comprised from 10 percent to 16 percent of the work force. In comparing only adults working underground, the ratio of women to men was extremely high, 1 to 3 in the Mid Lothian and East Lothian coal fields and averaging 1 to 5 in the others. The ratio is the highest in Wales in the Pembrokeshire coal mines where there was one woman working for every two men (1842[380]XV:39). As a whole, John (1980) estimates the number of women and girls employed both in and at the top of coal mines was between 5,000 and 6,000 (25). Clearly, women were working underground in the coal mines of Great Britain but not in all the coal mines as the children were.

In contrast, the number of women working in metal mining was comparable to the number of children and youths employed. Unlike the children, however, very few women worked underground in metal mines while the majority were occupied on the surface. Women were employed in most of the metal mines in Cornwall and within a given metal mine there was a higher percentage of women working than in coal mines. According to commissioners, Lemon's paper on "The Statistics of the Copper Mines in Cornwall" contained a complete list of the mines worked in Cornwall in 1836 and 1837 (1842[381]XVI:769). Women were working in 70 percent of the 125 tin, copper and lead mines in Cornwall in 1836 and 1837. In the mines where women were employed, women comprised from as little as 2 percent to as much as 45 percent of the work force, as Table 5.2 in Chapter 5 has shown. Women were working in the some of the smallest operations as well as many of the largest. For example, 44 percent of the 16 workers at Trevarthen Downs were women, 45 percent of the 380 workers of South Roskear consisted of women and 40 percent of the 1,004 employees of East Wheal Crofty were women.

Although it appears that more women were working in the smaller mines than in the larger ones, the relationship is not statistically significant. A cross tabulation of the percent of women workers with the size of the establishment's work force supports this observation. Fifty-five percent of the smallest mines (with 300 or fewer workers) employed a high percentage of women (31-45 percent) while only 11 percent of the largest mines (with over 600 workers) employed as many women, see Appendix 10. The Chi-square Pearson coefficient (7.27) is not significant at the 90 or 99 percent confidence level. Similarly, the relationship between the size of the establishment and the number of child workers is not significant. The Chi-square for the cross tabulation of the percent of child workers with the size of the work force is 1.66, considerably below the critical value of 13.28. Herein lies one of the similarities among women and child workers; women and children tended to be employed in both small and large metal mines. There were a few mines, however, where women were working while no children were (Wheal Bolton, Tresavara and United Hills) and several where the reverse was true; children and youths worked but women were absent (Wheal Andrew, Boscean, Bosorn, Baldue, Ballowall, Cardaze, Wheal Clinton and West Dolcoath to name just a few).

Clearly, women were members of the new industrial labor force in Great Britain, and many of them worked in the same industries where a disproportionate number of children and youths were employed. In the textile factories, women workers outnumbered men workers while in the coal and metal mines the opposite was true. In particular, the fastest growing textile industry, cotton, relied heavily upon the work of women and children. What types of jobs did these women have in the textile factories and mines? Were they performing the same operations as children or were they doing something entirely different? Did employers consider women's labor as a substitute for child labor or was it instead complementary?

Women Working in the Textile Industry

Women and children were both substitutes and complements in the production of finished cotton, worsted and silk goods. Women, like children, worked in every stage of the process of making cloth: cleaning the raw material, carding the raw material into roving, spinning the roving into thread, weaving the thread into cloth as well as finishing. In several of these processes, women and children had identical tasks while in others they performed quite distinct operations in the same department. Horner's Directory of a Cotton Factory presented in Table 4.3 of Chapter 4 and Stanway's Report on the 151 cotton mills in his district presented in Table 4.7 yield considerable insight into the types of occupations held by women. Women were "pickers" and "batters" in preparing the raw material for carding. Women were "Jack-frame tenters," "Bobbin-frame tenters" and "Drawing-frame tenters" in replacing the full cans of sliver from the carding machine with empty ones. Women were spinners, primarily working with the Throstle frame or smaller common mules, as well as "reelers" and "winders" after the thread had been spun. Women were weavers once the power-loom was adopted. In the last stage of production, women were bleachers, dyers and calico printers and put the finishing touches on the cloth (1842(31)XXII:85). Based on the ages given by Horner, younger women between the ages of sixteen and twenty were "tenters" and throstle spinners while females aged sixteen and older were mule spinners and weavers. The testimony of women workers to the factory inspectors during the investigation of children's employment produces a list of occupations consistent with Horner's classifications. For example, Margaret Flanagan (age twenty) was a "picker," Janet Mackenzie (age nineteen) a spinner and Sophia Martin (age twenty-one) a power-loom weaver (1833[450]XX).

Although women shared many of these jobs with men there was a division of labor by gender that persisted in most departments in the majority of cotton, woollen and silk factories. In looking back at the information presented in Table 4.7, a clear pattern emerges for the cotton factories in England in 1833. Carding, throstle-spinning and reeling were predominantly women's work while mule spinning was predominantly men's work. On the other hand, the gender of workers in weaving was more evenly distributed between men and women, although there were more women weavers than men weavers in all districts except Oldham.[2] No pattern emerges for the cleaning and spreading of cotton, however. In Manchester and Bolton, women clearly dominated the work force while in Stockport, Hyde and Glossop more men were employed (1834(167)XIX:124-131).

The division of work along gender lines was most pronounced for the workers in silk factories. Women were "winders," "warpers" and "throwers" while men were weavers, overseers and messengers (1823(H.L.86)CLVI; Adams, Bartley, Lown and Loxton 1983; Malmgreen 1985 and Rendall 1990). According to the returns from thirty-seven silk mills in Macclesfield, Congleton and Manchester in 1834 women outnumbered men in the throwing department by a ratio of 2 to 1 while the number in weaving was evenly distributed (1834[167]XIX:146,149-50). Within each department, the men were employed in highly skilled positions or as managers while women and children filled the majority of the unskilled positions. Most of the boys who had been "reelers" and "winders" left the mill once they were young men, and those who remained became mechanics, weavers or overseers (Adams, Bartley, Lown and Loxton 1983:15). Nevertheless, as the girls grew older some remained "winders" while others became spinners and power-loom weavers. A few women called "Danters" had managerial positions and supervised the children in winding. Although it was unusual to find women in positions of power, it is not surprising since women and children had been employed in various branches of silk manufacture since the Norman Conquest (Warner 1922:20). Some factory owners and commissioners believed that the work in silk mills was not "fitting employment for any considerable number of grown-up Men" (Adams, Bartley, Lown and Loxton 1983:16). This feeling was shared by hand-loom weavers in general as the following statement from the Select Committee on Hand-Loom Weavers' Petition in 1834 reveals, "No man would like to work a power loom, there is such clattering and noise it would almost make some men mad" (1834(556)X quoted in Adams, Bartley, Lown and Loxton 1983:15).

Were the women who worked in factories married? How were the women and children who worked in the factories related in society? Were they from the same family and did they work together or were mothers at home while their children were in the factories? Estimates by Anderson (1971) and Tuttle (1990) place the labor force participation of married women in 1851 between 23 percent and 31 percent for all occupations. These proportions seem fairly representative of the situation in the textile industry. Using a random sample of *1851 Census* households in Lancashire, Hewitt (1958) finds that 27 percent of the women cotton operatives were married. Clearly, married women did work during the period of industrialization in Great Britain, but were they occupied outside the home?

Based on observations of contemporaries and employment figures from the *Parliamentary Papers*, mothers and married women did work in the textile factories. In 1844, Charles Bray collected employment records from 412 cotton mills with a work force of 16,281 people. He reported that 52 percent (61,098) of the workers in these mills were women and 18 percent (10,721) of these women were married. Roughly half of these women (5,314) had husbands who also worked in the factories while 3,927 had husbands who worked in other trades and 821 had husbands who had no regular employment (Bray 1857:16). Although Scott and Tilly seemed to downplay the employment of married women in their work on Lancashire, they found in 1841 that 25 percent of female cotton workers were married (1982:47). Horrell and Humphries' figures for the labor force participation of women during the nineteenth century confirms that married women worked. They estimated the economic activity of women from a data set compiled from fifty-nine sources which includes 1161 cases of married women whose husband was present and working (1995:90-91). Their estimates show that married "women in factory areas showed steadily increasing participation rates after the postwar decline" (100). The *1851 Census of Great Britain* contains, moreoever, additional evidence that married women worked in textile factories. In a sample from the *1851 Census*, 6.7 percent of working married women listed occupations indicating they were employed as skilled textile workers; spinner, throstle spinner and weaver. In this same sample, 10 percent indicated they were unskilled textile workers performing the duties of "minder," "assistant in the textiles," "helper," "winder," "picker" and "scourer" (Tuttle 1990:Table 7).

Factory Inspectors and contemporaries noted the employment of married women because of their concern for the preservation of the family and a woman's and mother's proper role in society. Bray believed a woman's work was to feed, clothe, bear children into the world, educate and nurse her family as well as to make a home "what it ought to be" (1857:12). He argued that women should not be trained for work in the trades, manufactures or professions but should learn to do their job at home better (1857:18). He was very disturbed by the presence of married women in the factories and remarked, "The factory system, and the way in which women are employed in England, make a home impossible, and with it goes every social and moral tie, and society falls to pieces" (16). Others feared that the child labor laws would increase the employment of married women, "By many others it was stated that the restriction of the hours of infant labour would compel the mothers of families to work in the mills; a consequence which is much deprecated as extremely mischievous" (1833(450)XX:63). Factory inspectors noted the employment of married women despite the focus on child labor by many of the commissions. *The Report on Proposed Changes in Hours and Ages of Employment in Textile Factories* confirms the employment of married women as late as 1873. The report states that many cotton and worsted weavers were not only married women but were mothers as well.

> Most weavers are women, many of them married women. They can attend 4 looms with the help of a child. They are paid by the piece (1873[c.754]LX:32).

> Most weavers were women, many of them married women and they return to work within a month after giving birth. They can attend 2 looms and spend much of their time undoing knots caused by defects in the yarn (1873[c.754]LX:48).

Surgeons, medical officers and private practitioners stated their objection to the employment of married women in the textiles industry when employment seemed to be preferred over nurturing an infant. Many compiled "lists" of married women who were working in the factories in their district.[3] In a letter to the Children's Employment Commission (1833(519)XXI:A3 70), a medical officer provides valuable information on the characteristics of the married women employed in New Lanark. The married women who worked were either widowed with children or young mothers.

> Dear Sir,   7th June

> I have at length the pleasure of forwarding to you the accompanying lists, which you requested. That of the married females in the works consists principally of widows with small families, of those in poor circumstances and whose husbands are not employed, and of those recently married, with one or at most two children.

> > Believe me to remain,
> > Your obedient servant,
> > Charles Walker

Of the 171 medical officials asked to testify in 1873, seventy-one said that mothers returned to work in less than a month after delivering a baby and forty-seven said it was more than a month. Regardless of the time frame, they all agreed that returning to work was a "terrible practice." They suggested that a list of women who recently bore a child should be circulated so employers would not hire them (1873[c.754]LX:54). This controversy provides hints about the nature and extent of married women working in the textile factories. Clearly, some married women and mothers did work in the textile factories of Great Britain. In addition, some women worked while they were pregnant and returned to work soon after the baby was born. What was factory work like for these women? Did mothers work alongside their children or were they separated?

Women Laborer and Child Laborer: Complements or Substitutes ?

The only instance where women and children were complements in production was in the spinning department. The young children who worked as "piecers" and "doffers" worked with women spinners in some cases and male spinners in others. Typically, women spinners worked with the improved spinning jennies, small common mules and the throstle frame. Men, on the other hand, were mule spinners and worked with the large common or hand mules. The reason for this differentiation by gender appears to have been related to strength and societal values and not skill. Feminist scholars have shown that whether a job required "skilled" or "unskilled" labor depended more upon the gender of the workers who were to fill these positions than on the objective technical skills needed for completion of the task (Cockburn 1985; Hall 1982; Rose 1992 and Valenze 1995). The subjective nature of "skilled work" is described by Phillips and Taylor (1980):

> . . .the classification of women's jobs as unskilled and men's jobs as skilled or semi-skilled frequently bears little relation to the actual amount of training or ability required for them. Skill definitions are saturated with sexual bias. The work of women is often deemed inferior simply because it is women who do it. Women workers carry into the workplace their status as subordinate individuals, and this status comes to define the value of the work they do. Far from being an objective economic fact, skill is often an ideological category imposed on certain types of work by virtue of the sex and power of the workers who perform it (79).

By applying Phillips and Taylor's reconceptualization of "skill" to the period of industrialization in Britain, Rose (1992) and Valenze (1995) have argued that women's work in the textile industry changed very little during the eighteenth and early nineteenth century.[4] Instead, what changed when production moved outside the home was how society perceived and valued women's work. Hence, despite the high level of coordination and deftness necessary for spinning, female spinners were considered unskilled, low paid, inferior workers. In the discussion that follows, technical and mechanical expertise will be used to replace the word "skill."

All of these spinning machines, except for the throstle frame, required a high level of technical and mechanical expertise and coordination to operate. In addition, some physical strength was necessary to move the wheel or lever that stretched, twisted and wound the thread onto the spindles. As the number of spindles grew from 48 to 100 to 400, this task became more difficult, and only the muscles of men could manage the larger and longer mules. Nonetheless, women did manage at least 288 spindles on the throstle spinning frame without difficulty (Ure 1861:104).[5] This machine was a simpler and compact version of the water frame. Because it was powered by a water wheel it required very little strength to operate.[6]

In every other area of women's work in textile factories, women and children performed similar tasks and were employed in identical occupations. Instead of working together as complementary inputs in production, they worked independently alongside one another as interchangeable laborers. Both women and children were hired as "pickers" and "batters," "sorters" and "scourers," "breakers," "reelers" and "winders" in the various preparatory processes of making cotton, wool and worsted, flax and silk thread. These tasks required very little technical expertise but quickness, good eyesight and nimble fingers were necessary. Although it is impossible to determine whether women and children were perfect substitutes in this type of work, one could imagine some employers may have preferred the energy and low wages of children and youths while others valued the carefulness and thoroughness of women. Similarly, both women and children "tenters" were responsible for tending the carding engines and replacing full cans of sliver with empty ones. This task was neither difficult nor strenuous although the "tenter" did have to constantly stoop to pick up the cans off the floor. In this case, the trade-off to employers would have been the greater strength of women versus the greater durability of children's backs.

It was in the spinning department where the differences in technical expertise and strength between women and children mattered in working with the new machines. Children spun on Hargreaves' original jenny because the number of spindles was limited (to twelve), and they could stand upright and turn the horizontal wheel. As the jenny was improved and more spindles were added and the horizontal wheel was replaced with a vertical one, women proved to be better spinners (Chapman 1904:54). More technical expertise was necessary to spin thread of uniform thickness on as many as 100 spindles at the same time. As technology progressed and machines replicated the skillful movements of the spinner's hands and water and steam power replaced human muscle, child labor was in demand again. It was children and not women who tended the water frame which spun as many as 1,000 spindles simultaneously. To spin on the water frame, dexterity was more important than technical expertise and the low frames gave children the comparative advantage over women (as well as other adults). Once the common mule was developed the demand for strong and adept spinners returned, however, and adults (particularly men) were preferred to children. Therefore, it was not until the common mule became automated in 1829 that women and children worked side by side as spinners using the same machinery. Many youths and women were employed as self-actor spinners replacing the adult male mule spinner. In this case women appeared to be perfect substitutes for children in spinning on the self-actor.

Although hand-loom weaving was an adult male occupation, both women and youths became weavers once the power-loom was adopted. The employment of women and youths as weavers is clear in the *Report from Commissioners on Hand-loom Weavers*.

Some of the weavers (hand-loom), it was stated, had found employment in the power-loom factories; but as far greater proportion of the hands in such establishments are females and young persons, the erection of power-loom factories does not, in the case of adult male weavers, furnish an adequate extent of employment to them which it deprives them of (1840[220]XXIV:607).

Based on the evidence presented in Chapter 4, it appears that women and youths were close substitutes as inputs in the process of power-loom weaving. Several economic historians have argued that women were preferred (Berg 1993; Hammond and Hammond 1920; Nardinelli 1990 and Rose 1992) while others argue that youths seemed to have the comparative edge (Chapman 1904; Smelser 1959; Unwin 1924 and Walton 1989). There is not evidence in the Factory Inspectors Reports to indicate that youths were better power-loom weavers than women. Manufacturers did remark how children were better spinners than adults but did not make similar comparisons about weaving. Moreover, witnesses before the *Select Committee on Hand-loom Weavers' Petition in 1834* testified that the power-loom used women and juvenile labor to the exclusion of men but did not identify youths as having a comparative advantage with the new machine (1834[556]X).

The explanation behind the increasing substitutability of youths and women for men during this period rests on the improvements in the construction of the original power-loom and the invention of the dressing frame. Originally, the power-loom invented by Cartwright (1785 and 1786) had a wooden frame similar to the hand-loom and was so cumbersome it required two strong men to operate it. As improvements were made and numerous variations built, the wooden frames were replaced with metal frames by Roberts in 1822. The machines were easier to use and capable of mass production (Benson 1983:22). Consequently, women and youths were employed as weavers in the factories and displaced many adult male hand-loom weavers. Mr. MacKenzie and Mr. Burges, two witnesses before the Select Committee, made the following observations regarding the new power-looms:

Many of the children of the hand-loom weavers are sent to the power-loom weaving; many of their daughters; and it is the support that they bring into the family that enables a weaver in the neighbourhood of Glasgow to live (1834(556)X:81).

. . .since the introduction of machinery I am given to understand the father and mother have been supported by the work of their children at the factory (1834[556]X:539).

In conclusion, there were many instances where women and children performed the same tasks in the textile factories and mills. They worked side by side in the preparation, spinning and weaving of cotton, worsted and silk. The technological innovations in carding, spinning and weaving reduced the technical expertise and strength necessary to complete each process. Women and children picked and cleaned the raw material and tended the carding engines. They spun on the self-actor and wove on the power-loom. In fact, their small and thin fingers, their agile bodies and quick reflexes made them better machine minders than men. A clear example of this was in the process of winding in the silk manufacture. The comparative advantage of women and children over men is apparent in the factory commissioner's description of the two processes:

(1) The ends break constantly, so that the work and the motion of the fingers is continual. It requires very sharp sight, and we noticed several cases of squint in one of the rooms where this process was going on.

(2). . . to separate the silk and put on a bobbin is done by women and girls because the men's fingers are too clumsy (1873[754]LV:34).

The physical attributes of women, however, made it impossible for them to be substitutes for child "piecers" and "doffers." The tiny fingers and short bodies of children were best suited to piece together the broken threads on the improved spinning jennies, common mules, water frames and throstle frames. Hence, women and children worked together as complements in spinning departments before the self-actor was invented. Women working with the improved spinning jennies, the small mules and the throstle hired and paid the children just as the male spinners on the longer mules did. The quantity and quality of their daily output depended upon the ability of their assistants. Thus, the subcontract system was not gender exclusive and prevailed for women spinners as well as men. As in the case with men, when mothers hired their own children to "piece" for them, the competitive labor market model will not capture changes in the productivity or demand for child labor. This interdependence among family members was not present in the other work they performed in the factories. In the cases where mothers hired their own children as "piecers," the demand for child labor represents the desires and needs of the mother rather than employers to enhance the production process. Unlike other child laborers in the factory, child "piecers" were hired, supervised and paid by their mother (or father). By assisting their mother, children increased the amount of thread she could spin in a given period of time (i.e., increasing the mother's productivty). Consequently, the decision made by mothers to hire their children was based on the desire to maximize her output and hence the family's income.

Women Working in the Mining Industry

Women, like children and youths, did not work in all stages of coal and metal mining. The diversity of jobs performed by women in coal mines is revealed in Mr. Brough's statement about the women workers at the Begelly Colliery he managed in South Wales. He stated that, "The women work very hard, both above and below ground. The nature of their employment was severe. They had great strength and patience. Working at the windlasses below ground, wheeling and skreening coals above, formed their usual occupation" (1842[382]XVII:575). Women worked the "windlasses" underground and prepared and transported the coal above ground.[7] Women also worked as "drawers," as shown in Diagram 6.1. R. H. Franks, a commissioner, provides the following description to accompany the diagram.

In this case a woman is the drawer (for males and females are employed indiscriminately), and a little boy is assisting behind as a thrutcher. . .The mine where this drawing was taken being rather steep, a rope was attached to a post at the top, and by taking hold of this the woman assists herself in ascending to the place where the collier was at work (1842[382]XVII:161).

Underground, women were employed in loading and hauling but rarely worked in hewing. In the eighteenth and nineteenth centuries, hewing was an adult male occupation in Great Britain as it continues to be in the twentieth century. Traditionally, boys worked their way from "foal" to "half marrow" to "headsmen" to "put and hewer" and then finally became a full-time hewer (Ashton and Sykes 1929:20-21). In some cases, these advancements became entrenched due to custom while in others the process was formalized through apprenticeships and bonding. The system of apprenticeships for children and young persons was practiced in South Staffordshire, Yorkshire, Lancashire, West of Scotland and Halifax. Children and youths, particularly from workhouses and orphanages, were bound to a collier until they reached the age of twenty-one (1842[380]XV:41-44). For example, in the West Riding of Yorkshire "hurriers" were apprenticed by the Board of Guardians from the age of eight until twenty-one (1842[381]XVI:70). Thus, it was rare to find women hewers. Not surprisingly, the majority of women who testified before the Committee on the Employment of Children in the Mines were "drawers" like Jane Johnson and "putters" like Isabel Wilson and Elizabeth M'Neil. As Humphries points out, women like Margaret Boxer became hewers only under "extenuating circumstances" (1981:10). Her husband was sick and she took over his job in the mine to support their seven children (1842[381]XVI:475).

Apart from hewing, the tasks underground were not gender-specific as they had been in the textile factories. Women, lasses and lads, girls and boys all worked as "fillers," "putters" and "drawers" performing the same tasks. The subcommissioner from West Riding of Yorkshire, J. C. Symons, commented on this indiscriminate organization of labor. He noted, "There is no distinction of sex, but the labour is distributed indifferently among both sexes, excepting that it is comparatively rare for the woman to hew or get the coals, although there are numerous instances in which they regularly perform even this work" (1842[380]XV:24). Kennedy made similar remarks concerning the employment in his districts. In Lancashire and Cheshire he said, it "is the general custom for girls and women to be employed in the ordinary work of the mines" and in North Lancashire that "girls and women were regularly employed just as boys and men" (1842[380]XV:26,27).

Although women and children were both employed in the loading and hauling, there were a few tasks they did not share. Women were not employed as "trappers" (opening and closing the trap doors), "slackboys" (sweeping the loose pieces of dirt), or drivers (riding the underground ponies). Children were chosen as "trappers" and "slackboys" because they could squeeze into small openings behind the air doors and could maneuver in the tight spots where hewers often worked. Similarly, children were better suited as drivers because they could sit upright on top of horses as they

DIAGRAM 6.1 Woman Drawer in Coal Mines in England

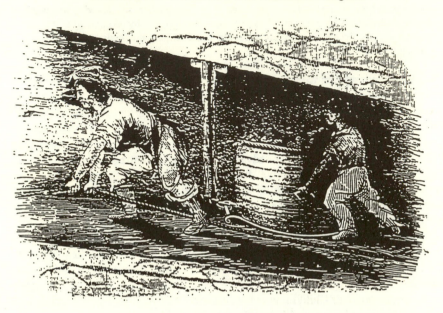

traveled through the low passageways. Women, on the other hand, worked as "windlasses." The muscles of children were insufficient to move the cranks that wound up the loads of coal while those of women had such potential. This crude method of raising coal to the surface was practiced in Wales while in the coal fields of England whim gins (powered by horses) and eventually steam engines were used. Women did not work underground in the metal mines of Cornwall or Devonshire but worked on the surface in "dressing the ores" (1842[380]XV:207).

In the nineteenth century, women worked on the surface in "preparing the coals" and in "dressing the ores."[8] On the surface of coal mines, women filled the same occupations as youths as "wailers" and "screeners" separating the dirt and small coal from the large coal.[9] Moving the screens back and forth required some coordination and strength but no technical expertise. In contrast, women and children did not perform the same tasks on the surface of metal mines. Most of the processes of "dressing the ores" were age- and gender-specific. Girls worked as "riddlers" (separating large ore from small ore) and "pickers" (separating smaller ore from worthless material) while boys worked as "washer uppers" (washing the ore in water); whereas, women worked as "cobbers" (breaking the stones open with a hammer), "buckers" (reducing the size of the stones with anvils) and "samplers" (examining the isolated ore). Most of the work on the surface was considered light and suitable for children and youths too weak to work underground. The process of breaking the stones and isolating the ore with a hammer or anvil (cobbing and bucking, respectively) required strength and stamina. Since the men and lads were occupied underground, women filled the more strenuous jobs on the surface.

The sight of women working on the surface of tin and copper mines in Cornwall had become a familiar one and, for some, picturesque. Dressed alike with a "yard of cardboard" covering their heads and a "garibaldi" tucked inside their skirts, these Cornish bâl maidens worked together under the long open sheds for as many as ten hours a day.[10] These women had a unique socio-economic status as a class of laborers and were admired by contemporaries. Leifchild (1857) marveled in the "grass-work" of the women and believed their singing was a reflection of how much they enjoyed their work. He exclaimed, "There they (the women and children) sit, 'spalling, jigging', 'buddling and trunking', and doing all manner of mining mysteries, and delighting in them too. Hark! well, I declare, the whole set are positively singing a hymn, and singing it in parts too! Listen!" (164). Their revered status is summed up by Jenkin when he reported, "The Cornish bâl maidens formed a class of workwoman to themselves, a class, as a whole, shrewd, honest, respectable, and hard working" (1927:237).

Did married women work in the mines? How were the women and children who worked in the mines related in society? The observations from contemporaries and coal viewers and the personal testimonies from women in the *Parliamentary Papers* indicate that mothers and married women did work in the coal mines until the legislation in 1842 forbid it. Although there is a dearth of statistical evidence on the employment of married women in mining, Horrell and Humphries's figures for the economic activity of women during the nineteenth century confirms that married women worked. Their estimates show that married women did work in mining but that their labor force participation was declining after 1840 (1995:100). The timing of the decline is not surprising since the regulation which prohibited women from working in mines passed in 1842. By 1851, almost ten years after the legislation, a sample from the *1851 Census* reveals that very few women worked in mining (2 out of 2,018 working women) and none were married (Tuttle 1990:Table 7).

Although the number of married women working in mining was not as extensive as it was in the textile factories, family-based employment was more widespread in mining than it was in the textile industry. Jenkin, is his research on metal mining in Cornwall, concluded that "whole families looked to the mines for their support" in the eighteenth century (1927:131). As Humphries points out, "coalminers had for centuries turned to their own families for help" (1981:12). J. Fletcher, a commissioner investigating the employment of children in mines, reveals how widespread this custom was,

> In some few instances the young people are employed by the proprietors, but generally they are employed by the colliers or getters themselves; and if the members of their own families can do the work, they are always preferred. The getters are paid according to the quantity of coals they send to the bottom of the pit, and they may employ whomsoever they please to bring them there (1842[382]XVII:820).

The dependence of the men on their wives and children became apparent to others when the 1842 Mines Regulation Act was passed which forbade females and young children from the pits. The manager of Shott's Iron and Coal Works in Lanarkshire observed that with the family pitching in the men could work fewer hours and earn just as much as they did when they worked alone for longer hours. Mr. C. J. Baird reported that,

> When the Act passed we had females down the pits. Most of them worked with members of their own family. The only disadvantage to the men from the change is, that is they would put out the same quantity of coal they must work longer, or pay a boy to help them. When they had the women to help them they worked eight to nine hours a day; now they work from ten to eleven, earning the same amount per week (1844[592]XVI:45).

The existance of family-based employment in coal and metal mining offers another explanation for the employment of married women and children. If fathers turned to their wives and children for assistance in hauling and isolating the valuable coal and minerals, they could increase their total output without having to reduce family earnings. Whether or not the father paid his wife and children a wage is inconsequential because the earnings stayed within the family rather than going to workers belonging to another family. The competitive labor market model is no longer applicable in the situations where fathers hired their wives and children to work for them. In this case, the demand for married women's labor and child labor represents the desires and needs of fathers to maximize output rather than employers. Theoretically, the demand for married women's labor (and child labor) becomes a doubly derived demand and is not directly measurable in the labor market. This means that the demand for married women's labor (and child labor) is a derived demand from the demand for the father's labor which is derived from the total demand for the coal or ore in the economy. This implies that the employment of married women and children may be high in mining towns due to custom, not technology or poverty.

The testimony of women who worked underground provides additional evidence that married women were engaged in mining during the period of industrialization. Unfortunately, the commissioners did not collect employment figures on the number of married women working underground and on the surface of mines. They did, however, question several female witnesses who were older than eighteen during their investigation of the employment of women in mining. The testimony of these women is proof of their employment as well as an insightful commentary on their work experience. Jane Peacock Watson, aged forty, was a "coalbearer" at Bearings pits, Harlow Muir, Coaly-Burn in Pebblesshire. She confessed,

> I have wrought in the bowels of the earth 33 years. Have been married 23 years, and had nine children; six are alive, three died of typhus a few years since; have had two dead borns; think they were so from the oppressive work; a vast number of women have dead children and false births, which are worse, as they are not able to work after (1842[380]XV:93).

Jane Sym, aged twenty-six and waggonner at Mr. Craig's in Blackrod said,

> I am a drawer; I am a married woman; I work night and day, week about, that is, I work

in the day one week and in the night the next; I don't like working in the night shift; it makes me very tired sometimes, and I am ill with it, but I must keep my turn, or 'clem' [go without food] (1842[380]XV:84).

Betty Wardle tells of working and giving birth to her children in the pits,

I have worked in a pit since I was six years old. I have had four children, two of them were born while I worked in the pits. I worked in the pits whilst I was in the family way. I had a child born in the pits, and I brought it up the pit-shaft in my skirt; it was born the day after I were married - that makes me to know (1842[380]XV:27).

Robert Bald a contemporary and eminent coal-viewer observed,

In surveying the workings of an extensive colliery underground, a married woman came forward, groaning under an excessive weight of coals, trembling in every nerve, and almost unable to keep her knees from sinking under her. On coming up she said, in a plaintive and melancholy voice, 'Oh, Sir, this is sore, sore, sore work. I wish to God that the first woman who tried to bear coals had broke her back, and none would have tried it again!' (1842[380]XV:94).

Unlike the textile factories in which overseers and proprietors hired the children, most families worked together in the mines because the mining masters and agents only hired the hewers or "getters" (the fathers). The method of extraction and isolation of the coal or ores was a decentralized system where hewers hired, supervised and paid their own helpers. The practice of bringing one's family to the mine to work was quite common in England, Scotland and Wales. This is clear in the testimony of miners, mining agents and medical officers from the *Report on Children's Employment in the Mines*. Mr. William Strange, a medical assistant at Llanvabon stated, "They [the people] certainly had a bad practice here of taking children down as soon as they can creep about, many as early as five or six years of age" (1842[380]XV:471). Mr. Samuel Jones, a cashier of the Waterloo Colliery noted, "Fathers carry their children below at four or five years of age" (1842[380]XV:471). Mrs. Mary Lewis, a mother of a mining family exclaimed, "My youngest boy, Lewis, was taken down at five years and three months old, and has been down ever since" (1842[380]XV:471). Mr. William Jenkins, an under-agent to the Gelligaer Collieries added,

Children are taken down as soon as they can crawl. Perhaps it is unnecessary to adduce further testimony in proof of a custom so general and pernicious, and I shall add only the evidence of Mr. John Hoare, the cashier of the extensive works at Cwmavon -'Colliers take their children down to early and labourious employment; and where infants open and shut the air-doors there is very little hope of amendment in the passing generation' (1842[380]XV:471).

There were numerous advantages to hiring family members in the mining industry. Mining required people to work underground in multiple locations, simultaneously. Supervision of the workers in this highly decentralized system was inordinately difficult. It would have been extremely costly and ineffective to have supervisors wandering through the tunnels in order to monitor the worker's progress and productivity. In the textile factories, however, supervision was considerably easier and more efficient because an overseer could roam the aisles of the mill and identify slackers quickly. Consequently, the managers of collieries placed supervision in the hands of the most effective person, the father. Family members were easier to discipline and control and far more dependable because the father was in charge. In addition, the tradition of the family economy instilled in the wives and children a sense of collective purpose in generating income for the family. After examining all the reasons for hiring family members in mining, Humphries argues "the overwhelming incentive to employ family labour was that the wage did not then have to be shared with outsiders" (1981:14). Humphries showed that families were not only compelled to promote their own economic welfare but would also be more likely to rescue one another if an accident occurred (1981:13).

There were many compelling reasons for a family-based employment system in mining. A family-based employment system satisfied the needs of the manager for a diligent, disciplined, dependable work force. It also met the needs of the family in achieving the maximum family income without sacrificing familial interaction and interdependence. Hence, in mining towns, women worked with their families in the mines. Young women, single women, married women, mothers and widowers worked in the mining industry during the Industrial Revolution. But what did they do? Did they work with their husbands and children or were they segregated into different types of jobs?

Women Laborer and Child Laborer: Complements or Substitutes?

Women and children were imperfect substitutes working underground in the coal mining industry. Women, children and youths were used as "human asses" underground to haul coal from the hewer to the main roads or to the shafts. Women pulled, pushed, dragged and carried on their backs loads of coal varying in weight from 2 to 10 cwt.[11] Women were not adverse to hard work as this statement of a mining oversman at Arnsiton Colliery reveals, "Women always did the lifting or heavy part of the work, and neither they nor the children were treated like human beings, nor are they where they are employed. Females submit to work in places were no man or even lad could be got to labour in: they work in bad roads, up to their knees in water, in a posture nearly double" (1842[381]XVI:453-454). The work of a "drawer," "putter" or "coal-bearer" was considered strenuous and although the commissioners were appalled by the women performing such tasks, the colliers appeared to prefer them to lads. Peter Gaskell, a collier in Lancashire, believed women were more productive workers because: "...they were better to manage, and keep the time better; they will fight and shriek and do everything but let anybody pass them, and they never get to be coal-getters, that is another good thing" (1842[382]XVII:217). Others preferred them because their tenure in the job was longer since they rarely became hewers. This preference is revealed in J. L. Kennedy's remarks about the employment of women in Lancashire and Cheshire coal mines:

> Women were employed as drawers, not one woman in a hundred ever becomes a coal-getter, and that is one of the reasons the men prefer them (1842[382]XVII:205).

> They make far better drawers than lads; they are more steady. When a lad gets to be half, he is all for getting coal; but a lass never expects to be coal-getter, and that keeps her steady to her work (1842[382]XVII:215).

Women worked in conditions where lads refused; they lifted heavy loads and remained "drawers" until they left the pit. Based on these types of statements, it is unclear whether the preference for women over young men was due to their productivity or because they posed no threat to the hewer's status. Whichever the case, it is clear that women were relegated to the same tasks as the children and youths. Further, it is entirely plausible that women were preferred to haul coal in the main roads because they could push or pull heavier loads while children were preferred to haul coal in the auxiliary roads because they could maneuver better in tight spots. Numerous commentaries of commissioners confirm that a further subdivision of labor among women and children working existed underground. The necessity of using people of small stature as "haulers" in tight spots is implicit in Commissioner Frank's statement about the coal mines of South Wales. He reported, "The hauler is generally from 14 to 17 years of age, his size is a matter of importance, according to the present height and width of main roads" (1842[381]XVI:474). This was also the case in ironstone mines where the beds were thin but the loads of calcined ironstone heavier than the loads of coal. As a result, children were employed in bringing the ironstone from the workings to the shaft "in consequence of the thinness of the beds, horses and asses cannot be employed" (1842[380]XV:196). Women, on the other hand, were hired as "haulers." A commissioner of the ironstone mines remarked, ". . .the drawing in the ironstone-pits is never done by children, being too heavy for them. It is often, however, very improperly made the work of women, and in other cases migratory Irishmen commence working under ground by engaging as drawers of ironstone, being the business easiest learned" (1842[380]XVI:327).

In Scotland where the largest proportion of women were working underground, the most primitive methods of transporting coal were used. Women, children and youths were "coal-bearers" and carried coal on their backs in baskets or sacks, along unrailed roads and up ladders to the surface.

> The business of these females is to remove the coals from the hewer, who has picked them from the wall-face, and, placing them either on their backs, which they invariably do when working in edge-seams, or in little carts when on levels, etc., to carry them to the main road, where they are conveyed to the pit bottom, where, being emptied into the ascending basket of the shaft, they are wound up by machinery to the pits mouth (1842[381]XVI:383).

This must have required considerable strength and balance as the sacks were often overflowing as the sketches in Diagrams 6.2 and 6.3 illustrate. Contemporaries discovered women doing this work as early as 1793 and were shocked by this class of women "coal-bearers." Robert Bald of Edinburgh had written in 1808 that their labor was "severe, slavish, and oppressive in the highest degree" (1842[381]XVI:384). As a subcommissioner from Wales reported in 1842, this system had become obsolete in all other districts and replaced by methods depending on horse or steam power. He said, "The coal is transported from the different workings by successive windlasses, or balances, working on inclined planes, which plan entirely obviates the necessity of having recourse to the slavish and degrading employment of female labour at present in practice in the collieries in the East of Scotland" (1842[381]XVI:383). Robert Brown describes these strong women in 1851 in a letter to the Duchess of Hamilton, "Muscular strength in a female,-not beauty,-was the grand qualification by which she was estimated, and a strong young woman was sure of finding a husband readily. There is an old Scotch saying, 'She is like the collier's daughter, better than she is bonny,'-proving the value put upon this description of excellence" (1851[1406]XXIII:49).

DIAGRAM 6.2 "Coal-Bearers" in Scotland

DIAGRAM 6.3 "Coal-Bearers" in Scotland

[Janet Cumming.]

[Girl carrying Coals.]

DIAGRAM 6.3 (continued)

[Load dropping on ladder while ascending.]

It is difficult to discern from the evidence available if women and children as "coal-bearers" were close substitutes. Obviously women could carry heavier loads than children, but children and youths had more energy and could make more trips. The amount of coal, however, transported or brought to the surface varied considerably among the children and youths questioned by the subcommissioners in the *Second Report*. Surprisingly, the amount of coal carried and the number of trips made in a day did not seem to depend on the "coal bearer's" age from this scanty evidence. For example, Agnes Moffat who was seventeen, carried 4-1/2 cwt. and made five journeys a day while Isabella Read who was only eleven, carried 4-1/4 cwt. and made four journeys a day. While in this case girls of different ages accomplished similar work in a day, there are also cases where girls close in age did not. In particular, Mary Duncan who was sixteen, carried 2 cwt. and made forty to fifty journeys a day while Margaret Jaques, age seventeen, carried 2 cwt. but made only thirty "rakes" a day (1842[381]XVI:439-464). Unfortunately, the testimony of the women "coal-bearers" did not include the weight or number of trips taken in a day. If the total tonnage of coal transported at the end of the day was comparable, girls, young women and adult women would have been very close substitutes in the underground coal mines of Scotland.

On the surface of mines, women, children and youths were substitutable inputs in the process of "screening the coals" while they were complementary inputs in the process of "dressing the ores." In coal mining, women and children performed identical tasks in "screening the coals." Both were occupied as "wailers," picking out stones and slate from the hewn coal and as "screeners" separating the large coal from the small coal and dust. It was repetitive, monotonous work that required no technical expertise and minimal strength and would have been performed equally well by women and children. Because the commissioners were primarily concerned with child labor, there is very little evidence on the numbers of women employed on the surface of coal mines.[12] The only mention of women working on the surface by commissioners was in the coal mines of South Staffordshire and North Wales where they were "bankswomen."[13] In South Staffordshire the Commissioners Robert Saunders, Thomas Tooke, T. Southwood Smith and Leonard Horner note: "But although no girls or women are employed in the underground work of the colliery in this district, yet it is not uncommon for them to be occupied on the surface in certain descriptions of work connected with the coal pits" (1842[380]XV:35). Similarly, in North Wales they give the impression that the employment of women on the surface was not extensive.

Though in some parts of this district girls and women are employed in particular kinds of work at the surface, no female of any age is allowed to descend into the mines for the purpose of engaging in underground labour. . .The number who work on the surface is comparatively few, and the custom of employing females at all is confined to the district around Wrexham (1842[380]XV:36).

Based on the generality of these statements, it is difficult to substantiate or refute Flinn's claim that few women were employed in this manner. Flinn argued, "Since most surface workers were craftsmen or other skilled workers, however, it is unlikely that women ever formed a substantial portion of the surface labour force" (1984:336). In contrast, there is evidence that large numbers of children and youths were employed on the surface (1842[380]XV:88).

Women and children performed noncompeting jobs in an assembly-type line preparing the metallic ore for sale. The ore was passed from the "riddler" to the "picker" to the "washer upper" and then on to the "cobber" and "bucker." Once pulverized, the ore was washed again (often 100 times) at which point it reached the end of the line and the preparer would divide it into several portions which were then dispersed to the lord, the adventurer and the tributer (Jenkin 1927:135).[14] The size of these piles and the quality of the ore contained in them depended as much upon the "dressers" as it did on the tributer. "Dressers," however, were not usually paid by the piece as tributers were but instead by the day or week. The custom at most metal mines in Cornwail was to contract at so much per bing of dressed ore and the contractor would hire and pay the women and children working for him (1842[381]XVI:846). Even when surface laborers were paid by the tributers or by piece work, care was taken to assure that regular monthly wages were paid (1842[381]XVI:850). This evidence implies that women and children were interdependent laborers in the way that workers on a modern assembly line are today.

In summary, the production relationship between women, children and youths working underground was quite different from those working on the surface. Women, children and youths performed similar tasks underground in loading and hauling coal. As human asses they pulled, pushed, dragged and carried loads of coal from the workings to the main roads or shaft. Women may have moved heavier loads while children and youths made more frequent trips. Both were partially displaced when rolleyways replaced barren floors and horses were utilized underground (1842[381]XVI:444,450). More women may have lost their jobs than children since children could drive the horses and remained the only laborers small enough to transport coal in tight spots. It is difficult to conjecture just how long women, children and youths would have continued to be employed as haulers with the advances in the technology of hauling since restrictive labor legislation was passed.

The 1842 Mines Regulation Act prohibited girls and women from working underground. Women and girls were discharged as this first piece of discriminatory labor legislation in Great Britain was enforced and inspectors of the mines were appointed. Interestingly enough, this did not put an end to the employment of women underground. Several commissioners reporting on the Mining Districts in 1850 discovered that some women were sneaking down before daylight while others were disguising themselves by dressing in men's clothing. H. Seymour Tremenheere was told that women had returned to the coal mines in Monmouthshire, Brecon and Glamorganshire (in Wales): "I was lately informed that at the large and important works of Blaenavon, Clydach, Nantyglo, Beaufort, Blaina, Coalbrook and probably one or two more, females were again at work below ground" (1850[1248]XXIII:59). Similarly, in a letter to Her Grace the Duchess of Hamilton the principal agent of the Hamilton Estates Robert Brown wrote: "Indeed, the poor women, finding themselves unfit for other employment, often eluded the overseers, and stole into the mines dressed in men's clothes, in order to gain a few days' wages for the sake of bare subsistence" (1851[1406]XXIII:50).

On the surface of tin and copper mines where the division of labor created age and gender-specific jobs, women, children and youths performed quite different tasks. Women did the heavier work of cobbing and bucking while girls had the lighter jobs of riddling and picking and boys had the monotonous job of washing the ore. Women and children did work together, but they were not easily interchangeable laborers because they had specialized in very different operations. Instead, they were complements in "dressing the ores" although unlike the spinner and "piecer," some were paid by the owners. This was particularly true in Cornwall while in the Alston Moor District, Scotland and North Wales the surface workers were paid by the contractor or master (1842[381]XVI:786; 1842[382]XVII:369,746). The speed, quality and accuracy of the children and youths in the early stages affected the productivity of the women in the succeeding stages as well as the amount of valuable ore produced for sale.

Women and Children: Complements, Substitutes and Co-Workers in Production

Although previous historians have recognized that thousands of women worked in the textile factories, their role and their relationship to the child workers had not been developed. In fact, between one fourth and one third of the work forces of cotton, flax and silk manufactures were women in the 1830s and 1840s. The number of women, moreover, working in the textile industry grew dramatically from 1841 to 1851. According to the Census, the number of women working in all branches of cotton manufacture nearly doubled from 1841 (82,083) to 1851 (143,268) as shown in Table 6.4. The number working in wool, flax and silk more than doubled for this same period while the number employed in worsted increased by a factor of four. Clearly, women's contribution to the production of textiles in the factories and mills of the eighteenth and nineteenth century cannot be ignored. Although fewer in number, the women who broke with tradition and worked in the predominantly male occupation of mining were just as important. Several thousand women worked underground and on the surface during this period of industrialization. Women took jobs that required considerable strength and stamina. They were employed as haulers and "coal-bearers," "screeners" and bâl maidens and their numbers increased from 1841 to 1851. According to the *1841* and *1851 Census*, the employment of women in the mining industry increased remarkably in a decade. As the totals in Table 6.4 reveal, the number employed in coal mining rose by 30 percent from 1,495 in 1841 to 1,943 in 1851. The increases in employment in tin and copper mining outpaced the increases in coal with 70 percent more women working in copper and 1,140 percent more women working in tin by 1851! Thus, although women workers did not dominate the

TABLE 6.4 The Employment of Women in Textiles and Mining

Occupation	Number of Adult Females Employed[a]	
	1841	*1851*
Textile Manufacture		
Cotton	82,083	143,268
Woollen	14,872	30,554
Worsted	6,151	26,352
Flax and Linen	15,013	31,589
Silk	18,780	43,018
Mining		
Coal-heaver, labourer	310	589
Coal miner	1,185	1,354
Copper miner	913	1,565
Tin miner	68	843

[a]An adult includes anyone 20 years and older.

Source: 1844[587]XXVII, pp. 31-44. 1852-53[1691-I]LXXXVIII, Table 53 pp. cxxi-cxlix.

work forces of coal and metal mines as they did the factories, they were obviously not a dying breed that disappeared by 1850.

Future research on the role of women and children during the Industrial Revolution must recognize that as laborers they were not synonymous. Large numbers of women and children worked in the textile factories, some worked together and others worked independently side by side. In the spinning department, children helped women as "piecers" and "doffers." Women spun on the improved spinning jennies, the small hand mules, and the automated throstle frame. They depended upon the nimble fingers and quickness of their young assistants to increase the quality and amount of thread they could spin. In all the other departments, however, women, children and youths performed identical tasks -- in preparing the raw material, in spinning on the self-actor and in weaving on the power-loom. Similarly, the relationship between women and children working in mining included instances where they were complements and others where they were substitutes. On the surface of metal mines, women, children and youths had distinct, but interconnected, tasks. The amount of ore women isolated by hammering and crushing depended on how carefully the valuable portions of rock had been separated from the waste by the children and youths. Although the productivity of the women "spallers" depended upon the carefulness and thoroughness of the child "pickers" and "riddlers," their wages were not connected. Typically "dressers" were paid by the day or month by a surface tributer or contractor based on age and ability, not output.

The situation underground in coal mines was quite different. Women were hired to execute similar tasks as the children and youths performed. In the districts of England and Scotland where women worked underground, they loaded and hauled the coal from the hewer to the shafts. As long as human asses were used for transporting coal underground, these female "drawers" had the same responsibilities as the children and youths who worked as "hurriers," "putters" and "trammers." Women and children were close substitutes because while women could pull or carry heavier loads, children and youths could make more trips and could maneuver in smaller passageways. Furthermore, the employment of women and children in these occupations continued despite technological advances and restrictive legislation. The 1842 Mines Regulation Act tried to put an end to the employment of women, girls and young children underground but was only moderately successful by 1850. Women and young children were still working as haulers in coal mines in Wales and Scotland in 1850.

Notes

1. See Clark (1995), Corr and Jamieson (1990), Folbre (1991), Hewitt (1992), Hudson and Lee (1990), Smith and Valenze (1988) and Vickery (1993) for recent developments on the role of women at home and in the labor market.

2. Recent research by Rose (1992) and Valenze (1995) thoroughly develops the role of gender in the reorganization of work force in the textile industry as industrialization proceeded.

3. Charles Walker, Dr. Loudon and Dr. Mitchell included lists of married women who worked in their reports (1833(519)XXI).

4. Elson and Pearson (1989) and Milkman (1987) apply these ideas to women's employment in multinational companies in Europe and to auto and electrical manufacturing industries during World War II, respectively.

5. By 1873 the women who minded the throstle frames superintended between 400-600 spindles (1873[754]LV:31).

6. Textile mills in the United States adopted the throstle frame over the mule and employed primarily women (Goldin and Sokoloff 1982).

7. The earliest reference to a woman working underground was in Derbyshire in 1322 (John 1980:20).

8. In the seventeenth and eighteenth century the majority of employees on the dressing floors in tin and copper mines were boys from seven to eighteen years of age (Jenkin 1927:105,133).

9. Women working on the surface of coal mines were called "pit brow" women. The number of tasks they performed expanded during the second half of the nineteenth century (John 1980:77-85).

10. A detailed description of the dress of a Cornish bâl maiden can be found on page 238 in Jenkin (1927).

11. The loaded corves weighed between 2 and 5 1/2 cwt. in England and between 3 and 10 cwt. in Scotland (1842[380]XV:66 and 1842[381]XVI:435).

12. Although the *1841* and *1851 Census* counted the number of women employed in coal mining, it did not distinguish between underground and surface work. In 1874, of the 110,218 people who worked on the surface of coal mines 6,899 were women (John 1980:70).

13. Women who were employed in "banking the coal" unhooked the skip, pushed it forward and emptied it when it reached the surface.

14. Throughout the eighteenth century tin miners were paid in tin stuff while copper miners were paid in money (Jenkin 1927:135).

7

Is Child Labor a Fading Memory?

The employment of children and youths decreased by the end of the nineteenth century but had not disappeared altogether. Many boys and girls were still working in the textile factories while young men continued to work in the coal and metal mines. A *Report on Proposed Changes in Hours and Ages of Employment in Textile Factories* (1873[754]LV) revealed that despite child labor legislation a large number of children were still employed. The figures in Table 7.1 show the number of children over the age of nine who were working in textile factories and mills up to ten hours a day in Great Britain in 1870. The largest number of children--333,041--were employed in the cotton factories, although a considerable number still worked in flax, worsted, wool and silk mills. In fact, over seventy-five percent of the workers in the cotton, flax, worsted and silk manufactories were still children. Clearly, child labor had not disappeared from the textile industries of Great Britain by 1870.

In coal and metal mining, boys and young men were still working underground by mid-century. Based on the commissioners' observations and a few selected enumerations, the presence of children and youths in coal and metal mines is confirmed. After examining the coal fields of Monmouthshire, Brecon and Glamorganshire, Commissioner H. Seymour Tremenheere reported, "The employment underground of boys under 10 years of age had also been resumed in several works by admission of the managers and their mineral agents. At Blaenavan, the mineral agent very frankly stated that there were at least 30 out of 120 boys underground under the legal age" (1850[1248]XXIII:63). Similarly, Commissioner Tremenheere's report of South Staffordshire and Worcestershire coal fields gives the impression that young children were still working underground in 1851.

The crying reproach, however, in regard to the great mass of the mining population of the district, and of those engaged in analogous occupations, remains in full force-that of sacrificing the best interests of their children by sending them to work at the earliest possible age, in order to profit by the small sums they can earn. The excuse that such additions to the receipts of the family are necessary can seldom be valid in this neighborhood, where wages are so high. . .(1851[1406]XXIII:3).

TABLE 7.1 Employment of Children in Textiles in 1870

Industry	Total Employed	Under Factory Acts
Cotton	450,087	333,041
Flax	124,037	100,037
Worsted	109,557	84,607
Wool & Shoddy	128,946	47,302
Silk	48,124	39,071
Jute	17,570	14,943
Print Works	29,567	13,181
Bleaching & Dye Works	31,427	11,393
Hosiery	9,692	6,020
Lace Works	8,370	4,217

Source: 1873[754]LV, p. 6.

Furthermore, the statistics furnished by the Coal Trade Office in Newcastle provide additional evidence that boys and young men were employed extensively in the mines of Northumberland and Durham after the passage of the Mines Regulation Act of 1842. Table 7.2 replicates part of this report which contained returns from 119 coal mines in 1844. Because the two categories of workers, which include boys and young men, stretch beyond the threshhold of eighteen years of age, the totals overestimate the extent of child labor in these mines. These figures, combined with the observations made by the commissioners, however, undoubtedly included many young men between the ages of thirteen and eighteen and several boys under thirteen years of age. The proportion, moreover, of the work force who are occupied as assistants ("putters," "trappers," "fillers," etc.) is high, ranging from one seventh to two fifths and is consistent with the evidence from 1842.

Declining Employment in Textiles and Mining

The proportions of children and youths in the work forces of the textile factories and coal mines were moderately less by the end of the century than they had been for the first three decades. In Booth's (1886) publication, "On the Occupations of the People in United Kingdom," the decline of child labor is irrefutable. Table 7.3 reproduces his employment figures for the textile and mining industries from 1851 to 1881. The employment of children under fifteen in textiles was notable until 1871 when there was a drop from 15 percent of the work force in 1851 to 11 percent of the work force in 1881. By 1881, there were 58,900 boys and 82,600 girls under fifteen still working in textiles and dyeing. The employment of children in mining dropped 50 percent during the second half of the century from 13 percent in 1851 to 6 percent in 1881. Only 30,400 boys and 500 girls under fifteen were still working in the mines by 1881,

Table 7.2 Employment in Collieries in 1844

Colliery	Hewers	Putters, Trappers and Boys under 20 years	Overmen, Deputies Wasteman, & c.	Bankmen, Brakemen, Enginemen, & c.	Carpenters, Smiths, Masons, & c.	Boys of all kinds under 20 years	Persons Employed in Shipping Coals, & c.	Total
River Tyne
Andrew's House	40	32	10	14	4	5	7	112
Benwell	55	78	3	19	18	39	–	212
Burradon and Wideopen	145	109	42	34	26	20	25	401
Coxlodge	92	129	10	47	36	36	–	350
Cramington	245	201	78	104	32	37	17	714
East Holywell	87	54	12	19	6	8	10	196
Elswick	45	50	21	11	10	6	3	146
Fawdon	76	100	42	33	17	15	10	293

(continues)

Table 7.2 (continued)

Colliery	Hewers	Putters, Trappers and Boys under 20 years	Overmen, Deputies Wasteman, & c.	Bankmen, Brakemen, Enginemen, & c.	Carpenters, Smiths, Masons, & c.	Boys of all kinds under 20 years	Persons Employed in Shipping Coals, & c.	Total
Fenham	58	48	15	13	10	5	2	151
Greencroft	34	22	4	8	4	8	6	86
Hebburn	113	109	29	34	22	42	12	361
Holywell	63	38	9	15	5	6	7	143
Jarrow	90	46	27	30	9	16	14	232
Killingworth	105	85	30	27	24	12	20	303
Manor W. E.	134	177	54	42	22	27	15	471
Mickley	75	53	23	10	5	7	21	194
Oakwellgate	36	22	7	6	8	6	3	88
Pelaw Main	88	95	29	52	17	32	11	324
Percy Main	90	107	59	37	13	–	12	318

Seaton Burn	152	80	26	20	10	8	–	296
Seghill	252	135	60	86	32	14	21	600
Spital Tongues	90	71	21	28	7	4	7	228
South Tanfield	56	49	12	10	7	11	8	153
Stormont	65	67	40	18	4	–	7	201
Tanfield Moor	35	63	–	26	15	6	–	145
Tyne Main and Woodside	73	53	55	40	18	16	10	265
Walbottle	99	82	36	43	28	15	56	359
Walker	100	103	56	44	27	17	10	357
West Cramlington	140	69	35	38	12	9	12	315
West Townley and Stella	82	64	30	21	14	15	62	288
Wylam	82	53	20	15	10	7	5	192
Bedlington	120	50	6	19	7	4	11	217

(continues)

Table 7.2 (continued)

Colliery	Hewers	Putters, Trappers and Boys under 20 years	Overmen, Deputies Wasteman, &c.	Bankmen, Brakemen, Enginemen, &c.	Carpenters, Smiths, Masons, &c.	Boys of all kinds under 20 years	Persons Employed in Shipping Coals, &c.	Total
Hartley	102	70	28	34	18	7	11	270
River Wear								
Arbour House	48	25	6	15	5	6	6	112
Belmont	70	53	17	15	16	6	8	185
Castle Eden	244	74	46	40	18	16	12	450
Elvet	78	45	9	19	4	5	6	166
Garmonsway	78	54	28	23	10	13	3	209
Hetton	302	181	126	91	50	36	82	868
Hetton South	157	124	64	77	39	42	15	518
Keepier Musgroe	100	45	24	11	3	14	6	203
Lambton	398	290	149	297	82	118	69	1,403

Monkwear- mouth	100	120	76	64	44	10	46	460
Shield Row	40	15	5	8	2	2	–	72
Shotton	293	194	61	63	21	33	11	676
Thornley	338	244	152	87	46	55	20	942
Washington	65	59	27	19	7	7	10	194
Whitwell	177	58	24	26	13	17	10	325
Murton	146	87	76	68	37	41	–	455
River Tees								
St. Helen's, Aukland	84	65	19	35	8	16	–	227
Black Boy	204	110	28	42	15	19	12	430
Copy Crooks	72	46	17	14	12	13	–	174
Deanery (Pease)	106	49	13	31	11	19	–	229

(continues)

Table 7.2 (continued)

Colliery	Hewers	Putters, Trappers and Boys under 20 years	Overmen, Deputies Wasteman, &c.	Bankmen, Brakemen, Enginemen, &c.	Carpenters, Smiths, Masons, &c.	Boys of all kinds under 20 years	Persons Employed in Shipping Coals, &c.	Total
Etherly and Lands	101	66	15	35	19	15	6	257
Norwood	35	18	6	9	6	5	–	79
Woodhouse Close	76	90	15	20	5	9	–	215
Clarence Hetton	42	32	12	8	2	6	–	102
Willington	66	28	10	10	8	5	6	133
Branspeth	47	21	5	14	9	4	11	111
Hunwick	77	33	11	21	7	3	–	152

Source: 1847[844]XVI, pp. 37-39.

TABLE 7.3 Child Labor in Great Britain 1851-1881

Industry & Age Cohort	*1851*	*1861*	*1871*	*1881*
Mining				
Males under 15	37,300	45,100	43,100	30,400
Males 15-20	50,100	65,300	74,900	87,300
Females under 15	1,400	500	900	500
Females over 15	5,400	4,900	5,300	5,700
Total under 15	38,700	45,600	44,000	30,900
as % of work force	13%	12%	10%	6%
Textiles and Dyeing				
Males under 15	93,800	80,700	78,500	58,900
Males 15-20	92,600	92,600	90,500	93,200
Females under 15	147,700	115,700	119,800	82,600
Females over 15	780,900	739,300	729,700	699,900
Total under 15	241,500	196,400	198,300	141,500
as % of work force	15%	19%	14%	11%

Source: Booth (1886) "On Occupations of the People in United Kingdom, 1801-81," *Journal of the Royal Statistical Society*, XLIX, pp. 353-399.

a far cry from the 28 percent and 30 percent enumerated in the *1841 Census* and *1851 Census*.

In 1870, the composition of the operatives working in cotton factories was noticeably different from the composition in 1835; there were fewer children and male youths but more females over the age of thirteen. As Table 7.4 illustrates, the percentage of boys and girls of the work force fell from 13.2 percent in 1835 to 9.6 percent in 1870. The trend, however, did not continue downward as one might have expected. Instead, the number of child cotton operatives declined from 1835 to 1850 and then began to increase again reaching another peak in 1869 of 10.4 percent before falling slightly by 1870. The trend for female youths, however, is harder to track because the factory inspectors combined the cohorts of young women and women. Thus, without knowing the relative composition of this aggregated category, it is impossible to discern the percentage of female youths employed during this period. Nevertheless, data on male youths is unambiguously clear. The number of young men operatives aged thirteen to eighteen was half as large by 1870 (8.5 percent) than it had been at its peak in 1838 (16.6 percent). Here the downward trend was smooth and continuous. If the employment of young women moved like that of young men, the

TABLE 7.4 Percentage of Male and Female Operatives In Cotton Factories

Cohort	1835	1838	1847	1850	1856	1867	1869	1870
Children, M & F	13.2	4.7	5.8	4.6	6.5	8.8	10.4	9.6
Male, 13 to 18	12.5	16.6	11.8	11.2	10.3	9.1	8.6	8.5
Female, over 13	47.9	53.8	55.3	55.8	55.7	55.0	55.9	53.9
Male, over 18	26.4	24.9	27.1	28.7	27.4	26.4	26.0	26.0

Source: S. J. Chapman (1904), p. 112, from Returns to Factory Inspectors.

number of women operatives must have increased to produce the higher proportions for females over thirteen shown in Table 7.4. Otherwise, it may have been a combination of more young women and older women who filled the employment opportunities in Great Britain's cotton factories.

The composition of miners working underground also changed after 1835. Fewer young boys (under ten) were employed and more young men (aged twelve to eighteen) worked as "putters," drivers and fillers. For coal mines, the reports on sessions 1847-48 and 1849 in *Mining Districts I* and the reports on sessions 1850 and 1857-58 in *Mining Districts II* contain hints that the number of young children employed underground had diminished. As Commissioner Tremenheere noted, "It is generally in the monotonous occupation of opening and shutting air-doors that boys under age are liable, if at all, to be employed" (1847-48[993]XXVI:3). He added in his next report, "It is, I believe, only in the portion of the Yorkshire coal-field where the seams are very thin (from 18 inches to 2 feet) that this clause in the Act is not generally attended to" (1849[1109]XXII:20). Because the commissioner was primarily concerned with enforcement of the Mines Regulation Act of 1842, very little attention was directed to the proportion of boys over ten years of age still employed. Nevertheless, on an aggregate level, Booth's figures reveal that the employment of young men (aged fifteen to twenty) increased from 50,100 in 1851 to 87,300 in 1881. This supports the view that the composition of the mining work force changed as young men replaced boys.

In metal mining, statistics on the composition of the work forces of tin, copper and lead mines after 1842 are incomplete.[1] Jenkin argues that the decline of child labor in the copper and tin mines of Cornwall began in 1870 and by 1890, only a few boys were still working underground. He observed the scores of women and children working on the surface in "dressing the ores" had entirely disappeared by the twentieth century. Young children, moreover, ceased to work underground as they had in coal mines, "Boys no longer go to work underground at the early age which was formerly common. Few will now be found under sixteen years, whilst most of them are older" (1927:309).

Why did the employment of children and youths in factories and mines decrease? Was it the social legislation or economic conditions that led to a decrease in the employment of children as the industrialization process continued? Or was the decline inevitable due to changes in technology?

Social, Economic or Technological Change?

Several explanations for the diminishing role of child labor as industrialization proceeded have been put forth by historians and economic historians. Social historians argue that the rise of the domestic ideology of the "breadwinner - homemaker household" meant a reduction in the employment of women and children. Some economic historians believe the rising standard of living which accompanied the Industrial Revolution increased many families' incomes making the contribution of their children no longer essential. Others believe the employment of children and youths declined because of government intervention in passing child labor laws and schooling laws. Others argue the return to education began to increase with children going to school instead of working in factories and mines. Still others argue that the decline in child labor was inevitable with continued advances in technology and improvements in machinery that reduced the demand for unskilled labor. In reviewing the literature, each of these explanations has some merit and together they provide the most accurate picture of why child labor gradually declined from its peak in the 1830s and 1840s. Both the demand and the supply of child labor decreased by mid-century thereby decreasing the number of children employed in the factories and mines. This is illustrated graphically in Figure 7.1 where employment has dropped from L^* to L' because of the leftward shift in demand, from D_L to D_L' and supply, from S_L to S_L'.

FIGURE 7.1 The Decline in Child Labor

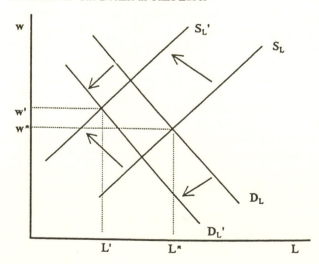

The demand for child labor declined because of child labor laws and technological change. The supply of child labor declined because more and more families were deciding that children should not work as adult wages rose and schooling became a more attractive alternative.

Several social historians associate the decline in child (and women's) labor with the emergence of the domestic ideology that emphasized man's duty to support his family (Davin 1982, De Vries 1994, Land 1980, Levine 1985, Rose 1992, Tilly and Scott 1976 and Valenze 1995). Initially, the movement began among the middle class where "prosperity allowed children and wives to be progressively exempted, not only from wage labour but also partly or wholly from domestic labour, performed by servants" (Davin 1982:639). As these gender distinctions spread from the middle class to the working class, the role of men, women and children in the family economy changed. Men were considered "respectable" if they could provide for their family and allow the wife to devote herself solely to domestic duties and child rearing (Rose 1992:187). Many argue that industrialization and the rise in adult male wages caused the family to become more dependent upon the success of its chief breadwinner (Davin 1982, Levine 1985, Tilly and Scott 1976 and De Vries 1994). Additionally, families' preferences changed so that home-based, time-intensive goods were valued more highly than goods purchased in the market (De Vries 1994:263). The value of a "neat and tidy" home, healthy, curious and learned children increased in the eyes of the mother and father. This shift in preferences changed the role of children in the household from paid laborers with bargaining power in family decision-making to dependent individuals requiring nurturing and education. De Vries describes these changes in family preferences using Becker's model of the allocation of time and his definition of "Z,"[2] "As real earnings rose in the second half of the nineteenth century (the timing varied by social class and country), a new set of Z commodities associated with hygiene and nutrition, the health and education of children, and the achievement of new standards of domesticity and comfort in the home came to appear superior to the available range of market provided goods and services" (263).

The existing model of the family production unit where women and children worked and contributed to the family's income and household decision-making was gradually replaced by the model of the modern patriarchal family. Middle-class values and the new field of political economy espoused by Adam Smith and T. R. Malthus "presumed that the 'worker' was male, and, as a breadwinner, supported a wife and children at home" (Valenze 1995:129). The ideal family was one where men became the sole breadwinners of the household and women became homemakers. Children were to be cuddled and fussed over rather than sent to work. As Davin describes it, the traditional family economy was replaced by a family where men and women lived and reigned in "separate spheres," "Central to it (the ideal family) was the notion of 'separate spheres' - to men the public world of commerce, industry and politics; to women the domestic world, where patriarchal authority was still over-riding, but women had the compensation of moral force, and still had the responsibility for order and stability within the household and family" (1982:639). This division and separation of duties created a hierarchical division of labor within the family and meant that children could no longer be breadwinners nor were they expected to work full time. As children's contribution to family income fell, so too did their bargaining power in household decision-making. Once their contribution was negligible, household interactions and decision making changed; whereby, parental preferences drove consumption and allocation of time decisions.[3] The timing of this transformation of the family economy to the capitalist patriarchy coincides with the decline in child labor. Most historians concur that the "breadwinner - homemaker household" emerged in the first half of the nineteenth century in the upper and middle classes and became a widespread household norm towards the end of the nineteenth century (De Vries 1994:262 and Valenze 1995:102). Therefore, children and youth may have left the factories and mines voluntarily because society and, more importantly their families, no longer wanted them to work all day. This explanation, however, cannot stand alone in explaining the decline in child labor. Quite clearly, most social historians connect the change in family preferences to a change in an economic factor - the rising wages of adult workers.

Just as poverty led families to send their children into the market for work, rising family income reduced the need for children's wages. When families were poor, their children's contribution was often essential for their survival.

> A single child, then, in the middle of the nineteenth century could earn between 10 and 30 percent of an adult male's wage, and such a significant potential contribution to family income would have been further amplified by the presence of more than one working child in the family (Mitch 1982:293).

> When weavers' wages had sunk to 6s. 6d. a week, the earnings of his children in the factory became an integral part of the family income, and parish relief was refused if he had children whom he could send into the mill (Hammond and Hammond 1937:108).

In families where the adults earned an adequate income to provide food, clothing, housing and other necessities, the financial contribution of the children was not essential or necessary. Theoretically, an increase in the income generated by other family members alters the optimal allocation of time so that the child will spend less time in the market working. This is true regardless of how the family's income increases - whether the wage rate of the mother or father increases, or if a parent or kin previously unemployed secures market employment or even if the family obtains some additional nonlabor income (such as inheritance or rental income). In Becker's allocation of time framework, an increase in income generated by parents and other family members is viewed as an increase in the child's nonlabor income. Subsequently, an increase in nonlabor income for the child has a "pure income effect" on the child's allocation of time shifting the labor supply curve inward. Thus, the child may withdraw from the labor force entirely or will spend fewer hours working in the market for wages.

Were wages and family income increasing during the nineteenth century in Great Britain? Unfortunately, the answer to this question is not simple or straightforward. Considerable debate remains surrounding the existence and timing of rising incomes during the Industrial Revolution. The literature on the standard-of-living controversy continues to be interesting and engages many of the best economic historians (Brown

1990, Crafts 1985, Feinstein 1981, Lindert and Williamson 1983 and 1985, Von Tunzelmann 1979). The facet of the debate relevant to an explanation of the decline in child labor is whether and when adult wages began increasing. There is consensus that real wages rose, but some argue the increase was small before 1850 while others believe it was substantial. Flinn (1974) concluded that the gains in real wages during the second quarter of the nineteenth century were less than 1 percent per year. Lindert and Williamson (1985) estimated real wage growth for this period to be 80 percent for all "blue collar workers" and 116 percent for "all workers" (187). Recently, Brown (1990) has estimated that real factory earnings rose 50 percent. He argues, however, that the standard of living increased "at best 10%" during the first half of the century once the welfare costs of urbanization and the decline in hand-loom workers' wages were taken into account (613). Brown concludes that improvements in the living standards of textile workers began to appear during the 1840s and not earlier. Concurring with Brown, Huck finds when correcting for biases in earlier studies, that "1850, or some point in the 1840s, should be seen as the key turning points, as opposed to 1820s" for improvements in living standards (1992:22).

Although some historians argue advances in the standard of living began as early as 1820, others believe it happened nearly two decades later; all would agree that real wage gains were considerable during the second half of the century. Wood's calculations of real wages between 1850 and 1909 revealed, "The Standard of Comfort of the British wage-earner is now, on the average, not less than 50 percent, and probably nearer 80 percent, higher than that of his predecessor in 1850, and that of this advance more than one-half has been obtained during the past quarter of a century" (1909: 101). More recent research has confirmed Wood's findings that real wages grew more rapidly after 1850 than during the Industrial Revolution. Williamson (1985) found the real wages of "blue-collar workers" increased by nearly 64 percent from 1851 to 1911 or 1.06 percent per year (28). Feinstein's estimates show the average real wage rose 31 percent, at 1.58 percent per year between 1882 and 1899 and by 0.29 percent per year from 1899 to 1913 (Feinstein 1990:344). MacKinnon analyzed Bowley's (1937) and Feinstein's (1990) estimates and concludes real wages rose gradually because the increase in full-time earnings in many sectors was tempered by rising prices after 1900 (1994:275). Whether real wages rose more or less than 1 percent each year after 1851, clearly there was a sustained increase in real wages for nearly five decades. Thus, it is plausible that during the later half of the century adults' rising real wages could have contributed to the observed decline in child labor. As the breadwinners' wages grew, families worked their way out of poverty and no longer needed the children's wage to survive.

Historians agree that mandatory schooling requirements were not responsible for the decline in child labor. The first mandatory schooling legislation was passed by Parliament in 1876, several decades after the employment of children had begun to fall in the textile factories and the mines. Furthermore, it was not until the Free Education Act of 1891 that education was provided for the poor. Several historians argue, however, that more parents were sending their children to school instead of to the factories. Both Mitch (1982) and West (1975) concur that there was an increase in the enrollment of children in school during the nineteenth century. According to

Mitch, the number of scholars on registers increased by nearly 50 percent from 1833 to 1851 and then increased more gradually during the second half of the century.[4] Citing evidence from the *1851 Census Special Report on Education* (1852- 53[1692]XC), West concludes more people were attending school (about 12 percent of the population in 1851) and remaining in school longer.

Perhaps an increasing number of children and youths were leaving the labor force and going to school for other reasons. West has identified the spread of education with the growing interest and willingness on the part of working-class parents to pay for school fees and enroll their children in evening schools. Working-class parents believed the value of education was increasing. This perceived increase in the social marginal product of investment in human capital would result in more children and adolescents enrolled in school. Families, searching for a new pareto efficient solution, made entirely different decisions about the allocation of children's time than they had previously. If the future value of educating their children exceeded their children's current earnings, more of the children's time would be allocated to school and less to work. West discovered that Henry Brougham's Select Committee Report in 1820 stated that, "In 1818 about one in 14 or 15 of the population was being schooled. This considerable improvement since the beginning of the century was attributable partly to the energy of ecclesiastical groups, but more importantly as we shall see, to the willingness of parents to pay fees, which indeed in most cases at this time covered the whole cost" (1975:75).

Hopkins identifies this transition from work to school as the most important change in the life of working-class children in the nineteenth century. He concludes, "This enormous economic change (the Industrial Revolution) is the key to so much which happened, and especially firstly the widespread presence of young children in paid employment, and subsequently their being sent to school, not solely on humanitarian grounds, but also because society could afford to educate them, in the hope of their contributing usefully to the economy in later life" (1994:314). The idea of school became more familiar to working-class children and their parents. By the end of nineteenth century, school became a reality for most children.

> We can only guess at the attitude of children to school in these changed circumstances, but it seems a fair assumption that there must have been a far wider acceptance of school by then as a part of the growing-up process. It was no longer something which might or might not happen. Further, the restrictions placed on child labour meant that school was more and more becoming the necessary experience before starting work, and was no longer a possible alternative to work (Hopkins 1994:238).

Families may have seen education as enhancing their children's future income potential because schools began to teach "occupations" in addition to reading, writing and arithmetic. Some of the "topics" taught had a clear connection to the types of employment opportunities the British economy offered. Several hours a week were devoted to teaching the children "fraying stuff," "bead threading," "stick laying," "plaiting mats" and "paper folding" (Hopkins 1994:252). School inspectors noticed the change in the content of what was taught in school. Hopkins quotes Cartwright, an inspector for Northants, from the *Reports of the Committee of Council on Education, 1844-1900,*

> The contrast between the old and new styles would be startling to a teacher of 20 years ago . . . Associated as all our teaching now is with kindergarten principles and varied occupations, and the three R's being taught on rational and scientific principles, and with regular lessons on common objects from the collections in the school museums which have now so largely taken the place of pictures, our schools have greatly increased the powers of observation of the children (1994:255).

Mitch, on the other hand, attributes the rise in the literacy rates and the fall in the labor force participation of children to increasing living standards. He concludes rising income may have contributed more to the increase in school attendance than the existence of any legislation (1982:320-328). In general, whether it was changing tastes of parents and children, social institutions or rising income which encouraged more children to attend school, the ultimate result was the same - a decline in child labor.

Several economic historians, however, have argued that the reduction in children's employment was partly due to labor legislation. Plener (1873) studied the response of factory owners and concluded the effect of the Factory Acts was not only to reduce the number of hours children worked but also to cause a reduction of all labor hours in general. In addition, he argues that by reducing a significant portion of the factories' labor force, the labor laws gave a "direct impulse to the introduction of many of the time-saving machines" (98). Chapman (1904) reported that the factory inspectors' survey showing the percentage of children under thirteen fell dramatically from 13.2 percent in 1835 to 4.75 percent in 1838 (112). Although this decline cannot solely be attributed to the enforcement of the Factory Act of 1833, Chapman clearly believed the legislation had a large impact. He declared, "Children had been displaced by the Act of 1833; the simpler regulations of the Act of 1844 caused their recall" (1904:93).

Marvel (1977) examined the enforcement of the Factory Act of 1833 using an econometric model. He concluded that water-powered-dominated districts were more likely to be charged with offenses and subjected to stiffer penalties (402). He argues that although the clause for enforcement in the Factory Act of 1833 had substance and did impose a cost to factory owners for employing young children, it did not charge all offenders equally.

> The Scottish state of affairs stood in contrast to the situation in England where First Inspector Robert Rickards, and later Horner, brought a number of charges and were reasonably successful in obtaining convictions. Fines, when levied, were variable, ranging from substantial sums (one Halifax millowner was fined 200 pounds) to the minimum penalty of twenty shillings. The vigor of enforcement was evidenced by Ashley's observation that in only two years of enforcement, one of every eleven millowners in Great Britain had been convicted of a violation (1977:384).

Using data from the Inspector's Reports in the *Parliamentary Papers,* Marvel showed the enforcement of the Act was uneven and biased toward the mills which used water power instead of steam engines to move the machinery. Marvel does not address the issue of whether the factories and mills complied with the law or the consequences of compliance but concludes the Factory Act of 1833 "did have a selective impact" (402).

More recently, Nardinelli examines this theory in his 1980 paper, "Child Labor and the Factory Acts," and his book, *Child Labor and the Industrial Revolution* (1990), and concludes that the role of legislation in reducing the employment of children has been exaggerated. He argues, "child labor was already declining relative to adult labor and the Factory Act only speeded up the change" (1980:743). Thus, although fewer children under the age of thirteen were employed by textile factories by 1838, Nardinelli claims that the Factory Act of 1833 was not singlehandedly responsible. Instead he believes technology "played the leading role in reducing the demand for children after 1835" (1980:746).

Contemporaries believed technological change was responsible for displacing the male, female and <u>child</u> laborer. P. Gaskell's research on the influence of machinery on the value of human labor led him to conclude that, "The object of every mechanical contrivance is, to do away with the necessity for human labour, which is at once the most expensive and troublesome agent in the production of manufactured articles" (1836:312). According to T. J. Howell, a factory inspector, the spinning and weaving machinery in textile factories were displacing labor.

> I observe a market reduction in the number of hands employed in the cardroom, in consequence of improved machinery. I have shown that the number of adults employed in the spinning-rooms has been greatly diminished by the introduction of self-actors, and by coupling and double decking. The improved machinery which is applied to the process of dressing will, I am informed, if it should succeed, eventually displace from 50 to 75 per cent of the men employed in that department; as the power-loom has displaced the adult male weaver (1842[410]XXII:13).

I have argued, however, technological change during the Industrial Revolution increased the demand for child labor through the 1840s. In the textile industry, much of the new spinning and weaving machinery increased the employment of children and youths as both helpers and as "machine tenders." The automation of other machinery in the preparatory, spinning and weaving stages (by steam) increased the substitutability of young workers for adults and, consequently, increased the employment of children and youths. Furthermore, the adaptation of steam engines to pump up water from the mines, to raise workers and minerals and to improve ventilation created additional opportunities for children and youths to work as "trappers," "putters" and "pushers."

How can technological change both increase and decrease the demand for child labor? One explanation lies in understanding the process of industrialization that took place in Great Britain. Initially, the male artisans produced goods for sale in their cottages or in small family operated businesses. Considerable expertise and strength were required to use the tools and simple machines that created a unique product. In the first stage, innovations and inventions changed the method of production. Automated machines replicated human movement and reduced the strength necessary to perform various operations. The specialization and the division of labor reduced tasks to simple procedures requiring very little skill. Consequently, women and children with "watchful eyes and nimble fingers" were employed to operate the machines. In the final stage, innovations continued and the machines were improved until they ran independently and required only highly-skilled mechanics to adjust and repair their parts. Therefore, the process of industrialization in Great Britain was labor-intensive before it became labor-saving. This implies that industries caught in the first stage will employ more labor but a different kind of labor - child labor. The textile industry during the first half of the nineteenth century in Great Britain is a perfect example of this.

More than a hundred years later, other economic historians arrived at the same conclusion. Levine (1987) analyzed the path of industrialization and concluded, "Child labour had been an integral component of the first phase of industrialization, it was a marginal one in the second phase" (173). Mokyr (1993) clearly pinpoints the comparative advantage of child workers in the early factories when he asserts, "Factories needed dexterity and discipline, and women and children provided these disproportionately before 1850" (94). Berg and Hudson (1992) go so far as to claim technological innovation was endogenous when they conclude, "The peculiar importance of youth labour in the industrial revolution is highlighted in several instances of textile and other machinery being designed and built to suit the child worker" (36). This seems at least feasible for many of the new textile machines (the original spinning jenny, the water frame and the self-actor) but would not ring true in all cases.

Evidence from contemporaries and *Parliamentary Reports* reveals the textile and mining industry had entered the second stage by the end of the nineteenth century. In the textile industry improvements in the spinning and weaving machinery gradually reduced the number of assistants and operators necessary per machine. Because the industry utilized unstandardized machinery in various stages of modernization, however, textile manufacturers still required the special "skills" of child laborers. Thus, the two main types of improvements taking place after 1850, reduced but did not totally eliminate, the work of children and youths.

In spinning, improvements were aimed at increasing the number of spindles and the speed at which the spindles moved. Dr. J. H. Bridges's and Mr. T. Holmes's report on textile factories in 1873 (1873[754]LV) gives concrete examples of the advances in spinning and weaving machinery. In cotton, the number of spindles more than doubled on the self-actor. In 1833, mules with between 300-350 spindles were commonly found while by 1873, mules had between 400-1,284 spindles with an average of 738 spindles per mule. Factory Inspector Horner recognized the impact such progress had on the number of workers per machine.

The superseding of manual labour by mechanical contrivances is going on rapidly. I have seen an instance of it very recently. On the 29th of March I visited a factory, where I found the following changes. It was one newly built, to which the owner had removed from another mill. In his old mill he had seven pairs of mules, viz. four of 420 spindles on each carriage, one of 450, one of 324, one of 320, - in all 5548; which were worked by 7 spinners and 25 piecers. He has now three pairs only, but each carriage is 126 feet long, and has 1184 spindles, in all 7104; and these are worked by 3 spinners and 18 piecers (1842(31)XXII:6).

In addition, the speed of the spinning machinery had increased because both the velocity of the rotating spindles had risen and the carriage moved to and fro more quickly. The effect on child labor was that, "The number of hands employed in piecing threads at the mule has not increased in proportion to the number of spindles" (1873[754]LV:10). Consequently, two "piecers" were required per spinner on the self-actor in 1873 compared to eight in 1834 (10-11). This places the reduction in the number of assistants considerably later than Nardinelli concluded in his 1980 article. He argued that the reduction in "piecers" took place around 1835 because "the self-actor broke fewer threads" (746). In fact, according to Bridges and Holmes, the faster moving mules broke more threads, typically ten to twelve per minute per "piecer." They reported "In 1873, they witnessed a 'more swiftly moving mule and a larger number of spindles to each hand . . . but a considerably greater number of threads breaking than would seem to have been the case' in 1833" (1873[754]LV:13). Thus, they conclude that the work of the full-time "piecer" was actually harder at the end of the century than it had been decades earlier. Upon reflection they noted, "The piecer of the present day superintends a larger number of spindles moving at a higher rate of speed than his predecessor of forty years ago" (1873[754]LV:12).

In weaving, several improvements were made on the power-loom which made the machines more efficient and permitted them to run faster. The invention of the weft-fork, self-acting templets and the use of a regulator to keep the speed of the shuttle constant helped to produce a more uniform cloth in a shorter period of time. In Britain, however, the specific improvements and their timing varied considerably since "most British machines were produced in hundreds of variants as models were updated regularly" (Benson 1983:27). For example, the invention of the Northrop, which replaced the weft automatically without stopping the loom, was almost universally used in American looms by 1930 while only 5 percent of British looms adopted it (27). Nevertheless, numerous microinventions improved the power-loom by increasing its speed and reducing the labor necessary to operate it. The speed increased from 90-112 picks per minute in 1833 to 170-200 picks per minute in 1873. During this same time period, the number of looms allotted to each weaver increased from two looms per weaver to four (1873[754]LV:16). Thus, as the power-looms in a given factory improved, the number of weavers necessary in the production process fell. As these adjustments and improvements spread from factory to factory, the demand for youths, mostly female, decreased.

The technological advances occurred more rapidly and to a greater extent in cotton and worsted than in wool and flax. The adaptation of the power-loom to textiles occurred first in cotton and worsted. A dramatic increase in the number of power-looms did not occur in woollen and flax until 1868. As Table 7.5 shows, the number of spindles per factor was substantially larger in the spinning of cotton than in worsted or flax. In 1868, the average number of spindles per factor in cotton was 18,300, while it was considerably less than half that in woollen, worsted and flax. In addition, the power-loom was used more extensively in weaving cotton cloth and required less

TABLE 7.5 Advances in Machinery by 1868

The number of power-looms in use in factories

	1850	*1856*	*1868*
Cotton	249,627	298,847	379,329
Woollen	9,439	14,453	46,204
Worsted	32,617	38,956	71,666
Flax	3,670	7,689	31,040
Silk	6,092	9,260	14,625

Average number of spindles per factor

	1850	*1856*	*1868*
Cotton	14,000	17,000	18,300
Woollen	--	--	3,000
Worsted	2,200	3,400	4,600
Flax	2,700	3,700	6,430

Average looms per weaver in 1868 in factories

Cotton	2.5 looms
Woollen	1.3
Worsted	2.2
Flax	1.3
Silk	2.3

Source: 1868-69[4093]XIV, pp. 12-14.

labor than the other textile fabrics. In cotton, worsted and silk, one weaver could tend nearly 2.5 looms while in woollen and flax the average was only 1.3. Because of the differences in the thickness and strength of the thread, woollen power-looms were substantially slower than worsted and cotton looms.[5] Due to these differences and the variations in the spinning and weaving machinery, children and youths continued to work in textile factories and the reduction in the demand for child "piecers" and power-loom weavers was gradual.

In mining, the improvements made to underground tramways and the mechanization of "dressing the ores" eliminated the jobs that children had occupied both under ground and above ground.   The children who had worked as "putters," "pushers," haulers and "drawers" were replaced by horses and engines which conveyed the loads of coal from the hewer to the shaft. This improved technology of hauling was present in the coal fields of Northumberland and Durham in 1849. The commissioner, Seymour Tremenheere, noted this in his report, "The arrangements of mechanical power on the tramway, etc. is so complete, that the labour of one horse only is required in the whole of these extensive works" (1849[1109]XXII:10). Several years later he attributes the declining employment of young boys to the advances in technology.

> . . .and I understand that the tendency of the more scientific working of the collieries, which was becoming more general even before the Act passed enabling the Secretary of State to appoint Inspectors of Coal Mines, and which, under the judicious supervision of those gentleman, is, I believe, rapidly extending, is to make the labour of very young boys far less necessary underground than it use to be (1857-58[2424]XXXII:8).

Unfortunately, the precise nature of the "more scientific working of the collieries" is impossible to glean from Tremenheere's reports. Simonin, however, provides a more detailed account of the changes in his book, *Underground Life*, written in 1869. He maintains by 1860 the technology had advanced to the extent that in some collieries horses were used to draw the waggons on the underground railways in the main roads while in others the trains or trams were conveyed by locomotive engines or drawn by stationary engines (when working on inclined planes). In addition, some of the waggons, carts and trams used for carrying the coal were made of sheet-iron instead of wood and all types ran on four wheels (125-129). Simonin's description of how the method of working mines had improved by 1869 is particularly enlightening:

> No more square-work or falls; no more narrow, winding, and badly-kept roads; no more conveyance on the backs of men: but a methodical setting off of stalls, or a regular system of working away the mineral by long-work, and a rapid conveyance along good roads on underground railways, either by horses or by engines. With all these improvements the cost of winning and raising the coal has been diminished by one-half, and the lives of the men have been less exposed to risks (122).

Advances in the method of "dressing the ores" on the surface of metal mines occurred nearer the end of the nineteenth century. The process of riddling, bucking, cobbing and washing had been mechanized. Belts powered by steam engines moved the metal sieves back and forth to separate the rock and metal (riddling) and raised the hammers and anvils which crushed and pulverized the ore (bucking and cobbing). Water ran continuously with the aid of pumps over the metals to wash away dirt and impurities (washing). Machines performed the tasks which had employed hundreds of the young women and children on the surface of metal mines. The jobs of "riddlers," "buckers," "cobbers" and "washers" were becoming obsolete as mines modernized the dressing process. In reminiscing about the loss of the Cornish "bâl maidens," Jenkin passionately describes these changes in 1927:

> Gone are the ramshackle wooden buildings below the stamps, where scores of women and children formerly earned a hardy living, shifting sand with their long-hilted shovels, or tending the jigs, trunks, strips, hand-frames, square buddles, and other paraphernalia of the old style of tin-dressing. In place of them have arisen crude buildings of galvanized iron and floors of concrete wherein elaborate machinery is driven by belts from a network of

shafting overhead. Human labour, now become so expensive, is in the minority in these new surface-workings, and in great buildings wherein scores of persons would once have found employment the buzz of machinery has taken the place of the "maidens" song and but two or three men may be seen, attendant on the engines (307).

Although the advances in technology for mining fell short of completely automating the industry, as they did in textiles, the production process became more capital intensive and involved fewer auxiliary workers. In particular, the new methods of hauling coal underground and dressing the metal ores on the surface reduced the demand for child labor and female labor. The job of the hewer was lightened with the invention of the machine drill in 1910, but the process of extraction even to this day remains labor intensive.

Child-Intensive Phase and Adult-Intensive Phase of Production

Great Britain went through a child-intensive phase of production as it industrialized from an agricultural economy into a manufacturing economy. This phase, moreover, was industry-specific and lasted over forty years. Children and youths in poor and working-class families had worked for centuries helping on the farm, with domestic chores and with small family enterprises run from their homes. Children and youths helped their parents by doing a wide variety of tasks such as weeding the garden, picking the fruit and vegetables, feeding the horses, fetching water, sweeping the floor, watching the baby, running errands, spinning thread and sewing on buttons. Children and youths were helpers - secondary workers who increased the overall production of the household but never had a central role in production or in generating income. Children and youths were very useful to their families in the production of farming products, domestic goods and final products to be sold in the market. Their contribution, however, was not essential to production. Without their children's help, parents were still able to successfully complete their trade or craft and produce the intermediate or final goods. The production process may have taken longer and required more effort and energy of the parents but it still would have been completed. During the British Industrial Revolution, however, the nature of children's work changed dramatically. Children and youths worked outside of the home in textile factories and coal and metal mines as workers - primary workers who had an essential role in the overall production of the product. Children and youths operated the spinning and weaving machines once they were automated and hauled coal and rocks with imbedded minerals in underground mines. Children swept under machines, tended the combing and dressing machines and opened and closed the air doors in mines. Children and youths worked on their own, and the jobs they held were essential to the successful production of textiles and extracted coal and minerals. They were no longer merely supplementary helpers; they were primary workers. Therefore, the methods of production in the textile industry and mining offered new opportunities for children to work as independent laborers who were contracted to work for a specific wage. Their contribution to production was essential and they were not easily replaced. Thus, the technological innovation which accompanied the Industrial Revolution in the textile industry and mining industry created a child-intensive phase of production markedly different from the previous adult-intensive phase of production.

In the preindustrial phase of the British economy skilled craftsmen and artisans produced goods and services for sale while children were merely helpers. They worked in their home, in someone else's home or in a small cottage making cloth, bonnets, shoes and furniture or cutting hair, sharpening knives, putting on horse shoes and canning food. This was an adult-intensive phase of production because workers needed strength and/or expertise to use the tools in creating an unique product. The quality of the products and services produced reflected the level of craftsmanship of its producer. After years of practice men and women performed their trade while their children assisted in every way possible. Women would spin cotton thread on the wooden spinning wheels while children would fill up the basket with raw cotton. Women would stitch the lace onto the rim while children would weave the straw plait into a bonnet. Men would weave the thread into cloth while children would dye the cloth and hang it out to dry. Men would cut the stiff leather sole while children would hammer it onto the shoe. Children helped their parents by doing simple tasks while youths accomplished more difficult tasks and began to learn the trade. Parents could have performed the children's tasks and probably did on the days when the children were ill. With the help of their children, parents were able to produce more. The contribution of the children, however, was not essential to the production process. Products would still be made and services provided without the children's assistance. This implies that the production process of most goods and services was adult-intensive during this preindustrial phase of development.

During the proto-industrial stage of development skilled labor was still a prerequisite for the production of most goods and services. Skilled craftsmen, tradesmen and artisans used their expertise, strength and experience to produce goods and services for sale while children helped with auxiliary tasks. In several industries, however, some mechanization and division of labor occurred which allowed skilled and unskilled labor to work in tandem. This still remained an adult-intensive phase of production because the workers needed strength and/or expertise to use the new machines. At the same time, these innovations created more opportunities for the unskilled laborer who worked alongside the skilled worker. As the production process was divided into distinguishable tasks, production moved out of individual homes and into workshops, small- and medium-scale manufactories. Some innovations applied to the production processes made it feasible to employ child labor in the cotton industry, the metal trades, calico printing and button making. Children assisted as "piecers" with the larger spinning jennys, as "doffers" with the spinning mule and as "drawboys" for the hand-loom. Children assisted in making nails, pounding studs, dyeing cloth, printing patterns on cloth as well as making buttons. Children and youths helped the skilled adult artisan by performing simple repetitive tasks. Adults could have performed the children's tasks but were able to specialize and become very productive workers with the children's assistance. Thus, the contribution of the children was important but not imperative. Products would still be made without the children but their quality. and uniformity may have been compromised and their numbers diminished.

In the early stages of industrialization the types of technological advances applied to the production of textiles and the extraction of coal and metallic ore displaced skilled labor. Mechanization, automation and the division of labor in textile factories made it possible for unskilled workers to mass produce goods with some uniformity. Several macroinventions and microinventions mechanized the spinning and weaving processes until no expertise was required to spin cotton into thread or weave thread into cloth. Once the water wheel and the steam engine automated these spinning and weaving machines, the "jobs" of spinning and weaving no longer required any strength. And finally, as the principle of specialization and the division of labor was applied to the entire process of making cloth, the number of separate simple one-step tasks proliferated. Children and youths were no longer merely helpers but they became workers whose tasks were central to production. Technological innovation made it possible for children and youths to accomplish in the textile factories what their parents had been doing in cottages. Hence, the child laborers in the factory replaced the adult workers in the home. They operated the spinning (water frame and self-actor) and the weaving (power-loom) machines. They tended the combing machines (for wool), the winding machines (for silk) and the dressing machines (for cotton). Innovations in the production process had created tasks that required stamina and dexterity instead of strength and skill. This was the child-intensive phase of production because child labor was ideally suited for the work in these new factories and mills. Children and youths were unskilled workers whose supple little bodies, nimble fingers and docile nature could survive the monotonous ceaseless demands of the new industrial regime.

Similarly, mechanization and the division of labor made it possible for unskilled workers to increase the production of coal, tin and copper from the mines of England and Scotland. The macroinvention of the steam engine made it possible to ventilate the underground workings of the mine and raise the extracted coal and ore-ridden rock such that larger and deeper mines were excavated. Larger and deeper mines increased the distance between the hewer and the main shaft to the surface of the mines. This implied that the number and length of underground tunnels multiplied requiring more workers to haul the coal and precious ore from the hewer to the main shaft. Several microinventions which produced wooden carts, wheeled corves and underground railways reduced the strength necessary to haul the coal, rock and dirt underground. Applying the principle of the division of labor to the production processes of moving and isolating the valuable minerals and metals dramatically increased the number of simple separate tasks. Children and youths were no longer merely helpers but they became workers whose jobs were critical to the operation of the mines. Little children worked as "trappers" sitting in a crouched position to open and shut the air doors at the critical moment in order to let the miners pass without jeopardizing the ventilation of the air. Children worked as "fillers" placing the chunks of coal and rock into the carts as the hewer freed them from the earth's clutches. Unskilled youths were particularly good haulers because of their small stature and growing strength. The "putters" and " drawers" made numerous trips crawling through the tunnels from the hewer to the main shaft. Once wooden wagons and wheeled corves replaced the wheelbarrows and wooden sledges, youths could haul underground since the carts required less strength to push or pull through the tunnels. On the surface, moreover, children and youths were employed "preparing the coals" or "screening the ores." As the job of separating the valuable coal and ore from the dirt and rock was divided into many separate simple tasks, children were able to perform the functions of filtering, separating and washing in order to isolate the final product. This was not only a labor-intensive phase of coal and ore extraction it was a child-intensive phase because child labor was ideally suited to work in these coal and metal mines. Children and youths were unskilled workers especially suited to work underground because of their short, small, supple bodies that allowed them to move freely in narrow tunnels and maneuver in confined places.

As industrialization progressed and modern industry was born, adult workers operated the machines which produced the goods and services for sale while children were of little use. Adults worked in factories, mills and large-scale manufactories producing intermediate goods (such as thread, cloth, engines, steel) and finished goods (such as clothes, automobiles, computers, sporting goods). This was an adult-intensive phase of production because workers needed some combination of expertise, physical coordination and intelligence to operate, maintain and repair the machines which mass produced identical goods. The quality of the products and services produced reflected the ingenuity of the mechanist and the creativity of the entrepreneur. As technological innovation continued, the machinery got larger and more complicated until eventually it could run without being watched. Children and youths were no longer needed to "tend" the machines. As production became fully modernized in many industries, the machines became highly sophisticated and moved faster and with fewer problems than their predecessors. Children and youths were no longer needed to assist the adults. The child "piecers" who tied broken threads, the "doffers" who removed full bobbins and the "dressers" who prepared the cloth for the weaver on the low wooden spinning and weaving machines could not reach high enough to perform these duties on the new tall metal spinning and weaving machinery. They were replaced by adults who did not require helpers because they operated the machines, corrected any flaws and replaced full bobbins with empty ones. Therefore, the technological innovation associated with fully modernized industries lead to an adult-intensive phase of production dramatically different from the child-intensive phase of earlier industrialization. Child labor disappeared because there did not appear to be any role for children and youths in this new phase.

Is Child Labor Only a Memory?

Child labor is a part of Great Britain's history and it is also a reality of many developing countries today. Interestingly, many current issues surrounding the use of children in developing countries resemble the features of child labor in Great Britain as it industrialized. Presently, children and youths are put to work in only partially modernized labor-intensive enterprises. Some work as assistants to adults while others have the responsibilities of primary workers. They perform simple one-step tasks but often rely on keen eyesight and "nimble fingers." They work long days in poor conditions and earn almost nothing. Pharis Harvey, the executive director of the International Labor Rights Education and Research Fund believes that, "Child labor is growing as a partially-hidden, seldom acknowledged part of industrial and agricultural strategies for global competition" (Child Labor Monitor 1993III:3). According to the ILO, "Child labour is primarily a developing country problem" with the largest number of children employed in Africa, Asia and Latin America. They believe, moreover, that child labor is increasing in the transition economies, especially in Central and Eastern Europe (labornet@igc.org 1998:1). In 1989, the ILO reported the fastest growing area of child labor employment in developing countries is in the informal sector in the brickmaking, construction, handicrafts and food service industries (ILO 1989:38). In 1996, the International Confederation of Free Trade Unions (ICFTU) Report found that:

> at least 15 million children are producing goods for international markets, in agriculture and in industrial production. A much larger number is providing goods and services for domestic consumption, working in the formal and informal sectors. The largest single sector is agriculture, accounting for as many as half of all child workers, many of whom are engaged in subsistence farming, not knowing from one month to the next if there will be enough to eat (ICFTU 1994:1).

Predominantly, children and youths are employed in the small, unregistered enterprises which are either exempt from or not covered by child labor regulations governing larger businesses. Some multinational companies are unaware their products are made by children because of the complex subcontracting arrangements used by their suppliers. Several regional and local studies estimate the participation rates for children and youths range from 20 - 60 percent.[6] As Table 7.6 illustrates, the participation rate varies tremendously from country to country with less than 10 percent of children working in Malaysia and more than 50 percent working in rural Cote d'Ivoire. In several cases, the labor force participation rate in rural areas exceeds 40 percent; such is the case in rural Egypt (43 percent), in rural Nigeria (42-50 percent), and in rural Cote d'Ivoire (54 percent). On the other hand, these studies show the percentage of children working in the market (or for wages) is usually lower than on the farm or in the home. Only 22 percent of the children aged seven to twelve were involved in market work in the Bicol region in the Philippines while as many as 44 percent of the children aged thirteen to seventeen were involved in market work.

The *World Development Report 1995* (WDR) presents similar estimates of the labor force participation of workers in different countries. The ILO defines participation as involvement in "income-generating activities, whether in the home, on the family farm or enterprise, or in the labor market" (WDR 1995:24). Uganda has the highest labor force participation rate for children aged ten to fourteen; 40 percent for boys and 30 percent for girls. Pakistan has the next to highest with 10 percent of boys aged ten to fourteen working and 5 percent of girls aged ten to fourteen working. Not surprisingly, youths have a higher labor force participation rate than children.

TABLE 7.6 Labor Force Participation of Children in Various Countries

Country and source	*Children*	*Participation Rate*
Rural Egypt, 1975	Ages 6-11	17%
(Levy 1985)	Ages 12-14	43
Rural Nigeria, 1992	Work on farm	42-50
two villages	Work at home	52-61
(Okojie 1993)	Trading	24-27
	Craftwork	16-21
	Food processing	26-30
Philippines, 1983	Market work:	
Bicol region	Ages 7-12	22
(DeGraff et al. 1993)	Ages 13-17	44
	Home production:	
	Ages 7-12	49
	Ages 13-17	68
Rural Pakistan, 1990	Boys	19-25
(Sathar 1993)	Girls	22-32
Pakistan, 1985	Ages 10-14:	
(Cochrane et al. 1990)	Boys	31
	Girls	7
Rural Maharashtra, India	Household work:	
one district	Boys	34
(Jejeebhoy 1993)	Girls	65
	Family work:	
	Boys	24
	Girls	16
	Wage Work:	
	Boys	9
	Girls	6
Malaysia, 1980	Ages 10-14:	6
(Jomo 1992)	Boys	7
	Girls	4
Cote d'Ivoire, 1986	Ages 10-14	
(Cochrane et al. 1990)	Urban:	
	Boys	5
	Girls	6
	Rural:	
	Boys	55
	Girls	54

(continues)

TABLE 7.6 (continued)

Country and source	Children	Participation Rate
Peru, 1986	Ages 10-14:	
(Cochrane et al. 1990)	Boys	41%
	Girls	38

Source: Grootaert and Kanbur (1995), Table 1:190. Reprinted with permission.

Boys aged fifteen to nineteen have a higher participation rate than girls of the same age; where 80 percent of boys in Uganda are working, 60 percent in Pakistan and Brazil are working, 40 percent in Romania are working and 20 percent in Japan are working (WDR 1995:24). The labor force participation rate for girls aged fifteen to nineteen is considerably lower with 58 percent in Uganda working, 40 percent in Romania working, 28 percent in Brazil are working and less than 20 percent in Japan and Pakistan working (WDR 1995:24). These figures, however, may be an underestimate since the domestic work many girls perform (in their own home or in other people's homes) goes unreported because it is not always included in surveys as work. The U. S. Department of Labor claims that domestic service "is a commonplace and widely-accepted practice throughout Asia, the Americas, and Africa. Because many child domestics work and live within the confines of private homes, they are perhaps the most invisible of all child workers. While there are no reliable national or international figures on the number of children engaged in domestic services, the figure is estimated to be in the millions worldwide and possibly on the increase" (1995:144-145). Obviously, child labor is not only a mere memory from the eighteenth and nineteenth centuries but it is also a reality of the twentieth century.

The Employment of Children in Developing Countries

Where are the child laborers in developing countries working and what are they doing? In India children work in several labor-intensive industries producing goods for export. They weave carpets, throw silk, clean gemstones, sew clothes, condition leather and make matches. Child labor is important in the glass bangle industry in Firozabad, the jewelry industry in West Bengal and Gujarat, the slate-making industry in Madhya Pradesh and in the carpet and brick-kiln industries throughout the country (Kanbargi 1988:93). The employment of children is also prevalent in the fireworks and match industries in Sivakasi, the manufacture of shoes in Agra and the glassware industry in Ferozabad (U. S. Dept. of Labor 1994:73-93). In 1993 it was reported that, "Throughout South Asia some 55 million child laborers toil away their days. They work in many export industries, including glass blowing, brass and garment manufactory. In Carpet weaving alone, over one million children are forced to work in slave-like conditions" (Child Labor Monitor 1993III:4). Most of the children who work in the hand-knotted carpet industry spend six to twelve hours a day in small earthen shacks or sheds in villages. They often begin work at age six as an unpaid apprentice or a bonded laborer.[7] The children who work in glass factories begin work at age eleven. They toil long hours to produce bangles, chandeliers, wine glasses, beads, bulbs and crockery. According to the International Labor Rights Education and Research Fund, these children work in "Dante's Inferno" where the heat reaches 1,600 Celsius, broken glass litters the floor, electric wires hang from the ceiling and workers do not wear shoes, gloves or goggles (U. S. Dept. of Labor 1994:80). The young children who make India's matches work ten to twelve hour days, seven days a week. The children, mostly girls, must "rapidly pound match sticks on their chests" as part of the match-making process (American Federation of Teachers (AFT) 1998:5). They work for subcontractors in small factories or sheds which are usually not registered with the government.

Establishing a precise figure for the number of children and youths who work in these industries and their labor force participation rate is problematic. Parents may lie about their child's age and employers have an incentive to under report because of child labor laws. The government of India estimated in 1985 that 17.5 million children were working while at the same time, the Operations Research Group - Baroda concluded that 44 million children were working. Recently, the Center for Concern for Working Children approximated the number of children not attending school and concluded that 100 million children work (U. S. Department of Labor 1994:73). Regardless of the exact number, India has the largest number of child laborers in the world. The labor force participation rate, moreover, of children in India is extremely high. A survey by the Indian Labour Ministry stated that 25 percent of the children between the ages of five and fifteen are working (AFT 1998:3). The composition of the work force, however, in most of the industries is an enigma. Some estimates seem rather low given other existing information while others may be outdated. The National Council for Applied Economic Research estimated from a survey in 1992 that "8% of the total work force in hand-knotted carpet industry is child labor" (U. S. Dept. of Labor 1994:74). This estimate is not consistent with Juyal research on the carpet industry in Mirzapur-Bhadohi where the ratio of adult to child workers was 1:2.254 (1993:33). In addition, the contrast of the 1992 estimate with a government estimate in 1985 is surprising. In 1985, the government reported child workers constituted 37.5 percent of the total labor force in the carpet industry and the absolute numbers were growing (Kanbargi 1988:96).

In Columbia, research has uncovered the extensive use of children and youths in the Bogota Quarries and in small brickmaking enterprises. The brickmaking industry makes intensive use of family labor and relies on minimal technologies and low levels of capital investment. Salazar (1988) found that children and youths participate in virtually all tasks connected with making bricks but spend most of their time transporting and stacking bricks. She reported, "They pile up the bricks after they have dried in the sun, carry them to and load the kiln, remove the bricks from the kiln, stack them again after firing and load them on to the trucks" (55). David Parker, a specialist in occupational health and safety, witnessed this wearisome form of child labor when he photographed children working in a variety of occupations in Mexico, Thailand, Nepal, Bangladesh and India. The caption next to a picture of a young brick worker named Kathmandu in Nepal on January 29, 1993 read, "The brick factories are one of the more brutal work places I have visited. In the factories, children and adults work side by side. A child such as the one seen in this picture may over the course of a day carry over 1,000 bricks on top of his head and earn 20 rupees or about 60 cents. Each brick weighs about one kilogram (2.2 pounds)" (Parker 1994:39).

Youths are also employed in the cut flower industry in Bogota. They begin work at age eleven although some children assist their parents beginning at age nine. Salazar's recent research found children working on plantations in the areas of cultivation, packaging and classification (1994, Part 2.2:4). Children are busy debudding, packaging and rubber-banding the carnations, roses and pompoms. The small-scale coal mines in Northwestern Colombia employ families who bring their children along to work with them. Children are most likely to be working in these informal and marginal mining operations which produce most of Columbia's coal. Two to eight workers (usually family or friends) use manual equipment and explosives in chamber and post underground operations to remove the coal. The children work from 4:00 a. m. to 12:00 midnight five or six days a week (U. S. Dept. of Labor 1994:52). These Colombian children have many of the same types of hauling and filling jobs as their predecessors in Great Britain.

> Children are involved in all of the mining tasks, with the youngest engaged in carrying water out from the mines, taking the mules loaded with coal to the road, and packing the coal into bags. The older children are primarily engaged in the more physically demanding tasks such as carrying heavy bags of coal on their backs, dragging tins of coal to the shoulder from the inside of the mines to the outside, driving the electric car to take coal out of the mine, and digging charcoal with a pike inside the mine (U.S. Dept. of Labor 1994:52).

Guillen-Manoquin (1988) estimated that approximately 20 percent of the workers in gold production in Peru are young people aged eleven to eighteen. Children and youths perform hauling and cleaning operations similar to the children who worked in the coal and metal mines of Great Britain. Gold panning, like mining, is divided into a series of distinct activities. Children and youths participate in "Descargue" and push small carts of the soil removed to uncover the area to be mined along wooden ramps. In addition, they use a wooden sieve (or tolva) to sort and wash the gravel from the gold which is similar to the "riddlers" of the nineteenth century (63-65).

Child labor was extremely prevalent in Kenya as early as 1946 when children comprised 21percent of the labor force (Onyango 1988:162).[8] Although evidence from Ooko-Ombaka's paper shows that child labor has declined since Independence, children continue to work as domestic servants, as plantation workers and in forestry. Despite labor laws which prohibit paid child labor in industry, children and youths continue to be employed in the market economy. The largest form of paid labor in industry is on coffee plantations where boys between the age of twelve and seventeen help in the planting, cultivation and harvesting of coffee beans.[9] In addition, many girls in Kenya work on the rice plantations wading through the insect-infested swampy ground (Onyango 1988:162).

In Pakistan, children and youths are primarily occupied in the agriculture sector, carpet industry, sporting goods industry and the manufacture of surgical instruments.

In addition, millions of bonded child laborers work in brick kilns, fisheries, stone/brick crushing, shoe-making, refuse sorting as well as in the carpet industry and agriculture (U.S. Dept. of Labor 1994:126). Children, like Iqbal Massih,[10] work twelve-hour days at a weaving loom tying knots for hand-knotted carpets. Jonathan Silvers, a reporter, describes the process and the comparative advantage of child weavers;

> A hand-knotted carpet is made by tying short lengths of fine colored thread to a lattice of heavier white threads. The process is labor-intensive and tedious: a single four-by-six-foot carpet contains well over a million knots and takes an experienced weaver four to six months to complete. The finest, most intricate carpets have the highest density of knots. The smaller the knot the weaver can cram into his lattice and the more valuable the finished carpet. Small knots are, of course, made most easily by small hands (1996:87).

Children also use their hands to stitch soccer balls for the sporting goods industry. Boys and girls ranging in age from twelve to fifteen work eighty hours a week in cramped cottages. In the town of Sialkot, younger children aged five to ten work in "near-total darkness and in total silence" (AFT 1998:83). The foreman explains the darkness keeps costs down and photographers away while the silence ensures product quality (83). A child can usually stitch three soccer balls a day and earn 20 rupees (75 cents) per ball.

Estimates of the number of children and youths working in Pakistan range from two to nineteen million. The Pakistan Labor Force Survey in 1991 placed the number of children and youths (aged ten to fourteen) at two million while the Pakistan Institute of Development Economics believes this figure to be a gross underestimate due to under-reporting and the exclusion of children under ten. Economists at the Institute "estimate there are 19 million children working, 7 million below the age of 10 and 12 million between 10 and 14 years old" (AFT 1998:126). The Human Rights Commission of Pakistan put the estimate within this range at eleven to twelve million, with at least half of the Pakistani children under the age of ten (AFT 1998:81). Although research has not revealed any figures for the labor force participation of children in Pakistan, there is some information on the composition of the work force in the carpet and sporting goods industry. According to a UNICEF and Government survey, ninety percent of the one million workers in the carpet industry were children in 1992 (U.S. Dept. of Labor 1994:127). Many of these child laborers, moreover, were under the age of ten. The proportion of children working in the Pakistan carpet industry far surpass even the highest figures for textile mills in Great Britain (at 60 percent). The percentage of children and youths working in the sporting goods industry is substantial but considerably lower than in the carpet industry. Children and youths comprise nearly one fourth of the work force in the cottages where soccer balls are made (U.S. Dept. of Labor 1994:130).

Child labor is employed in the footwear, textile and garment industries of Brazil. In the footwear industry, children begin work at age seven for independent contractors who have converted homes, garages, yards and verandas into workshops. The workshops are cramped and noisy and lack proper lighting and ventilation. The children perform a variety of tasks in the production of shoes: cutting, trimming, folding, gluing, hand sewing, hammering studs and sanding soles for eight hours a day (U. S. Dept of Labor 1994:37). According to a government survey in 1990, more than 50 percent of the children and youths under the age of fourteen employed in the textile and garment industry work as weavers who operate heavy machinery (U. S. Dept. of Labor 1994:37). Children and youths also work underground in tin mines. The Confederacao Geral dos Trabalhadores reported in 1991 that, "Women, adolescents, and children can be found manually digging exploratory tunnels and searching for cassiterite veins in the mud of mining areas of Amazonia which are rich with malaria" (U. S. Dept. of Labor 1994:37).

The Brazilian Institute for Geography and Statistics (IBGE) discovered that roughly two million children and youths work in Brazil. Specifics on the extent of child labor in the textile, garment and tin industries are not available although thorough documentation does exist on the 1,300 children illegally working in the footwear industry (U. S. Dept. of Labor 1994:36). According to an unofficial source, however, children and youths constitute 18 percent of the work force in those establishments and manufacturers which utilize child labor (Wright 1994:1). In addition, the IBGE estimates the labor force participation rate of children and youths between the ages of ten and thirteen is 14.3 percent in Brazil (U. S. Dept. of Labor 1994:36). Although this estimate seems small, the labor force participation rate in Brazil is the highest in Latin America and is comparable to estimates for Peru and India which were calculated for larger age ranges.

Why are children still working? Are they working for the same reasons they did over a hundred years ago in Great Britain? Based on recent research on child labor in developing countries it appears the reasons for employment are similar. Family poverty, the cultural views of childhood and cost of labor are offered as explanations for the persistence of child labor in developing countries despite labor legislation aimed to curb it. Just as the poor working-class families of Great Britain needed their children's wages for subsistence, the poor families of India, Brazil, Columbia and Peru depend on their children's contribution for survival. Both the International Labor Organization and the World Bank identify poverty of the household as an important factor contributing to the employment of children. In their newest publication *Child Labour: Targeting the intolerable*, the ILO places poverty as the primary factor affecting the supply of child labor. They clearly state that, "Poverty is the most important reason why children work. Poor households need the money which their children can earn, and children commonly contribute around 20-25 per cent of family income. Since by definition poor households spend the bulk of their income on food it is clear that the income provided by working children is critical to their survival" (1996:17). The *World Development Report of 1995* under causes of child labor states unequivocally, "A high prevalence of child labor is linked to poverty and to poor quality or availability of education. Children in poor families work because the family needs the extra income, especially if the parents' major source of revenue is uncertain" (1995:72).

Several development economists concur with the conclusions of the ILO and the World Bank that poverty is the root of the problem. Rodgers and Standing believe children's work is a part of a family survival strategy in the case of poverty or when a major household crisis occurs and the principal breadwinner dies, leaves or becomes unemployed (1981:22). Similarly, Luz Silva emphasizes the economic causes of child work in her research on Chile and argues that children work mainly in lower-class urban and rural families. When the parents cannot provide for their children's needs the children must, "Take on adult work to assist their parents, or take their parents' place as the family breadwinners on a virtually permanent basis" (1981:163). In addition, a study by the Institute of Industrial Relations at the University of Philippines on child labor in the wood-based and clothing industry determined that, "Poverty is the most pervasive factor in child employment" (1981:86). In considering other important contributors to child labor, such as the perceived returns of education relative to work, the levels of technology in industry and the cost of labor, the study concludes, "Child labour is rooted in poverty. Children with unemployed parents or children whose parents do not have social security must work to help in the family's struggle for survival" (85). Salazar's research on the employment of children in Colombian coal mines also concludes that the family's income status had a significant impact on whether children worked. Most of the children who worked in the mines came from poor families where the parents had little education. Given their importance of the child's contribution to family income, parents placed a higher value on their children's work than on their education (1994 Part 2.3:15).

Some experts on child labor and nongovernmental organizations have begun to argue that child labor causes poverty and not that poverty causes child labor. At the basis of the explanation is the human capital theory and the effect of education and training on an individual's earning power.[11] In simple terms, the theory states that the higher the investment a person makes in himself or herself through education and training, the higher his/her potential income. Thus, if children work instead of going to school, they do not increase their human capital which restricts their earning power in the future. When the conditions of employment are hazardous to the health and safety of the children, their human capital may even decrease the more they work.[12] If children do not obtain the skills necessary to move into higher wage occupations as adults, the vicious cycle of poverty continues. The U.S. Dept. of Labor espouses this view in their conclusion of the section on "Contributing Factors."

In summary, children work for a variety of reasons. Some work simply to survive. Others, in the absence of free or compulsory schooling, lack a meaningful educational alternative. Tragically too many children - those bonded labor - work to repay debts incurred by their parents. Still others are kidnapped, or recruited by unscrupulous agents to work away from home as a source of cheap labor in many industries. Nonetheless, most apologists for child labor cite poverty as the cause. However, the amount of money earned by most child workers is generally a small contribution to the family income. Although children work because they are victims of poverty, by working instead of being educated, they tend to perpetuate the cycle of poverty (1994:7).

In many cultures, children are expected to contribute to family income by either working independently in the market for wages or by helping adults with their work. The custom of putting children to work began centuries ago when children helped at home or on the farm. Sending children to work in the factories, workshops and mines is the natural evolution of this traditional practice in the twentieth century. Imran Malik, the vice chairman of the Pakistan Carpet Manufactures and Exporters Association, proported this view when questioned by a reporter for the *Atlantic Monthly*. He made the observation that, "For thousands of years children had worked alongside their parents in their villages. The work they now do in factories and workshops is an extension of this tradition, and in most ways an improvement on it. The children earn more than they would elsewhere. They contribute significantly to their family's security and raise their standard of living" (Silvers 1996:79). Thus, in many cultures, childhood is a time for learning information and skills that will be necessary for survival in the future. This learning can take the form of apprenticeships, informal schooling, formal schooling and on-the-job training. The age at which this learning begins and the form it takes depends upon the cultural traditions of the people within a local, regional or national sphere. For example, working in India is founded in tradition. The people believe that the learning process starts soon after conception when the human body is soft, flexible and pliable. It is believed this is the ideal time to prepare for a profession because the child can learn to twist, bend, stretch or assume different positions as required by specific jobs. Many adults do not feel that working children are exploited or deprived of their childhood (Gathia 1983:78 and Kanbargi 1988:106). Instead, making children work is considered an integral part of the family economy and necessary for personal development. The importance of training is clear in the following quote by Dube, "Craftsmen and artisans hold similar ideas and so ensure that their children start acquiring skills early. The nimble fingers and keen eyesight of children are greatly valued. In hereditary crafts like carpet weaving, paper mache, cotton and silk weaving with intricate designs, woodcarving, embroidery, etc., training starts at an early age" (1981:188).

Finally, several development economists argue that children and youths are hired because they are cheap labor and allow an industry to grow and compete (Dube 1981, Gathia 1983, Kulshreshtha 1978, Rodgers and Standing 1981). This form of "sweated labor" keeps the cost of labor low in a typically labor-intensive industry. According to Rogers and Standing, "The growth of wage labour and capitalist relations of production had been associated, in the industrialised countries, with a long-run decline in child employment. But in the early stages children were used in many guises to further capital accumulation and intensify exploitation" (1981:16). Kulshreshtha believes the low cost of child labor is one of the causes of the widespread use of children in India. After examining employment and wage statistics from the 1971 Census of India he observes, "Mostly employers think that a lot of work can be done by the children in their establishment and this labour of children is very cheap labour in comparison to that of men. In fact, it ensures them more margin of profit over less investments" (1978:16). Linda Golodner, president of the National Consumers League and co-chair of the Child Labor Coalition has proclaimed that, "Child Labor--once a mainstay in many local economies--has emerged as a profitable economic strategy in world trade" (Capitol Hill Briefing 1992:24). Without hesitation she blames employers whose profit maximizing behavior leads them to hire children in order to compete internationally, "The fact remains that child labor is desirable--and is preferred over adult employment--because it is cheap labor" (Capitol Hill Briefing 1992:25). This capitalist motive is clear in a Rawalpindi landowner's remarks about why he employs child labor. He replied candidly to a reporter, "Children are cheaper to run than tractors and smarter than oxen" (Silvers 1996:79).

Research has documented that children in Chile, Pakistan and Jamaica are paid indirectly through a "supplementary wage" given to their parents (Luz Silva 1978, Hafeez 1979 and Standing 1978). When children are paid directly, their wages are one third to one half adult wages (Child Labor Monitor 1993III:7 and Luz Silva 1978). In the case of apprentice and bonded labor, children do not get paid at all (U. S. Dept. of Labor 1994: 9-26). There is no doubt that children are cheaper laborers than adult men, but are they as productive? In many of these countries, moreover, where a labor surplus exists and unemployment is widespread, the wages of all workers must be low according to the competitive labor market model. So why employ so many children? Could the technology argument still be operative? Are the technologies utilized in these developing countries biased toward the employment of children as they were in the textile and mining industry of Great Britain during the Industrial Revolution?

The idea that certain methods of production and specific technologies employ more children and youths than others has been alluded to by researchers investigating child labor in developing countries. In developing a model of the labor market for children, Grootaert and Kanbur (1995) incorporate the technology of production as a major determinant of the demand for child labor. They draw on examples that span nearly two centuries and reveal the importance of technology as a country industrializes.

> Many of the cases where this factor (technology) plays an extreme role are those that incite reports in the press and by voluntary agencies. Examples are the employment of boys in mines (because the tunnels are too small for adults to crawl through) or as chimney sweeps (for similar reasons); the employment of girls to weed and pick cotton; and the employment of children to weave carpets because they have more nimble fingers and can tie smaller knots than can adults (195).

They recognize how changes in technology can lead to an increase in child labor in some instances while in others the demand for child labor will fall. Therefore, in the quarries of Bogota, children were displaced by the adoption of wheelbarrows; whereas, assembly line production in multinationals in the electronics and electrical appliance industries has increased the demand for "nimble fingers" (196). Rodgers and Standing identify the mode of production as one of the two main factors determining the varying economic roles of children in developing countries (1981:13). Dube believes that the establishment of certain kinds of industry, the reorganization of many cottage industries and crafts on nonfamilial and commercial basis and the capitalization of agriculture has expanded the scope for the exploitation of child labor in India (1981:182).

The study on child labor in the Philippines by the Institute of Industrial Relations mentions the level of technology in an industry as a possible determinant of child labor in the Philippines (1988: 85). In addition, Pharis Harvey identified technological innovation as one of the three causes of the "explosion of exploitation of children" in his report on "International Child Labor: A Global Crisis" in 1992. He argues that poverty, industrialization and urbanization have increased the use of child labor worldwide. Specifically, he associates the types of technological advances present during the early stages of industrialization, mechanization and the division of labor, with increases in employment opportunities for children. Harvey argues, "The industrial revolution brought an immense increase, however, in the level of exploitation involved by mechanization and the organization of work into simple, repetitive tasks in the making and assembling of goods. This made it possible for children to do more valuable tasks without great physical strengths or craft skills" (1992:21). Very little research, however, has been done to develop this theory as it relates to the child labor in India, Chile, Columbia or Peru. Industry studies which focus on the state of technology and the application of the principles of specialization, division of labor and automation to production could shed considerable light on the impact technology has on child labor in our world today.

Several employers have mentioned the "special skills" of children in working with the technology as justification for the employment of children. In a field study of Nepal's carpet factories, weavers reported children were employed "because small hands tie intricate knots more easily" (AFT 1998:8). Anju Shrestha, program officer with the Nepal Center for Women and Children Affairs, highlighted this practice in an interview with John-Thor Dahlburg for the *LA Times*, "The bosses prefer children, their hands are considered to be defter, and they are more patient" (*LA Times* 7/12/94, World Report:1). In the interview he also learned that country girls make the best carpet makers because they are submissive and quiet (*LA Times* 7/12/94, World Report:1). A carpet master in Pakistan has similar preferences and actively recruits young boys. He told a reporter, "They make ideal employees. Boys at this stage of development (aged 7 to 10) are at the peak of their dexterity and endurance, and their wonderfully obedient- they's work around the clock if I asked them" (Silvers 1996:79). Manufacturers in India believe, like their predecessors in England, children make particularly good weavers because of their excellent eyesight, "nimble fingers" and supple bodies. According to the Report of the National Commission on Labor in 1969, some employers insisted that children had a comparative advantage in weaving because of their "nimble fingers" (386). Kanbargi (1988) highlights this point in his research on the carpet industry of Varanasi, "The manufacturers, weavers and others involved in the industry said that children had nimble fingers and keen eyesight, which are essential for accuracy" (97) and, "The weaver has to adopt a squatting position for hours at a time without support for the back, concentrating hard on the design and colour chart placed in front" (100). In addition, boys work in coal mining in the region of the Khasi tribe in northeast India. They assist the hewer by hauling the coal out of the tunnel. Although the mines are not nearly as deep or complex as those in nineteenth-century Britain, children have a comparative advantage in this type of work because of their small stature. In her examination of the economic roles of children in India, Dube argues, "In the operations connected with mining, children, mostly boys, have an important role to play. While men do the digging inside the tunnel, boys carry the coal outside. In point of fact, children below 12 years are preferred because their height permits them to walk inside the tunnel without bending or without much difficulty; they are lithe and do the running about effortlessly" (1981:203).

The ILO has attempted to disprove this "nimble fingers" argument by pointing out that in most of the industries where children's dexterity is necessary, adults are also performing the same tasks. Based on recent studies and information on hazardous work in India, the ILO argues that child labor is replaceable. They offer the following evidence:

> Even in the hand-knotting of carpets, which calls for considerable dexterity, an empirical study of over 2,000 weavers found that children were not more likely than adults to make the finest knots. Some of the best carpets, with the greatest density of small knots, are in fact woven by adults, and if a child's "nimble fingers" are not essential in such demanding work, it is difficult to imagine in which trades the claims might be valid (ILO 1996:19).

Although this evidence is convincing, it is not compelling. More research would be fruitful in this area to determine the validity of the "nimble fingers" argument as it applies to other industries and other developing countries.

Lessons from the British Experience

Will the uses of child labor continue in developing countries in Asia, Africa, and Latin America and in transition economies in Central and Eastern Europe? What can be done to protect children from abuses and exploitation in the work place? The British experience offers some answers to these questions. If the labor market is competitive as it was in Great Britain, the employment of children and youths will continue to increase in many developing countries.[13] Certain economic, social and technological factors exist which increase both the supply and demand for child labor. Poverty increases the supply of child labor. If a family lacks sufficient income to purchase the necessities, more members of the family will work. If the breadwinner of the family, moreover, gets sick or becomes disabled and can no longer work, other members of the family will have to work in his/her place. Children, as many researchers have noted, can make a sizeable contribution to the family's income. The more children in the family, the more substantial the collective contribution. In addition, if opportunities arise for children to earn money or learn a trade, custom in many cultures dictates they take advantage of those opportunities and go to work. In the family labor supply model, tradition will increase the supply of child labor. Figure 7.2 illustrates the impact these factors have on wages and employment, ceteris paribus. The supply of child labor, S_L, shifts to the right to S_L^* and the wage falls to w^* while the level of children's employment increases to L^*. The demand for child labor is increasing as well. In situations where children and adults are substitutable, profit-maximizing employers will choose to hire children and youths to keep costs down. In labor-intensive methods of production, "cheap" labor will greatly reduce the capitalist's total costs. This will increase the demand for child labor. In situations

FIGURE 7.2 The Market for Child Labor in Developing Countries

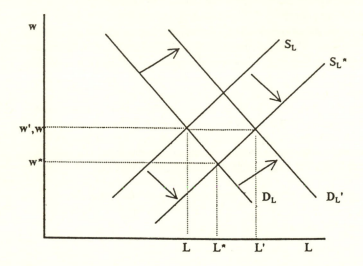

where children and adults are not substitutable and children have a comparative advantage, children will be hired over adults. Children will be hired to lean over carpet looms and stoop at spinning machines. The adoption of certain types of technology will shift the demand for child labor rightward. Furthermore, children may be hired for their "nimble fingers" or supple bodies to sew soccer balls and crawl in underground tunnels. The comparative advantages of the child worker will also shift the demand for child labor rightward. The demand for child labor, D_L, shifts rightward to D_L'. Although the net result on the child's wage is inconclusive, the level of employment increases further to L'. Therefore, the labor model predicts the employment of children and youths will increase in countries where any of these socioeconomic factors exist.

To curb the increase in child labor in Great Britain, Reformers pushed for legislation that would forbid young children from working and youths from working long hours. Most developing countries have adopted the same tactic to reduce the employment of children in the economy with one important difference. Most of developing countries have also passed schooling laws which set age limits for compulsory education. Table 7.7 gives an overview of the child labor laws and education laws in the developing countries discussed in this book.[14] The majority of countries have set standards for the beginning age of employment consistent with the ILO's Convention 138 on Minimum Age for Employment (1973) which states, "The minimum age . . . should not be less than the age of compulsory schooling and, in any case, should not be less than 15 years. Convention 138 allows countries whose economy and educational facilities are insufficiently developed to initially specify a minimum age of 14 years and reduce from 13 years to 12 years the minimum age for

TABLE 7.7 Child Labor Restrictions and Compulsory Education Ages for Various
Countries in 1996

Country	Minimum Age for Work	Age Limits for Compulsory Education
Bangladesh	12 to 15	6-10
Brazil	14	7-14
Colombia	14	6-12
Egypt	12	6-11
Guatemala	14	7-14
India	14	6-14
Indonesia	14	7-13
Mexico	14	6-14
Morocco	12	7-13
Nepal	14	6-11
Pakistan	14 to 15	----
Peru	12 to 16	6-16
Philippines	15	7-13
Portugal	16	6-15
Thailand	13	6-11
Zimbabwe	–	7-15

Source: ILO, 1996, Table 4, pp. 39-46.

light work" (U.S. Dept. of Labor 1994:1). The existence of these laws is an obstacle
to employers wanting to hire children and to parents who want to send their children
to work instead of school. Theoretically, they would have the same effect on child
labor as the Factory Laws had in Great Britain (recall Figure 2.3). The fines
established for violations of the laws would act as an implicit tax on the employers or
as a reduction in income on parents to deter the employment of children.
Unfortunately, the reality resembles what happened in Great Britain during the
nineteenth century - the laws are not enforced.

Child labor laws in many developing countries are not effective in curbing the
employment of children because the laws are not enforced. The child labor laws are
not enforced in agriculture, domestic service or the informal sector where many
children are working. In addition, the problems of enforcement in the formal sector
are very similar to the problems experienced by Great Britain. Child labor laws are
not effective because too few inspectors exist, the fines are too small and the
conviction rate is low. In India, the number of labor inspectors enforcing child labor
laws is grossly inadequate. According to the ILO, all countries have some form of
inspection, but many inspectors have a host of other responsibilities in addition to
checking child labor violations (1996:91). In the carpet industry alone where the
employment of children is rampant, there are only six inspectors (U. S. Dept. of Labor
1994:85). Similarly, in Pakistan, enforcement of child labor laws "is hampered by the
lack of manpower and expertise in the Dept. of Labor and a general acceptance of
child labor" (U.S. Dept. of Labor 1994:131). There were 6,803 inspections between

January 1995 and March 1996. Although the inspectors registered 2,531 cases of child labor, only 774 resulted in convictions with fines (ILO 1996:94). The effectiveness of Kenya's enforcement is worse. Of the 2,982 inspections, 8,074 children were found working illegally. Only 5 of the 8,074 cases were prosecuted resulting in merely 2 convictions (ILO 1996:94). In Mexico, the enforcement system is feeble and "the fines are small and considered by business owners as a cost of doing business" (U.S. Dept. of Labor 1994:110). According to a development economist, Kenneth Klothen, the weakness of the system is apparent in the minute number of cases appealed to the court (U.S. Dept. of Labor 1994:110). Consequently, the impact of child labor laws is minimal because, for many developing countries, the "monitoring of child labor laws remains an enormous challenge" (U. S. Dept. of Labor 1994:140). The situation in Bangladesh appears to be common among many developing countries. The U.S. Department of Labor reports that, "The government agency responsible for enforcing child labor laws, the Bangladesh Dept. of Labor and Inspectorate of Factories, lacks sufficient resources, staff and logistical support to adequately perform the task of monitoring child labor laws" (1994:31).

The compulsory education laws, like the child labor laws, have been entirely ineffective in removing children from workshops, factories, fields and mines. Although requiring children to attend school has the potential of removing children from the labor force until a certain age, the laws are ineffectual if there are no schools for the children to attend. In India, the education law has not been implemented and Professor Myron Weiner from MIT "attributes the prevalence of child labor in India largely to the failure of the educational system" (U. S. Dept. of Labor 1994:86). In Pakistan, primary education became compulsory in 1962 but none of the provinces have complied. Consequently, less than 65 percent of school age children attend primary school and at least half of them drop out before completion (U. S. Dept. of Labor 1994:132). In Bangladesh and the Philippines, the desire to educate children is hampered by the relatively high cost of school supplies. Bangladesh set a goal to have compulsory education in 50 percent of the country by 1995 and 100 percent by the year 2000. The effort has not been successful because parents find the cost of uniforms and books to be a financial burden (U. S. Dept. of Labor 1994:32). Although Philippinos have free education through sixth grade, only 60 percent of the children attend school. The stumbling block in this case is the cost of food and transportation (U. S. Dept. of Labor 1994:140). Thus, parents perceive education laws as a sharp reduction in family income (due to the loss of the child's contribution and the fees and supplies) rather than as a viable alternative for their children. What can be done to reduce the employment of children if legislation and compulsory schooling are not enough?

International organizations, government officials and labor leaders have addressed the problem of child labor by creating new initiatives and launching global programs. The ILO's Minimum Age Convention (No. 138) in 1973 established a minimum age for work and by 1996 was ratified by forty-nine nations. The adoption of the United Nations Convention on the Rights of the Child in 1989 gave additional momentum to the struggle against child labor. In addition, the ILO's International Programme on the Elimination of Child Labour in 1992 has become operational in more than twenty-five developing countries. The governments of participating countries have agreed to review and update their national child labor laws and have adopted pragmatic measures to curtail the employment of children (ILO 1996:7). The International Confederation of Free Trade Unions launched a global campaign for the elimination of child labor in 1994. This measure will increase the impact of the ILO Convention No. 138 by establishing provisions prohibiting the use of child labor in the production of certain goods. Increasing efforts from manufacturers and consumers mount an effective assault on the use of child labor in the production of goods exported to the United States as well. Despite progress, considerable work remains before the ILO accomplishes its goal of eliminating the employment of children in dangerous and hazardous occupations.

The International Labor Office and International Confederation of Free Trade Unions have made several recommendations for the future. The recommendations as outlined in Table 7.8 are a combination of suggestions to strengthen the effectiveness of existing legislation and conventions and to create new obstacles to the employment

TABLE 7.8 A Program for the Elimination of Child Labor

Recommendations of the International Labour Office

1. A new Convention on child labour.
2. Time-bound programs of action to eliminate child labour.
3. Immediate suppression of extreme forms of child labour.
4. Prohibition of work for the very young (under 12 or 13 years).
5. Permanent removal of children from hazadarous work.
6. Preventive measures.
7. Designation of national authority responsible for child labour.
8. Making a crime against a child anywhere a crime everywhere.
9. Increased financial aid to fight against child labour.

Source: ILO (1996), p. 116.

Recommendations of the International Confederation of Free Trade Unions

1. Provision for proper primary education coupled with a provision for free school meals.
2. Replacement of child laborers with an unemployed adult worker of the same family.
3. National legislation prohibiting the use of child labor and the prevention of imports produced by child labor. Strengthening of the inspection system to increase enforcement.
4. Community awareness through public campaigns of companies using child labor and collective agreements of trade unions prohiting the use of child labor.
5. Ratification on International Conventions.
6. Prohibition of child labor in trade agreements.
7. Boycotts and labeling of products.
8. Investigations by multinationals into their work forces.

Source: ICFTU (1994), p. 15.

of children. The ratification of existing International Conventions and designation of the national authority responsible for child labor could strengthen the political deterrents already in place in many Third World Countries. A new convention, moreover, on child labor which capitalizes on the growing public sentiment against the employment of children could establish new standards for countries to meet. Increasing the involvement of consumers and multinationals could be an effective tool to reduce the demand for and supply of goods produced by child labor. Campaigns like RUGMARK can reduce the employment of children indirectly by closing off the export markets to manufacturers in developing countries. The most important deterrent, however, is the provision of an inexpensive education for children of poor families. If children have the option of going to school and parents view this alternate use of their children's time as beneficial, the transformation of childhood which took place in Great Britain can occur in developing countries. Whether the process of removing children and youths from the work place is gradual as it was in Britain or more dramatic, it is irreversible (Hopkins 1994:94). Once education is a viable alternative, the childhood of working-class and poor children is spent in school, not in factories, workshops or mines. Pharis Harvey articulates the importance of education in the fight against child labor in an article published in *The Christian Century*,

> The most important task is to increase the opportunity and the requirement for free public education. Lack of schooling leads to massive employment; irrelevant schooling leads to massive dropout rates, then to child employment. International development policy should assist, in upgrading and universalizing basic education as the first line of offense against child servitude (4/5/95:364).

The ILO believes education will help reduce child labor over the long run because,

> Educated persons are more aware of their rights and so less likely to accept hazardous working conditions; educated persons make more informed and active citizens; educated persons (especially women) have fewer, better educated and healthier children when they themselves become adults, and these smaller family sizes and education expectations should reduce child labour in future generations; and educated persons are more productive workers and so help increase economic growth rates and wealth (ILO 1996:105-106).

It appears history is repeating itself. Children and youths are hard at work in the brickyards, carpet factories, gold mines and garment manufactories of the Third World. More than one hundred years ago, children and youths were hard at work in the textile mills, coal and metal mines of Great Britain. The forces which encourage child labor today seem as compelling as those in Britain during the early nineteenth century. Poverty, tradition and competition have either pushed or pulled children and youths into employment instead of school. In poor households, children's contribution to family income is often essential for survival. In some cultures, putting children to work at a young age has been the custom instituted to insure independence in adulthood. In industries which export, children's comparative advantage over adults is an irresistible enticement to the profit-maximizing manufacturer. Reformers, Pessimists, Radicals, workers and benevolent mill owners fought an uphill struggle to remove young children from British textile factories and mines and to reduce the working hours of youths. The ILO, UNICEF, ICFTU and other international organizations fight the same battle today.

Must every country or industry which industrializes pass through a stage which is child labor-intensive? Can this stage be avoided? Could developing countries move more quickly from the labor-intensive production modes of handicraft enterprise to the capital-intensive production mode of modern industry? Part of the answer to these questions lies in the nature of the technological innovation experienced by industry. In certain instances, the division of labor, the expansion of production, the adoption of new machinery and the limits imposed by space can lead to an increase in the demand for child labor. The special qualities of children - their keen eyesight, nimble fingers, limber bodies, high energy level and obedient nature makes them ideal laborers for certain jobs. Child labor died a slow death in Great Britain despite restrictive legislation. If society can learn from Britain's experience, the removal of children from hazardous work places and the elimination of young children from factories, workshops and mines could occur more rapidly. The welfare of the world's children depends on it.

Notes

1. The cost-book accounts of mining companies in Cornwall have recently been archived by the Duchy of Cornwall Office at Buckingham Gate and when available will be a rich source of time series data on employment and pay of the miners.

2. Recall from the theoretical model developed in Chapter 2 that Becker use "Z" to represent the basic commodities that enter directly in a household's utility function (Becker 1965:495).

3. Theoretically, household behavior could be represented by Becker's unitary model. The efficient household model is no longer appropriate because decisions are made by the father.

4. Mitch estimates enrollment rates from 1818 to 1901 in his 1982 paper (Table 1.1:10).

5. In the 1850s the woollen power-looms wove at 48 picks per minute while the worsted looms could weave at 160 picks per minute (Benson and Warburton 1986:10).

6. The ILO defines child labor as the economically active population under the age of fifteen (Ashagrie 1993).

7. It has been confirmed that a large number of children work as bonded laborers in the carpet industry. Recruiters give parents a cash advance or "loan." The child works to pay off the family debt. The debt may carry on for generations (U. S. Department of Labor 1995:85).

8. According to Onyango, the labor force is defined as the economically active population.

9. The largest occupation of paid labor for children is urban domestic work where children work in other people's homes (Onyango 1988:162).

10. Four-year-old Iqbal Massih was sold into bondage to a carpet maker. Freed at age ten, he began a successful crusade against child labor and was honored by the ILO. In 1995 he was murdered at the age of twelve (Silvers 1996:88-90).

11. For a development of the human capital theory see Becker (1964).

12. There are numerous examples in the U.S. Dept. of Labor's Report where child laborers become sick, maimed or deformed after working in deplorable conditions.

13. It appears that the labor market for children is competitive in many developing countries with the exception of a few industries where families work together (e.g., mining, flower industry). Apprentice and bonded labor are traded in a separate market.

14. For a complete list of all countries see the 1996 publication of the ILO entitled, *Child Labour: Targeting the intolerable*, Table 4:39-46.

Appendix 1
The Number of Textile Factories in Great Britain

ENGLAND AND WALES

Type	Counties	1836	1850
Cotton	Chester	109	145
	Cumberland	13	11
	Derbyshire	60	74
	Lancashire	683	1,235
	Staffordshire	4	10
	Yorkshire	126	227
Woollen	Brecon	7	9
	Cardigan	2	9
	Carmarthen	5	18
	Chester	15	12
	Cumberland	15	11
	Derbyshire	4	2
	Glamorganshire	11	31
	Gloucestershire	118	80
	Herefordshire	2	3
	Lancashire	98	na
	Merioneth	7	16
	Monmouthshire	3	9
	Montgomery	52	54
	Oxfordshire	9	8
	Salop	2	3
	Somersetshire	28	31
	Westmoreland	14	8
	Wiltshire	59	36
	Yorkshire	402	880

(continues)

Appendix 1 (continued)

Type	Counties	1836	1850
Worsted	Lancashire	8	11
	Salop	1	1
	Staffordshire	1	1
	Worcester	6	11
	Yorkshire	199	418
Flax	Cumberland	7	7
	Durham	5	3
	Lancashire	18	9
	Northumberland	2	1
	Westmoreland	4	5
	Yorkshire	67	60
	Chester	84	97
	Derbyshire	1	24
	Gloucestershire	2	7
	Lancashire	23	29
	Somersetshire	8	15
	Staffordshire	11	10
	Warwickshire	5	23
	Wiltshire	2	3
	Worcester	8	13
	Yorkshire	8	16

IRELAND

Type	Counties	1836	1850
Cotton	Antrim	9	3
	Armagh	3	1
	Dublin	6	3
	Kildare	2	1
	Waterford	1	1
	Wexford	1	1
Woollen	Cork	7	1
	Dublin	13	2
	Kilkenny	5	1
	King's Country	2	1
	Queen's Country	2	3
	Waterford	na	1
Worsted	Dublin	na	2
Flax	Antrim	14	38
	Armagh	5	4
	Dublin	1	1

(continues)

Appendix 1 (continued)

Type	Counties	1836	1850
	Kildare	1	1
	Meath	1	1
	Monaghan	1	2
SCOTLAND			
Cotton	Aberdeenshire	4	2
	Ayrshire	2	4
	Bute	2	4
	Dumbartonshire	5	4
	Lanarkshire	88	94
	Kirkcudbright	1	1
	Linlithgowshire	1	1
	Perthshire	3	3
	Renfrewshire	49	51
	Stirlingshire	3	4
Woollen	Aberdeenshire	6	22
	Ayrshire	18	16
	Clackmannanshire	19	23
	Fifeshire	1	2
	Kincardine	2	3
	Kirkcudbright	-	4
	Lanarkshire	3	8
	Linlithgowshire	1	1
	Perthshire	4	14
	Renfrewshire	2	3
	Roxburgh	13	21
	Selkirk	11	15
	Stirlingshire	7	22
Worsted	Ayrshire	-	4
	Lanarkshire	-	1
	Renfrewshire	-	1
Flax	Aberdeenshire	4	4
	Ayrshire	1	3
	Edinburghshire	3	4
	Fifeshire	49	43
	Forfarshire	82	101
	Lanarkshire	-	4
	Kincardine	9	7
	Perthshire	17	19
	Renfrewshire		4

(continues)

Appendix 1 (continued)

Type	Counties	1836	1850
Silk	Lanarkshire	3	4
	Renfrewshire	3	1

Source: 1836(24)XLV, pp. 3-93 and 1850(745)XLII, pp. 2-21.

Appendix 2
The Number of Coal Collieries in Great Britain

ENGLAND AND WALES

Counties	1842	1855
Pembrokeshire	10	19
Glamorganshire & Monmouthshire	80	227
Flintshire	–	30
Denbighshire	–	25
Anglesea	–	5
Devonshire	–	2
Gloucestershire & Somersetshire	–	85
Shropshire	–	48
South Staffordshire	–	393
North Staffordshire	–	123
Nottinghamshire	–	17
Warwickshire	–	15
Leicestershire	–	11
Derbyshire	48	123
Yorkshire	80	276
Lancashire	164	333
Cheshire	–	30
Cumberland	–	23
Durham & Northumberland	119	225

SCOTLAND

Counties		
Lanarkshire	–	153
Ayrshire	–	78
Fifeshire	38	34
Clackmannanshire	11	8
Haddingtonshire	–	11
Edinburghshire	–	11
Linlithgowshire	–	15
Stirlingshire	15	34
Dumbartonshire	2	11
Renfrewshire	–	7

(continues)

Appendix 2 (continued)

Counties	1842	1855
Other counties	–	6
IRELAND	–	19

*This total is for 1844 not 1842.

Source: 1842: 1842[381]XVI, pp. 379-381, 556, 558, 766-769. 1842[382]XVII, pp. 94-95, 194-196, 251-252, 469-471. 1844:1847[844]XVI, pp. 37-39 Appendix B. 1855: Hunt, 1856, p. 320.

Appendix 3
Efficient Household Model

Households seek to maximize

$$U_F = \{ \propto (p, w_c, w_a) U_a(Z_i) + [1-\propto (p, w_c, w_a) U_c(Z_i)] \}$$

where $Z_i = f_i(x_i, L_i; E_i)$ Production Function

and where $\propto (p, w_c, w_a)$ represents the weight of the parents in bargainning process

subject to budget constraint

$$\sum p_i \, x_i \leq \sum w_c L_i + \sum w_a L_i + y_c + y_a$$

and subject to time constraint

$$\sum L_i^c + \ell^c = 24$$
$$\sum L_i^a + \ell^a = 24$$

where p is a price vector
y_c is the child's non-labor income
y_a is the adult's non-labor income
w_c is the child's market wage
w_a is the adult's market wage
U_a, U_c are the adult's and child's utility function
Z_i are commodities produced by goods (x_i),
labor hours (L_i) and other factors (E_i)
ℓ^c is the child's leisure hours
ℓ^a is the adult's leisure hours
L^c is the child's labor hours
L^a is the adult's labor hours

This problem yields demand functions in the following form:

$$x^c = x^c (p, w_c, w_a, y_c, y_a)$$
$$L^c = L^c (p, w_c, w_a, y_c, y_a)$$

$$x^a = x^a (p, w_c, w_a, y_c, y_a)$$
$$L^a = L^a (p, w_c, w_a, y_c, y_a)$$

Appendix 4
Exports of Textile Manufactures in Great Britain

Year	Cotton Thread (mill. lb)	Cotton Piece Goods (mill. yds)	Wool and Worsted Yarn (000 lb)	Wool and Worsted Goods (000 yd)	Silk Thread (000 lb)
1815	0.2	253	–	12,173	269
1816	0.2	189	–	7,112	205
1817	0.3	237	–	6,614	203
1818	0.3	255	–	8,997	241
1819	0.3	203	14	6,488	—
1820	0.4	251	11	4,791	—
1821	0.5	266	18	6,322	276
1822	0.6	304	31	8,436	287
1823	0.6	302	18	8,140	225
1824	0.6	345	20	7,338	—
1825	0.7	336	77	7,804	—
1826	0.8	267	131	4,941	—
1827	1.3	365	256	6,461	—
1828	1.3	363	437	6,816	—
1829	1.1	403	590	5,298	—
1830	1.2	445	1,108	5,562	—
1831	1.5	421	1,592	5,798	—
1832	1.7	461	2,204	6,011	—
1833	1.9	496	2,107	7,456	—
1834	2.3	556	1,862	6,689	—
1835	2.3	558	2,237	7,907	—
1836	2.2	638	2,546	9,100	—
1837	2.2	531	2,514	5,923	—
1838	2.5	690	3,086	6,912	—
1839	3.0	731	3,320	8,164	—
1840	2.8	791	3,797	8,164	622
1841	2.8	751	4,903	—	638
1842	2.5	734	5,962	—	369
1843	2.8	919	7,410	—	398
1844	3.2	1,047	8,272	—	488
1845	2.9	1,092	9,406	—	470

(continues)

Appendix 4 (continued)

Year	Cotton Thread (mill. lb)	Cotton Piece Goods (mill. yds)	Wool and Worsted Yarn (000 lb)	Wool and Worsted Goods (000 yd)	Silk Thread (000 lb)
1846	2.8	1,065	8,631	—	470
1847	3.5	943	10,065	—	620
1848	3.7	1,097	8,429	—	411
1849	5.0	1,338	11,773	—	818
1850	4.4	1,358	13,794	—	1,186

Source: Mitchell and Deane (1962), pp. 182, 195-96, 209-10. Reprinted by permission.

Appendix 5
Production Processes in Textile Industry

The Process of Cotton Manufacture

Clean and loosen raw cotton

(Willow, Scutcher)

Carding

(carding engine)

Spinning

(spinning jenny, water frame,
common mule, self-actor)

Weaving

(hand loom, flying shuttle,
power loom, dressing machine)

Finishing

Bleaching, Dyeing, Calico Printing

The Process of Wool & Worsted Manufacture

Sort & Scour Wool

Wool	Worsted
Carding	Wash & Dry
(willy, scribbler, slubbing Billy)	(plucker)
Spinning	Combing
(spinning jenny, self-actor)	(combing machine, breaking machine)
Weaving	Spinning
(hand loom, power loom)	(throstle spinning frame)
Scour & Burl	Weaving
	(hand loom, power loom)
Fulling	Finishing

```
┌─────────────────────────────────┐
│            Tentering            │
└─────────────────────────────────┘


┌─────────────────────────────────┐
│            Teasling             │
└─────────────────────────────────┘

              (gig mill)

┌─────────────────────────────────┐
│          Shearing or            │
│           Cropping              │
└─────────────────────────────────┘

          (shearing frame)

┌─────────────────────────────────┐
│            Pressing             │
└─────────────────────────────────┘

          (pressing machine)
```

```
┌─────────────────────────────────────────┐
│                 Reeling                   │
└─────────────────────────────────────────┘
```

```
┌─────────────────────────────────────────┐
│                 Winding                   │
└─────────────────────────────────────────┘
```

(winding engine)

```
┌─────────────────────────────────────────┐
│                 Cleaning                  │
└─────────────────────────────────────────┘
```

(scissor mechanism)

```
┌─────────────────────────────────────────┐
│                 Spinning                  │
└─────────────────────────────────────────┘
```

Doubling

(doubling frame)

Throwing or Twisting

(Piedmantese throwing machine)

Weaving

(Jaquard loom, power loom)

Finishing

Breaking

Heckle or Hackle

(automatic heckling machine)

Sorting

Carding

(carding engine)

Drawing & Roving

(automatic roving machine)

Wet Spinning

(fly spinning frames)

Dyeing

Reeling & Winding

(winding machine)

Dressing & Sizing

(dressing machine)

Dry Spinning

Weaving

Finishing

Appendix 6
The Invention of the Spinning Jenny

It is unclear from the records remaining whether it was Hargreaves intention to employ children on his spinning jenny. An earlier version, however, based on a similar principle, patented by Richard Haines, claimed to be made specifically with the employment of the young, sick and elderly in mind. He proposed that his machine, if placed in a Working-Almshouse for the manufactory of linen cloth, would provide "employment for the weakest people, viz. women and children and decrepit or aged people" (465). These Working-Almshouses would relieve parish rates "since now the Parishes need not so much fear a charge, knowing a Means how to employ all their Children, as fast as they come to be five or six years old" (469). Therefore, it seems at least plausible that a spinning engine like the jenny, which worked on the principle of multiplying the actions of the spinning wheel, could be worked by children. This view is strengthened by statements made by several of Hargreaves' contemporaries. John Aikin seems almost apologetic in his confirmation of the employment of children on the jenny in 1795 in his *Description of the Country from 30 to 40 miles round Manchester*. Apparently having some preference for adult spinners he observes that, "At first, it is true, jennies containing at most twelve spindles were worked by children of nine to twelve years of age; but these machines were soon displaced by larger jennies both because the latter proved cheaper and also because the spinning done by children was unsatisfactory when a higher level of quality in yarns began to be expected" (quoted in Chapman 1904:54). John Kennedy, in a paper entitled "Observations on The Rise and Progress of the Cotton Trade in Great Britain" that he read before the Literary and Philosophical Society of Manchester in 1815, stated that youths worked the jenny. Kennedy was particularly knowledgeable about spinning machinery since he began his career as a machine-maker and mule spinner and later built three cotton mills with his partners Sanford and McConnell. In tracing the improvements in machinery, he said, "This was followed by another machine, called the Spinning Jenny, invented in 1767 by Mr. Hargreaves, of Blackburn; by means of which a young person could work ten or twenty spindles at once" (9). By the end of the eighteenth century, Marsden published a book on cotton spinning (1884) in which he draws an important distinction between Hargreaves' original jenny and the improved versions with 120 spindles, "Hargreaves' jennies were generally worked by women and children, as also were Arkwright's water frames. The successive improvements and enlargements, however, began to make them complicated and cumbrous for females to handle, and hence necessitated a change in this respect" (224-225).

Appendix 7
Produce of British Tin and Copper Mines from 1790-1855

Year	Tons of Tin	Tons of Copper
1790	3193	–
1791	3470	–
1792	3809	–
1793	3202	–
1794	3351	–
1795	3440	–
1796	3061	4950
1797	3240	5210
1798	2820	5600
1799	2862	4923
1800	2522	5187
1801	2365	5267
1802	2668	5228
1803	2960	5615
1804	3041	5374
1805	2785	6234
1806	2905	6863
1807	2465	6716
1808	2371	6795
1809	2548	6821
1810	2036	5682
1811	2385	6141
1812	2373	6720
1813	2324	6918
1814	2611	6369
1815	2941	6525
1816	3348	6697
1817	4120	6498
1818	4066	6849
1819	3315	6804
1820	2990	7508
1821	3373	8514

(continues)

Appendix 7 (continued)

Year	Tons of Tin	Tons of Copper
1822	3278	9140
1823	4213	7927
1824	5005	7823
1825	4358	8226
1826	4603	9026
1827	5555	10311
1828	4931	9921
1829	4434	9656
1830	4444	10890
1831	4300	12218
1832	4323	12099
1833	4065	11185
1834	2989	11224
1835	4228	12271
1836	4054	11639
1837	4790	10823
1838	5130	11527
1839	–	12451
1840	–	11038
1841	–	9987
1842	–	9896
1843	–	–
1844	–	–
1845	–	12883
1846	–	11850
1847	–	12754
1848	6613	12241
1849	6952	11683
1850	6729	12253
1851	6143	11807
1852	6287	11776
1853	5763	–
1854	5947	–
1855	6000	–

Sources: For Tin: 1790-1837 Carne (1839), pp. 261-262. 1838-1855 Hunt (1856), p. 206. For Copper: 1796-1837 Lemon (1838), p. 70. 1838-1842 McCulloch (1847), p. 615. 1845-1852 Leifchild (1857), p. 232.

Appendix 8
The Process of Coal & Metal Mining

```
┌─────────────────────────────────────────────┐
│                   Hewing                      │
└─────────────────────────────────────────────┘

┌─────────────────────────────────────────────┐
│                   Loading                     │
└─────────────────────────────────────────────┘

┌─────────────────────────────────────────────┐
│                   Hauling                     │
└─────────────────────────────────────────────┘

┌───────────────────────────────────────────────────────┐
│            Raising Coals & Metals to Surface            │
└───────────────────────────────────────────────────────┘
```

Coals

```
┌─────────────────────────────────────────────┐
│                   Slating                     │
└─────────────────────────────────────────────┘

┌─────────────────────────────────────────────┐
│                  Screening                    │
└─────────────────────────────────────────────┘

┌─────────────────────────────────────────────┐
│               Transport for Sale              │
└─────────────────────────────────────────────┘
```

Hewing

Loading

Hauling

Raising Coals & Metals to Surface

Metals

Riddling

Picking

Washing Up

Cobbing

Bucking

Jigging

Washings

Sampling

Transport for Sale

Appendix 9
Cross-Tabulation of Children in Mining

Cross-Tabulation of Seam Size with % of Children Employed

% of Work Force Under 13

Size of seam in inches	0 - 20%	21 - 40%	41 - 65%
11 - 35"	20.6 Row Pct. 16.7 Col. Pct.	58.8 71.4	20.6 100.0
36 - 70"	75.0 57.1	25.0 28.6	
71 - 114"	100.0 26.2		

Chi-Square
Pearson   32.51471*   4 d.f
Likelihood Ratio   39.66841   4 d.f.

Cross-Tabulation of Seam Size with % of Youths Employed

% of Work Force Aged 13-18

Size of seam in inches	0 - 20%	21 - 40%	41 - 67%
11 - 35"	20.6 Row Pct. 28.0 Col. Pct.	61.8 47.7	17.6 75.0
36 - 70"	40.6 52.0	56.3 40.9	3.1 12.5
71 - 114"	45.5 20.0	45.5 11.4	9.1 12.5

Chi-Square
Pearson   6.46658*   4 d.f
Likelihood Ratio   6.91380   4 d.f.

*significant at the 99 percent confidence level

Source: 1842[381]XVI, pp. 210-211 Appendix B.

Appendix 10
Cross-Tabulation of Women in Mining

Cross-Tabulation of Size of Establishment with % of Women Employed

% of Work Force Women

Total Number of Workers	0 - 15%	16 - 30%	31 - 45%
2 - 300	60.0 Row Pct. 83.0 Col. Pct.	32.3 67.7	7.7 55.6
301 - 600	46.7 14.9	33.3 16.1	20.0 33.3
601 - 3200	14.3 2.1	71.4 16.1	14.3 11.1

Chi-Square
Pearson   7.2662   4 d.f.
Likelihood Ratio   7.2876   4 d.f.

Cross-Tabulation of Size of Establishment with
% of Children Employed

% of Work Force under 13

Total Number of Workers	0 - 15%	16 - 30%	31 - 50%
2 - 300	32.1 Row Pct. 81.8 Col. Pct.	61.9 81.3	6.0 62.5
301 - 600	28.6 12.1	57.1 12.5	14.3 25.0
601 - 3200	28.6 6.1	57.1 6.3	14.3 12.5

Chi-Square
Pearson   1.6619   4 d.f.
Likelihood Ratio   1.4364   4 d.f.

Source: Table 5.2 in text. Lemon (1838) Tables XVI and XVII, pp. 78-79.

References
Primary Sources

Aikin, John. 1795. *A Description of the Country from 30 to 40 Miles Round Manchester*. Piccadilly, London: John Stockdale.

Alfred (Samuel Kydd). 1857. *The History of the Factory Movement*. London: Simpkin, Marshall, and Co.

Arnold, R. A. 1864. *The History of the Cotton Famine*. Otley: Saunders.

Baines, Edward. 1835. *History of the Cotton Manufacture of Great Britain*. London: H. Fisher, R. Fisher, and P. Jackson. (Second edition, London: Cass 1968.)

Birmingham Reference Library, Wyatt MSS. I: 31-2.

Booth, C. 1903[1897]. *Life and Labour of the People of London*. IX London.

_____. 1886. "On Occupations of the People of the United Kingdom, 1801-81." *Journal of the Royal Statistical Society* (J. S. S.) XLIX: 314-436.

Boulton and Watt MSS. "Account of the State of the Principal Mines of Cornwall at the Time of the Introduction of Mr. Watt's Engines." in the Collection at the Royal Cornwall Polytechnic Society, Falmouth.

Bray, Charles. 1857. *The Industrial Employment of Women*. London: Longman and Company.

British Almanac. 1834. "Wages and Prices." *British Almanac and Companion*. Pp. 33-61.

Brown, William. 1980[1823]. "Early Days in a Dundee Mill 1819-23," in John Hume, ed., *Dundee Abertay Historical Society Publication Number 20*. Dundee: Stevenson Limited.

Carne, Joseph. 1839. "Statistics of the Tin Mines in Cornwall and of the Consumption of Tin in Great Britain." *Journal of Royal Statistical Society* II: 260-268.

Chambers, Ephraim. 1741. *Cyclopaedia*: or, a universal dictionary of arts and sciences. 5th edition, 2 vols.

Chadwick, D. 1860. "On the rates of wages in Manchester and Salford and the manufacturing districts of Lancashire during the twenty years from 1839 to 1859." *Journal of the Statistical Society* XXIII: 1-36.

Chapman, S. J. 1904. *The Lancashire Cotton Industry*. Manchester: Manchester University Publications.

Checkland, S. G. and E. O. A. 1974[1834]. *The Poor Law Report of 1834*. Penguin Books.

Clapham, J. H. 1907. *The Woollen and Worsted Industries*. London.

Crump, W. B. ed. 1931. *The Leeds Woollen Industry, 1780-1820*. Leeds.

Daniels, G. 1917-18. "The Cotton Trade at the Close of the Napoleonic War." *Translations of the Manchester Statistical Society*. Pp. 1-31.

Davies, David. 1811. *A New Historical and Descriptive View of Derbyshire*. Belper.

Davies, David. 1795. *The Case of Labourers in Husbandry*. London.

Defoe, Daniel. 1742. *A Tour Through the Whole Island of Great Britain*. Third edition, 4 vols. London.

Dunckley, Henry. 1854. *Charter of the Nations*. London: W. and F. G. Cash, 5, Bishopgate Without.

Eden, F. M. 1966[1797]. *The State of the Poor*. Volume I, II, III. London.

Ellis, William. 1826. "Effects of the Employment of Machinery on the Happiness of the Working Classes." *Westminster Review* V.

Ellison, Thomas. 1858. *Hand-book to the Cotton Trade*. London: Longman, Brown, Green, Longmans and Roberts.

Engels, Frederick. 1926[1845]. *The Condition of the Working Class in England.* Translated by the Institute of Marxism-Leninism, Moscow. E. J. Hobsbaum, ed., 1969 London.

Freeman, Arnold. 1980[1914]. *Boy Life and Labour: The Manufacture of Inefficiency.* London: P.S. King and Son.

Gaskell, Elizabeth. 1848. *Mary Barton.* London: Everyman.

Gaskell, Peter. 1836. *Artisans and Machinery.* London: John W. Parker, West Strand.

_____. 1833. *Manufacturing Population of England.* London: Baldwin and Cradock.

Gilboy, Elizabeth W. 1934. *Wages in Eighteenth Century England.* Cambridge, MA: Harvard University Press.

Guest, Richard. 1823. *A Compendious History of the Cotton-Manufacture.* Manchester.

G., W. and M(ather) R(alph). 1780. *An Impartial Representation of the Case of the Poor Cotton Spinners in Lancashire, etc.*

H[aines], R[ichard]. 1677. *Proposals for Building in Every Country, A Working-Almshouse or Hospital.* Reprinted in *Harleian Miscellany,* 2nd ed. 1745, 4: 465-469. London.

Hall, G. Stanley. 1904. *Adolescence: Its Psychology and Its Relations to Physiology, Anthropology, Sociology, Sex, Crime, Religion and Education.* I and II New York: Appleton.

Hoffmann, Walther G. 1955. *British Industry, 1700-1950.* Oxford: Basil Blackwell.

Horner, Leonard. 1840. *On the Employment of Children in Factories and Other Works in the United Kingdom and in Some Foreign Countries.* London: Bancks and Co.

House of Commons Papers: (British Parliamentary Papers)

1808 (177) II Cotton, Weavers (England) petitions. Sel. Cttee. Rep. (Thomas Stanley)

1816 (397) III Children, Mills and Factories. Sel. Cttee. Mins. of ev. (Sir Robert Peel)

1817 (400) VI Children, Sweeping Chimneys, Sel. Cttee. Rep. (H. Grey Bennett)

1830 (9) VIII Coal Supply and Coal Duties. Sel. Cttee. HL Rep., Mins. of ev. (Earl Bathurst)

1830 (590) X Factory Inspectors' reps.

1831 (348) XVII Population, Great Britain. Comparative account, 1801-31.

1831-32 (706) XV Children, Mills and Factories Bill. Sel. Cttee. Rep., Mins. of ev. (T. Sadler)

1833 (149) XXXVI Census, 1831, Enumeration abstract.

1833 (450) XX Factories, employment of children. R. Com. 1st rep., Mins. of ev. (Lord Ashley).

1833 (519) XXI Factories, employment of children. R. Com. 2nd rep. (Thomas Took and Edwin Chadwick).

1834 (44) XXVII Administration and Operation Poor Laws. App. A, pt. 1

1834 (44) XXXVI Administration and Operation of Poor Laws. App. B. 2, pts. III, IV, V

1834 (167) XIX Factories, employment of children. Supplementary rep. (Thomas Took and Edwin Chadwick).

1834 (167) XX Factories, employment of children. Supplementary rep.

1834 (556) X Hand-Loom Weavers, petitions. Sel. Cttee. Rep., Mins. of ev. (John Maxwell)

1834 (596) XLIII Factory Inspectors' reps.

1835 (603) V Coal Mines, Accidents in Mines. Sel. Cttee. Rep., Mins. of ev. (Joseph Pease).

1836 (254) XLV Factories, Accounts and Papers, Persons employed, children, etc.

1839 (159) XIX Factory Inspectors' reps.

1840 (203) X Factories, Operation of the Factory Act. Sel. Cttee. 1st rep. (Lord Ashley).

1840 (220) XXIV Hand-Loom Weavers, p. V, West of England, Wales, Scotland.

1840 (227) X Factories, Operation of the Factory Act. Sel. Cttee. 2nd rep. (Lord Ashley).

1841 (52) II Great Britain (1841 Census). Population Statements.

1841 (56) IX Factories, Operation of the Factory Act. Sel. Cttee. Rep. (Lord Ashley).

1841 [311] X Factories, Accidents to children and young persons. Inspectors special reps.

1842 (31) XXII Factory Inspectors' reps.

1842 [380] XV Children's Employment (mines). R. com 1st rep. (Thomas Took and T. Southwood Smith).

1842 [381] XVI Children's Employment (mines). App. to 1st rep., pt. 1, Subcommissioners' reps.

1842 [382] XVII Children's Employment (mines).App. to 1st rep., pt. II. Subcommissioners' reps.

1842 [410] XXII Factory Inspectors' reps.

1843 (197) LII Factories, Memorials and Petitions of master spinners and manufacturers of West Riding and county of York, for limitation of hours of labour.

1843 [430] XIII Children's Employment (Trade and Manufactures). R. Com. 2nd rep. (Thomas Took and Southwood Smith).

1843 [431] XIV Children's Employment (Trade and Manufactures). App. to 2nd rep., pt. I.

1843 [432] XV Children's Employment (Trade and Manufactures). App. to 2nd rep., pt. II.

1843 (496) XXII England, Wales, Islands. Enumeration abstract.

1843 (508) XIII Mines and Collieries. Midland Mining Commission 1st rep. (Thomas Tancred).

1843 [510] XII Report of the Employment of Women an Children in Agriculture.

1844 [587] XXVII Great Britain (England, Wales, Islands). Occupation Abstract.

1845 [639] XXV Factory Inspectors' reps.

1847 [844] XVI Mines and Collieries, Mining Districts. Commissioner's rep. (Tremenheere).

1847-48 (522) LI Factories, Relay System. corresp.

1847-48 [993] XXVI Mines and Collieries, Mining Districts. Commissioner's rep. (Tremenheere).

1849 (613) VII Coal Mines, Accidents in Mines. Sel. Cttee. HL Rep., mins. of ev. (Lord Wharncliffe).

1849 [1017] XXII Factory Inspectors' reps.

1849 [1109] XXII Mines and Collieries, Mining Districts. Commissioner's rep. (Tremenheere).

1850 (745) XLII Returns of the Number of Cotton Factories.

1850 [1141] XXIII Factory Inspectors' reps.

1850 [1248] XXIII Mining Districts. Commissioner's rep. (Tremenheere).

1851 [1304] XXIII Factory Inspectors' reps.

1851 [1406] XXIII Mining Districts. Commissioner's rep. (Tremenheere).

1852-53 (691) XX Coal Mines, accidents. Sel. Cttee. 1st rep., mins. of ev. (E. J. Hutchins).

1852-53 [1631] LXXXV Census of Great Britain, 1851. Population tables pt. 1, vol. 1.

1852-53 [1632] LXXXVI Census of Great Britain, 1851. Population tables pt. 1, vol. II.

1852-53 [1633] LXXXVII Census of Great Britain, 1851. Population tables, index.

1852-53 [1690] LXXXIX Census of Great Britain, 1851, religious worship.

1852-53 [1691-I] LXXXVIII Census of Great Britain, 1851. Tables on ages, civil condition, etc.

1852-53 [1692] XC Census of Great Britain, 1851, education (England and Wales).

1854 (169) IX Coal Mines, accidents. Sel. Cttee. 1st rep. mins. of ev. (E. J. Hutchins).

1857 (151) XI Bleaching, Dyeing, and Print works, employment of women and children. Sel. Cttee. 1st rep., ins. of ev. (Lord John Manners and Isaac Butt).

1857-58 [2424] XXXII Mines and Minerals. Commissioner's rep. (Tremenheere)

1859 [2563] XXIX Factory Inspectors' rep.

1861 [2895] LXII Factory Inspectors' reps.

1863 [3170] XVIII Children's Employment (trade and manufactures). R. com. 1st rep.

(Tremenheere).

1864 [3414] XXII Children's Employment (trade and manufactures). R. com. 2nd rep. (Tremenheere).

1865 [3548] XX Children's Employment (trade and manufactures). R. com. 4th rep. (Tremenheere).

1866 [3622] XXIV Factory Inspectors' reps.

1866 [3678] XXIX Children's Employment (trade and manufactures). R. com. 5th rep. (Tremenheere).

1867 [3796] XVI Children's Employment (trade and manufactures). R. com. 6th rep. (Tremenheere).

1868-69 [4093] XIV Factory Inspectors' reps.

1871 (c.348) XIV Factory Inspectors' reps.

1871 (c.446) XIV Factory Inspectors' reps.

1873 (c.754) LV Factory Textiles, changes in hours and ages of employment. J. J. Bridges and T. Holmes rep. to Local Government Board.

1875 [c.1184] XVI Factory Inspectors' reps.

1887 (c.5172) LXXXIX Wage rates (19th century), United Kingdom. Return.

1889 (c.5807) LXX Wages, Textile Trade Rates, United Kingdom. Return.

House of Lord Papers:

1818 (90) XCVI or 1819 (90) XCVI

1819 (24) CX

1823 (86) CLXI

Hunt, Robert. 1978 [1887]. *A Historical Sketch of British Mining*. West Yorkshire, England: EP Publishing Limited.

Hunt, Robert. 1856. "The Present State of the Mining Industries of the United Kingdom." *Journal of the Royal Statistical Society* XIX: 201-218, 311-325.

James, John. 1857. *History of the Worsted Manufacture in England*. Bradford.

Jenkin, A. K. Hamilton. 1927. *The Cornish Miner: An Account of His Life Above and Underground From Early Times*. London: George Allen and Unwen, Ltd.

Kennedy, John. 1830. *A Brief Memoir of Samual Crompton: With a Description of His Machine Called the Mule and of the Subsequent Improvements of the Machinery by Others*. Manchester.

_____. 1826. "Observations on the Influence of Machinery upon the Working Classes of the Community." (Read before the Literary and Philosophical Society of Manchester on February 10, 1826) Manchester.

_____. 1819. "Observations on the Rise and Progress of the Cotton Trade in Great Britain." *Memoirs of the Literary and Philosophical Society of Manchester*, Second Series, vol. III.

Labor Statistics. 1887. *Returns of Wages Published Between 1830 and 1886*. London: HMSO.

Leach, J. 1844. *Stubborn Facts from the Factory*. London: Ollivier.

Leeds Intellengencer. August 13, 1804.

Leeds Intellengencer. March 1, 1802.

Leifchild, J. R. 1857. *Cornwall: Its Mines and Miners*. London: Longman, Brown, Green, Longmans and Roberts.

_____. 1853. *Our Coal and Our Coal Pits*. London: Longman, Brown, Green and Longmans.

Lemon, Sir Charles. 1839[1838]. "The Statistics of the Copper Mines of Cornwall." *Journal of the Royal Statistical Society* I: 65-84.

Lists, the regulation of wages by, in the Cotton Industry-Spinning. Report to the British

Association. 1887.

Lists, the regulation of wages by, in the Cotton Industry-Weaving. Report to the British Association. 1887.

Mallalieu, Alfred. 1836. "The Cotton Manufacture and the Factory System." *Edinburgh Magazine* July, Part II, XL: 11.

Marsden, Richard. 1895. *Cotton Weaving: Its Development, Principles, and Practice.* London: George Bell & Sons.

_____. 1884. *Cotton Spinning: Its Development,, Principles, and Practice.* London: George Bell & Sons.

Marx, Karl. 1912[1906;1909]. *Capital.* I Chicago: Charles H. Kerr & Company.

McCulloch, J. R. 1839, 1847. *Statistical Account of the British Empire.* Third edition. vol. I and II. London: Longman, Brown, Green and Longmans.

_____. 1832. "Cotton." *Dictionary of Commerce and Commercial Navigation* London.

Mill, John Stuart. 1965[1848]. *Principles of Political Economy,* with some of their applications to social philosophy. London: J. W. Parker.

Montgomery, James. 1832. *The Carding and Spinning Masters Assistant* or *The Theory and Practice of Cotton Spinning.* Glasgow: Niven.

NEI Buddle 25/111. *North of England Institute of Mining and Mechanical Engineers.* Buddle MSS, (54 volumes) 25: 111.

The New Moral World. 1836. 4 June, vol. II, no. 84, pp. 640-1.

Ogden, James. 1887 [1783]. *A Description of Manchester by a Native of the Town.* Manchester. Reprinted as *Manchester a Hundred Years Ago.* (Ed. W. E. A. Axon) 1887. London: John Heywood.

Plener, Ernst Elder Von. 1873. *English Factory Legislation.* London: Chapman and Hall.

Porter, G. R. 1851. *Progress of the Nation.* Second edition. Albermarle Street, London: John Murray.

Public Records Office, Chancery Lane, London. 1733.

P.R.O. SP 44/254, pp. 380-1; patent 542.

P.R.O. SP 36/41, fol. 212; patent 562.

S.P.D. Geo II, 41; Defense of Arkwright's patent.

Radcliffe, William. 1828. *Origin of the New System of Manufacture or Power-Loom Weaving.* Stockport.

Rees, A. 1819. *The Cyclopaedia.* London.

Recensement General. 1846. *Statisque de la Belgique.* Volume: Industrie. Brussels: Ministere de l'Interieur.

Shuttleworth, A. 1843. *The Report of the Twelfth Meeting of the British Association for the Advancement of Science.* London.

Simonin, L. 1869. *Underground Life; or Mines and Miners.* London: Chapman and Hall.

Sims, James. 1849. "On the Economy of Mining in Cornwall" from H. English, *The Mining Almanack for 1849.* Pp. 120-130. London. Reprinted in Roger Burt, ed., 1969. *Cornish Mining.* Newton Abbot: David and Charles.

Statistical Department of Board of Trade. "Tables of Revenue, Population, and Commerce." (years prior to 1853).

Statistical Department of Board of Trade. "Miscellaneous Statistics of the United Kingdom." (commenced in 1857).

Smith, Adam. 1976[1776]. *Wealth of Nations.* Oxford.

Taylor, John. 1837. "On the Economy of Mining." *Quarterly Mining Review* 10: 261-272. Reprinted in Roger Burt, ed., 1969. *Cornish Mining.* Newton Abbot: David and Charles.

_____. 1814. "On the Economy of the Mines of Cornwall and Devon." *Transactions of the Geological Society* 12: 309-327. Reprinted in Roger Burt, ed., 1969. *Cornish Mining*. Newton Abbot: David and Charles.

Thornley, T. 1906[1894]. *Practical Treatise Upon Self-Acting Mules*. Manchester, Heywood.

Toynbee, Arnold. 1969 [1884]. *Toynbee's Industrial Revolution: A Reprint of Lectures on the Industrial Revolution*. New York and Newton Abbot: David and Charles.

Trollope, Frances. 1840. *Michael Armstrong: The Factory Boy*. London: Cass.

Union Pilot. April 17, 1830.

Unwin, George. 1924. *Samuel Oldknow and the Arkwrights*. Manchester: Manchester University Press.

Ure, Andrew. 1861[1835]. *The Philosophy of Manufactures*. London.

_____. 1861[1836]. *The Cotton Manufacture of Great Britain*. London.

_____. 1860[1839]. *Dictionary of Arts, Manufactures and Mines*. 3 vols., London: Longman, Orme Brown, Green and Longmans.

Wadsworth, A. P. and J. de L. Mann. 1965[1931]. *The Cotton Trade and Industrial Lancashire, 1600-1870*. Manchester: Manchester University Press.

Warner, Sir Frank. 1922. *The Silk Industry of the United Kingdom*. London: Drane's.

Webb, S. and Webb, B. 1898. *Problems of Modern Industry*. London: Longmans, Green.

_____. 1919. *Industrial Democracy*. London: Longmans, Green.

White, Walter. 1861 [1855]. *A Londoner's Walk to the Lands End and a Trip to the Scilly Isles*. London: Chapman and Hall.

Wood, G. H. 1910. *The History of Wages in the Cotton Trade*. London: Sherratt and Hughes.

_____. 1910. "The Statistics of Wages in the United Kingdom During the 19th Century." XVI, XVIII The Cotton Industry. Section II, IV. *Journal of the Royal Statistical Society* April Pp. 128-63, 411-34.

_____. 1909. "Real Wages and the Standard of Comfort Since 1850." *Journal of the Royal Statistical Society* March 72:.91-103.

Secondary Sources

Adams, Carol; Bartley, Paula; Lown, Judy and Loxton, Cathy. 1983. *Under Control: Life in a Nineteenth-Century Silk Factory*. London: Cambridge University Press.

American Federation of Teachers. 1998. *Child Labor: A Selections of Materials on Children in the Workplace*. Washington: International Affairs Department.

Anderson, Michael. 1988. "Households, Families, and Individuals: Some Preliminary Results from the National Sample from the 1851 Census of Great Britain." *Continuity and Change* 3, no. 3: 421-438.

_____. 1971. *Family Structure in Nineteenth Century Lancashire*. Cambridge: Cambridge University Press.

Anti-Slavery Society for the Protection of Human Rights. 1978. *Child Labour in Morocco's Carpet Industry*. London: Anti-Slavery Society.

Apps, Patricia and Rees, Ray. 1997. "Collective labor supply and household production." *Journal of Political Economy* 105, no. 1: 178-191.

Aries, Philippe. 1962. *Centuries of Childhood*. New York: Alfred A. Knopf.

Ashagrie, Kebebew. 1993. "Statistics on Child Labor: A brief paper." *Bulletin in Labour Statistics* no. 3, Geneva.

Ashton, T. S. 1964[1948]. *The Industrial Revolution 1760-1830*. New York: Oxford University Press.

Ashton, T. S. and Sykes, J. 1929. *The Coal Industry of the Eighteenth Century*. Manchester.

Aspin, Chris. 1982. *The Woollen Industry*. Buckinghamshire: Shire Publications Ltd.

_____. 1981. *The Cotton Industry*. Buckinghamshire: Shire Publications Ltd.

_____. 1968. "New Evidence on James Hargreaves and the Spinning Jenny." *Textile History* 1, no. 1: 119-21. Plymouth: Latimer Trend and Company Limited.

_____. 1964. *James Hargreaves and the Spinning Jenny*. Helmshore Local History Society.

Ayala, U. 1982. *El trabajo infantil en Bogota*. vol I. Bogota: Departamento Nacional de Planificacion (DNP).

Becker, Gary. 1997. "Is There Any Way to Stop Child Labor Abuses?" *Business Week*. May 12: 22.

_____. 1981. *A Treatise on the Family*. Cambridge, MA: Harvard University Press.

_____. 1973. "A Theory of Marriage: Part I." *Journal of Political Economy* July/August 81: 813-46.

_____. 1965. "A Theory of the Allocation of Time." *Economic Journal* 75, no. 299: 493-517.

_____. 1964. *Human Capital: A Theoretical and Empirical Analysis*. New York: National Bureau of Economic Research.

Bennett, Alan. 1991. *A Working Life: Child Labour Through the Nineteenth Century*. Oxford: The Alden Press.

Bennett, Judith. 1988. "History that Stands Still: Women's Work in the European Past." *Feminist Studies* 14: 269-83.

Benson, Anna and Warburton, Neil. 1986. *Looms and Weaving*. Buckinghamshire: Shire Publication Ltd.

Benson, Anna P. 1983. *Textile Machines*. Buckinghamshire: Shire Publications Ltd.

Bequele, Assefa and Boyden, Jo. eds. 1988. *Combating Child Labour*. Geneva: International Labour Office.

Berg, Maxine. 1993. "Small Producer Capitalism in Eighteenth Century England." *Business History* 35, no. 1: 17-39.

_____. 1993. "Women's Property and the Industrial Revolution." *Journal of Interdisciplinary History* XXIV, no. 2: 233-250.

_____. 1993. "What Difference did Women's Work Make to the Industrial Revolution?" *History Workshop Journal* 35: 20-44.

_____. 1985. *The Age of Manufactures, Industry, Innovation and Work in Britain 1700-1820*. Oxford: Basil Blackwell Ltd.

_____. 1980. *The Machinery Question and the Making of Political Economy 1815-1848*. Cambridge.

Berg, Maxine and Hudson, Pat. 1992. "Rehabilitating the Industrial Revolution." *Economic History Review* 2nd series, XLV: 25-50.

Berg, Maxine; Hudson, Pat and Sonenscher eds., 1983. *Manufacture in Town and Country Before the Factory*. Cambridge: Cambridge University Press.

Berg, Maxine, ed. 1991. *Markets and Manufacture in Early Industrial Europe*. London: Routledge.

Berg, Maxine, ed. 1979. *Technology and Toil in Nineteenth Century Britain*. London: CSE Books.

Bergstrom, Theodore. 1996. "Economics in a Family Way." *Journal of Economic Literature* XXXIV: 1903-1934.

Berkow, Ira. 1996. "Jordan's Bunker View on Nike." *The New York Times*. July 12, Sports Friday: 1.

Berlanstein, Lenard R. ed. 1992. *The Industrial Revolution and Work in Nineteenth Century Europe*. New York and London: Routledge.

Best, G. F. A. 1964. *Shaftesbury*. New York: Arco Publishing Company, Inc.

Binmore, K. 1985. "Testing noncooperative bargaining theory: a preliminary study." *American Economic Review* 75: 1178-80.

Black, Eugene C. 1974. *Victorian Culture and Society*. New York: Walker and Company.

Blaug, Mark. 1961. "The Productivity of Capital in the Lancashire Cotton Industry During the Nineteenth Century." *Economic History Review* 2nd series, 13: 358-381.

Bolin-Hort, Per. 1989. *Work, Family and the State: Child Labor and the Organization of Production in the British Cotton Industry*. Lund University Press.

Bourguignon, F., Browning, M. and Chiappori, Pierre-Andre. 1995. "The Collective Approach to Household Behavior." *Working Paper 95-04*, Paris: DELTA.

Bourguignon, François and Chiappori, Pierre-Andre. 1992. "Collective Models of Household Behavior: An Introduction." *European Economic Review* 36, no. 2-3: 355-365.

Bowley, A. L. 1937. *Wages and Income in the United Kingdom since 1860*. Cambridge: Cambridge University Press.

Branigin, William. 1996. "Honduran Girl Asks Gifford to Help End Maltreatment." *Washington Post* 5/30/96: A29.

Brown, John C. 1990. "The Condition of England and the Standard of Living: Cotton Textiles in the Northwest, 1806-1850." *Journal of Economic History* 50, no. 3: 591-615.

Browning, Martin and Chiappori, Pierre-Andre. 1997. "Efficient Intra-Household Allocations: a General Characterization and Empirical Tests." *Econometrica*, forthcoming.

Browning, Martin; Bourguignon, François; Chiappori, Pierre-André and Lechene, Valérie. 1994. "Income and Outcomes: A Structural Model of Intrahousehold Allocation." *Journal of Political Economy* 102, no. 6: 1067-1096.

Burke, Gill. 1986. "The Decline of the Independent Bal Maiden: The Impact of Change in the Cornish Mining Industry," in Angela V. John, ed., *Unequal Opportunities: Women's Employment in England 1800-1981*. Oxford: Basil Blackwell.

Burke, Laura E. 1997. *Child Development*. Fourth edition. Boston, MA: Allyn and Bacon.

Burnett, John; Vincent, David and Mayall, David. 1984. *The Autobiography of the Working Class: An Annotated, Critical Bibliography*. I: 1790-1900. New York: New York University Press.

Burt, Roger and Waite, Peter. eds. 1988. *Bibliography of the History of British Metal Mining*. University of Exeter and the Natural Association of Mining History Organizations.

Burt, Roger. ed. 1969. *Cornish Mining: Essays on the Organisation of Cornish Mines and the Cornish Mining Economy*. Newton Abbot: David and Charles.

Burton, Anthony. 1989. "Looking forward from Aries? Pictorial and material evidence for the history of childhood and family life." *Continuity and Change* 4, Part 2: 203-229. Cambridge: Cambridge University Press.

Bush, Sarah. 1987. *The Silk Industry*. Buckinghamshire: Shire Publications Ltd.

Capdevila, Gustavo. 1998. "Labor: It's Up to Governments to Eliminate Child Labour." www. one world.org/ips2/ May 98, p. 1.

Capitol Hill Briefing. 1992. "Children Who Work – Challenges for the 21st Century." *A Report on the Proceedings of the Child Labor Coalition*. February 26 Washington: National Consumers League.

Challis, James and Elliman, David. 1979. *Child Workers Today*. Middlesex, England: Quartermaine House, Ltd.

Chapman, Stanley D. 1970. "Fixed Capital in the Cotton Industry." *Economic History Review* XXIII: 235-266.

_____. 1967. *Early Factory Masters.* Newton Abbot.

Chaippori, Pierre-André. 1997. "Introducing Household Production in Collective Models of Labor Supply." *Journal of Political Economy* 105, no. 1: 191-211.

_____. 1992. "Collective Labor Supply and Welfare." *Journal of Political Economy* 100, no. 3: 437-468.

Child Labor Coalition. 1993. "Child Labor Update and Recommendations for Action." April Washington: National Consumers League.

Child Labor Monitor, A National Consumers League Publication for the Child Labor Coalition. Washington: National Consumers League.

Vol. III, No. 1, Winter 1993

Vol. III, No. 2, Summer 1993

Vol. IV, No. 2, June 1994

Vol. IV, No. 3, September 1994

Vol. V, No. 1, April 1995

Vol. VII, No. 1, July 1997

Clapham, Sir John. 1964[1939; 1926]. *An Economic History of Modern Britain.* Vol. I and II. Cambridge: Cambridge University Press.

Clark, Anna. 1995. *The Struggle of the Breeches: Gender and the Making of the British Working Class.* Berkeley: University of California Press.

Clark, Gregory. 1987. "Why Isn't the Whole World Developed? Lessons from the Cotton Mills." *Journal of Economic History* XLVII, no. 1: 141-173.

Cockburn, Cynthia. 1985. *Machinery of Dominance: Women, Men and Technical Know-How.* London.

Cochrane, S.; Kozel, V.; Alderman, H. 1990. "Household Consequences of High Fertility in Pakistan." *World Bank Discussion Paper* no. 111. Washington, DC.

Collier, Francis. 1964. *The Family Economy of the Working Classes in the Cotton Industry 1784-1833.* R. S. Fitton, ed., Manchester: Manchester University Press.

_____. 1941-3. "Samuel Greg and Styal Mill." *Memoirs and Proceedings of the Manchester Literary and Philosophical Society* LXXXV.

Corr, Helen and Jamesian, Lynx. eds. 1990. *The Politics of Everyday Life: Continuity and Change in Work and Family.* London: Macmillan.

Crafts, N. F. R. 1985. "English Workers' Real Wages During the Industrial Revolution: Some Remaining Problems." *Journal of Economic History* 45: 139-144.

Crawford, Harriet . ed. 1979. *Subterranean Britain.* New York: St. Martin's Press.

Cressy, David. 1980. *Literacy and the Social Order: Reading and Writing in Tudor and Stuart England.* Cambridge: Cambridge University Press.

Cruickshank, Marjorie. 1981. *Children and Industry.* Manchester: Manchester University Press.

Cunningham, Hugh. 1990. "The Employment and Unemployment of Children in England, c. 1680-1851." *Past and Present* 126: 115-150.

Dahlburg, John-Thor. 1994. "Trading With Tiny Hands: Nepal and Many Other Poor Countries Have Become Dependent on Child Labor." *Los Angeles Times.* Home Edition, 7/12/94. World Report.

Davidoff, Leonore. 1995. *Worlds Between: Historical Perspectives on Gender and Class.* Cambridge, U. K.: Polity Press.

Davin, Anna. 1982. "Child Labour, The Working-Class Family, and Domestic Ideology in 19th Century Britain." *Development and Change* 13: 633-652.

Deane, P. and Cole, W. A. 1967. *British Economic Growth, 1688-1959*. Cambridge: Cambridge University Press.

DeGraff, D. S.; Bilsborrow, R. E.; Herrin, A. N. 1993. "The Implications of High Fertility For Children's Time Use in the Philippines." in C. B. Lloyd , ed., *Fertility, Family Size and Structure - Consequences for Families and Children*. Proceedings of a Population Council Seminar, June 9-10. New York.

De Vos, George A. 1973. *Socialization for achievement: essays on the cultural psychology of the Japanese*. Berkeley: University of California Press.

De Vries, Jan. 1994. "The Industrial Revolution and the Industrious Revolution." *Journal of Economic History* 54, no. 2: 249-70.

Dube, Leela. 1981. "The Economic Roles of Children in India: Methodological Issues," in Gerry Rodgers and Guy Standing, eds., *Child Work, Poverty and Underdevelopment*. Pp. 179-213. Geneva: International Labour Office.

Dyehouse, C. 1981. *Girls Growing up in Late Victorian and Edwardian England*. London.

Eckenfels, Edward J. 1976. "Several Selves and Many Homes: Black Youth's Adaption to Geographical and Cultural Mobility," in Estelle Fuchs, ed., *Youth in a Changing World: Cross-Cultural Perspectives on Adolescence*. Pp. 125-136. Paris: Mouton Publishers.

Edwards, M. M. and Lloyd-Jones, R. 1973. "N.J. Smelser and the Cotton Factory Family: A Reassessment," in N. B. Harte and K. G. Ponting, eds., *In Textile History and Economic History*. Essays in Honour of Miss Julia de Lacy Mann. Manchester: Manchester University Press.

Elson, D. and Pearson, R. 1989. "Nimble Fingers and Foreign Investments," in *Women's Employment and Multinationals in Europe*. Pp. 1-12. London: MacMillan Press.

Erikson, E. H. 1968. *Identity, Youth and Crisis*. New York: Norton Publishing.

Erikson. E. H. 1963. *Childhood and Society*. Second edition. New York: Norton Publishing.

Feinstein, Charles. 1981. "Capital Accumulation and the Industrial Revolution," in Roderick Floud and Donald N. McCloskey, eds., *The Economic History of Britain Since 1700*. vol. I. Cambridge: Cambridge University Press.

Fine, Ben. 1990. *Segmented Labour Market Theory: A Critical Assessment*. London: Thames Polytechnic and North East London Polytechnic.

Fitton, R. S. and Wadsworth, A. P. 1958. *The Strutts and the Arkwrights 1758-1830*. Manchester.

Flinn, M. W. 1984. *The History of the British Coal Industry, 1700-1830: The Industrial Revolution*. vol. II. Oxford: Clarendon Press.

_____. 1974. "Trends in Real Wages, 1756-1850." *Economic History Review* XXVII: 395-413.

Floud, Roderick and McCloskey, Donald. eds. 1981. *The Economic History of Britain Since 1700*. Cambridge: Cambridge University Press. (Second edition, 1994).

Folbre, Nancy. 1991. "The Unproductive Housewife: Her Evolution in Nineteenth Century Economic Thought." *Signs: Journal of Women in Culture and Society* Spring issue 16, no. 3: 463-484.

Ford, P. and Ford, G. 1972. *A Guide to Parliamentary Papers*. Ireland: Irish University Press.

_____. 1970. *Hansard's Catalogue and Breviate of Parliamentary Papers, 1696-1834*. Ireland: Irish University Press reprint.

_____. 1970. *Select List of British Parliamentary Papers, 1833-1899*.

Franca, Valeria and Carvalho, Joaquim de. 1996. "Tragedy, Success, and Precocity: Brazil's 7.5 Million Young Workers." *World Press Review* 43: 10-12.

Freudenberger, Hermann; Mather, Francis J. and Nardinelli, Clark. 1984. "A New Look at the

Early Factory Labour Force." *Journal Economic History* 44: 1085-90.

Fuchs, Estelle. ed. 1976. *Youth in a Changing World: Cross-Cultural Perspective on Adolescence.* Paris: Mouton Publishers.

Fuchs, Estelle and Havighurst, Robert J. 1972. *To Live on This Earth: American Indian Education.* New York: Doubleday.

Galler, J. R.; Ramsey, F., and Solimano, G. 1985. "A follow-up study of the effects of early malnutrition on subsequent development: I. Physical growth and sexual maturation during adolescence." *Pediatric Research* 19: 518-523.

Gangrade, K. D. and Gathia, J. A. eds. 1983. *Women and Child Workers in Unorganised Sector.* New Delhi: Concept Publishing Company.

Gathia, J. A. 1983. "Child Workers in the Informal Sector: Role of NGOs - Some Reflections," in K. D. Gangrade and J. A. Gathis, eds., *Women and Child Workers in Unorganized Sector.* Ch. 7. New Delhi: Concept Publishing Company.

Gillis, J. R. 1974. *Youth and History: Tradition and Change in European Age Relations, 1770-Present.* London.

Gokulanathan, K. S. 1976. "Adolescence in a Matriarchal Society: Changing Cultural and Social Patterns After Industrialization," in Estelle Fuchs, ed., *Youth in a Changing World: Cross-Cultural Perspectives on Adolescence.* Pp. 253-257. Paris: Mouton Publishers.

Goldin, Claudia and Sokoloff, Ken. 1982. "Women, Children and Industrialization in the Early Republic: Evidence from the Manufacturing Censuses." *Journal of Economic History* XLII, no. 4: 741-774.

Goldstone, Jack A. 1983. "A New Historical Materialism." *Contemporary Sociology* 12, no. 5: 487-490.

Griffiths, Trevor; Hunt, Philip A. and O'Brien, Patrick K. 1992. "Inventive Activity in the British Textile Industry, 1700-1800." *Journal of Economic History* 52, no. 4: 881-906.

Gronau, R. 1977. "Leisure, Home Production, and Work - The Theory of the Allocation of Time Revisited." *Journal of Political Economy* 85: 1099-1123.

Grootaert, Christiaan and Kanbur, Ravi. 1995. "Child Labour: An economic perspective." *International Labour Review* 134, no. 2: 194-198.

Guillé-Marroquin, Jesús. 1988. "Child Labour in Peru: Gold Panning in Madre de Dios," in Assefa Bequele and Jo Boyden, ed., *Combating Child Labour.* Pp. 61-77. Geneva: International Labour Office.

Hafeez, S. 1979. *Child Labor in Pakistan.* Geneva: International Labour Office.

Hall, Catherine. 1982. "The home turned upside down? The working-class family in cotton textiles 1780-1850," in Elizabeth Whitelegg, et al., eds., *The Changing Experience of Women.* Oxford: Martin Robertson.

Hammond, J. L. and Barbara. 1937. *Town Labourer.* New York: A Doubleday Anchor Book.

_____. 1920. *The Skilled Labourer, 1760-1832.* London: Longmans, Green and Company.

Hartwell, R. M. 1971. *The Industrial Revolution and Economic Growth.* London: Methuen.

Harvey, Pharis. 1995. "Where Children Work: Child Servitude in the Global Economy." *The Christian Century* April 5, 112, no. 11: 362-366.

_____. 1992. "International Child Labor: A Global Crisis," in *Children Who Work - - Challenges for the 21st Century.* Pp. 20-23. Capitol Hill Briefing.

Havighurst, Robert J. 1976. "Future Time Perspectives and Attitudes of New Zealand Maori and Pakeha Adolescents," in Estelle Fuchs, ed., *Youth in a Changing World: Cross-Cultural Perspectives on Adolescence.* Pp. 167-185. Paris: Mouton Publishers.

Hendrick, Harry. 1990. *Images of Youth: Age, Class, and the Male Youth Problem, 1880-*

1920. Oxford: Clarendon Press.

Hewitt, Nancy. 1992. "Compounding Differences." *Feminist Studies* 18, no. 2: 313-326.

Hewitt, Margaret. 1958. *Wives & Mothers in Victorian Industry*. London: Loxley Brothers Ltd.

Heywood, Colin. 1988. *Childhood in Nineteenth-Century France*. New York: Cambridge University Press.

Higgs, Edward. 1992. "Women Workers in Agriculture." Paper presented at a conference in February on "Gender and History" in honor of Leonore Davidoff.

———. 1989. *Making Sense of the Census: The Manuscript Returns for England and Wales, 1801-1901*. Public Record Office. London: HMSO.

———. 1987. "Women, Occupations and Work in the Nineteenth-Century Censuses." *History Workshop* 23: 59-80.

———. 1986. "Domestic Service and Household Production," in Angela V. John, ed., *Unequal Opportunities: Women's Employment in England 1800-1918*. Oxford: Basil Blackwell.

Hill, Bridget. 1989. *Women, Work, and Sexual Politics in Eighteenth-Century England*. Oxford: Basil Blackwell.

Hills, R. L. 1979. "Hargreaves, Arkwright and Crompton, Why Three Inventors." *Textile History* X: 114-126.

Hobsbawm, E. J. 1964. *Labouring Men*. New York: Anchor Book.

Hohenberg, Paul. 1991. "Urban Manufactures in the Proto-Industrial Economy: Culture Versus Commerce?" in Maxine Berg, ed., *Markets and Manufacture in Early Industrial Europe*. Oxford: Basil Blackwell Ltd.

Holleran, Philip M. 1993. "Child Labor and Exploitation in Turn-of-the-Century Cotton Mills." *Explorations in Economic History* 30, no. 4: 485-500.

Hopkins, Eric. 1994. *Childhood Transformed: Working Class Children in Nineteenth-Century England*. Manchester: Manchester University Press.

Horrell, Sara and Humphries, Jane. 1995. "The Exploitation of Little Children: Child Labor and the Family Economy in the Industrial Revolution." *Explorations in Economic History* 32, no. 4: 485-516.

———. 1995. "Women's Labor Force Participation and the Transition to the Male-Breadwinner Family, 1790-1865." *Economic History Review* XLVIII, no. 1: 89-117.

———. 1992. "Old Questions, New Data, and Alternative Perspectives: Families' Living Standards in the Industrial Revolution." *Journal of Economic History* 52, no. 4: 849-880.

Huck, Paul. 1992. Infant Mortality and the Standard of Living During the Industrial Revolution. Ph. D. Thesis., Northwestern University.

Hudson, Pat and Lee, W. R. eds., 1990. *Women's Work and the Family Economy in Historical Perspective*. Manchester: Manchester University Press.

Hudson, Pat. ed. 1989. *Regions and Industries*. Cambridge: Cambridge University Press.

Hudson, Pat. 1975. *The West Riding Wool Textile History: A Catalogue of Business Records*, vol. 3, Edington.

Humphries, Jane. 1991. "Lurking in the Wings...: Women in the Historiography of the Industrial Revolution." *Business and Economic History* 20: 32-44.

———. 1990. "Enclosures, Common Rights, and Women: The Proletarianization of Families in the Late Eighteenth and Early Nineteenth Centuries." *Journal of Economic History* L, no. 1: 17-43.

———. 1987. "...The Most Free From Objection...The Sexual Division of Labor and Women's Work in 19th Century England." *Journal of Economic History* XLVII, no. 4: 929-950.

———. 1981. "Protective Legislation, the Capitalist State and Working-Class Men; the Case of the 1842 Mines Regulation Act." *Feminist Review* 7: 1-33.

_____. 1977. "Class Struggle and the Persistence of the Working Class Family." *Cambridge Journal of Economics* 1, no. 3: 241-58.

Humphries, S. 1981. *Hooligans or Rebels? An Oral History of Working-Class Childhood and Youth*. London.

Hunt, E. H. 1981. *British Labour History, 1815-1914*. London.

Institute of Industrial Relations, University of the Philippines. 1988. "Child Labour in the Philippines: Wood-Based and Clothing Industries," in Assefa Bequele and Jo Boyden eds., *Combating Child Labour*. Pp. 79-91. Geneva: International Labour Office.

International Congress of Free Trade Unions. 1998. "ICFTU Report: Child Labor Around the World." www.labornet@igc.org., June 14, p. 1.

International Confederation of Free Trade Unions. 1994. "The Best Kept Secret: Child Labour Round the World," in American Federation of Teachers. 1998. *Child Labour: A Selection of Materials on Children in the Workplace*. Pp. 1-15. Washington: International Affairs Department.

International Labour Office. 1996. *Child Labour: Targeting the intolerable*. Geneva: International Labour Office Publications.

_____. 1989. "Still So Far To Go: Child Labour in the World Today." Pp. 37-39. Geneva: International Labour Organisation.

Jacobson, Jodi L. 1992. "Slavery (Yes, Slavery) Returns." *World Watch* January-February, 5, no. 1: 9-34.

James, Jeffrey. 1993. "New Technologies, Employment and Labour Markets in Developing Countries." *Development and Change* 24, no. 3: 405-437.

Jejeebhoy, S. J. 1993. "Family size, outcomes for children, and gender disparities: The case of rural Maharashtra," in C. B. Lloyd, ed., *Fertility, Family Size and Structure - Consequences for Families and Children*. Proceedings of a Population Council Seminar, June 9-10. New York.

Jenkins, D. T. and Ponting, K. G. 1982. *The British Wool Textile Industry 1770-1914*. London: Heinemann Educational Books Ltd.

John, Angela V. ed. 1986. *Unequal Opportunities: Women's Employment in England 1800-1918*. Oxford: Basil Blackwell.

John, Angela V. 1980. *By the Sweat of Their Brow: Woman Workers at Victorian Coal Mines*. London: Croom Helm.

Jomo, K. S. ed. 1992. *Child Labour in Malaysia*. Kuala Lumpur: Varlin Press.

Kalu, Wilhemina. 1976. "Impact of Urbanization on the Life Patterns of the Ga Adolescent," in Estelle Fuchs, ed., *Youth in a Changing World: Cross-Cultural Perspectives on Adolescence*. Pp. 137-160. Paris: Mouton Publishers.

Kanbargi, Ramesh. 1988. "Child Labour in India: The Carpet Industry of Varanasi," in Assefa Bequele and Jo Boyden, eds., *Combating Child Labour*. Pp. 93-108. Geneva: International Labour Office.

Kanefsky, J. and Robey, J. 1980. "Steam Engines in 18th-Century Britain: A Quantitative Assessment." *Technology and Culture* 21: 161-186.

Kett, J. F. 1977. *Rites of Passage: Adolescence in America, 1790 to the Present*. New York.

Krause, J. T. 1958-59. "Changes in English Fertility and Mortality, 1781-1850." *Economic History Review* Second Series, XI.

Kresz, Maria. 1976. "The Community of Young People in a Transylvanian Village," in Estelle Fuchs, ed., *Youth in a Changing World: Cross-Cultural Perspectives on Adolescence*. Pp. 207-212. Paris: Mouton Publishers.

Kulshreshtha, J. C. 1978. *Child Labour in India*. New Delhi: Ashish Publishing House.

Kurian, George. 1976. "Problems of Socialization in Indian Families in a Changing Society," in Estelle Fuchs ed., *Youth in a Changing World: Cross-Cultural Perspectives on Adolescence*. Pp. 259-272. Paris: Mouton Publishers.

Kussmaul, Ann. 1990. *A General View of the Rural Economy of England, 1538-1840*. Cambridge: Cambridge University Press.

_____. 1981. *Servants in Husbandry in Early Modern England*. Cambridge: Cambridge University Press.

Land, Hilary. 1980. "The Family Wage." *Feminist Review* no. 6: 55-77.

Landes, David. 1969. *The Unbound Prometheus*. Cambridge.

Landes, W. and Solomon, L. C. 1972. "Compulsory Schooling Legislation: An Economic Analysis of Law and Social Change in the Nineteenth Century." *Journal of Economic History* 32, no. 1.

Lawson, John and Silver, Harold. 1973. *A Social History of Education in England*. London: Methuen.

Lazarus, Mary. 1969. *Victorian Social Conditions and Attitudes, 1831-71*. New York: St. Martin's Press.

Lazonick, William. 1979. "Industrial Relations and Technical Change: The Case of the Self-Acting Mule." *Cambridge Journal of Economics* 3: 231-262.

Leadbeater, Eliza. 1979. *Spinning and Spinning Wheels*. Buckinghamshire: Shire Publications Ltd.

Levine, David. 1987. *Reproducing Families: The Political Economy of English Population History*. Cambridge: Cambridge University Press.

_____. 1985. "Industrialization and the Proletarian Family in England." *Past and Present* 107: 168-203.

_____. 1977. *Family Formation in an Age of Nascent Capitalism*. New York: Academic Press.

Levy, Victor. 1985. "Cropping pattern, mechanization, child labor, and fertility behavior in a family economy: Rural Egypt," in *Economic Development and Cultural Change* 33, no. 4, July, Chicago.

Lindert, Peter and Williamson, Jeffrey. 1985. "English Workers' Living Standards During the Industrial Revolution: A New Look," in Joel Mokyr, ed., *The Economics of the Industrial Revolution*. Totowa, N. J.: Rowman and Littlefield.

_____. 1983. "English Workers' Living Standards During the Industrial Revolution: A New Look." *Economic History Review* Second Series, 36, no. l: 1-25.

Litchfield, Burr. 1978. "The Family and the Mill: Cotton Mill Work, Family Work Patterns and Fertility in Mid-Victorian Stockport," in Anthony Wohl, ed., *The Victorian Family*. London: Croom Helm.

Lofts, Norah. 1979. *Domestic Life in England*. New York: Doubleday and Company, Inc.

Longmate, Elizabeth. 1981. *Children at Work 1830-1885*. Essex: Longman Group, Ltd.

Lown, Judy. 1990. *Women and Industrialization: Gender at Work in Nineteenth-Century England*. Minneapolis: University of Minnesota Press.

Lundberg, Shelly and Pollak, Robert. 1994. "Noncooperative Bargaining Models of Marriage." *American Economic Review* 84, no. 2: 132-137.

Luz Silva, Maria de la. 1981. "Urban Poverty and Child Work: Elements for the Analysis of Child Work in Chile," in Gerry Rodgers and Guy Standing, eds., *Child Work, Poverty and Underdevelopment*. Pp. 159-177. Geneva: International Labour Office.

_____. 1978. *Antecedentes sobre el trabajo de los menores en Chile*. Documento de Trabajo PREALC/163. Santiago, Chile: ILO/PREALC.

Lyons, John. 1989. "Family Response to Economic Decline: Handloom Weavers in Early

19th-Century Lancashire." *Research in Economic History* 12: 45-91.

Macfarlane, Alan. 1970. *The Family Life of Ralph Jesselin, A Seventeenth-Century Clergyman.* Cambridge: Cambridge University Press.

MacKinnon, Mary. 1994. "Living Standards, 1870-1914," in Roderick Floud and Donald McCloskey, eds., *The Economic History of Britain Since 1700.* 2nd edition, vol. 2: 1860-1939. Pp. 265-290. Cambridge: Cambridge University Press.

MacLeod, Christine. 1988. *Inventing the Industrial Revolution: The English Patent System.* Cambridge.

Maday, Bela C. and Szalay, Lorand B. 1976. "Psychological Correlates of Family Socialization in the United States and Korea," in Estelle Fuchs, ed., *Youth in a Changing World: Cross-Cultural Perspectives on Adolescence.* Pp. 273-286. Paris: Mouton Publishers.

Madeira, Felicia Reicher. 1986. "Youth in Brazil: old assumptions and new approaches." *CEPAL Review* no. 29: 55-78.

Malmgreen, Gail. 1985. *Silk Town: Industry and Culture in Macclesfield 1750-1835.* England: Hull University Press.

Manser, Marilyn and Brown, Murray. 1980. "Marriage and Household Decision-Making: A Bargaining Analysis." *International Economic Review* 21, no. 1: 31-44.

Mantoux, Paul. 1928. *The Industrial Revolution in the Eighteenth Century.* New York: Harper Torchbooks. (Revised edition 1961.)

Mathias, Peter. 1983. *The First Industrial Nation.* Second edition. New York: Methuen.

Marvel, Howard P. 1977. "Factory Regulation: A Reinterpretation of Early English Experience." *Journal of Law and Economics* 20, no. 2: 379-402.

McElroy, Marjorie. 1985. "Joint Determination of Household Membership and Market Work: The Case of Young Men." *Journal of Labor Economics* 3: 293-316.

McElroy, Marjorie and Horney, Mary. 1981. "Nash-Bargained Household Decisions: Toward a Generalization of the Theory of Demand." *International Economic Review* 22, no. 2: 333-349.

McKendrick, Neil. 1976. "Home Demand and Economic Growth: A New View of the Role of Women and Children in the Industrial Revolution," in *Historical Perspectives: Essays in Honor of J.H. Plumb.* Manchester: Manchester University Press.

McKeown, T. and Brown, R. G. 1955. "Medical Evidence Related to English Population Change in the Eighteenth Century." *Population Studies* IX.

Medick, H. 1976. "The Proto-Industrial Family Economy: The Structural Function of Household and Family During the Transition from Peasant Society to Industrial Capitalism." *Social History* 3: 291-315.

Milkman, Ruth. 1987. *Gender at Work: The Dynamics of Job Segregation by Sex During World War II.* Chicago: University of Illinois Press.

Mitch, David. 1993. "The Role of Human Capital in the First Industrial Revolution," in Joel Mokyr ed., *The British Industrial Revolution.* Oxford: Westview Press.

_____. 1992. *The Rise of Popular Literacy in Victorian England: The Influence of Private Choice and Public Policy.* Philadelphia: University of Pennsylvania Press.

_____. 1984. "Underinvestment in Literary? The Potential Contribution of Government Involvement in Elementary Education to Economic Growth in Nineteenth-Century England." *Journal of Economic History* 44: 557-566.

_____. 1982. The Spread of Literacy in Nineteenth Century England. Ph. D. Thesis, University of Chicago.

Mitchell, B. R. 1988. *British Historical Statistics.* Cambridge: New York University Press.

Mitchell, B. R. and Deane, P. 1962. *Abstract of British Historical Statistics.* Cambridge: Cambridge University Press.

Moehling, Carolyn. 1996. Work and Family: Intergenerational Support in American Families, 1880-1920. Ph. D. Thesis, Northwestern University.

Mokyr, Joel. 1990. *The Lever of Riches: Technological Creativity and Economic Progress.* New York: Oxford University Press.

_____. 1983. "Three Centuries of Population Change." *Economic Development and Cultural Change* 32, no. 1: 183-192.

Mokyr, Joel, ed. 1993. *The British Industrial Revolution.* Oxford: Westview Press.

Morris, William, 1981. *The American Heritage Dictionary of the English Language.* Boston: Houghton Mifflin Company.

Munoz, C. and Palacios, M. 1977. "Aportes al trabajo infantil: Evolucion de la fuerza de trabajo infantil en Columbia, 1951, 1961, 1973," in Defense for Children International, eds. *Child Labour: A Threat to Health and Development.* Second edition. Geneva.

Nardinelli, Clark. 1990. *Child Labor and the Industrial Revolution.* Bloomington: Indiana University Press.

_____. 1988. "Were Children Exploited During the Industrial Revolution?" *Research in Economic History* II: 243-276.

_____. 1982. "Corporal Punishment and Children's Wages in Nineteenth Century Britain." *Explorations in Economic History* 19, no. 3: 238-295.

_____. 1980. "Child Labor and the Factory Acts." *Journal of Economic History* XL, no. 4: 739-755.

Nash, J. F. 1953. "Two-Person Cooperative Games." *Econometrica* 21: 128-40.

The National Trust. 1985. *Quarry Bank Mill and Styal.* Cheshire: The National Trust.

Nef, John Ulric. 1932. *The Rise of the British Coal Industry.* vol I and II. London: George Routledge & Sons, Ltd.

Nixon, Nigel and Hill, Josselin. 1986. *Mill Life at Styal.* Cheshire: Willow Publishing.

Nunes de Castillo, M. I. 1980. "Child Labour in Sao Paulo, Brazil." *Anti-Slavery Society Report.* mimeo. London.

Okojie, C. 1993. "Micro-consequences of high fertility in Nigeria," in C. B. Lloyd, ed., *Fertility, Family Size and Structure - Consequences for Families and Children.* June 9-10. Proceedings of a Population Council Seminar, New York.

Oko-Ombaka, O. 1983. "The Law and child labour in Kenya, 1900-1980." *Journal of Eastern African Research and Development* Nairobi: Kenya Literature Bureau, no. 13: 171-178.

Onyango, Philsta P. M. 1988. "Child Labour Policies and Programmes in Kenya" in Assefa Bequele and Jo Boyden, eds., *Combating Child Labour.* Geneva: International Labour Office.

Oosterhout, Henk van. 1988. "Child Labour in the Philippines: The Muro-Ami deep-sea fishing operation," in Assefa Bequele and Jo Boyden. eds., *Combatting Child Labour.* Geneva: International Labour Office.

Owen, Robert. ed. 1969. *A New View of Society and Report to the County of Lanark.* V.A.C. Gattrell, Harmondsworth.

Parker, David L. 1994. "Stolen Dreams: Portraits of The World's Working Children." *Labor's Heritage Quarterly of the George Meany Memorial Archives* 6, no. 1: 22-45.

Peterson, John. 1976. "Mississippi Choctaw Youth," in Estelle Fuchs, ed., *Youth in a Changing World: Cross-Cultural Perspectives on Adolescence.* Pp. 161-165. Paris: Mouton Publishers.

Phillips, A. and Taylor, B. 1980. "Sex and Skill: Notes Towards a Feminist Economics." *Feminist Review* no. 6: 79-88.

Pinchbeck, Ivy. 1969. *Women Workers and the Industrial Revolution 1750-1850.* London:

Frank Cass and Company Limited.

_____. 1930. *Women Workers and the Industrial Revolution, 1750-1800*. London: George Routledge and Sons.

Pinchbeck, Ivy and Hewitt, Margaret. 1973. *Children in English Society*. vol. I and II. London: Routledge and Kegan Paul.

Plumb, J. H. 1975. "The New World of Children in Eighteenth Century England." *Past and Present* 67.

Pollard, Sidney. 1980. "A New Estimate of British Coal Production, 1750-1850." *Economic History Review* 33, no. 2: 212-232.

_____. 1965. *The Genesis of Modern Management*. Cambridge, MA.: Harvard University Press.

_____. 1964. "Fixed Capital in the Industrial Revolution in Britain." *Journal of Economic History* XXIV, no. 3: 299-314.

Pollock, Linda. 1983. *Forgotten Children: Parent-Child Relations from 1500 to 1900*. New York: Cambridge University Press.

Razzell, P. E. 1965. "Population Change in Eighteenth Century England: A Reinterpretation." *Economic History Review* Second Series, XVIII.

Read, Douglas A. 1976. "The Decline of St. Monday, 1776-1867." *Past and Present* 71: 76-101.

Redford, Arthur. 1926. *Labour Migration in England 1800-1850*. Manchester: Manchester University Press.

Rendall, Jane. 1990. *Woman in Industrializing Society: England 1750-1880*. Oxford: Basil Blackwell.

Richards, Eric. 1974. "Women in the British Economy." *History* 59: 337-347.

Roberts, Elizabeth. 1988. *Women's Work 1840-1940*. London.

Rodgers, Gerry and Standing, Guy. eds. 1981. *Child Work, Poverty and Underdevelopment*. Geneva: International Labour Office.

Rose, M. E. 1981. "Social Change and the Industrial Revolution," in R. Floud and D.N. McCloskey, eds., *The Economic History of Britain Since 1700*. vol. 1: 253-75. Cambridge.

Rose, Sonya O. 1992. *Limited Livelihoods: Gender and Class in Nineteenth-Century England*. Berkeley: University of California Press.

_____. 1988. "Proto-Industry, Women's Work and the Household Economy in the Transition to Industrial Capitalism." *Journal of Family History* 13, no. 2: 181-193.

Rosenzweig, Mark and Stark, Oded, eds., 1997. *Handbook of Population and Family Economics*. Amsterdam: North Holland.

Rowe, John. 1953. *Cornwall in the Age of the Industrial Revolution*. Liverpool.

Rubinstein, Ariel. 1982. "Perfect Equilibrium in a Bargaining Model." *Econometrica* 50: 97-109.

Rule, John. 1981. *The Experience of Labour in Eighteenth Century English Industry*. New York: St. Martin's Press.

Salazar, Maria Christina et al. 1994. *Child Labour in Industrial Sectors in Columbia*. Colombia: Santafe de Bogota.

Salazar, María Cristina. 1988. "Child Labour in Colombia: Bogotá's Quarries and Brickyards," in Assefa Bequele and Jo Boyden eds., *Combating Child Labour*. Pp. 49-60. Geneva: International Labour Office.

Saleeby, C. W. 1911. *The Methods of Race Regeneration*. London.

Saleeby, C. W. 1909. *Parenthood and Race Culture*. London.

Santrock, John W. 1998. *Adolescence*. Seventh edition Boston: McGraw Hill.

298

Samuel, Ralph, ed. 1977. *Miners, Quarrymen and Saltworkers.* History Workshop Series. London: Routledge and Kegan Paul.

Samuel, R. 1977. "The Workshop of the World: Steam Power and Hand Technology in Mid-Victorian Britain." *History Workshop Journal* III.

Sanderson, Allen. 1974. "Child-Labor Legislation and the Labor Force Participation of Children." *Journal of Economic History* 34: 297-99.

Sanderson, Michael. 1972. "Literacy and Social Mobility in the Industrial Revolution in England." *Past and Present* 56: 75-104.

_____. 1968. "Social Change and Elementary Education in Industrial Lancashire, 1780-1840." *Northern History* 3: 131-154.

_____. 1967. "Education and the Factory in Industrial Lancashire, 1780-1840." *Economic History Review* 20: 266-279.

Sathar, Z. A. 1993. "Micro-consequences of high fertility: The case of child schooling in rural Pakistan," in C. B. Lloyd, ed., *Fertility, Family Size and Structure - Consequences for Families and Children.* June 9-10. Proceedings of a Population Council Seminar, New York.

Schaie, K. Warner and Willis, Sherry. 1991. *Adult Development and Aging.* Third edition. New York: Harper Collins.

Schanberg, Sydney. 1994. "Six Cents an Hour." *Life Magazine* June, p. 37.

Scott, Joan and Tilly, Louise. 1982. "Women's work and the family in nineteenth-century Europe," in Elizabeth Whitelegg et al. , eds., *The Changing Experience of Women.* Oxford: Martin Robertson.

Schultz, Paul. 1990. "Testing the neoclassical model of family labor supply and fertility." *Journal of Human Resources* 25: 599-634.

Sen, Arunava. 1991. "Virtual implementation in Nash equilibrium." *Econometrica* 59: 997-1021.

Sharpe, Pamela. 1991. "Poor Children as Apprentices in Colyton 1598-1830." *Continuity and Change* 6, Part 2.

Shorter, Edward. 1975. *The Making of the Modern Family.* New York: Basic Books, Inc.

Silvers, Jonathan. 1996. "Child Labor in Pakistan." *The Atlantic Monthly* February, pp. 79-92.

Slaughter, J. G. 1910. *The Adolescent.* London.

Smelser, Neil. 1959. *Social Change in the Industrial Revolution.* Chicago: University of Chicago Press.

Smith, R. L. And Valenze, Deborah. 1988. "Mutuality and Marginality: Liberal Moral Theory and Working-Class Women in Nineteenth Century England." *Signs: Journal of Women in Culture and Society* Winter 13, no. 2: 277-98.

Sokoloff, Ken. 1984. "Was the Transition from the Artisanal Shop to the Nonmechanised Factory Associated with Gains in Efficiency?" *Explorations in Economic History* 21: 351-382.

Springer, Jane. 1997. *Listen to Us: The World's Working Children.* Ontario: Douglas & McIntyre Ltd.

Springhall, J. 1986. *Coming of Age: Adolescence in Britain, 1860-1960.* Dublin.

_____. 1977. *Youth, Empire and Society: British Youth Movement, 1883-1940.* London.

Standing, G. 1978. *Labour commitment, sexual dualism and industrialisation in Jamaica.* Geneva: International Labour Organization.

Stickland, Irina. 1973. *The Voices of Children 1700-1914.* Great Britain: Basil Blackwell.

Stoch, M. B.; Smythe, P. M.; Moodie, A. D. and Bradshaw, D. 1982. "Psychosocial outcome and CT findings after growth undernourishment during infancy: A 20-year developmental study." *Developmental Medicine and Child Neurology* 24: 419-436.

Stone, Lawrence. 1977. *The Family, Sex and Marriage in England 1500-1800*. London: Weidenfeld and Nicolson.

Tang, M. C. 1976. "Parental Authority and Family Size: A Chinese Case," in Estelle Fuchs, ed., *Youth in a Changing World: Cross- Cultural Perspectives on Adolescence*. Pp. 239-252. Paris: Mouton Publishers.

Taylor, A. J. 1961. "Labour Productivity and Technological Innovation in the British Coal Industry, 1850-1914." *Economic History Review* Second Series, XIV, no. 1: 48-70.

Thompson, E. P. 1966. *The Making of the English Working Class*. New York: Vintage Books.

Tillott, P. M. 1972. "Sources of Inaccuracy in the 1851 and 1861 Censuses," in Anthony E. Wrigley, ed., *Nineteenth-Century Society*. Pp. 82-133. Cambridge: Cambridge University Press.

Tilly, L. A. and Scott, J. W. 1978. *Women, Work and Family*. New York: Holt, Rinehart, and Winston.

_____. 1976. "Women's Work and the Family in 19th Century Europe." *Comparative Studies in Society and History* 17: 36-64.

Trevelyan, G. M. 1946. *English Social History*. London: Longmans, Green and Company.

Tuttle, Carolyn. 1998. "A Revival of the Pessimist View: Child Labor and the Industrial Revolution." *Research in Economic History* 18: 53-82.

_____. 1993. "Biased Technological Change During the British Industrial Revolution and the Demand for Child Labor." *Working paper*, Lake Forest College.

_____. 1990. "Married Women in the Home or in the Market: A Statistical Analysis of Working Women in Great Britain in 1851." *Working Paper*, Lake Forest College.

_____. 1986. Children at Work in the British Industrial Revolution. Ph. D. Thesis, Northwestern University.

UNICEF. 1997. *The State of the World's Children 1997*. Oxford: Oxford University Press.

U. S. Department of Labor. 1995. "By the Sweat and Toil of Children: The Use of Child Labor in U.S. Agriculture Imports and Forced and Bonded Child Labor." II. Washington: Bureau of International Affairs.

_____. 1994. "By the Sweat and Toil of Children: The Use of Child Labor in American Imports," I. Washington: Bureau of International Labor Affairs.

Unwin, George. 1924. *Samuel Oldknow and the Arkwrights*. Reprint ed. 1968. New York: Augustus Kelley.

Valenze, Deborah. 1995. *The First Industrial Woman*. Oxford: Oxford University Press.

Vernon, Sally. 1977. "Trouble up at T' Mill: The Rise and Decline of the Factory Play in the 1830s and 1840s" *Victorian Studies* Winter.

Vickery, Amanda. 1993. "Golden Age to Separate Spheres? A Review of the Categories and Chronology of English Women's History." *Historical Journal* 36, no. 2: 383-414.

Vivian, John. 1990. *Tales of the Cornish Miners*. Penryn, Cornwall: Tor Mark Press.

Von Tunzelmann, G. N. 1981. "Technical Progress During the Industrial Revolution," in Roderick Floud and Donald McCloskey, eds., *The Economic History of Britain Since 1700: Volume I, 1700-1860*. Cambridge.

_____. 1979. "Trends in Real Wages, 1750-1850, Revisited." *Economic History Review* Second series 32: 37-49.

_____. 1978. *Steam Power and British Industrialization to 1860*. Oxford: Clarendon Press.

Wall, Richard. 1987. "Leaving Home and the Process of Household Formation in Pre-Industrial England." *Continuity and Change* II, no. 1: 77-101.

_____. 1978. "The Age at Leaving Home." *Journal of Family History* III, no. 2: 181-202.

Walton, John K. 1989. "Protoindustrialization and the First Industrial Revolution: The Case of Lancashire," in Pat Hudson, ed., *Regions and Industries: A Perspective on the Industrial Revolution in Britain*. Cambridge: Cambridge University Press.

Walvin, J. 1982. *A Child's World: A Social History of English Childhood, 1800-1914*. London.

Ward, J. T. 1962. *The Factory Movement 1830-1855*. London: MacMillian and Company Ltd.

Weissbach, Lee Shai. 1989. *Child Labor Reform in Nineteenth-Century France*. Baton Rouge: Louisiana State University Press.

West, E. G. 1978. "Literacy and the Industrial Revolution." *Economic History Review* 31: 369-383.

_____. 1975. *Education and the Industrial Revolution*. London: B. T. Batsford, Ltd.

_____. 1971. "The Interpretation of Early Nineteenth-Century Educational Statistics." *Economic History Review* 24: 633-652.

Whitbourne, S. K. 1986. *The Me I Know: A Study of Adult Identity*. New York: Springer-Verlag.

Whitelegg, Elizabeth et al., eds. 1982. *The Changing Experience of Women*. Oxford: Martin Robertson.

Williamson, Jeffrey. 1990. *Coping with City Growth During the British Industrial Revolution*. Cambridge: Cambridge University Press.

_____. 1985. *Did British Capitalism Breed Inequality?* Boston: Allen & Unwin.

World Bank. 1995. *World Development Report 1995: Workers in an Integrating World*. Oxford: Oxford University Press.

Wright, Robin. 1994. "The Littlest Victims of Global 'Progress.'" *Los Angeles Times* 1/11/94 World Report, col. 2, p. 1.

Wrigley, E. Antony. 1988. "The Character of the Industrial Revolution in England." *Continuity, Chance and Change* Cambridge: Cambridge University Press.

_____. 1987. *People, Cities and Wealth, The Transformation of Traditional Society*. Oxford: Basil Blackwell.

_____. 1978. "Fertility Strategy for the Individual and the Group," in Charles Tilly, ed., *Historical Studies in Changing Fertility* Princeton: Princeton University Press.

Wrigley, E. Antony., ed. 1972. *Nineteenth-Century Society*. Cambridge: Cambridge University Press.

Wrigley, E. A. and Schofield, R. S. 1981. *The Population History of England 1541-1871: A Reconstitution*. Cambridge, MA: Harvard University Press.

Zavalloni, Marisa. 1976. "Students and Society: A Cross-National Comparison of Youth Attitudes and Values," in Estelle Fuchs, ed., *Youth in a Changing World: Cross-Cultural Perspectives on Adolescence*. Pp. 315-334. Paris: Mouton Publishers.

Index